PERSONAL TAXATION

Finance Act 2010 & Finance (No 2) Act 2010

Study Text

In this edition

- Plenty of **exam focus points** to ensure you focus on the exams you will be facing in 2011

- A **question and answer bank** including preparatory and exam standard short and long form questions and pilot paper questions for this syllabus. Marking schemes have been added to some of the answers so that you can gauge how well you are doing

- A **general index**

- **Icons** which highlight relevant chapters for study in the ATT's law manual 'Essential Law for the Taxation Technician'.

- **Thorough** and **reliable** updating for the **first two 2010 Finance Acts** with changes highlighted in the text

FOR EXAMS IN MAY AND NOVEMBER 2011

TQT
Tax Qualification Training

Contents

Fifth edition September 2010
Printed text 9780 7517 9116 7
e text ISBN 9780 7517 9286 7

British Library Cataloguing-in-Publication Data

A catalogue record for this book
is available from the British Library

Published by

BPP Learning Media Ltd
BPP House, Aldine Place
London W12 8AA

www.bpp.com/learningmedia

Printed in the United Kingdom

A note about copyright

Dear Customer

What does the little © mean and why does it matter?

Your market-leading TQT books, course materials and e-learning materials do not write and update themselves. People write them: on their own behalf or as employees of an organisation that invests in this activity. Copyright law protects their livelihoods. It does so by creating rights over the use of the content.

Breach of copyright is a form of theft – as well as being a criminal offence in some jurisdictions, it is potentially a serious breach of professional ethics.

With current technology, things might seem a bit hazy but, basically, without the express permission of BPP Learning Media:

- Photocopying TQT materials is a breach of copyright.

- Scanning, ripcasting or conversion of TQT digital materials into different file formats, uploading them to Facebook or emailing them to your friends is a breach of copyright.

You can, of course, sell your books, in the form in which you have bought them – once you have finished with them. (Is this fair to your fellow students? We update for a reason.) But the i-pass CDs are sold on a single user license basis: we do not supply 'unlock' codes to people who have bought them second hand.

TQT
Tax Qualification Training

Using your ATT texts

The ATT texts aim to ensure your success in the 2011 exams.

Key features of this text include:

- **Exam focus points** to help ensure you focus your efforts on the exams you will be facing in 2011.

- Changes introduced by the first two **2010 Finance Acts** highlighted throughout the text. This enables you to identify material that may have changed since your previous studies.

- **Relevant legislative references** provided throughout the text. As you are permitted to take your legislation into the examination room, it is important that you develop the habit of looking up references in the legislation as you study. Publications taken into the examination must be bound copies. They can be **underlined, sidelined and highlighted. Annotating, use of 'post-its' and tagging is NOT allowed.**

- **Icons** highlight when to study areas of the ATT's law manual 'Essential Law for the Taxation Technician'.

- **Worked examples** throughout the text.

- **Chapter roundups** at the end of each chapter summarising the key points covered in the chapter.

- **Quizzes** at the end of each chapter designed to test your grasp of the principles explained. Solutions to the quiz follow immediately.

- **A separate short form and long form Question and Answer section**. At the end of every chapter there are short form and long form questions that you should attempt. Some of the long form questions are preparatory questions and others are exam standard. Some of the answers contain marking schemes which will help you gauge how well you are doing.

- A **general** index is included at the back of the text.

The Examination Papers

Overview of the examination structure

The examination

The ATT examination offers a choice from seven free-standing Certificates of Competency in a modular structure. It is possible to take an examination in one topic only. This will lead to the award of a Certificate of Competency in that topic.

The certificate papers are:

1   Personal Taxation
2   Business Taxation & Accounting Principles
3   Business Taxation: Higher Skills
4   IHT, Trusts & Estates
5   VAT
6   Business Compliance
7   Practice Administration & Ethics

Relevant law and accounting issues will be examined in each paper.

The papers may be sat on a modular basis, ie they may be sat as and when the candidate decides.

Certificates of Competency

A certificate will be valid for a three-year period but will be renewable for any number of further three-year periods.

Members

Membership can be applied for by those who have passed the examination requirement in four Certificates of Competency which must include Personal Taxation, Business Taxation & Accounting Principles and Practice Administration & Ethics and who can demonstrate at least two years' acceptable current practical experience in UK taxation.

Examination pass mark

To pass a Certificate paper a candidate is required to achieve 50% of the total marks available.

Those who fail a paper will be permitted to re-sit any subsequent examination, provided that they submit an examination entry form and fee at each attempt and are registered as a student at the time of re-sitting.

Reference works and calculators for the examination

Pocket calculators (except those with an alpha-numeric keyboard) may be brought into the examination. Candidates are also allowed to bring into the examination room:

*   Tolley's Yellow Tax Handbook and Orange Tax Handbook: or
*   CCH Editions Ltd Tax Statutes and Instruments including the Index Volume; or
*   HMSO copies of taxing statutes.

Publications brought into the examination must be bound copies. They can be underlined, sidelined and highlighted. Annotating, use of 'post its' and tagging is **not** allowed.

No other written material or calculation aid will be permitted.

Candidates will be provided with a sheet giving the tax rates and tables required for the examination.

TQT
Tax Qualification Training

Format and syllabus of Certificate papers

Each Certificate paper is three hours in length.

Questions will not be set which require knowledge of:

- any statute receiving Royal Assent or any statutory instrument made less than 5 months before the examination date,

- with the exception of Inheritance Tax, any legislation repealed or suspended more than 5 months before the examination date,

- any case reported less than 3 months before the examination date.

Questions may be set:

- on prospective legislation passed more than 5 months before the examination date even if it is not in force,

- on matters which are not specifically listed in the syllabus but which are related to topics within the syllabus (for example, accountancy principles for the computations of business income),

- on matters which require a knowledge of taxes which are not specifically within the syllabus of a particular paper but are within the syllabus as a whole.

Certificate papers will be a mixture of computational and written questions and no question choice. The short-form questions will carry marks of between 2 and 4 marks each and in total will account for 40% of the available marks. There will therefore be between 10 and 20 such questions in each paper. The remaining available marks will be accounted for by between 3 and 5 longer questions carrying from 10 to 20 marks each. Questions requiring a knowledge of law will normally attract between 10% and 15% of the available marks in each of the technical papers (either as an element of questions or as a stand alone question).

You can find a detailed syllabus on the ATT's website (www.att.org.uk). Just click on 'Students' in the left hand navigation bar, then 'How to become a member (Prospectus)'. From here you should be able to click on the link to 'ATT Prospectus' which contains the detailed syllabus. Please make sure that you are looking at the syllabus for the **2011 examinations** which will be published online in the Autumn of 2010.

The overall and specific objectives of each of the papers are as follows.

Paper 1: Personal Taxation

Overall objectives

- To prepare the information of income and capital gains to be included in the self assessment (SA) personal tax return
- To prepare any associated computations in relation to the above
- To be able to submit the return and computations under UK self assessment
- To be able to complete a client's claim for tax credits

Specific objectives

- To be able to identify all relevant forms of income and to prepare the income tax computations for an individual

- To be able to identify capital gains transactions and calculate the computations and liability

- To be able to prepare the appropriate entries on tax returns for both income tax and capital gains

- To understand both the differences and similarities between the self assessment and tax credit systems

- To show awareness of professional ethics issues

- To deal with the administration process of SA returns

- To demonstrate understanding of relevant legal issues/implications when dealing with the tax affairs of individuals

- To be able to communicate with clients in a professional manner in written correspondence

Paper 2: Business Taxation & Accounting Principles

Overall objectives

- To prepare the information to be included in SA tax returns for sole traders or partners
- To prepare the information to be included in the SA partnership tax return
- To prepare the information to be included in CTSA returns for companies
- To prepare any associated computations in relation to the above
- To be able to submit returns and computations under self assessment and CTSA

Specific objectives

- To prepare the income tax computations for trades and professions for all aspects of the business life-cycle

- To prepare corporation tax computations for individual companies

- To be able to identify those transactions which have a capital gains impact and compute the liabilities

- To be able to complete the appropriate entries on tax returns

- To demonstrate an understanding of accounts which form the basis for tax computations

- To be able to prepare basic accounts

- To show awareness of professional ethics issues

- To deal with the administration process of SA and CTSA returns

- To demonstrate understanding of legal issues/implications when dealing with the tax affairs of the self-employed and companies

- To be able to communicate with clients in a professional manner in written correspondence

Paper 3: Business Taxation: Higher Skills

Overall objective

- To be able to deal with all aspects of the Paper 2 syllabus in more complex situations

Specific objectives

- To be able to identify the tax implications of setting up, or disposing of, a business including the consideration of alternative mediums

- To be able to advise on the tax implications of the incorporation of a business

- To demonstrate understanding of legal issues/implications when dealing with the incorporation of companies

- To be able to advise on the tax implications of changes in the membership of a partnership

- To demonstrate understanding of the tax treatment of Limited Liability Partnerships

- To be able to advise on the tax implications of the legislation relating to personal service companies

- To be able to advise on the tax implications of family owned companies

- To be able to advise on the taxation treatment of groups of companies

- To show awareness of professional ethics issues

- To demonstrate understanding of legal issues/implications when dealing with the tax affairs of the self-employed and companies

- To be able to communicate with clients in a professional manner in written correspondence

Paper 4: Inheritance Tax, Trusts & Estates

Overall objectives

- To prepare the information to be included in the SA Trust & Estate Tax Return
- To prepare any associated computations in relation to the above
- To be able to submit the return and computations under UK self assessment

Specific objectives

- To demonstrate understanding of the distinction between types of trusts to complete the appropriate entries on tax returns
- To be able to distinguish between the entries required on all relevant forms
- To be able to prepare all relevant computations to complete the above
- To be able to calculate the tax liability on income arising to the estate of a deceased person
- To be able to compute the capital gains tax for trustees, executors and beneficiaries
- To be able to identify the IHT implications of lifetime gifts for individuals
- To be able to prepare basic computations of the inheritance tax liability arising on a death
- To show awareness of professional ethics issues
- To deal with the administration process of SA returns
- To demonstrate understanding of legal issues/implications when dealing with trusts
- To be able to communicate with clients in a professional manner in written correspondence

Paper 5: Value Added Tax

Overall objectives

- To prepare the information to be included in the VAT Return for a taxable trader
- To be able to compute any annual or periodic adjustments to be included within a VAT return
- To be aware of any special schemes available for taxable traders generally, and to be able to complete returns where such schemes apply

Specific objectives

- To understand the accounting and other documents and records required to be maintained for VAT
- To identify traders requiring registration or able to deregister for VAT
- To define a taxable person; supply; time of supply and place of supply
- To be aware of the basis of valuation of supplies
- To be able to identify different types of supplies
- To be able to prepare a computation involving partial exemption using the standard method, and to be able to compute annual adjustments
- To be aware of the VAT treatment of imports and exports including international services
- To be able to determine deductible input tax
- To understand the provisions relating to transfers of a going concern
- To be able to compute the adjustments necessary for the capital goods scheme
- To be able to identify the VAT implications of land transactions
- To be able to prepare a VAT return where a special scheme applies
- To be able to explain the rules relating to groups of companies and group registration
- To understand the regime of penalties and interest on late payment and the implications of other irregularities for VAT
- To show awareness of professional ethics issues
- To demonstrate understanding of relevant legal issues/implications affecting VAT transactions
- To be able to communicate with clients in a professional manner in written correspondence

Paper 6: Business Compliance

Overall objectives

- To be able to deal with employer obligations under PAYE, NIC and related matters under the tax system
- To be able to complete and submit VAT returns

Specific objectives

- To compute PAYE and NIC deductions and ERNIC liabilities
- To be able to identify the correct treatment of non-cash items, travel expenses and lump sum payments
- To prepare computations on benefits in kind
- To be able to identify and distinguish the various forms of share options and the related tax and NIC liabilities
- To be able to complete all relevant forms in relation to PAYE and NIC on the above
- To be able to deal with all aspects of payroll administration, including all deductions and credits.
- To be able to demonstrate knowledge of UK VAT and related calculations
- To be able to prepare a basic VAT return
- To deal with the VAT administration process
- To show awareness of professional ethics issues
- To demonstrate understanding of legal issues/implications affecting business compliance
- To be able to communicate with clients in a professional manner in written correspondence

Paper 7: Practice Administration & Ethics

Content

The paper will cover the following areas:

- Administration of taxation
- The legal framework in which the tax adviser operates
- Ethical rules and practice guidelines

Administration of taxation

Candidates will be expected to have a thorough understanding of the processes by which the taxpayer notifies that they are within the charge, through to returns, assessments/self assessments, and enquiries. Detailed knowledge of the process of pursuing an appeal through to the Tribunals and beyond would not be required.

Much of the administration is generic and will apply as much to corporate as to personal tax.

Some basic knowledge of the way VAT, IHT and PAYE is administered will also feature. Even if a candidate does not sit the specific paper on these topics it is not unreasonable to require a prospective member to be able to relay to a client at least the very basics of compliance in these areas.

Candidates will also be required to deal, at a fairly basic level, with questions of what should be disclosed and why, and also how to deal with errors, both by HMRC and by the adviser.

Tax administration is not an area on which students generally spend enough time studying; they will avoid it as much as possible in examinations. Given that the whole tax system is built on providing information to HMRC, it is essential that prospective members give this area the attention it deserves.

The legal framework in which the tax agent operates

This involves not only the relationship between the agent and HMRC, but also some of the basic framework which exists between a client and an adviser. Candidates will be expected to understand something of the nature of the duty of care owed to a client and the normal contractual arrangements regulating an engagement.

The majority of the Association's members will be employees and therefore candidates need to understand something of the quadripartite relationship between client, tax authority, adviser and employee.

Ethical rules and practice guidelines

The Association's publication: *Professional Rules and Practice Guidelines* will form the basis of the syllabus. Some of this material is covered in the discussion of the legal framework above, but there is much which does not fit into this category. All of that publication which relates to the activities likely to be carried on by an Association member is potentially examinable.

HOME STUDY PLANNER

1 Introduction

This TQT Home Study Programme will guide you through this 2010 edition of the TQT Study Text. This Home Study planner is intended for use by students who are studying on their own. If you are attending a taught course, your course provider may provide you with a different programme of studies.

2 Using the Home Study Programme

This Home Study Programme is made up of 21 **Study Periods**.

The tax and law in each study Period should take about 3 hours. In addition you are directed to read various parts of the ATT's professional rules and practice guidelines. Experience shows that the best way of studying these documents is to approach them little and often.

Exams

If you are a home study student you will have two course exams.

To gain the greatest benefit from the exams, you must set aside a period of three hours and fifteen minutes during which you will have no interruptions.

By sitting these exams, you will increase your chances of passing the real exams by 30%.

Please note, these exams are available only as part of the home study package. If you are attending a taught course, your provider may provide you with other exams to sit at different times during your studies.

3 Getting ready to Study

To get off to the best possible start to your study, you should take time to read the following guidance.

Before you begin your studies, you may want to spend some time thinking about how to approach them. Consider the following.

(a)   **The study environment.** Studying while working is very different from studying full time. Time management is crucial.

(b)   **Types of subject.** You need to think about the form the exam will take and the skills it will draw on. For example, does it test knowledge, numerical skills, application of knowledge or application of theory?

(c)   **What is your learning style?** Your learning preferences should affect the way you approach this study material.

(d)   You need to think about **how to work through the text**, how to take notes and how to do examples.

(e)   How will you approach your **revision**?

(f)   You need a technique for dealing with **common types of question**.

(g)   You must approach the exam in a **methodical manner**.

Approaching Personal Taxation

This guidance describes what the paper seeks to achieve, the skills you are expected to demonstrate and how you can improve your chances of passing the paper.

Paper 1, Personal Taxation seeks to test the liability of individuals to:

- Income tax,
- National Insurance Contributions, and
- Capital gains tax.

The exam may also contain questions on the ethical considerations of being in practice, and the following areas of legal knowledge:

- Property Law
- Land Law
- Working relationships

We have indicated where you should also study from the 'Essential Law for the Tax Technician (Third edition)' text book and the ATT Professional Rules and Practice Guidelines (2006 version), ATT Professional Conduct in Relation to Taxation and Engagement Letters for Tax Practitioners (10 March 2009).

Because you are not expected to have any previous knowledge of these subjects, we will be introducing them to you from first principles. If you have any previous knowledge of personal taxation, perhaps as a result of work experience, you can modify the amounts of time you send on each topic, to take account of your knowledge.

The examination

The examination is made up of two parts:

Part I – which is made up of a number of short form questions (SFQs), with mark allocations ranging from 2 to 4 marks. There are 40 marks available in Part I of the exam. As you work through the study text you will encounter SFQs at the end of each chapter. By practising this kind of question you can help prepare for the real exam as you go along. SFQs can be on any syllabus area and Part I of the exam typically includes a cross section of questions taken from all areas of the syllabus.

Topics covered in the last five actual Past Papers are set out below:

	May 2008	November 2008	May 2009	November 2009	May 2010
1	IT: Calculation of IT liability	IT: Property income	IT: Living accommodation	IT: Property income	IT: Exempt income
2	CGT: Married couples	CGT: Overseas aspects	Overseas: Income tax for non-UK domiciliary	CGT: Connected persons	CGT: Chattels
3	Accrued income scheme and CGT on loan stock	IT: Taxation of a REIT	Self assessment: Enquiries	CGT: Gift relief	IT: Accrued income scheme
4	CGT: 31 March 1982 asset and taper relief	IT: Allowances	CGT: Chattels	CGT: Chattels	NIC: Employee NICs and age limits
5	Self assessment: Penalties, interest and surcharges	State benefits: Taxable benefits	IT: VCT investment and dividends	IT: Personal pension contributions	IT: Pension contributions
6	CGT: Overseas aspects	CGT: Rights issue shares	CGT: PPR	CGT: Overseas aspects	IT: EMI share options
7	IT: Life assurance policies	Self assessment: Filing returns & keeping records	Overseas: Remittance basis charge	CGT: PPR relief	IT: Tax credits

	May 2008	November 2008	May 2009	November 2009	May 2010
8	Self assessment: Determinations	Tax credits: CTC & WTC	IT: Restrictive covenants	IT: Accrued income scheme	ISA tax advantages
9	CGT: Chargeable disposals	CGT: Overseas aspects	IT: Termination payments	IT & CGT: Gift of shares	Self assessment: Return filing deadlines
10	IT: Pre owned assets	CGT: Chattels & use of capital loss	CGT: DTR	IT: Estate income	CGT: Negligible value claim & loss relief for unquoted shares
11	IT: Employment benefits	CGT: PPR relief	CGT: Insurance	IT: Restricted shares	CGT: Deductible expenditure
12	Ethics: Fee arrangements	Ethics: Data protection	Overseas: residence definition	IT: Life assurance policy gain	IT: Termination payments
13		Ethics: Money laundering	CGT: Connected persons	Law: Data protection	Law: Jointly owned property
14			Law: Property law		

Part II of the exam is made up of between three to five long form questions with a total of 60 marks. The marks are shared between the questions, but ATT have indicated that they may not be allocated evenly. However, on all the past papers 20 marks have been allocated to each question.

You must be prepared to answer long form questions, as you cannot pass the exam from the short form questions alone, and practising the questions at the end of each Study Period and in the Course Exams, will help with this.

Make sure you consider how long a question is supposed to take. Where a question has a mark allocation this will be an indication of the time it is expected to take. As an estimate, the exam is 3 hours long, so each mark should take, on average, 1.8 minutes of your time. Therefore, a 20 mark question should take around 36 minutes to answer. This is only a rough guide, but it helps you to allocate your time in the exam so that you do not spend more time on a question than it should take to gain the available marks, as this is likely to make your answers to later questions weaker.

Topics covered in Real Past Papers

	May 2008	November 2008	May 2009	November 2009	May 2010
Q1	Tax credits: CTC & WTC. IT payable calculation. Law: Employment law.	Taxable benefits, investment income, IT computation, payment of tax Law: Employment law	Law: Employment, CTC, Pension, SAYE, Ethics: Tax avoidance vs evasion, Admin: Late filing penalty.	IT & CGT computation for non-UK domiciled individual, remittance basis claim, payment date	IT payable calculation Law: Employees' obligations
Q2	CGT disposals including land, chattels, compensation. Loss relief for unquoted shares.	CGT disposals involving leases IT property income Law: Property law	IT calc, Admin: Penalty for late tax payment, Losses, Pension, Ethics: Professional privilege & negligence	Income calculation including benefits, CGT disposals including chattel, shares, part disposal Law: consultancy contract clauses Tax credits	Income from jointly owned assets CGT on separation & divorce Duty of confidentiality
Q3	EIS: IT and CGT implications.	Approved share schemes: IT and CGT implications for SIP, CSOP and SAYE.	IT: Car benefit, CGT: Connected persons, EIS investment, CGT: Capital distribution & bonus issue.	IT and CGT summary of tax efficient investments VCT approval conditions Money laundering regulations	CGT disposals including paper for paper treatment & insurance CGT & IT reliefs for EIS subscription FSMA regulated activities

All the questions set in the Pilot Paper issued by the ATT are included within the Question Bank.

Detailed Home Study Planner

Use this planner and your exam timetable to plan the dates on which you will complete each Study Period.

At the end of each Study Period you will be advised to study a section from the separate publications issued by the ATT in relation to professional rules and practice guidelines. Students often say they find studying from these ATT publications very hard going. We find that by studying a little and often you will find the task a little less daunting

Study Period	Guidance through Study text	Attempt Questions
1 **Taxable income**	You must thoroughly understand how the basic income tax computation works. Subsequent Study Periods will deal with the calculation of the different types of income subject to income tax. This Study Period introduces the basic knowledge of how an income tax computation is put together and how income tax is calculated. This knowledge will be tested throughout the exam. The last seven exams have included an income tax computation as part of a long form question. Tax credits are also a popular exam topic, covered in the short form questions in the sample, May 2007, November 2007 and November 2008 exam papers, and May 2010 paper. They were also tested in Part II of the sample paper, the May 2008 and 2009 exams and the November 2009 paper.	SFQ 1.1 – 1.20 LFQ 1.1 – 1.3
Examined: May 2007 November 2007 May 2008 November 2008 May 2009 November 2009 May 2010	Please read Chapter 1 after reading the guidance here. This essential Study Period is likely to take longer than 3 hours, so you may wish to split the period into two: Sections 1 – 6 and then Sections 7 – 14. Read through Section 1 to gain background knowledge about the UK tax system. This is not usually examined but will help your understanding. Read through Section 2 to familiarise yourself with who pays income tax in the UK. You will return to the overseas aspects of income tax in a later Chapter. Read through Sections 3 to 9 in detail, making notes and working the examples. Take note of the step by step approach to building up an income tax computation in the right order in Section 3. Work through the Illustrations and Examples carefully to understand the rates of tax. Ensure you understand the order in which income is taxed. Illustration 3 in Section 9 shows the complete computation. Learn the format. Child and working tax credits in Section 10 and social security benefits in Section 11 are examined frequently so work carefully through Examples 7, 8 and 9. Take note of the key income tax planning idea in Section 12.3 for jointly owned property, which was examined in a long question in May 2010, and work carefully through the illustration in Section 13 on income from the estate of a deceased person (which was tested for the first time in a SFQ in November 2009). You must be able to identify exempt sources of income in Section 14.	

Study Period	Guidance through Study text	Attempt Questions
Professional Rules and Practice Guidelines	Now revise Chapters 1 and 2 of your ATT Professional Rules and Practice Guidelines • Introduction • Professional Rules	
2 **Savings income**	You are likely to be asked to calculate income tax for individuals in both the short form and the long form questions. The rates of tax you will use differ depending on whether the income being taxed is non savings, savings or dividend income. You will be expected to be able to identify the different types of income and calculate tax at the appropriate rate. You may also be expected to deal with more complex investments. For example, the accrued income scheme for securities is an examiner's favourite, while the taxation of life assurance policies was tested in a SFQ in November 2009 and a LFQ in May 2010.	SFQ 2.1 – 2.9 LFQ 2.1 – 2.7
Examined: Sample Paper May 2007 November 2007 May 2008 November 2008 May 2009 November 2009 May 2010	Please read Chapter 2 after reading the guidance below: • Read through the introduction to understand the meaning of what is included as savings income. • Read through Sections 2 and 3 and note that interest can be received either gross (ie with no tax deducted before it is paid to the investor) or net (of 20% tax) and that dividends are **always** received net (of 10% tax). Make sure you understand that all income is included gross in the income tax computation. Read through Section 4 and make notes on how savings and dividend income is taxed, the order in which income is taxed and the rates of tax used. Pay particular attention to the three column format of the computation. Attempt Examples 1 to 4 to check you have understood this section. Review the illustration in Section 5 to check you understand how interest and dividends fit into the income tax computation and then attempt Example 5. Read carefully through Section 6. Note the way that income from trusts is taxed, and the associated tax credits available to the recipient of trust income. Take time to understand how the accrued income scheme works as this has been a popular topic over the last few papers. Work through Example 7 which tests life assurance policies. Finally note the 'catch all' category of miscellaneous income. Refer to the rates and allowances in the Tax Tables included at the front of the Study text as you go along so that you know what information you will be given in the exam.	
Professional Rules and Practice Guidelines	Now revise Chapter 3 of your ATT Professional Rules and Practice Guidelines • Practice Governance	

Study Period	Guidance through Study text	Attempt Questions
3 **Income from UK land and buildings**	This Study Period considers how to calculate the amount of income arising from UK property and the legal aspects of property law. In the exam, property income calculations can come up in both the short form and the long form questions. An example of these can be found on Part I of the sample, November 2008 and 2009 exam papers, and Part II of the May 2007, November 2008 and May 2010 exam papers. You may also be asked factual questions, such as the conditions for rent a room relief to apply. Questions may combine the income tax and capital gains tax aspects of owning and disposing of land and buildings (capital gains tax will be covered in later Study Periods) and the legal aspects of owning property.	SFQ 3.1 – 3.10 LFQ 3.1 & 3.2
Examined: Sample Paper May 2007 November 2007 November 2008 May 2009 November 2009 May 2010	Please read through Chapter 3 of the Study text, after reading the guidance here. Read through Sections 1 – 8 which deal with how to compute property income. You need to be able to calculate: • Property income net of allowable expenses (and capital allowances) (please try Example 1) • Property losses • The portion of a lease premium received on a short lease that is taxable on the landlord (please try Examples 2 and 3). You need to be able to state: • How to set off property losses. • The conditions for, and the tax implications of, a property being treated as a furnished holiday letting. • The conditions for rent a room relief to apply and the tax implications of this relief applying. • How a landlord of a UK property, who is not resident in the UK, is taxed on the property income received. • The tax implications of receiving rental income from a Real Estate Investment Trust. Read through the topics Property Law and Land Law in the ATT manual Essential Law for the Taxation Technician.	
Professional Rules and Practice Guidelines	Now revise Chapter 4 of your Professional Rules and Practice Guidelines • New clients	

Study Period	Guidance through Study text	Attempt Questions
4 **Tax efficient investments**	You will be expected to be able to identify the main tax efficient investments and to understand the tax implications of investing in them. Questions could cover the conditions for a particular investment to qualify for a tax efficient scheme, the tax implications of investing in a scheme or calculating the tax position of an individual making such an investment. The EIS and VCT schemes have become very popular topics with the Personal taxation examiner. The tax advantages of investing in ISAs is also a common SFQ.	SFQ 4.1 – 4.4 LFQ 4.1
Examined: May 2007 May 2008 May 2009 November 2009 May 2010	Please read Chapter 4 of the Study Text after reading the guidance below: Read through Section 1 of the Chapter and note the main tax free investments. You need to be able to identify these in questions so that you can tell the examiner that income arising from them is not taxable in the income tax computation. Read through Section 2 on ISAs. Make notes on the key points such as who can invest and how much can be invested (see Illustration 1). You should understand that an ISA is effectively a tax free wrapper, so income and gains within it are tax free. Read carefully through Section 3 on the Enterprise Investment Scheme (EIS), highlighting the key conditions in your legislation as you go (see ss.156 – 234 ITA 2007). Also, find the EIS investment limit and rate of relief in the Tax Tables at the front of this Text. You must understand the tax relief available and the circumstances in which, and consequences of, the relief will be withdrawn. Attempt Example 1. Read through Section 4 on venture capital trusts (VCTs), again following through with the legislation and highlighting key conditions. Locate the investment limit and rate of relief in the Tax Tables. You have a lot of information at your fingertips in the exam itself. Make sure that you can distinguish, and understand the differences, between the two schemes. Finally read through Section 5. The pre-owned asset rules are not concerned with tax efficient investments as such, but with the tax treatment of an individual who believes that he has escaped taxation on income by giving away cash or an asset but can still benefit from it. In certain circumstances such a gift is ineffective and you must be able to recognise the situation and calculate the income tax charge, so work through the examples carefully.	
Professional Rules and Practice Guidelines	Now revise Chapter 5 of your Professional Rules and Practice Guidelines • Client Service	

Study Period	Guidance through Study text	Attempt Questions
5 **The employed earner**	This Study Period deals with the calculation of the employment income figure that an employed earner must include in his income tax computation. Questions have appeared in every examination sitting so far and can focus on many different aspects of the employed earner. For example, understanding the basis of assessment for employment income, identifying and calculating taxable employment income, including the tax value of benefits received and identifying tax free benefits. You may also be required to show your understanding of the taxation of termination payments received when leaving employment.	SFQ 5.1 – 5.23 LFQ 5.1 - 5.6
Examined: Sample Paper May 2007 November 2007 May 2008 November 2008 May 2009 November 2009 May 2010	Please read Chapter 5 of the Study text, after reading the guidance below: • Read through Section 1 to understand the types of income that makes up employment income. Make sure that you can explain how the receipts basis, which determines the tax year that employment income is taxed, applies. Work through Example 1. • Then work through Section 2, making notes on how to calculate the taxable value of the benefits that are taxable on all employees, regardless of their income level. Try Examples 2, 3 and 4. • Next, read through Section 3 and make notes on how to calculate the taxable value of benefits only taxable on directors and employees earning £8,500 pa or more. The benefits of a company car and private fuel are an examiner's favourite. Try Examples 5 to 10. • Read through Section 4 and make sure you can identify the benefits that can be received tax free. • Read through Section 5 and ensure you understand when expenses can be deducted from employment income. The 'wholly, exclusively and necessarily' test is key. Try Example 11. • Finally, read through Section 6, making notes on how the different categories of termination payment are taxed. Make sure you can identify which payments are fully taxable, those that are completely exempt and those that are partially exempt from tax. Try Example 12. Also try to understand the effect of foreign service on termination payments.	
Professional Rules and Practice Guidelines	Now revise Chapter 6 of your Professional Rules and Practice Guidelines • Conflicts of Interest	

Study Period	Guidance through Study text	Attempt Questions
6 **Share remuneration**	You need to be able to calculate the amount that must be included as part of an employee's taxable employment income in respect of shares they receive from their employer. In particular you must understand: • The rules applying to the different share schemes, especially the approved schemes, although the November 2009 paper included a SFQ on restricted shares. You must be able to apply these rules and determine what figure should be included as employment income. • Employment law issues, as these have been examined in **every** paper so far, either in a SFQ or as part of a LFQ.	SFQ 6.1 – 6.3 LFQ 6.1
Examined: Sample Paper May 2007 November 2007 May 2008 November 2008 May 2009 November 2009 May 2010	Read through Chapter 6 after reading the guidance below: Read Section 1 to obtain a general understanding of the difference between: • An employer giving free or cheap shares directly to an employee, and • The employer granting an option to an employee to buy shares in the future, usually at a favourable, low price. Read Section 2 which deals with shares given directly to employees by their employer. There is an income tax charge if the shares are completely free or the employee pays less than the market value for them. Other tax charges apply if there are any restrictions on the shares. Then read Section 3 on the tax implications of an employer granting an option under an unapproved share option scheme. Try Example 1. Section 4 covers the four approved share schemes. An approved scheme is one where, to obtain favourable tax treatment, certain conditions must be satisfied before HMRC will give their approval. Make notes ensuring that you know how each scheme works, the tax implications of each scheme and what profit is charged when the employee sells the shares. You also need to be aware of the National Insurance Contribution (NIC) aspects of share schemes in Section 5. You should return to this section once you have covered NIC in the next chapter. Read through the topic, 'Working Relationships' in the ATT Manual Essential Law for the Taxation Technician, after reading the guidance below: • Read through the sections which introduce the subject of employment law, and the tests that may be used to determine whether an individual is employed or self employed. • Read through the section on contracts of employment and make notes on the format of employment contracts, including express and implied terms. • Read through the sections on termination of employment to understand the law surrounding this topic.	
Professional Rules and Practice Guidelines	Now revise Chapter 7 of your Professional Rules and Practice Guidelines • Other client handling issues	

Study Period	Guidance through Study text	Attempt Questions
7 **National insurance contributions** Examined: May 2010	In this Study Period we look at National Insurance Contributions (NIC). You need to be able to identify the different classes of NIC payable by employers and employees and also those paid by the self employed. This topic was added to the syllabus for the first time for the 2010 exams, and was tested in SFQ 4 of the May 2010 paper. The entire topic is examinable at the principles level so an awareness of the topic is all that is required. However, if you do need to make a simple NIC calculation in the exam, the rates are provided in the ATT's Tax Tables. Read through Chapter 7 on National Insurance Contributions. Make notes on the different classes of NIC payable by employers, employees and the self employed and make sure you are aware of how the NIC contributions are calculated in both cases (Sections 1 to 6). Pay particular attention to what is included in 'earnings' for NIC purposes in Section 2.2 and note that it includes not just cash payments, such as salary and bonuses, but also the employment income figure you calculated in the previous chapter for share schemes. You should also be aware that lower NIC contributions are paid by individuals who 'contract out' of the State second pension (this is a newly added topic for the 2011 exams). Finally, read quickly through Section 7 which covers the annual maximum amount of NICs payable by someone with more than one employment or with both employment and self employment income (the 'annual maxima'). This should be a relatively short Study Period, so take this opportunity to return to the Share Remuneration chapter and revise how NIC applies to taxable amounts from the various share schemes. Also, review any other topics that you have covered so far that you have found challenging or difficult.	SFQ 7.1 – 7.3 LFQ 7.1

Study Period	Guidance through Study text	Attempt Questions
8 **Pensions**	You may be asked to: • Calculate the amount of pension contributions that an individual can make to either an occupational or a personal pension scheme • Explain the tax implications of making contributions to a scheme, the timing of the contributions and on drawing the pension once the individual retires.	SFQ 8.1 – 8.6 LFQ 8.1 – 8.3
Examined: Sample Paper May 2007 November 2008 May 2009 November 2009 May 2010	Read through Chapter 8 of the Study text after reading the following guidance: Read through section 1 of the Chapter to gain background knowledge and understand the distinction between occupational and personal pension schemes. Make sure you understand that a pension is (like an ISA) a tax free wrapper around investments, so there is no income tax or capital gains tax on investments within a pension. However, the downside is that an individual cannot take the investment out of the pension until they retire. Read through Sections 2 and 3 and make notes on the following aspects for both occupational and personal pension schemes: • Whether payments are made net or gross of tax. • How tax relief is given for pension contributions. In particular make sure you understand how this affects the income tax computation you studied in Study Periods 1 and 2. Try Example 1. Read through Section 4 so that you understand how pension income is taxed on retirement.	
Professional Rules and Practice Guidelines	Now revise Chapter 8 of your Professional Rules and Practice Guidelines • Charging for services	

TQT
Tax Qualification Training

Study Period	Guidance through Study text	Attempt Questions
9 **Overseas aspects of income tax**	So far all the individuals we have considered have been UK resident. You may also be examined on: • Definitions and explanations of terminology used for discussing overseas matters (May 2009 SFQ 7 & 12) • Determining the status of an individual, to decide if they are liable to UK income tax (November 2007 LFQ 3) • Understanding the tax implications of individuals coming to and leaving the UK (Sample Paper SFQ 13, May 2007 SFQ 11) • Deciding when overseas income will be taxable on non-UK domiciled individuals in the UK (May 2009 SFQ 2) • Comparing the tax payable both with and without a remittance basis claim (November 2009 LFQ 1) • Calculating the amount of double tax relief available on foreign income.	SFQ 9.1 – 9.3 LFQ 9.1
Examined: Sample Paper May 2007 November 2007 May 2009 November 2009	Read through Chapter 9 of the Study text after reading the following guidance: Refer back to Section 2.4 of Chapter 1 to get a feel for the UK tax implications of residence and domicile status. Now read Section 1 of Chapter 9 and make notes on the meaning of residence, ordinary residence and domicile for UK tax purposes. Make sure you understand how they are interpreted where individuals are leaving or coming to the UK. Try Examples 1 and 2. Read Section 2 which covers how UK and overseas income is taxed depending on the taxpayer's residence, ordinary residence and domicile status, paying particular attention to overseas dividend income. Then read Section 3 which deals with the remittance basis of taxation, which allows the overseas income of a not ordinarily resident or non-UK domiciled taxpayer to be taxed only when it is brought into the UK. Can you determine whether it applies automatically or if the taxpayer has to make a claim for it to apply? When does a taxpayer have to pay the £30,000 remittance basis charge? You should find the flowchart at the end of the section helpful here. Try Example 3. Read Section 4 quickly, noting which non-UK residents are entitled to personal allowances and how the allowances of non-UK domiciled individuals are affected by a remittance basis claim. Finally, read Section 5 on double taxation relief (DTR) and make notes on how relief is given against the UK Income tax liability on foreign source income for tax paid overseas. You may be asked to calculate double tax relief in the exam. Try Examples 4 and 5 to check whether you have understood this section.	
Professional Rules and Practice Guidelines	Now revise Chapter 9 of your Professional Rules and Practice Guidelines • Complaints	

Study Period	Guidance through Study text	Attempt Questions
10 **Administration of income tax**	Once we have calculated an individual's income tax liability we need to know: • Self assessment reporting requirements and due dates (Sample paper SFQ 11, May 2007 SFQ 9, November 2008 SFQ 7, May 2010 SFQ 9) • Due dates for tax payments. These are easy to learn and easy marks in the exam, so learn them! (May 2007 LFQ 3, November 2009 LFQ 1) • Penalties and interest for non-compliance with the rules (May 2007 SFQ 4, November 2007 SFQ 1, May 2008 SFQ 5, May 2009 LFQ 1 & 2) • HMRC's powers and taxpayer appeals (May 2009 SFQ 3). These could be examined as a SFQ or as part of a longer question.	SFQ 16.1 – 16.2 & 16.4
Examined Sample Paper May 2007 November 2007 May 2008 November 2008 May 2009 November 2009 May 2010	Read Chapter 16 of the Study text, after reading the following guidance: Chapter 16 considers the tax administration aspects of both income and capital gains tax (CGT). As you have not studied CGT yet, we will focus on the income tax aspects only at this stage and will return to the administration of capital gains tax in a later Study Period. For each section in this chapter, note down any deadlines or due dates. You may find it useful to locate the rules in your legislation. You already have so much to learn for the exam, you should use your legislation for this topic as much as possible. Remember you can highlight the text, so do that as you follow through with the Text. Concentrate on highlighting key words and figures, not whole paragraphs. You will see that a number of rules are new – the ATT has confirmed that these new rules are examinable, even though they may not be effective until after April 2011. You are examinable on these new rules **only**. Read Section 2 and note the deadline for notifying HMRC of your liability to income tax and the penalties for doing this late. Then read Section 3 and note the different deadlines for submitting paper and electronic self assessment tax returns and who can use the short tax return. You must also be able to state the penalties for submitting a tax return late. Note the time period for which records must be kept and the penalties for failing to keep records or submitting an incorrect return. Read Section 4 on taxpayer claims for relief (eg to transfer the married couples allowance) and for refunds of overpaid tax. Section 5 is an essential section as it deals with the payment of income tax. Note the payment dates and identify how payments on account are calculated (try Example 1) and reduced, where applicable. You do not need to read Section 5.5 at this stage. From Section 6 identify the situations when late payment interest and penalties are charged by HMRC and when the taxpayer can receive interest on a repayment of overpaid tax. Finally, read through Sections 7 and 8 which deal with HMRC's powers and how the taxpayer can appeal against an HMRC assessment or decision.	
Professional Rules and Practice Guidelines	Now revise Chapter 10 of your Professional Rules and Practice Guidelines • Ceasing to act	

TQT
Tax Qualification Training

Study Period	Guidance through Study text	Attempt Questions
11 **Course Exam**	Once you have completed the above study periods you are ready to sit Course Exam 1 on Income tax and NIC. To gain the most from this exam, set aside 3 hours and 15 minutes to complete it.	Course Exam 1 (Income tax and NIC)
12 **Outline of CGT**	Questions testing capital gains tax (CGT) may require a candidate to: • Determine whether CGT applies or not to a particular disposal (May 2008 SFQ 9) • Calculate the CGT liability for a tax year (Sample paper SFQ 5, November 2009 LFQ 1, May 2010 LFQ 3). The areas covered in this study period are essential to your knowledge of CGT and whilst they are unlikely to be examined in their own right, apart from the overseas aspects (May 2008 SFQ 6, November 2008 SFQ 2 & SFQ 9, May 2009 SFQ 10, November 2009 SFQ 6 & LFQ 1), they are essential to any question involving CGT.	SFQ 10.1 – 10.4 LFQ 10.1 – 10.2
Examined: Sample Paper May 2008 November 2008 May 2009 November 2009 May 2010	Read through Chapter 10 after reading the following guidance: Read Sections 1 and 2 of the Chapter, which form essential background knowledge to CGT, and make notes making sure you can identify: • Who pays CGT. • The rates of tax applicable to individuals (both before and after 23 June 2010). • Chargeable and exempt persons, disposals and assets. Try Examples 1 and 2. Section 3 is very brief. Note the date of payment of CGT – the administration of CGT is dealt with in more detail in Study Period 18. Read Section 4 on the overseas aspects of CGT, a key topic, making sure you understand: • The impact of residence and domicile status on the chargeability of an individual to UK CGT on the disposal of UK and overseas assets. • The impact of the remittance basis. • The rules for temporary non-residents. • When double tax relief will be available and how it is calculated (try Example 3). • How the location of assets (UK or overseas) is determined.	
Professional Rules and Practice Guidelines	Now revise Chapter 11 of your Professional Rules and Practice Guidelines • Training and CPD	

Study Period	Guidance through Study text	Attempt Questions
13 **Computing gains and losses**	You may be expected to calculate capital gains tax on a number of different disposals. You must be able to calculate gains/losses quickly and efficiently, as this is the basis of most questions on CGT. You may be examined on: • The basic gain computation. The use of capital losses (May 2008 LFQ 2, November 2008 SFQ 2, May 2009 LFQ 2, May 2010 SFQ 10) • Deductible capital expenditure (May 2010 SFQ 11) • Gains on transfers between connected persons, or between husband and wife or civil partners (May 2007 SFQ7, May 2008 SFQ 2, May 2009 SFQ 13 & LFQ 3, November 2009 SFQ 2) • Gains on part disposals (Sample Paper SFQ 4, November 2009 LFQ 2) • CGT treatment of debts and loans.	SFQ 11.1 – 11.10 LFQ 11.1 – 11.2
Examined Sample Paper May 2007 November 2008 May 2009 November 2009 May 2010	Read through Chapter 11 of the Study text after taking account of the following guidance: Section 1 is essential. It shows the basic computation of a capital gain. Attempt Example 1. Section 2 shows how to calculate and use a capital loss, and how the use differs depending on whether it is a current year loss or a loss brought forward from an earlier year. Try Examples 2 to 5. Work through Example 6 on the use of losses on death. Then carefully read through the details on share loss relief (another examiner's favourite) for losses arising on disposals of shares in EIS type companies, and work through Example 7 on the rules for losses of non-UK domiciled individuals. Next, carefully work through the valuation rules in Section 3 and attempt Examples 8 and 9. Sections 4 and 5 set out the rules for dealing with disposals between connected persons and married couples/ civil partners, particularly the rules for jointly owned property. Try Example 10. Section 6 deals with the fundamental topic of part disposals. You must understand how the cost is split if an asset is disposed of in more than one disposal (Examples 11 and 12). Read the Exam Focus Point after Example 12 and then try Example 13 to revise the chapter so far. Section 7 then stands alone as it explains the CGT implications of the disposal of a debt or a loan. This is a lower priority area than the rest of this study period.	
Professional Rules and Practice Guidelines	Now revise Chapter 12 of your Professional Rules and Practice Guidelines • Members in Employment	

TQT
Tax Qualification Training

Study Period	Guidance through Study text	Attempt Questions
14 **Shares and securities**	You may be examined on the special rules for calculating gains on the sale of shares and securities. You need to be able to: • Apply the matching rules and be able to identify which shares should be included in the share pool (Sample paper SFQ 6, May 2007 SFQ 3, November 2007 LFQ 2, November 2009 LFQ 2) • Deal with bonus issues and rights issues of shares (Sample paper LFQ 2, November 2008 SFQ 6, May 2009 LFQ 3) • Deal with capital distributions, reorganisations and takeovers (Sample paper LFQ 2, November 2008 SFQ 6, May 2009 LFQ 3, May 2010 LFQ 3) • You must also be able to deal with the CGT implications of selling shares received under an employer's approved or unapproved share scheme (November 2009 LFQ 3), so now would be a good time to revisit the Share Remuneration chapter Share disposal questions often involve a lot of facts. Take your time reading through the information given.	SFQ 12.1 – 12.3 LFQ 12.1 – 12.4
Examined: Sample Paper May 2007 November 2007 November 2008 May 2009 November 2009 May 2010	Read through Chapter 12 of the Study text after reading the following guidance: Section 1 explains why we need special rules for disposals of shares and securities. Read quickly for background knowledge. Read through Sections 2 and 3 carefully, attempting Examples 1 and 2. At the end of these sections you will be able to deal with calculating a capital gain on the sale of shares. This computation will form the basis of all questions on the disposal of shares. It is important to make sure you understand this part of the chapter well before you progress to the other sections of the chapter. Once you are happy with the basic computation on the sale of shares, you can then look at how we add to the basic rules in certain circumstances. In Section 4 you will learn about: • Bonus issues (Example 3) • Rights issues (Example 4) • Capital distributions (Example 5) • Reorganisations & takeovers (Examples 6 to 8). Make sure you understand and can identify each of these situations. Finally, read Section 5. This deals with the CGT on a disposal of gilts (ie Treasury Stock) and QCBs. Try Example 9.	
Professional Rules and Practice Guidelines	Now revise Chapter 13 of your Professional Rules and Practice Guidelines • Legal matters	

Study Period	Guidance through Study text	Attempt Questions
15 **Chattels and wasting assets**	This chapter also deals with special rules, this time for the disposal of special assets known as chattels and wasting assets (which includes leases). These calculations are frequently examined as a SFQ (Sample paper SFQ 2, May 2007 SFQs 2, 6 & 7, November 2008 SFQ 10, May 2009 SFQ 4, November 2009 SFQ 4 and May 2010 SFQ 2). The types of calculation involved make these calculations easy to examine as both a SFQ and also as part of a long question, including many different capital disposals (November 2007 LFQ 2, May 2008 LFQ 2 and November 2009 LFQ 2). In November 2008 the whole of LFQ 2 examined a number of lease disposals.	SFQ 13.1 – 13.7 LFQ 13.1 – 13.3
Examined: Sample Paper May 2007 November 2007 May 2008 November 2008 May 2009 November 2009 May 2010	Read through Chapter 13 after taking note of the following guidance: Read through Section 1 and make sure you can identify a chattel in the exam: it is simply an item of personal property. Understand that wasting chattels are exempt and also how the basic gain computation is affected if there is a sale of a chattel. Quickly note the general treatment of wasting assets (that are not chattels) from Section 2, as background knowledge. This is less likely to appear as a separate question but try Example 4 to test your understanding. Now read through Section 3 very carefully. You must understand the difference between 'assigning' (ie selling) a lease and granting a lease and what makes a lease a 'short' lease. Work through each of the five different situations and try Examples 5 to 8. Try and summarise in your own words how the normal CGT calculation is affected in each situation (eg What cost is used? What proceeds?) Don't waste too much time here – just note down the difference between the different types of computations. You will have time to practise these calculations later, which is the best way to learn and revise them.	
Professional Rules and Practice Guidelines	Now revise the remaining sections of your Professional Rules and Practice Guidelines • Advertising Publicity and Promotion • Appendices Now revise the ATT's Professional Conduct in Relation to Tax and ATT's Engagement Letters for Tax Practitioners (10 March 2009).	

TQT
Tax Qualification Training

Study Period	Guidance through Study text	Attempt Questions
16 **Principal private residence relief**	Having calculated a gain on disposal, you may then be tested on the occasions when those gains may either be exempted from tax completely or deferred (ie delayed) by the operation of a CGT relief. The only relief that **exempts** the gain is Principal Private Residence Relief. Questions are unlikely to focus on a property that is entirely exempt from tax. It is more likely that you will need to consider situations where a property may be partially exempt, perhaps where there has been a period of absence from the property, during which time the property may have been rented out, or where more than one residence was held at once (Sample Paper LFQ 3, May 2007 LFQ 2, November 2008 SFQ 11, May 2009 SFQ 6, November 2009 SFQ 7).	SFQ 14.1 – 14.3 LFQ 14.1 – 14.3
Examined: Sample Paper May 2007 November 2007 November 2008 May 2009 November 2009	Read through Chapter 14 of the Study text after reading the following guidance: Section 1.1 establishes the basic principle of when the relief applies. It is fundamental to your understanding of the rest of the chapter. Understand which periods are deemed to be occupation of the property for CGT purposes – find the rules in your legislation. Try Example 1. Read quickly through Section 2 and be aware of the rules where the taxpayer owns more than one residence. Next, read carefully through Section 3 and make sure you know when letting relief is available, how this relief fits into the calculation and the maximum relief given. Try Example 2 to make sure you have understood the principles. Finally, read quickly through Section 4 and try Example 3 to ensure you know how a period of business impacts the exemption.	

Study Period	Guidance through Study text	Attempt Questions
17 **Other CGT reliefs**	The reliefs in this Study Period allow the taxpayer to defer (or delay) paying their CGT, but do not exempt the gain. It will become chargeable at some point in the future. These reliefs can be tested in either a SFQ (Sample paper SFQ 3 & 7, May 2007 SFQ 14, November 2007 SFQ 6, May 2009 SFQ 11, November 2009 SFQ 3) or as part of a long form question (each sitting apart from November 2008).	SFQ 15.1 – 15.8 LFQ 15.1 – 15.7
Examined: Sample Paper May 2007 November 2007 May 2008 May 2009 November 2009 May 2010	Read through Chapter 15 from the Study Text, after reading through the following guidance: Read quickly through Section 1 to understand what we mean by 'deferral' reliefs. Read through Sections 2.1 to 2.3, which deal with the basic gift relief rules. This is an important area so make sure you understand the fundamentals of how CGT is deferred using the relief. Try Examples 1 and 2 to test your understanding so far. Then move on to Sections 2.4 to 2.7. These are additional rules for certain circumstances that build on the basics you have already learned. Pay particular attention to Section 2.5, sales at an undervalue, where the taxpayer sells an asset for less than it is worth – this is only partly a gift so the rules are modified slightly to deal with this. Try Examples 3 and 4. Read through Section 3 on EIS deferral relief – a common exam topic. You have already seen EIS relief from an income tax perspective – and the examiner likes to test both sets of rules together – so you may find it useful to refresh your memory at this point by returning to the relevant income tax chapter. For CGT, concentrate on the amount of relief available, the qualifying conditions for the relief to apply (which are not as strict as for income tax relief) and the occasions when the deferred gain crystallises (ie becomes chargeable again). Finally, read quickly through Section 4 which deals with the treatment of insurance proceeds (or 'compensation') received when an asset is damaged or destroyed. This is a less popular exam topic but has been examined in both an SFQ and in a number of LFQs. Try Examples 6 and 7 to make sure you have understood the basic rules.	

TQT
Tax Qualification Training

Study Period	Guidance through Study text	Attempt Questions
18 **Administration of CGT**	Once CGT has been calculated for an individual we need to know : • Self assessment reporting requirements and due dates. • The due date for payment of CGT. • Penalties and interest for non-compliance with the rules. • HMRC's powers and taxpayer appeals. These could be examined as a SFQ or as part of a longer question.	SFQ 16.3
Examined: May 2007 November 2009	Read Chapter 16 of the Study text, after reading the following guidance: You have already studied the administration of income tax in Study Period 10 and in most cases the rules are identical. Read Sections 2 to 4 for revision. Read Section 5 to revise the payment dates for income tax and capital gains tax and understand how payments on account are calculated were there is both income tax and capital gains tax due (try Example 1). Most importantly, note when CGT may be paid by instalments in Section 5.5. Now identify from Section 6 the situations when interest is charged on overdue tax and note the penalties that may be due. You could also take this opportunity to revise the HMRC's powers and the rights of the taxpayer to appeal against an HMRC assessment or other decision in Sections 7 and 8.	
19, 20, 21 **Revision**	If you are a home study student attempt Course Exam 2 in Study Period 19. Use the exam to help identify areas where you are weak. Then spend the next session and any remaining time you have revising your weak areas. Just before you are about to start the 'revision phase' of your studies you should sit Course Exam 3. This exam is a good indicator of whether you are ready to move on to practising questions.	Course exams

Revision Phase

TQT provide you with the following material to assist with your revision phase:

Passcards

TQT's Passcards will be published in early 2011. TQT's Passcards follow the overall structure of the TQT Study Texts, but they are not just a condensed book, each card has been separately designed for clear presentation. Topics are self contained and can be grasped visually. **They are the perfect aid to your revision**.

i-pass CD Rom

TQT's i-Pass CD-Rom will also be published in early 2011. This is a useful tool which is designed to test the knowledge which is fundamental to your exam. It enables you to attempt tests, making it an ideal revision tool.

i-Pass has two modes. The first one is 'Test as you learn'. This allows you to test yourself on the areas that you are studying at the time or a combination of different areas. Use the sliders to choose the number of questions to do to fit the time you have available.

The second mode provides exam practice by creating an exam containing questions selected at random from those within 'Test as you learn' for you to answer.

Each mode gives you **comprehensive feedback on the questions and your performance**.

Revision Kit

TQT's Revision Kit is packed full of past examination questions and answers for you to practise. Plenty of question practice is the key to passing this exam. Many of the answers to questions in the Revision Kit have annotated marking schemes attached. This means that you can see where the easy marks are likely to be awarded on your examination and thus learn how to maximise your chances of passing. There are also a number of recap questions covering key areas of the syllabus.

TQT
Tax Qualification Training

ATT EXAMINATIONS
MAY AND NOVEMBER 2011
TAX TABLES

INCOME TAX	**2010/11**
Rates	**%**
Starting rate for savings income only	10
Basic rate for all income	20
Higher rate for non-savings and savings income only	40
Higher rate for dividends	32.5
Additional rate for non-savings and savings income only	50
Additional rate for dividends	42.5
Trust rate	50
Dividend trust rate	42.5
Thresholds	**£**
Savings income starting rate band	1 – 2,440
Basic rate band	1 – 37,400
Higher rate band	37,401 – 150,000
Standard rate band for trusts	1,000
Reliefs	**£**
Personal allowance[1]	6,475
– age 65–74[1]	9,490
– age 75 or over[1]	9,640
Married couple's allowance[2]	6,965
– Maximum income before abatement of relief - £1 for £2	22,900
– Minimum allowance	2,670
Blind person's allowance	1,890
'Rent-a-room' limit	4,250
Enterprise investment scheme relief limit[3]	500,000
Venture capital trust relief limit[4]	200,000
Employer supported childcare	£55 per week

Notes

(1) From 2010/11, the personal allowance of any individual with income above £100,000 is reduced by £1 for every £2 of income above the £100,000 limit.

(2) Only available where at least one partner was born before 6 April 1935. Relief restricted to 10%.

(3) Relief at 20%.

(4) Relief at 30%.

Income tax – Pension contributions

	Annual allowance	Lifetime allowance	Minimum pension age
	£	**£**	
2010/11	255,000	1,800,000	55

Basic amount qualifying for tax relief   £3,600

ITEPA Mileage Rates

Vehicles		**2010/11**
Car or van[1]	First 10,000 business miles	40p
	Additional business miles	25p
Motorcycles		24p
Bicycles		20p
Passenger payments		5p

Note   (1)   For NIC purposes, a rate of 40p applies irrespective of mileage.

Company cars and fuel – 2010/11

Emissions	Car benefit %[1][2][3]	
0g/km	0%	
1 – 75g/km	5%	
76 – 120g/km	10%	
121 – 130g/km	15%	
131 – 230g/km	15%	+ 1% for each additional whole 5g/km above 130g/km
Over 230g/km	35%	

Fuel benefit base figure[2]   **£18,000**

Notes
(1) Apply the car benefit percentage to list price of vehicle.
(2) Apply the same car benefit percentages to the fuel benefit base figure to calculate the fuel benefit.
(3) 3% supplement for diesel cars.

Taxable benefits for vans – 2010/11

	£
Van benefit – No CO_2 emissions	0
Van benefit – CO_2 emissions > 0g/km	3,000
Fuel benefit	550

2010/11 Official rate of interest   4.00%

TAX CREDITS

Working Tax Credit

		£
Basic element	(one per single claimant or couple)	1,920
Couple and lone parent element	(in addition to basic, one per couple)	1,890
30 hour element	(in addition to other elements, one per couple)	790
Disabled worker element	(in addition to other elements, one per couple)	2,570
Severe disability element	(in addition to other elements, one per couple)	1,095
50+ Return to work payment	(16-29 hours)	1,320
50+ Return to work payment	(30+ hours)	1,965
Childcare element – max eligible cost	(if one child in registered childcare)	£175 pw
Childcare element – max eligible cost	(if two or more children in registered childcare)	£300 pw
% of eligible childcare costs covered		80%

Child Tax Credit

		£
Family element	(one per family)	545
Baby element	(child under one year)	545
Child element	(in addition to baby element, paid for each child)	2,300
Disabled child element	(in addition to child element)	2,715
Severely disabled child element	(in addition to child and disabled child elements)	1,095

Income thresholds and withdrawal rates

First income threshold for those entitled to WTC only (or WTC and CTC)	£6,420
First threshold for those entitled to CTC only	£16,190
First withdrawal rate	39%
Second income threshold (if exceeded then entitled to family and baby elements only)	£50,000
Second withdrawal rate	6.67%
Income disregard	£25,000

STUDENT LOAN RECOVERY

Employee earnings threshold at which repayment of student loans begin is £1,250 per month.

Rate of student loan deductions is 9% of earnings above the threshold rounded down to the nearest whole pound.

TQT
Tax Qualification Training

STATUTORY MATERNITY PAY

Period	First 6 weeks	Remaining weeks
From 6 April 2010	90% average weekly earnings	Lower of 90% of weekly earnings & £124.88

STATUTORY SICK PAY

		Weekly rate
Year to 5 April 2011		£
Average weekly gross earnings	97.00 or more	79.15

NATIONAL INSURANCE CONTRIBUTIONS

Class 1 Limits

	2010/11		
	Annual	**Monthly**	**Weekly**
Lower earnings limit (LEL)	£5,044	£421	£97
Earnings threshold (ET)	£5,715	£476	£110
Upper accruals point (UAP)	£40,040	£3,337	£770
Upper earnings limit (UEL)	£43,875	£3,656	£844

Class 1 primary contribution rates	**2010/11**
Not contracted out	
Earnings between ET and UEL	11%
Earnings above UEL	1%
Contracted out	
Earnings between ET and UAP	9.4%
Earnings between UAP and UEL	11%
Earnings above UEL	1%
Rebate on earnings between LEL and ET	1.6%

Class 1 secondary contribution rates	**2010/11**
Not contracted out	
Earnings above ET	12.8%
Contracted out – salary related	
Earnings between ET and UAP	9.1%
Earnings above UAP	12.8%
Rebate on earnings between LEL and ET	3.7%
Contracted out – money purchase	
Earnings between ET and UAP	11.4%
Earnings above UAP	12.8%
Rebate on earnings between LEL and ET	1.4%

Other contribution limits and rates	**2010/11**
Class 1A contributions	12.8%
Class 1B contributions	12.8%
Class 2 contributions	
Normal rate	£2.40 pw
Small earnings exception	£5,075 pa
Class 3 contributions	£12.05 pw
Class 4 contributions	
Annual lower profits limit (LPL)	£5,715
Annual upper profits limit (UPL)	£43,875
Percentage rate between LPL and UPL	8%
Percentage rate above UPL	1%

TQT
Tax Qualification Training

CORPORATION TAX

Financial year	2010	2009
Main rate	28%	28%
Small profits rate	21%	21%
Augmented profits limit for small profits rate	£300,000	£300,000
Augmented profits limit for marginal relief	£1,500,000	£1,500,000
Standard fraction	$\frac{7}{400}$	$\frac{7}{400}$
Marginal rate	29.75%	29.75%

Research and development expenditure[1]

	SMEs	
	From 1.1.05	From 1.8.08
Employees	≤ 250	≤ 500
Turnover	≤ €50m	≤ €100m
Balance sheet assets	≤ €43m	≤ €86m

Note   (1) Small and medium sized enterprises (SMEs) must meet the employees criteria and *either* the turnover *or* the balance sheet assets criteria.

CAPITAL ALLOWANCES

	6.4.10 – 5.4.11[1]	6.4.09 – 5.4.10[1]
Annual investment allowance (AIA)[2]	100%	100%
First year allowance (FYA)[3]	-	40%
WDA on plant and machinery in main pool[4]	20%	20%
WDA on plant and machinery in special rate pool[5]	10%	10%
Writing down allowance on patent rights and know-how	25%	25%

Notes   (1) Dates for companies are 1 April - 31 March.

         (2) 100% on the first £100,000 (£50,000 in 2009/10) of investment in plant and machinery (except cars).

         (3) A FYA was available for expenditure in the main pool in 2009/10. The FYA was given after and in addition to the AIA.

         (4) A rate of 20% applies to cars with CO_2 emissions greater than 110g/km but not more than 160 g/km acquired on or after 6 April 2009 (1 April for companies).

         (5) A rate of 10% applies to cars with CO_2 emissions greater than 160 g/km acquired on or after 6 April 2009 (1 April for companies).

         (6) Cars acquired before 6 April 2009 (1 April for companies) continue to be written down based on cost rather than emissions.

100% First year allowances available to all businesses

1) New energy saving plant and machinery, and water efficient plant and machinery.

2) New cars registered between 16 April 2002 and 31 March 2013 if the car either emits not more than 110 g/km of CO_2 or it is electrically propelled.

3) Capital expenditure incurred by a person on research and development.

VALUE ADDED TAX

	From 4.1.11	From 1.1.10 to 3.1.11
Standard rate	20%	17½%
VAT fraction	1/6	7/47

Limits	From 1.4.10
Annual registration limit	£70,000
De-registration limit	£68,000

Thresholds	Cash accounting	Annual accounting
Turnover threshold to join scheme	£1,350,000	£1,350,000
Turnover threshold to leave scheme	£1,600,000	£1,600,000

INHERITANCE TAX

Death rate	40%	**Lifetime rate**	20%

Nil rate bands

6 April 1996 – 5 April 1997	up to £200,000	6 April 2003 – 5 April 2004	up to £255,000
6 April 1997 – 5 April 1998	up to £215,000	6 April 2004 – 5 April 2005	up to £263,000
6 April 1998 – 5 April 1999	up to £223,000	6 April 2005 – 5 April 2006	up to £275,000
6 April 1999 – 5 April 2000	up to £231,000	6 April 2006 – 5 April 2007	up to £285,000
6 April 2000 – 5 April 2001	up to £234,000	6 April 2007 – 5 April 2008	up to £300,000
6 April 2001 – 5 April 2002	up to £242,000	6 April 2008 – 5 April 2009	up to £312,000
6 April 2002 – 5 April 2003	up to £250,000	6 April 2009 – 5 April 2015	up to £325,000

Taper relief

Death within 3 years of gift	Nil%
Between 3 and 4 years	20%
Between 4 and 5 years	40%
Between 5 and 6 years	60%
Between 6 and 7 years	80%

Quick Succession relief

Period between transfers less than one year	100%
Between 1 and 2 years	80%
Between 2 and 3 years	60%
Between 3 and 4 years	40%
Between 4 and 5 years	20%

Lifetime exemptions

Annual exemption	£3,000
Small gifts	£250
Wedding gifts - Child	£5,000
- Grandchild or remoter issue or other party to marriage	£2,500
- Other	£1,000

CAPITAL GAINS TAX

	2010/11	
	From 23.6.10	**Until 22.6.10**
Annual exempt amount	£10,100	£10,100
CGT flat rate for individuals, trusts and PRs		18%

CGT rates for individuals[1],[2]

Gains qualifying for entrepreneurs' relief	10%
Gains falling within remaining basic rate band[3]	18%
Gains exceeding basic rate band	28%

CGT rates for trusts & individuals paying the remittance basis charge

Gains qualifying for entrepreneurs' relief	10%
Other gains	28%

CGT rate for PRs

All gains[4]	28%

Entrepreneurs' relief

Relevant gains (lifetime maximum)	£5 million	£2 million
Reducing fraction	NA	$\frac{4}{9}$

Notes   (1) For individuals, gains are taxed as if they are the top slice of income.

      (2) Capital losses and the annual exempt amount may be offset in the most beneficial manner, ie against gains not qualifying for entrepreneurs' relief first.

      (3) The remaining basic rate band is calculated as £37,400 less taxable income less any gains on which entrepreneurs' relief has been claimed.

      (4) Personal representatives of deceased persons cannot claim entrepreneurs' relief.

TQT
Tax Qualification Training

Lease percentage table

Years	Percentage	Years	Percentage	Years	Percentage
50 or more	100.000	33	90.280	16	64.116
49	99.657	32	89.354	15	61.617
48	99.289	31	88.371	14	58.971
47	98.902	30	87.330	13	56.167
46	98.490	29	86.226	12	53.191
45	98.059	28	85.053	11	50.038
44	97.595	27	83.816	10	46.695
43	97.107	26	82.496	9	43.154
42	96.593	25	81.100	8	39.399
41	96.041	24	79.622	7	35.414
40	95.457	23	78.055	6	31.195
39	94.842	22	76.399	5	26.722
38	94.189	21	74.635	4	21.983
37	93.497	20	72.770	3	16.959
36	92.761	19	70.791	2	11.629
35	91.981	18	68.697	1	5.983
34	91.156	17	66.470	0	0.000

Retail Prices Index

Where Retail Price Indices are required, it should be assumed that they are as follows.

	Jan	Feb	Mar	Apr	May	Jun	Jul	Aug	Sep	Oct	Nov	Dec
1982	–	–	79.44	81.04	81.62	81.85	81.88	81.90	81.85	82.26	82.66	82.51
1983	82.61	82.97	83.12	84.28	84.64	84.84	85.30	85.68	86.06	86.36	86.67	86.89
1984	86.84	87.20	87.48	88.64	88.97	89.20	89.10	89.94	90.11	90.67	90.95	90.87
1985	91.20	91.94	92.80	94.78	95.21	95.41	95.23	95.49	95.44	95.59	95.92	96.05
1986	96.25	96.60	96.73	97.67	97.85	97.79	97.52	97.82	98.30	98.45	99.29	99.62
1987	100.0	100.4	100.6	101.8	101.9	101.9	101.8	102.1	102.4	102.9	103.4	103.3
1988	103.3	103.7	104.1	105.8	106.2	106.6	106.7	107.9	108.4	109.5	110.0	110.3
1989	111.0	111.8	112.3	114.3	115.0	115.4	115.5	115.8	116.6	117.5	118.5	118.8
1990	119.5	120.2	121.4	125.1	126.2	126.7	126.8	128.1	129.3	130.3	130.0	129.9
1991	130.2	130.9	131.4	133.1	133.5	134.1	133.8	134.1	134.6	135.1	135.6	135.7
1992	135.6	136.3	136.7	138.8	139.3	139.3	138.8	138.9	139.4	139.9	139.7	139.2
1993	137.9	138.8	139.3	140.6	141.1	141.0	140.7	141.3	141.9	141.8	141.6	141.9
1994	141.3	142.1	142.5	144.2	144.7	144.7	144.0	144.7	145.0	145.2	145.3	146.0
1995	146.0	146.9	147.5	149.0	149.6	149.8	149.1	149.9	150.6	149.8	149.8	150.7
1996	150.2	150.9	151.5	152.6	152.9	153.0	152.4	153.1	153.8	153.8	153.9	154.4
1997	154.4	155.0	155.4	156.3	156.9	157.5	157.5	158.5	159.3	159.5	159.6	160.0
1998	159.5	160.3	160.8	162.6	163.5	163.4	163.0	163.7	164.4	164.5	164.4	164.4
1999	163.4	163.7	164.1	165.2	165.6	165.6	165.1	165.5	166.2	166.5	166.7	167.3
2000	166.6	167.5	168.4	170.1	170.7	171.1	170.5	170.5	171.7	171.6	172.1	172.2
2001	171.1	172.0	172.2	173.1	174.2	174.4	173.3	174.0	174.6	174.3	173.6	173.4
2002	173.3	173.8	174.5	175.7	176.2	176.2	175.9	176.4	177.6	177.9	178.2	178.5
2003	178.4	179.3	179.9	181.2	181.5	181.3	181.3	181.6	182.5	182.6	182.7	183.5
2004	183.1	183.8	184.6	185.7	186.5	186.8	186.8	187.4	188.1	188.6	189.0	189.9
2005	188.9	189.6	190.5	191.6	192.0	192.2	192.2	192.6	193.1	193.3	193.6	194.1
2006	193.4	194.2	195.0	196.5	197.7	198.5	198.5	199.2	200.1	200.4	201.1	202.7
2007	201.6	203.1	204.4	205.4	206.2	207.3	206.1	207.3	208.0	208.9	209.7	210.9
2008	209.8	211.4	212.1	214.0	215.1	216.8	216.5	217.2	218.4	217.7	216.0	212.9
2009	210.1	211.4	211.3	211.5	212.8	213.4	213.4	214.4	215.3	216.0	216.6	218.0
2010	217.9	219.2	220.7	222.8	223.6	225.0*	226.4*	227.8*	227.9*	229.3*	230.7*	232.1*
2011*	233.5	234.9	236.3	237.7	239.1	240.5	241.9	243.3	244.7	246.1	247.5	248.9

* = assumed

TQT
Tax Qualification Training

Personal Taxation

Part A
Personal Income Tax

TQT
Tax Qualification Training

The purpose of this chapter is to help you to:

- identify the UK's main taxes and sources of tax law
- identify who pays income tax
- follow the seven steps to calculating income tax
- understand the distinction between gross and net income
- identify which payments are deductible from total income
- identify the allowances available to reduce net income
- explain how tax relief is obtained for charitable donations
- identify and calculate the tax reductions available
- calculate the child and working tax credits
- calculate social security benefits
- understand the tax consequences of owning property jointly
- set out the tax position of beneficiaries of deceased person's estate
- identify the various categories of exempt income

References: ITA 2007 unless otherwise stated

Taxable income

1 Introduction

Exam focus point

Read through the introduction to gain background knowledge.

1.1 Taxes in the UK

The following are examples of the main UK taxes:

(a) Income tax
(b) National insurance
(c) Corporation tax
(d) Capital gains tax
(e) Inheritance tax
(f) Stamp taxes
(g) Value added tax
(h) Customs duty, tobacco, petrol and other expenditure taxes

Items (a) to (f) are known as **direct taxes**. Items (g) and (h) are **indirect taxes**. For direct taxes, Her Majesty's Revenue and Customs (HMRC) collects directly (we count the PAYE system as a form of direct collection) from the taxpayer, whereas for indirect taxes HMRC collects from an intermediary, who attempts to pass on the cost to the final consumer.

There are other classifications which may be helpful. Items (a) (b) and (c) are, in general, **taxes on income** whereas those under (d), (e) and (f) are known as **capital taxes**. The indirect taxes in (g) and (h) are often called **expenditure taxes**.

1.2 Sources of tax law

Tax law is made by statute – although it is interpreted and amplified by case law. The main taxes and their sources are set out below.

Tax	Suffered by	Source
Income tax	Individuals Partnerships Trustees	Income Tax Act 2007 (ITA 2007) Income Tax (Trading and Other Income) Act 2005 (ITTOIA 2005) Income Tax (Earnings and Pensions) Act 2003 (ITEPA 2003) Taxation (International and Other Provisions) Act 2010 (TIOPA 2010) Capital Allowances Act 2001 (CAA 2001)
Corporation tax	Companies	Corporation Tax Act 2009 (CTA 2009) Corporation Tax Act 2010 (CTA 2010) Taxation (International and Other Provisions) Act 2010 (TIOPA 2010) Capital Allowances Act 2001 (CAA 2001)
Capital gains tax	Individuals Companies (which pay corporation tax on capital gains)	Taxation of Chargeable Gains Act 1992 (TCGA 1992)
Value added tax	Businesses, both incorporated and unincorporated	Value Added Tax Act 1994 (VATA 1994)
Inheritance tax	Individuals	Inheritance Tax Act (IHTA 1984)

1.3 The legislative process

The **tax year** runs from 6 April to 5 April following. **For example, the 2010/11 tax year runs from 6 April 2010 to 5 April 2011.**

Finance Acts make changes which apply mainly to the tax year ahead. Usually there is only one Finance Act each year, for example, the Finance Act 2009 is concerned with the tax year 2009/10 for income tax purposes. However, due to the General Election taking place part way through 2010, there are three Finance Acts that deal with the 2010/11 tax year and 2010 financial year.

Exam focus point

This Study Text sets out the law as it stands in relation to the 2010/11 tax year, including the provisions of **the first two 2010 Finance Acts**, which students taking exams in May 2011 and November 2011 will be expected to know.

ATT has stated that the third 2010 Finance Act will only be examinable from the 2012 examinations onwards.

The annual Budget process commences with the Chancellor presenting a pre-Budget report around November/December, indicating areas of legislation which will be included in the Budget speech and subsequent

Finance Bill. This is followed by the Budget speech in the following March/April, announcing, amongst other things, the tax changes proposed for the coming tax year. A Finance Bill is printed and, after Parliamentary debate and various amendments, passes into law (by receiving Royal Assent to become a Finance Act) usually at the end of July, although in 2010 the third Bill is not likely to receive Royal Assent until later in the year.

The **Taxes Management Act 1970 (TMA 1970)** provides the authority and the framework for administering the income tax system. Other provisions are found in subsequent Finance Acts, particularly the 2007, 2008 and 2009 Finance Acts.

Statutory Instruments (SIs) are used by the government as a convenient way of introducing detailed legislation. They are numbered on a calendar year basis (eg SI 1989/469 is SI No. 469 issued in 1989).

2 Who pays income tax

2.1 General

The following are liable to income tax:

(a)   **Adults**
(b)   **Children**, however young, and
(c)   Each **partner** carrying on a business in the form of a partnership.

2.2 Husband and wife and civil partners

Married men and women, and same sex couples in a civil partnership, are taxable persons in their own right, each with their own allowances and bands of tax (see below).

If the husband, wife or civil partner was born before 6 April 1935, a married couple's allowance (MCA), is available to reduce the tax of usually whichever spouse or partner has the higher income (see below).

2.3 Children

A child is a taxpayer in his own right.

There is an **important exception** to this rule where investment income of a minor (under 18), unmarried child arises from a gift made by his parent (eg the parent sets up a bank account for their child). This income is treated as the parent's income if, in the year, it exceeds £100.

2.4 Residence, ordinary residence and domicile

A taxpayer may be UK:

(a)   Resident, and/or
(b)   Ordinarily resident, and/or
(c)   Domiciled.

If he was born in the UK of UK domiciled parents and has never left the UK for any length of time he is likely to be all three. Another individual may be non-resident or non-ordinarily resident or non-domiciled. Various combinations are possible and depend on the facts of each case as well as legislation and HMRC practice.

Later in this Text we set out the definitions of residence, ordinary residence and domicile in detail.

Generally, a UK resident person is liable to UK income tax on his UK *and* foreign income whereas a non-resident is liable to UK income tax only on income *arising* in the UK. If non-residents were treated identically to UK residents HMRC would try to collect income tax from French residents on their French income. You can imagine the reaction!

A UK resident, who is not domiciled or not ordinarily resident in the UK, may be able to use the *remittance* basis for his foreign income, ie it will only be liable to UK tax to the extent that such income is brought to the UK, possibly subject to paying a minimum annual £30,000 tax charge on the unremitted income in certain circumstances (see later in this Text).

2.5 Exempt persons

To conclude this section, here is a list of some of the persons or bodies **exempt from paying UK income tax**:

(a) Registered **pension** funds
(b) UK registered **charities**
(c) Representatives of foreign countries.

3 Calculating income tax

Exam focus point

Sections 3-9 explain how to prepare an income tax computation. There is usually one long question in the Personal Taxation examination testing this, so this is a high priority area.

There are **seven steps** to calculating an individual's income tax liability. [s.23]

Step 1   Identify the amounts of income on which the taxpayer is charged to income tax for the tax year. The sum of those amounts is '**total income**'.

Step 2   Subtract allowable deductible payments and available losses from total income to arrive at '**net income**'.

Step 3   Deduct the personal allowance (and blind person's allowance where relevant) to arrive at '**taxable income**'.

Step 4   Calculate tax at each applicable rate on the amount of taxable income left after Step 3.

Step 5   Add together the amounts of tax calculated at Step 4.

Step 6   Deduct from the amount of tax calculated at Step 5 any tax reductions to which the taxpayer is entitled for the tax year.

Step 7   Add to the amount of tax left after Step 6 specific tax charges related to pension schemes. The result is the taxpayer's liability to income tax for the tax year.

Below we look at each of these steps in further detail.

4 Step 1: Calculating total income

4.1 'Components' of total income

The most common types of income are listed below:

Non savings income:	
Employment income	Income earned from employment including salaries, bonuses and benefits
Pension income	Pensions, annuities and other income received from pension funds
Trade profits	Profits earned from a trade, profession or vocation
Property income	Rent etc, from all types of land and buildings
Discretionary trust income	Income from a discretionary trust

Savings income:	
Interest income	Interest received either 'net' or 'gross'
Dividend income:	
Dividend income	Dividends received

Each of these types (or 'components') of income, is added together to arrive at 'total income'. Each type is considered in detail later in this Study Text.

4.2 Gross and net income

The total income for a tax year (6 April to 5 April) is the *gross* amount (that is, including any tax deducted at source) and is in most cases the income arising in that year.

Some income is received in full ('gross'), with no tax deducted in advance. Other income is received after deduction of tax ('net').

Tax is deducted from employment income by the employer under the Pay As You Earn (PAYE) system.

Exam focus point

The salary figure in the exam will always be the **gross** amount and you will be given the amount of tax deducted under PAYE separately.

If income is received net of 20% tax, eg bank interest, it must be grossed up by $^{100}/_{80}$ to include the gross amount in the income tax computation.

UK dividend income is received net of a 10% tax credit so must be grossed up by $^{100}/_{90}$ before including it in the computation. Savings and dividend income are considered in detail in the next chapter.

Where an individual is the beneficiary of a discretionary trust, any income he receives from it, regardless of its source, is received net of 50% tax and must be grossed up by $^{100}/_{50}$ ($^{100}/_{60}$ in 2009/10), or simply multiplied by 2 to calculate the gross income.

If an individual is the beneficiary of an interest in possession trust he is taxed on all income arising in the trust regardless of whether it is paid to him or not. Income from an interest in possession trust is received net of 20% tax, or 10% tax if it is dividend income.

Income from estates in administration (see below) **is also received net** of 20% or 10% tax depending on whether it is non savings income, savings income or dividend income.

Exam focus point

In the exam you may be given either the net or the gross amount of income: read the question carefully! If you are given the **net** amount, gross up the figure at the appropriate rate. For example, if Jack receives net building society interest of £160 it is equivalent to gross income of £160 × 100/80 = £200 with tax deducted at source of £40 (£200 × 20%).

Examiner's report – Personal Taxation

May 07 – Part II LFQ 1

The main problem....was in grossing up the trust income and dividends using the appropriate rates.

---

5 Step 2: Deductible payments and losses

5.1 Introduction

A deduction is available for certain payments from total income to arrive at 'net income'.

The amount of relief available is the gross amount paid in the tax year.

These deductible payments include: [s.24]

(a) Gifts of shares and land to charity
(b) Certain interest payments
(c) Annual payments and patent royalties

Relief for losses, such as property losses (see later in this Text), is also deducted at Step 2.

5.2 Gifts of shares and land to charity

Relief is available for gifts of certain assets to charity if the asset gifted is: [ss.432 & 433]

(a) **Quoted shares or securities** (including shares dealt with on the Alternative Investment Market (AIM)).
(b) **UK freehold or leasehold land**.

Relief is given by deducting the market value of the assets (less any consideration given by the charity, plus any incidental costs of making the disposal) **from total income**.

There is no capital gains tax (CGT) on such gifts (see later in this Text).

Exam focus point

Examiner's report – Personal Taxation

November 2009 – Part I SFQ 9

Most candidates realised that there was income tax relief but were vague as to exactly how much; only a small minority knew that it was available for quoted but not unlisted companies.

5.3 Interest payments

Interest payments **paid** in a tax year are deductible from total income when a loan is used for the following purposes:

(a) **To buy plant or machinery for use in a partnership.** Interest qualifies for three years from the end of the tax year in which the loan was taken out. If the plant is used partly for private purposes, only a proportion of the interest is eligible for relief. [s.388]

(b) **To buy plant or machinery for employment purposes.** Interest qualifies for three years from the end of the tax year in which the loan was taken out. If the plant is used partly for private purposes, only a proportion of the interest is eligible for relief. Interest relief is not available for a loan to acquire a car which an employee uses for business purposes, as a mileage allowance is available for business mileage instead (see later in this Text). [s.390]

(c) **To buy an interest in a close company (ordinary shares)** (other than a close investment holding company) or to lend money to such a company for the purpose of its business. A close company is a company controlled by its shareholder-directors or by five or fewer shareholders.

When the interest is paid the borrower must *either* hold some shares and work full time as a manager or director of the company *or* have a material interest in the close company (ie hold more than 5% of the shares). [s.392]

Relief is not available if Enterprise Investment Scheme (EIS) (see later in this Text) relief is claimed on the shares.

(d) **To buy shares in an employee-controlled company**. The company must be an unquoted trading company resident in the UK with at least 50% of the voting shares held by employees. [s.396]

(e) **To invest in**, or contribute capital or make a loan to, **a partnership**. The borrower must be a partner (other than a limited partner), and relief ceases when he ceases to be one. [s.398]

(f) **To buy shares in or lend money to a co-operative** (a common ownership enterprise). The borrower must work for the greater part of his time in the co-operative or a subsidiary. [s.401]

(g) **To pay inheritance tax**. Interest paid by the personal representatives of a deceased person's estate qualifies for 12 months after the date that the loan was taken out. [s.403]

(h) The replacement with other loans qualifying under (c) to (f) above.

If the interest is paid wholly and exclusively for business purposes the taxpayer can instead deduct the interest when computing his trade profits, rather than from total income. The interest need not fall into any of the categories outlined above.

Interest on a loan taken out by an individual to buy a letting property will qualify as an expense when computing property income (see later in this Text).

Where interest is allowable in the computation of trade profits or property income, the amount *payable* (on an accruals basis) is deducted rather than interest *paid* in the tax year.

5.4 Patent royalties

The only examinable deductible payment that is paid *net* is a non-trade related patent royalty payment, ie it is paid net of basic rate income tax (20% × the gross amount). [s.448]

However, as it is always the *gross figure* that is shown in the payer's tax computation, the deductible patent royalty payment must be grossed up by $^{100}/_{80}$. Doing so, however, means that the taxpayer has obtained tax relief twice, so the tax deducted must be collected as part of the taxpayer's self assessment, even where they may not usually be required to submit a self assessment return.

Note that patent royalties paid for the purposes of a trade are deducted in calculating the individual's trading income and not as a deductible payment.

Example 1

For 2010/11 Brenda has earnings of £4,350 and pays non-trade related patent royalties of £800 (net amount).

What amount can Brenda deduct from her total income and how much tax must she add to her liability?

---

6 Step 3: Personal allowance and blind person's allowance

6.1 The allowances

The personal allowance and the blind person's allowance are deducted from net income (at Step 3) to arrive at 'taxable income'.

The amount of the allowances are the same in 2009/10 and 2010/11.

6.2 Personal allowance (PA)

6.2.1 Basic personal allowance

This section is new.

All individuals (including children) are entitled to an amount of tax free income, the personal allowance (PA), of £6,475.

However, from 6 April 2010, if an individual's 'adjusted net income' exceeds £100,000 the personal allowance is reduced by £1 for every £2 of excess income. It can be reduced to nil (once income reaches £112,950), but if any allowance remains it is rounded up to the nearest pound.

Adjusted net income is broadly net income, less a deduction for the gross value of: [s.58]

(a)   Gift Aid donations (see below)
(b)   Personal pension contributions (see later in this Text), and
(c)   Trade losses.

Example 2

Bart earns £126,250 in 2010/11 from his employment with Waltrade Ltd. This is his only income in the year. He makes a contribution of £15,000 (gross) to his personal pension.

Calculate Bart's taxable income.

6.2.2 Age allowance (AA)

An individual aged between 65 and 74 years (at any time in the tax year) is entitled to an age allowance of £9,490 instead of the ordinary PA of £6,475.

Where adjusted net income (see above) exceeds £22,900 the age allowance is reduced by one half of the excess over £22,900 in much the same way as the personal allowance (see above). The allowance cannot usually fall below £6,475 unless, from 6 April 2010, adjusted net income exceeds £100,000, in which case it can be reduced to £nil (see above).

Individuals aged 75 or over (at any time in the tax year) obtain a more generous age allowance of £9,640. The higher age allowance works in the same way as the basic age allowance, with the same adjusted net income limit of £22,900.

Someone who dies in the tax year in which they would have had their 65th or 75th birthday is treated as having reached that age during the year.

Example 3

Geoff is 68 and has income of £25,620. What is his personal allowance for 2010/11?

6.3 Blind person's allowance (BPA)

A taxpayer who is registered with a local authority as a blind person is entitled to an allowance of £1,890. This is given in addition to the personal allowance.

6.4 Persons resident abroad

In general, **non-UK residents are liable to tax on income arising in the UK, but are not entitled to allowances**. However, **certain people are entitled to allowances despite being non-resident**. These are: [s.56(3)]

(a)   Individuals resident in the Isle of Man or the Channel Islands
(b)   Former residents who have left the country for their own or a family member's health reasons
(c)   Current or former Crown servants and their widows or widowers
(d)   Employees in the service of any territory under Her Majesty's protection
(e)   Missionaries
(f)   EEA nationals (ie all 27 EU member states, plus Iceland, Liechtenstein and Norway).

From 2010/11 Commonwealth citizens only qualify for allowances if they are already entitled to them under one of the categories listed above.

The rules for non-residents apply both to allowances deducted from net income (the PA and the BPA) and to allowances that reduce tax (eg married couples' allowance, see below).

UK resident **individuals who claim the remittance basis of taxation on their foreign income** (eg a non UK domiciled individual) are **not entitled to personal allowances** (see later in this Text).

Exam focus point

Calculation of allowances is often tested in the short form questions. Make sure you are familiar with the rules.

7 Steps 4 & 5: Calculating income tax

7.1 The personal tax computation

We have now considered the fundamental elements of the *personal tax computation*. Here is an example of what that computation might look like so far.

Illustration 1

MRS A: INCOME TAX COMPUTATION 2010/11

	£
Employment income – salary (PAYE of £46,010 deducted)	140,200
Property income – rent from cottage	24,100
Taxed income from discretionary trust £1,350 × 100/50	2,700
Total income	167,000
Less: deductible payment (eg qualifying interest paid)	(1,017)
Net income	165,983
Less: personal allowance (adjusted net income > £112,950)	(Nil)
Taxable income	165,983

Income tax is charged on the figure of 'taxable income' according to the type (or component) **of income being taxed**.

In 2010/11 the first £37,400 of non-savings income is taxed at the basic rate of 20%. Taxable non-savings income between £37,400 and £150,000 is taxed at a higher rate of 40% and income above £150,000 is taxed at the additional rate of 50%.

In the above illustration all of the taxable income is taxed as non-savings income:

(a)   **On the first £37,400 at the basic rate (20%) = £7,480**
(b)   **On the next £112,600 (ie up to £150,000) at the higher rate (40%) ie £112,600 @ 40% = £45,040**
(c)   **On the excess above £150,000 at the additional rate (50%) ie £15,983 @ 50% = £7,991**

The total tax liability would be £60,511.

The tax bands and rates are provided in the Association's rates and allowances tables in the examination.

Different tax rates apply to savings income and dividends (see the next Chapter).

Example 4

Simone's taxable income (ie after the personal allowance) for 2010/11 is £49,035. All of her income is non savings income. Calculate Simone's tax liability for the year.

The tax calculation may be affected by cash payments to charity made under the Gift Aid scheme (see below) or to personal pension schemes (see later in this Text).

7.2 Gift Aid

Cash payments to charity made under the Gift Aid scheme affect the donor's income tax computation. [s.414]

All cash donations to UK and EU/EAA charities are treated as being paid net, ie after deduction of income tax at the basic rate (20%), so a donation of £780 is treated as a gross donation of £975 (£780 × $^{100}/_{80}$).

The donor's basic rate band, and higher rate band from 2010/11, is increased by this gross gift (£975 in our example above). This only affects higher and additional rate taxpayers.

However, **until 6 April 2011 a net donation of £780 is actually worth £1,000 to the charity,** as it can claim an additional supplement from the Government (to top up the tax reclaim to the amount it would have been had the basic rate of tax remained at 22%, ie the basic rate of tax before 2008/09).

The gross donation for the charity is £780 × $^{100}/_{78}$, so it can reclaim a total of £220 (£1,000 × 22%). The gross donation for the donor, however, remains £975, so his tax bands are increased by £975 as usual and not by £1,000.

In the following illustration the taxpayer pays a total of £1,920 to charity under Gift Aid.

Illustration 2

MR B: INCOME TAX COMPUTATION 2010/11

		£
Net income		48,090
Less: personal allowance		(6,475)
Taxable income		41,615

Tax liability	£	£
Basic rate band:	37,400 @ 20%	7,480
Extended basic rate band: £1,920 × 100/80	2,400 @ 20%	480
Higher rate:	1,815 @ 40%	726
	41,615	8,686

So, the taxpayer obtains relief on the Gift Aid donation at the higher rate of £480 (£2,400 × (40 – 20 = 20%)) as income that would otherwise be taxed at 40% is only taxed at 20%.

The charitable payment must not be repayable to the donor.

Benefits provided by the charity to the donor or any person connected with him must not be worth more than: [s.418]

(a)	For gifts ≤ £100:	25% × the donation
(b)	For gifts between £100 and £1,000:	£25
(c)	For gifts > £1,000:	lower of (i) 5% × the donation and (ii) £500

The taxpayer must complete a declaration form agreeing to pay the appropriate amount of tax to cover the amount that the charity will reclaim.

If a donor pays insufficient tax during the year his allowances must be restricted to ensure the basic rate tax being recovered by the charity is paid.

All cash payments to charity (other than those made under the Payroll Deduction Scheme – see later in this Text) are potentially relievable under the Gift Aid scheme. There are no maximum or minimum thresholds for Gift Aid payments.

Taxpayers may elect to carry back the Gift Aid payments to the previous tax year. This may enable them to obtain higher rate tax relief in the previous year if their income in the current year is not sufficient to obtain higher rate relief. [s.426]

Example 5

Zoë earned £50,000 in 2010/11 and expects to earn £30,000 in 2011/12. She has no other income. In May 2011, she paid £8,000 under the Gift Aid scheme. Zoë elects for the gift to be treated as made in 2010/11. Show Zoë's tax liability in both years assuming that rates and allowances for 2011/12 are the same as for 2010/11.

A claim for carry back must be made no later than the date on which the taxpayer files his return for the earlier year, and in any event no later than the filing date for electronic tax returns for that year (see later in this Text). A claim to carry back relief from 2010/11 to 2009/10 must be made by 31 January 2011.

Where an individual overpays tax he can complete the 'Giving your tax repayment to charity' form and send it to HMRC with his tax return so that HMRC sends the repayment directly to the charity of his choice.

8 Step 6: Tax reductions

8.1 Introduction

Tax reductions reduce the tax on the income once it has been calculated. The tax reductions are as follows.

	Tax reduction
Investment under the **Venture Capital Trust Scheme (VCT)** (see later in this Text)	30% of investment (maximum investment = £200,000)
Investment under the **Enterprise Investment Scheme (EIS)** (see later in this Text)	20% of investment (maximum investment = £500,000)
Maintenance payments following the breakdown of marriage	10% of payment
Married couple's allowance	10% of allowance

Married couple's allowance and relief for maintenance payments are only available where the individuals concerned were born before 6 April 1935 (ie were aged 76 by the end of the 2010/11 tax year).

8.2 Married couple's allowance (MCA)

8.2.1 The relief

The MCA is available for married couples and same sex couples within a civil partnership. [s.42]

The MCA is only available if either spouse or partner (or both) was born before 6 April 1935 (ie 76 in 2010/11). If this condition is satisfied a minimum allowance is available of £2,670.

The tax reduction is given at 10% so the minimum tax reduction is 10% × £2,670 = £267.

For couples who are married **before 5 December 2005** (the date civil partnerships were introduced), the **tax reduction is automatically allocated to the husband**.

For marriages and civil partnerships entered into **on or after 5 December 2005**, the **tax reduction is allocated to whichever partner has the higher income**.

The **maximum value of the MCA is £6,965** if *either* partner is over 76 by the end of the tax year **but is subject to an income restriction**.

When adjusted net income exceeds £22,900, the personal allowance given to an elderly person is reduced by half of the excess, as explained above. **Once that has been reduced to £6,475 (or lower if the individual has adjusted net income between £100,000 and £112,950), the married couple's age allowance is then reduced by the excess restriction, but not to below £2,670.**

For marriages before 5 December 2005, the reduction in the married couple's age allowance always depends on the *husband's* adjusted net income. For marriages and civil partnerships entered into after 5 December 2005, the restriction to the MCA depends on the adjusted net income of the partner with the higher income.

8.2.2 Elections to transfer the MCA

The wife (or for partnerships/marriages entered into after 5 December 2005, the lower earning partner) can unilaterally (ie alone) elect to have half of the MCA tax reduction set against her tax instead of her partner's. The election must be made by the start of the tax year.

Alternatively, the couple can jointly elect, by the start of the tax year, to transfer all of the MCA tax reduction to the wife (or for partnerships/marriages entered into after 5 December 2005, the lower earning partner). An election remains in force until revoked, and any revocation applies from the following 6 April. For the year of marriage/partnership, an election may be made during the year.

The elections can only apply in respect of the minimum £2,670 MCA even if a higher allowance is available.

Any MCA which turns out to be wasted (because either spouse or partner has insufficient tax to reduce) may then be transferred to the other spouse or partner.

8.2.3 The year of marriage

In the year of marriage/civil partnership, the MCA is reduced by $^1/_{12}$ for each full tax month (from the 6th of one month to the 5th of the next) **before the wedding/civil partnership**.

8.2.4 The year of death/separation

If a wife (or for partnerships/marriages entered into after 5 December 2005, the lower earning partner) dies during a tax year, her partner receives the personal allowance (PA) and a full MCA for that year. The wife or lower earning partner will have a full PA for the year of death.

When a husband (or for partnerships/marriages entered into after 5 December 2005, the higher earning partner) dies the full PA and MCA (subject to age) are available. Any election relating to the MCA becomes void in the year of death. The widowed spouse or partner obtains the PA for the year, as normal, and is entitled to any MCA that becomes surplus.

In the tax year in which separation takes place, the husband or higher earning partner receives the PA plus a full MCA. However, any MCA election remains valid.

8.3 Maintenance payments

Provided the payer or the recipient (or both) was born before 6 April 1935 a tax reduction is available for payments under court orders or written agreements, or for maintenance assessments by the Child Support Agency. [s.453]

All maintenance payments are made gross (without deduction of tax at source) and are not taxable on the recipient.

Provided that the payment is made to the former spouse/partner for the benefit of the former spouse/partner or of a child of the family (and not directly to a child of the relationship), the payer is entitled to claim a tax reduction of 10% of the lower of:

(a)   The payments *due* in the tax year, and
(b)   The minimum value amount of the MCA (£2,670 for 2010/11).

8.4 Giving tax reductions

The tax reduction for enterprise investment scheme or venture capital trust scheme investments, married couples' allowance and qualifying maintenance payments are calculated and deducted only if the individual has enough tax to reduce. For example, if the tax is £130 and the reduction is £200, the tax is only reduced to nil. The individual *cannot* claim a repayment of (£200 – £130 =) £70.

An individual may be entitled to several different tax reductions. They **must be applied in a set order** as follows:

(a)   Investments under the venture capital trust and then enterprise investment schemes
(b)   Maintenance payments
(c)   The married couple's allowance.

Using the MCA last enables any unused amount to be transferred to the other spouse/partner. The other tax reductions cannot be transferred in this way.

Example 6

Peter, a married man aged 77, pays maintenance of £3,000 a year to a former spouse. His current wife has no income and is younger than him. Show his tax position for 2010/11 if his income consists of:

(a)   Trading profits of £27,700 and rental income of £2,000,
(b)   Trading profits of £8,100 and rental income of £2,000.

Exam focus point

Do not confuse how relief is given for allowances and tax reductions. **Allowances** are deducted from **net income**. **Tax reductions** reduce **tax on income**.

---

9 Step 7: Tax liability

The final step in calculating tax liability is to add certain tax charges including (see later in this Text): [s.30]

(a)   The pension lifetime allowance charge, and
(b)   The pension annual allowance charge.

Any tax already suffered by deduction at source (or already paid on account under self assessment) can then be deducted from the tax liability to arrive at the tax payable by the taxpayer.

We have now completed the steps for calculating the tax liability. Let's look once more at Illustration 1 (Mrs A) for an example of what a full personal tax computation may look like.

Illustration 3

MRS A: INCOME TAX COMPUTATION 2009/10

	£
Employment income – salary (PAYE of £46,010 deducted)	140,200
Property income – rent from cottage	24,100
Taxed income from discretionary trust £1,350 × 100/50	2,700
Total income	167,000
Less: deductible payment (eg qualifying interest paid)	(1,017)
Net income	165,983
Less: Personal allowance (total income > £112,950)	(NIL)
Taxable income	165,983

TQT
Tax Qualification Training

	£
Income tax:	
£37,400 @ 20%	7,480
£112,600 @ 40%	45,040
£15,983 @ 50%	7,991
	60,511
Less: Tax reduction	
– EIS subscription (see later in this Text) £1,000 @ 20%	(200)
Tax liability	60,311
Less: Tax suffered at source:	
– PAYE	(46,010)
– Discretionary trust income £2,700 × 50%	(1,350)
Tax payable (under self assessment)	12,951

10 Tax credits

10.1 Introduction

Child Tax Credit (CTC) and Working Tax Credit (WTC) are designed to support single people and couples with children. It is not necessary to have a very low income to claim the Child Tax Credit, so it is available to many people with children. The Pension Credit is for those aged 60 or over to provide them with a minimum income.

The term 'credits' is a misnomer as they are not tax credits that appear in the individual's tax computation but are non-taxable amounts that are payable directly to the individuals who are entitled to receive them.

The table below sets out who is eligible for the CTC and WTC:

TAX CREDIT	AVAILABLE TO:
CTC	UK resident individual responsible for at least one child/qualifying young person
WTC	Employed/self employed individual on a relatively low income who is either:
	• ≥ 25 years and working ≥ 30 hours a week, or
	• ≥ 16 years, responsible for one or more children and working ≥ 16 hours a week, or
	• ≥ 16 years, disabled and working ≥ 16 hours a week

Single or separated individuals claim tax credits based on their individual circumstances. Married or co-habiting couples must make a claim based on their joint circumstances.

10.2 Income

Tax credits for any tax year are calculated based on the income of the last complete tax year before the year of the claim. Gross income less registered pension scheme contributions and Gift Aid donations is used to calculate entitlement.

Income includes cash remuneration (salary, tips, reimbursed expenses etc less any allowable employment expenses) and the following benefits:

- Mileage allowance over the HMRC approved rates
- Company car and fuel
- Reimbursed non-business expense payments
- Gifts of goods and assets from the employer (eg gifts of food and drink)
- Payments made by the employer directly to a third party (eg rent to the employee's landlord), and
- Taxable vouchers and credit card purchases.

It also includes taxable interest income, taxable rental income, and foreign income.

The first £300 of interest, dividends, rental and foreign income is excluded. This limit applies to a couple's joint income, not £300 each.

An annual adjustment is carried out at the year end to finalise the tax credit based on current year income if lower than the previous year, or if higher than the previous year by more than £25,000.

If income in the year of claim rises by less than £25,000, it does not affect the level of tax credit awarded, ie the claim is still based on the income of the previous year. The increased income affects the amount awarded for the following year. For example if in 2010/11 income is £12,000, the tax credit is based on the previous year's income of say £10,000. However in 2011/12 the £12,000 of income from 2010/11 will be used to calculate the tax credit.

Where income in the current year is more than £25,000 higher than the previous year, the tax credits are based on the income of the current year.

Where the income in the current year is lower than the previous year a higher credit may be due. The individual can either:

- Inform HMRC immediately, in which case the tax credit will be adjusted accordingly. If credits are then overpaid, they will need to be repaid at the year end, or

- Wait until the end of the year and receive a one off credit at the year end.

Entitlement to tax credits is **not** affected by capital (ie savings, investments, property etc).

10.3 Child tax credit

Those who receive Income Support or income-based Jobseeker's Allowance will automatically receive the full amount of CTC for which they qualify.

The maximum annual amounts of CTC for 2010/11 are:

Element	Applies	Maximum Annual amount
		£
Family element	(one per family)	545
Family element, baby addition	(per family if at least one child under 1)	545
Child element	(per child including those under 1)	2,300
Disabled child element	(in addition, per disabled child)	2,715
Severely disabled child element	(in addition to the disabled element, per severely disabled child)	1,095

A disabled child is one who is registered blind or receives Disability Living Allowance (DLA) (see below), while a severely disabled child must be receiving the DLA care component at the highest rate.

Ignoring WTC, for joint income up to £16,190 the maximum CTC is payable as detailed above.

For joint income between £16,190 and £50,000, the full family element of £545 is payable plus the £545 baby element, if applicable. However, above the income threshold of £16,190, the 'per child' element of £2,300 per child is reduced by 39% of the excess income.

Once joint income exceeds £50,000, the per child element has already been reduced to zero and now the family and any baby elements are also reduced by £1 for every £15 over the £50,000 threshold.

Example 7

Charlie and Helen are married with two children, one of whom receives the Disability Living Allowance. They had joint family income of £16,465 last year. This year, joint income is expected to be £17,000. They are not eligible for WTC. They also have joint interest income of £250. Calculate the CTC that they are entitled to.

Example 8

Megan and Llewelyn are married with four children and had joint family income of £54,600 last year. This year, joint income is the same. They are not eligible for WTC. They also have joint interest income of £700. Calculate the CTC that they are entitled to.

CTC is paid to the main carer. Where the claim is made by a couple the CTC can only be paid to the person in that couple who is the main carer for all the children of that couple.

Where there is a dispute as to whom the main carer is, HMRC will determine who, in fact, the main carer is.

CTC should not be confused with Child Benefit which is paid to all parents regardless of their level of income and is tax free.

10.4 Working tax credit

The maximum annual amounts of WTC for 2010/11 are:

Element	Applies	Maximum Annual amount
		£
Basic element	(one per single claimant or couple)	1,920
Couple's and lone parent element	(in addition to basic, one per couple)	1,890
Disabled worker element	(in addition, if joint claim each claimant is entitled if both satisfy conditions)	2,570
30 hour element	(in addition to other elements, one per couple and look at joint hours)	790
Severe disability element	(in addition to disabled element, do not need to be working)	1,095
Childcare element maximum eligible cost	(if one child in registered childcare)	£175 per week
	(if two children in registered childcare)	£300 per week
	% of eligible childcare costs recovered	80%
50+ return to work payment	(in addition, paid to each claimant who works 16 – 29 hrs – available for 12m)	1,320
	(alternatively, paid to each claimant who works 30+ hrs – available for 12m)	1,965

WTC is payable in addition to CTC. **The childcare element of the WTC is paid direct to the main carer together with any CTC**. To qualify for the childcare element a lone parent or a couple must work at least 16 hours per week in total.

WTC is paid to the person who is working 16 hours or more each week. Couples where both partners qualify must decide who will receive it. WTC cannot be paid to the unemployed.

The amount received depends upon the income of the family. Tax credits are payable in full where the income is less than £6,420. Excess income above £6,420 reduces entitlement to tax credits at the rate of 39%. The WTC is reduced first, then CTC.

Example 9

Sophie and Shaun are married with four children, two of whom receive Disability Living Allowance, and had joint family income of £13,000 last year. This year, joint income is expected to be £13,500.

Shaun works more than 30 hours per week. Sophie works 18 hours per week. The youngest child is placed with a childminder each week (cost £75pw). Calculate the tax credits that they are entitled to.

TQT
Tax Qualification Training

10.5 Claiming the CTC and WTC

Tax credits need to be claimed within three months of entitlement. Therefore claims for 2010/11 should be submitted by 6 July 2010.

Where a claim needs to be backdated, it can only be backdated for a maximum of 3 months. Supposing an individual earns £60,000 salary, he would probably not complete a form as he's above the upper limit to any entitlement. However, if he's made redundant in October the earliest he could backdate his claim to is July. Thus he would lose any entitlement to tax credits for April to June. **Clients with children are advised to make a protective claim to CTC even if at the start of the year they have joint income above the level at which entitlement is reduced to nil.**

10.6 Pension Credit

Pension Credit is available to people aged 60 or over. It **guarantees those aged 60 and over a minimum income** of at least:

- £132.60 a week for a single person, or
- £202.40 a week for a couple

There is an additional element intended to reward savings which is payable if the claimant (or their partner) is age 65 or over. The maximum additional benefit is £20.52 per week for a single pensioner and £27.09 per week for a couple.

Whether the full benefit is available depends on income, which for this purpose includes earnings and pension benefits (including State pensions) and some other benefits such as Carer's Allowance and Bereavement Benefit. The definition excludes Attendance Allowance, Disability Living Allowance, Housing Benefit and Council Tax Benefit (see below).

11 Social security benefits

11.1 Introduction

In certain situations individuals may be able to claim State benefits. We look at various benefits in this section.

11.2 Benefits available following a death

11.2.1 Bereavement payment

A bereavement payment is a non-taxable one off lump sum payment of £2,000. It is available to widows and widowers whose **late spouse made sufficient National Insurance (NIC) contributions** or died as a result of their job.

11.2.2 Widowed parent's allowance (WPA)

Widowed parent's allowance is a taxable weekly benefit of £97.65 available to individuals:

- Bringing up a child under 19 (or expecting their late husband's/ civil partner's baby), **and**
- They are under State Pension age (60 for women and 65 for men), **and**

- Their husband, wife or civil partner died and they paid National Insurance contributions (NICs), **or**
- Their husband, wife or civil partner died as a result of their work - even if they didn't pay NICs.

11.2.3 Bereavement allowance

Bereavement allowance is a taxable weekly benefit paid for up to 52 weeks after the death of the claimant's spouse/civil partner. It is available to widows and widowers whose **late spouse made sufficient NIC contributions. The claimant must be aged 45 or over at the death of the spouse, have no dependent children, and not be entitled to WPA.**

A claimant aged 55 or over when widowed gets the full rate of bereavement allowance (£97.65). Those aged between 45 and 54 receive a reduced amount based on their age at the date of death of their spouse/civil partner.

11.3 Benefits available on illness

11.3.1 Statutory sick pay (SSP)

SSP of £79.15 per week is payable to employees who are:

- Aged between 16 and 65
- Sick for at least four days in a row (weekends and bank holidays are included)
- Earning at least £97 a week on average (the NIC lower earnings limit).

SSP is limited to a maximum period of 28 weeks. Different periods of sickness less than eight weeks apart can be linked for this purpose. If incapacity continues after the end of the 28 week period then incapacity benefit may be claimed (see below).

SSP is subject to tax and NICs as normal earnings.

11.3.2 Incapacity benefit and Employment and support allowance

Individuals who have been unable to work due to illness or disability since before 27 October 2008 may be entitled to a weekly incapacity benefit.

It is available where for example SSP has ended, or the individual was self employed or unemployed, and the individual was:

- Paying National Insurance Contributions (NIC)
- Unable to work due to sickness or disability for at least four days in a row
- Getting special medical treatment and unable to work for two or more days out of seven consecutive days

There are three rates of incapacity benefit:

Weekly rate	Amount	Amount if over State Pension age
Short-term (lower rate – first 28 weeks)	£68.95	£87.75
Short-term (higher rate – weeks 29 to 52)	£81.60	£91.40
Long-term basic rate (from week 53)	£91.40	not eligible

Short-term lower rate incapacity benefit is not taxable. Other incapacity benefit is taxable.

From 27 October 2008 new claimants with an illness or disability are instead entitled to employment and support allowance (ESA). This helps individuals who are unemployed or self employed and not (or no longer) receiving SSP, to move into work, if they are able.

There are two phases: the assessment and the main phase. During the assessment phase the claimant undergoes a work capability assessment (a medical interview and sometimes a physical examination) to assess how the illness or disability affects them and their ability to work. The assessment phase rate is paid for the first 13 weeks of the claim while a decision is made on the capability for work.

The main phase rate starts from week 14 if the work capability assessment shows that the illness or disability does limit the ability to work. If the illness or disability has a severe effect on the ability to work, the claimant receives a support component in addition to the basic rate.

The rates of ESA for 2010/11 are:

Weekly rate	Amount
Assessment phase:	
- Basic rate – Single person aged 25 or over	Up to £65.45
- Basic rate – Single person aged under 25	Up to £51.85
Main phase:	
- Basic rate	Up to £91.40
- Including support component	Up to £96.85

11.4 Benefits available to those needing long term care

11.4.1 Disability living allowance (DLA)

DLA is a tax free benefit for children and adults who need help with personal care or have walking difficulties due to physical or mental disability. Individuals over the age of 65 may be eligible for attendance allowance (see below).

There are two components to the DLA:

- Care component – for those needing help looking after themselves or supervision to keep safe
- Mobility component – for those who cannot walk or need help getting around

There are three different weekly rates of the care component dependent upon the degree of care needed.

- Highest rate   £71.40
- Middle rate   £47.80
- Lowest rate   £18.95

There are two different rates of the mobility component.

- Higher rate   £49.85
- Lower rate   £18.95

11.4.2 Attendance allowance

Attendance allowance is a tax-free benefit for people aged 65 or over who need help with personal care due to physical or mental disability.

There are two weekly rates:

- Higher rate   £71.40
- Lower rate   £47.80

11.5 Benefits available to carers

11.5.1 Child benefit

Child benefit is a non-taxable benefit paid to people responsible for at least one child. It does not count as income for Tax Credit purposes (see above).

The following weekly amounts are payable in respect of each qualifying child:

- £20.30 a week for the eldest child
- £13.40 a week for each additional child.

The benefit can be claimed by anyone bringing up a child, regardless of their level of income, who is:

(a)   Under 16.
(b)   Under 19 and is studying full time up to A Level, Advanced Vocational Certificate of Education (AVCE) or equivalent.
(c)   16 or 17 and registered with the Careers Service for work or training.

11.5.2 Carer's allowance

This is a taxable benefit for those who spend at least 35 hours a week caring for someone who is in receipt of either attendance allowance or the disability living allowance at the higher or middle rate of the care component (see above).

Carer's allowance is not paid to claimants earning more than £100 per week.

The weekly rate is £53.90, reduced by the amount of certain other benefits, including State Pension, that the claimant receives. It is not payable at all if the claimant's other social security benefits exceed this amount.

11.6 Benefits available on retirement

11.6.1 State pension and state second pension (S2P)

Where sufficient NICs have been paid, a full basic State Pension, currently £97.65 per week for a single person and up to £195.30 a week for a couple, will become payable at State pension age. This is generally 65 for men and 60 for women although all individuals will have a State pension age of 65 by 2020.

A State second pension (S2P) will be earned by those **employees** who satisfy the entitlement conditions by having **paid sufficient NIC** contributions.

The self employed earn no State second pension benefit. **A widow or widower may inherit a State second pension (S2P) from their late spouse.**

Both the State Pension and the S2P are taxable.

12 Joint property

12.1 General principles

Income from assets held in spouses' or civil partners' joint names will usually be split equally between them for tax purposes if they are living together, even if they hold unequal shares in the assets.

They are treated as owing the property equally except if the income is:

(a)   Earned income, eg employment income
(b)   Profits from a business partnership
(c)   Dividends from jointly owned shares in a close company
(d)   Property income from a furnished holiday letting (FHL) (see later in this Text).

Where the couple separates, the equal shares rule no longer applies.

12.2 Joint declaration

The couple can make a joint declaration of their actual interests in an asset held in joint names if their actual entitlements to the asset and its income are unequal. **This will result in the income being assessed on each partner according to their actual share.**

Income will be split on the basis of the declaration from the date of the declaration. A declaration in respect of an asset cannot be withdrawn and remains in force until either the marriage/partnership comes to an end or the interests change.

If the interests do change the 'equal shares' rule applies until a further declaration is made. If an asset ceases to be held in joint names, the partner entitled to all the income from the asset will be assessed on it from the date of the change.

12.3 Planning

If one partner's marginal rate of tax (the rate on the highest part of his or her income) is higher than the other partner's marginal rate, **it is sensible to transfer income-yielding assets to the partner with the lower rate.** Income can then, for example, be taxed at 20% instead of at 40% or 50%. However, **an outright gift of the property (with no strings attached) is required.**

Recently HMRC has shown a clear intention to scrutinise the division of assets and income very closely. Where it feels the split is really tax avoidance, HMRC has the power to reassess the tax liability of both parties for the past four years.

13 Beneficiaries of deceased person's estate

13.1 Introduction

The deceased is liable for income tax on any income *receivable* up to the date of death, regardless of whether it is actually received before or after death.

The 'personal representatives' (PRs) are taxed on any income receivable during the 'administration period.' This starts on the date of the deceased's death and ends when the administration of the estate is completed.

A PR is a person who acts as executor (named in the deceased's will) or administrator (where the deceased died without having made a will (ie intestate)) of a deceased person's estate.

13.2 Specific gifts

A will may specify that a certain beneficiary (or 'legatee') should receive a particular asset or a set sum of money. Where the asset bequeathed is an **income producing asset, eg shares, the beneficiary is taxable on the income receivable on and after the date of death on an arising basis**.

Where the beneficiary is taxable on the income, the income will have first been taxed on the PRs who will provide the beneficiary with a statement of income (R185 (Estate Income)).

This shows:

(a)   The net income (ie after any tax has been taken off) for the beneficiary to report

(b)   Tax credits (eg 20% tax deducted from savings income at source) and tax paid by the PRs, which the beneficiary can deduct from his own liability.

13.3 Beneficiaries with an absolute interest in the residue

13.3.1 General principle

A beneficiary has an absolute interest in the residue if he is entitled to both the income and capital of the whole (or part) of residue. **The residuary beneficiary is taxable on the income of the residue after setting off the PR's income expenses.**

In some cases this will include income that arose before death but is received after death.

Expenses are set against dividend income first, then savings income, then non-savings income.

13.3.2 Assessments on the beneficiaries

Where the estate administration is carried on over a number of years, it is usual for the PRs to make interim payments to beneficiaries before the administration of the estate is completed. **When the PRs make an interim payment, the residuary beneficiary is taxable on the lower of:**

(a)   **The actual amount received from the estate, and**
(b)   **The estate's distributable income of a particular tax year.**

These interim payments are assessed on *a receipts* basis. They are treated as being made from non savings income, then savings income, and then dividend income. The amount of the receipt is grossed up at the appropriate rate for the type of income in question in the year of receipt by the beneficiary, regardless of the tax actually paid by the PRs.

If there is an excess of income left at the end of the administration period, it is treated as income of the year in which the administration ended, regardless of when it is actually paid over to the beneficiary.

Illustration 4

Paul died on 1 November 2010, leaving his entire estate to his wife, Christa. The PRs received a dividend of £6,750, bank interest of £1,600 and rental income of £3,000 in 2010/11.

The PRs had expenses of £540. They made an interim payment of £4,090 to Christa on 1 April 2011. The administration of the estate ended on 31 December 2011.

The assessable amounts and the statement of income given to Christa for 2010/11 will be as follows:

2010/11

The interim payment of £4,090 is treated as coming from non-savings income (ie property income) first, then savings income, then dividend income.

Gross income available for distribution

	Non Savings £	Savings £	Dividends £
Rental income	3,000		
Bank interest £1,600 × $^{100}/_{80}$		2,000	
Dividends £6,750 × $^{100}/_{90}$			7,500
Taxable income	3,000	2,000	7,500
Less: expenses (from dividends first) £540 × $^{100}/_{90}$			(600)
Income available for distribution	3,000	2,000	6,900
Less: distributed to Christa 2010/11			
(non savings first, then savings, then dividends)			
£2,400 × $^{100}/_{80}$	(3,000)		
£1,600 × $^{100}/_{80}$		(2,000)	
£ 90 × $^{100}/_{90}$			(100)
£4,090			
c/f to 2011/12	Nil	Nil	6,800

Note. The above shows how the income will be distributed to Christa and is NOT an income tax computation.

2010/11 statement of income

	Net £	Tax £	Gross £
Non savings income	2,400	600	3,000
Savings income	1,600	400	2,000
Dividend income	90	10	100

Christa will use the statement of income to report the income received and tax suffered on her income tax return. The balance of the income will be taxed when it is received or in the year the administration ends.

13.3.3 Beneficiaries with a limited interest in the residue

A beneficiary has a limited interest in the residue if he is only entitled to the income (and not the capital) of the whole (or part) of the residue. He will be taxed on the net income of the estate during the administration period, after the PRs expenses have been deducted. Again, if he is only entitled to part of the income of the estate, he will only be taxed on that part.

The same tax rules used for beneficiaries with absolute interests also apply for those with limited interests.

14 Exempt income

Here is a list of some of the **main types of income that are exempt from income tax**:

(a)   Scholarship income (in the hands of the scholar; taxable on parent if paid by parent's employer)

(b)   Winnings from betting and gaming (including the lottery)

(c)   Gifts

(d)   Many social security benefits, eg child benefit, return to work credit, in-work credit, CTC and WTC.

(e)   Interest or terminal bonus on National Savings & Investments certificates and prizes on premium bonds

(f)   First £30,000 of certain compensation payments received on termination of employment (see later in this Text)

(g)   Damages (and interest on damages) for personal injuries

(h)   A terminal bonus paid under a 'save as you earn (SAYE) scheme' (see later in this Text)

(i)   Interest on government stocks held by persons not ordinarily resident in the UK

(j)   Income arising from an Individual Savings Account (ISA) (see later in this Text)

(k)   Up to £4,250 gross letting income from letting furnished accommodation in the landlord's own main residence (see later in this Text)

(l)   Dividends on ordinary shares in a Venture Capital Trust (up to the permitted maximum £200,000 investment per year) (see later in this Text)

(m)   Employment pensions paid to individuals retiring through work-related illness or injury but only the amount in excess of an ordinary ill-health pension.

The exemptions in (b) and (c) do not derive from statute, but from the general principle that income is taxable only if, broadly, it arises from a *source*. Neither gambling winnings nor gifts have a source and hence they are non-taxable.

Chapter roundup

- Income tax is charged on the chargeable income of a chargeable person for a tax year.

- Adults and children are all liable to income tax on their income.

- All components of an individual's income are brought together in a personal tax computation.

- All figures in the computation must be included gross.

- Certain payments can be deducted from total income. The main deductions are payments to charity in the form of shares or land and interest on certain loans.

- *Net income* is a figure representing the taxpayer's assessable income from all sources, after deductible payments.

- The personal allowance is deducted to arrive at *taxable income*. The personal allowance is available to each individual. It is increased for certain aged individuals (subject to their level of income).

- Cash donations to charity under Gift Aid are made net (saving basic rate tax at source) and also reduce the higher/additional rate tax bill (by extending the basic rate and higher rate tax bands).

- Tax reductions, as their name implies, are deducted in arriving at the *tax liability*. These include the married couples' allowance (only available to individuals aged 76 and over) and VCT and EIS investments.

- The *tax payable* is the tax liability less tax suffered at source (and payments on account).

- Certain tax credits may be claimed by workers with low incomes and by families with children. The award depends on various factors and is scaled down by reference to income thresholds.

- Various state benefits may be available on death, illness, disability, unemployment and retirement.

- State benefits may also be available to those with children and those who look after the disabled.

- Married couples and civil partners are taxed equally (ie 50:50) on income from assets held jointly (except broadly shares in a close company) unless they have notified HMRC of an actual ownership percentage which is different.

- When someone dies, the person they leave their assets to (ie the beneficiaries or 'legatees' of their estate) is usually taxable on income arising from the assets they have been left.

- Certain types of income are exempt from income tax.

TQT
Tax Qualification Training

Quiz

1. A 'tax year' is a 12-month period running from 1 April to the following 31 March. True/False?

2. The income of a minor child (aged under 18) is always treated as income of his parent. True/False?

3. To what extent are the following individuals liable to UK income tax?

   (a) John Smith, resident, ordinarily resident and domiciled in UK, who has both UK and foreign source income.

   (b) Johann Schmidt, who has never been to the UK, but who receives rental income from a property in London in addition to his salary from his German employer. Johann has always lived in Germany.

4. Define 'net income'.

5. Daniel is 35, has trade profits of £46,040 and makes a Gift Aid donation of £500 (net). Calculate Daniel's tax liability.

6. On 31 December 2010 an individual receives income from a discretionary trust of £1,650. Show how much must be included in their income tax computation.

7. Sarah is 67 and has net income of £24,700. She makes a donation via Gift Aid to Oxfam of £560. To what personal allowance is Sarah entitled?

8. Jack (aged 63) is married to Elsie (aged 76). To what allowances and tax reductions is Jack entitled in 2010/11, assuming his net income is £23,700?

9. Maria is a single parent to Josh aged 12. They have no contact with Josh's father. Maria earns £15,000 pa as a secretary and has rental income of £20,000 per annum. Calculate Maria's tax payable for 2010/11 if she paid £1,705 in tax under PAYE and her entitlement to Child Tax Credit.

10. Oberon (age 76) and Titania (age 38) married on 24 December 2010. What allowances and tax reductions are they entitled to in 2010/11 assuming Oberon's income is £11,000 and Titania's income is £16,000?

11. Peter (aged 77) and Rita (age 57) separate on 1 July 2010. Thereafter, Peter pays Rita £250 per month in maintenance. Payments are made on the last day of each month.

    (a) Will Peter make the payments net of income tax or gross?
    (b) What tax reduction is Peter entitled to in 2010/11?

12. James has an investment property. He pays income tax at 40% on the rental income. His wife Jill has insufficient income to utilise her personal allowance so he wishes to transfer the income to her for tax purposes. Which of the following statements are correct?

    (a) He can transfer the property into her name, on condition she hands over the income to him, so the income will be taxed on her.

    (b) He can transfer the property into her name, let her use the income as she chooses but require her to leave the property to him in her will and the income will be taxed on her.

    (c) He can transfer the property into joint names with his wife, retain a 95% beneficial interest, and thereby transfer half the income to her.

    (d) Under (c) he could declare that 95% of the income was hers.

1.   False – it runs from 6 April to the following 5 April.

2.   False – the income is only treated as the parent's income (broadly) if it is derived from the parent and exceeds £100 (gross) in the tax year.

3.   (a)   John Smith is liable to UK income tax on all his income, regardless of where it arises.

      (b)   Johann Schmidt, being not resident in the UK, is liable to UK income tax only in respect of income arising in the UK, ie on his UK rental income.

4.   Net income: total income (from all sources) less deductible payments (eg qualifying interest).

5.

	£
Net income	46,040
Less: PA	(6,475)
Taxable income	39,565
Tax:	
£38,025 × 20%	7,605
£1,540 × 40%	616
Tax liability	8,221

      (W) Basic rate band extended to £37,400 + (£500 × 100/80) = £38,025

6.   £3,300 ie £1,650 × 100/50 (or × 2)

7.

	£
Personal Age Allowance (PAA)	9,490
Less: ½(£24,700 – £700 (W) – £22,900)	(550)
PAA	8,940

      (W) Gross donation to charity is £560 × 100/80 = £700. This is taken as a notional deduction from net income when calculating the restriction to the PAA.

8.   Personal allowance — £6,475

Married couples' allowance (given by reference to age of elder spouse)	£6,965
Less: ½ × (£23,700 – £22,900)	(400)
	£6,565

      Tax relief restricted to 10% (ie £657)

9.

	Non savings	Tax suffered
	£	£
Employment income	15,000	1,705
Property income	20,000	
Net income	35,000	1,705
Less: PA	(6,475)	
Taxable income	28,525	

Income tax	£
£28,525 @ 20%	5,705
Less: tax suffered at source	(1,705)
Tax payable by Maria	4,000

CTC

Maria's income of £34,700 (£15,000 + £19,700 (excess of investment income over £300)) reduces the per child elements to nil. She is, therefore, only entitled to the family element (with no restriction as her income does not exceed £50,000) of £545. This will be paid direct to her bank account.

10. **Oberon**:

Personal allowance: £9,640

Titania:

Personal allowance: £6,475

MCA: given as one spouse over 76, apportioned as they married part way through the tax year: £6,965 × 4/12 = £2,322

Tax reduction @ 10% = £232

Note. The marriage took place after 5 December 2005, so the MCA is allocated to the spouse with the higher income, Titania.

11. (a)   Gross

    (b)   Lower of

        (i)   Payments due: £250 × 9 = £2,250, and
        (ii)   £2,670

        ie £2,250

        Tax reduction £2,250 × 10% = £225

12. (a) and (b) are False as the property must be transferred without 'strings attached'.

    (c)   is True as income on jointly held property is deemed to be shared equally.

    (d)   is False. A joint declaration can be made to overturn the 50:50 split assumption but it can only change the split to the actual proportions of beneficial ownership.

Solution to Example 1

Brenda can deduct the gross patent royalty payment from her total income (£800 × 100/80 =) £1,000

She will need to include the tax retained on the payment (£1,000 × 20% =) £200 on her self assessment return.

Solution to Example 2

Income tax liability 2010/11

	£
Earnings/ Net income	126,250
Less: personal allowance (W)	(850)
Taxable income	125,400

Working

	£	£
Personal allowance		6,475
Total net income	126,250	
Less: gross pension contribution	(15,000)	
Adjusted income	111,250	
Less: limit	(100,000)	
	11,250	
Less: ½ × £11,250		(5,625)
Available PA		850

Solution to Example 3

	£
Net income	25,620
PAA (> 65)	9,490
Less: ½ × £(25,620 – 22,900)	(1,360)
PAA given	8,130

Solution to Example 4

	Income		Tax
	£		£
Basic rate:	37,400	@ 20%	7,480
Higher rate:	11,635	@ 40%	4,654
	49,035		12,134

Solution to Example 5

	2010/11	2011/12
	£	£
Salary	50,000	30,000
Less: personal allowance	(6,475)	(6,475)
Taxable income	43,525	23,525
Tax		
£37,400/£23,525 × 20%	7,480	4,705
£6,125 × 20%	1,225	
	8,705	4,705

Income is below the higher rate threshold of £37,400 in 2011/12, so if no claim were made no higher rate relief would be given on the Gift Aid donation in 2011/12.

The claim allows £6,125 of income in 2010/11 to be taxed at 20% rather than 40%, saving tax of £1,225. The basic rate band is extended by £10,000 (£8,000 × $^{100}/_{80}$) in 2010/11.

Solution to Example 6

	(a) £	(b) £
Trade profits	27,700	8,100
Property income	2,000	2,000
Net income	29,700	10,100
Less: personal allowance (W)	(6,475)	(9,640)
	23,225	460
Income tax		
£23,225/ 460 × 20%	4,645	92
Tax reductions		
Maintenance payment £2,670 (max) × 10%	(267)	(267)
	4,378	nil
Married couple's allowance £6,730 × 10% (W)	(673)	–
Income tax liability	3,705	nil

Tax reductions cannot lead to repayments of tax, so in (b) part of the relief for the maintenance payments and the MCA is wasted. If Peter's wife had income of her own, the surplus MCA could be transferred to her.

Working

Income restriction:

	(a) £
Net income	29,700
Less: income limit	(22,900)
Excess	6,800
Half	3,400
PA	9,640
Reduction (maximum)	(3,165)
Basic PA	6,475
Maximum MCA	6,965
Excess reduction £(3,400 – 3,165)	(235)
Available MCA	6,730

Solution to Example 7

Their maximum tax credit entitlement is:

• Child tax credit

	£
Family element	545
Two child elements: 2 × £2,300	4,600
Disabled child element	2,715
Total	7,860

As the interest income is below £300 it can be disregarded as relevant income. As the joint income is expected to rise by less than £25,000 this year, the tax credit awarded will be based on the income of the previous year:

	£
Annual income	16,465
Less: CTC only threshold	(16,190)
Excess income	275
Maximum tax credit	7,860
Less: 39% × £275	(107)
Annual award	7,753

Solution to Example 8

As the interest income is over £300, the excess of £400 needs to be included as income. As the joint income is the same in both years, the tax credit awarded will be based on £55,000 (54,600 + 400).

As joint income exceeds the £50,000 upper threshold, they are only entitled to the family element. This is tapered by $^1/_{15}$ of the excess:

	£
Family element	545
Less: (55,000 − 50,000) × $^1/_{15}$	(333)
Award	212

Solution to Example 9

Their maximum tax credit entitlement is:

	£
CTC	
Family element	545
Four child elements: 4 × £2,300	9,200
Disabled child elements: 2 × £2,715	5,430
Total	15,175
WTC	
Basic element	1,920
Couple's element	1,890
30 hour element	790
Childcare element: 80% of £75 × 52 weeks	3,120
Total	7,720
Total tax credits	22,895

As the income of the current year changes by less than £25,000, the amount awarded will be based on the income of the previous year:

	£
Annual income	13,000
Less: CTC & WTC threshold	(6,420)
Excess income	6,580
Maximum tax credit	22,895
Less: 39% × £6,580	(2,566)
Award	20,329

The family (and baby element if applicable) would not be reduced until income exceeds £50,000. These would then be reduced by $^1/_{15}$th of the income over £50,000.

Now try the following questions

Short Form Questions:

1.1 – 1.20 inclusive

Long Form Questions:

1.1	Mr Daphnis
1.2	Mr Rich
1.3	Tax Credits (Pilot Paper)

- identify the types of income treated as savings and dividend income
- recognise savings income received net of tax
- deal with the non-refundable tax credit received with dividends
- apply appropriate tax rates using the three column personal tax computation
- understand how income from trusts is taxed
- deal with income received under the Accrued Income Scheme
- understand the treatment of non-qualifying life assurance policies
- identify miscellaneous income

Savings and dividend income

1 Introduction

A distinction is made between non savings, savings and dividend income.

Savings income comprises mainly interest, including interest from banks, building societies, gilts, debentures and the National Savings & Investments (NS&I) Bank. **It includes all types of interest whether received gross or received net of basic rate tax**.

Rental income, discretionary trust income and non- trade related patent royalties received are categorised as non savings income.

Savings income is taxed after non savings income while dividends are usually taxed as the very top slice of income.

2 Savings income

2.1 Introduction

Savings income principally covers interest, whether received net or gross. **The income assessed in a tax year is the full amount received in that year** without any deductions for expenses.

2.2 Interest received gross

Examples are interest on:

(a) **National Savings and Investments (NS&I) accounts**
(b) UK government (Treasury) stocks (issued after 6 April 1998)
(c) Loans between individuals.

2.3 Interest received net of 20% tax

Most building society and bank deposit interest is paid net of 20% tax, but this tax is refundable to individuals if it exceeds their tax liability.

Bank and building society interest must therefore be grossed up by $^{100}/_{80}$ for inclusion in the income tax computation.

Interest received from debentures (corporate loan notes) is also received net of a 20% tax credit.

Individuals who are not liable to income tax (eg because their allowances cover their income) **can certify their status** (on Form R85) to any bank or building society at which they have an account **and interest will be credited gross**. Should the income later prove to be assessable, it remains taxable as savings income and the individual must declare it in the usual way and tax will be paid under self assessment.

NS&I bank interest is paid gross (see above).

Exam focus point

Examiner's report – Personal Taxation

November 2007 – Part I SFQ 9

Too many candidates went down the route of calculating the taxable interest on an accruals basis, thereby not realising that interest is taxed on a receipts basis.

May 2008 – Part I SFQ 3

Very few candidates realised that the interest received in May 2008 would fall to be taxed in part on Mark in the 2008/09 tax year. Many candidates misread the question and tried to calculate the interest for 2007/08.

---

3 Dividends

3.1 Introduction

UK dividends are treated as if received net of a deemed (or 'notional') 10% tax credit. This tax credit can only reduce the tax liability calculated on taxable income and cannot be refunded to the shareholder.

Dividends are grossed up by $^{100}/_{90}$ for inclusion in the computation.

3.2 Basis of assessment of dividends

The individual is taxed on the gross amount received during the tax year. The date on the dividend voucher is taken as the date of receipt regardless of when the cheque is cashed or when the bank transfer is made.

4 Taxation of savings and dividend income

Exam focus point

Make sure you know which items of savings income are received net and which are received gross. Work through this section and the examples that follow carefully. Make sure you understand which rates of tax to apply to the different sources of income and what amounts are deductible from the tax liability.

4.1 Introduction

We must distinguish between 'non savings', 'savings income' (essentially interest) and 'dividend income' as they are taxed at different rates.

UK or foreign interest, whether it has been received net of basic rate tax or received gross, is taxed at the savings income rates. UK dividends and foreign dividends are both taxed at the dividend income rates. The exception to this is foreign interest or dividends received by a non-UK domiciled or not ordinarily resident individual and taxed on the remittance basis (ie when it is brought into the UK) which are always taxed as non-savings income (see later in this Text).

'Savings income' is taxed after 'non-savings income'. 'Dividend income' is taxed as the 'top slice' of a taxpayer's income.

4.2 Savings income tax rates

If savings income falls in the 'starting rate band' up to £2,440 it is taxed at 10%.

If it falls in the basic rate band between £2,441 and £37,400 it is taxed at 20%.

If it falls in the higher rate band between £37,401 and £150,000, it is taxed at 40%.

If it falls in excess of the higher rate band, 50% tax on the gross amount of the savings income is payable.

The tax taken at source on bank/building society interest (20%) is deducted from the tax liability in the income tax computation. So, if £80 of interest is received net, it must be grossed up at $^{100}/_{80}$ to £100 for inclusion in the income tax computation and has a tax credit of £20. This tax credit can be deducted from the investor's tax liability and **can create a repayment.**

The 10% starting rate band for savings income is only available if the taxpayer has taxable non-savings income of less than £2,440. Non savings income, while always being taxed at 20%, 40% or 50%, uses the starting rate band in priority to savings income. So, if a taxpayer has taxable non-savings income of £5,000 and savings income of £500, the 10% band is not available and the total income of £5,500 is taxed at 20%.

To determine whether savings income falls in the higher rate band it is treated as the top part of the taxpayer's income, apart from dividends (see below).

4.3 Dividend income tax rates

Dividends falling in the basic rate tax band are taxed at 10%. As they come with a 10% deemed tax credit, no further tax is payable on dividends for basic rate taxpayers. Dividends falling into the higher rate tax band are taxed at 32.5%.

From 6 April 2010, individuals with taxable income exceeding £150,000 are taxed on their dividend income at 42.5%.

The 10% tax credit on dividends is deductible from the tax liability. So, a net dividend of £90 is grossed up at $^{100}/_{90}$ to £100 for inclusion in the income tax computation and has a tax credit of £10. **However, since it is not a real tax credit, although it can be deducted from the shareholder's tax liability, it cannot be repaid to him.**

Dividend income is usually treated as the top 'slice' of the taxpayer's income (see below).

4.4 Deductions

As a general principle, personal allowances and other reliefs which are set against an individual's total income may be set off in the way that minimises the individual's tax liability. **Deductible payments, losses and personal allowances should be set against non savings income first then savings income and finally against dividend income.**

4.5 Top slice of income

There are **two main exceptions** to the rule that dividend income is treated as the top slice of a taxpayer's income. Taxable gains on **life assurance policies** and the **taxable part of termination payments** are both taxed after dividend income, in that order. Therefore a taxpayer with £30,000 of salary, £15,000 of dividends and a £100,000 termination payment would still have some dividends within the basic rate band (and therefore taxable at only 10%) and the balance within the higher rate band taxed at 32.5%.

5 Typical personal tax computation

Below is a typical personal tax computation. Note the way in which it is set out.

Illustration 1

MR TAXPAYER: INCOME TAX COMPUTATION 2010/11

	Non savings income £	Savings income £	Dividend income £
Employment income	33,830		
Less: occupational company pension scheme contribution	(1,080)		
	32,750		
Rental income	2,000		
Dividends £12,600 × $^{100}/_{90}$			14,000
Bank deposit interest: £1,200 × $^{100}/_{80}$		1,500	
Building society interest: £288 × $^{100}/_{80}$		360	
Less: qualifying interest	(100)		
Net income	34,650	1,860	14,000
Less: personal allowance	(6,475)		
Taxable income	28,175	1,860	14,000

Income tax			£	£
Basic rate band	non savings income		28,175 × 20%	5,635
	savings income		1,860 × 20%	372
	dividend income £(37,400 – 30,035)		7,365 × 10%	736
			37,400	
Higher rate £(14,000 – 7,365)			6,635 × 32.5%	2,156
				8,899
Less: tax reduction: EIS subscription (£2,000 × 20%)				(400)
Tax liability				8,499
Less: tax deducted at source				
Tax credit on dividends £14,000 × 10%			1,400	
PAYE (say)			5,255	
Tax suffered on bank interest £1,500 × 20%			300	
Tax suffered on building society interest £360 × 20%			72	
				(7,027)
Tax payable				1,472

Remember: the income is split into three parts: non savings income, savings income and dividend income. Non savings income is taxed first, savings income (ie interest) second and dividends last.

Also note that the deductible payments and personal allowance have been set against non savings income in priority to savings income and dividend income.

Example 1

Albert has a salary of £11,200, £2,000 (gross) of building society interest and £3,000 (gross) of UK dividends. What is his tax liability?

Example 2

Barry receives net bank interest of £8,000, and UK dividends of £10,800. What is his tax liability assuming he has rental income of:

(a)   £25,185?
(b)   £135,000?

Example 3

Bertha has rental income of £1,500, bank interest (net amount received) of £8,000, and receives UK dividends of £10,800. What is her tax liability?

For the 10% credit to be available, the dividend income has to be chargeable to tax.

For example, if a taxpayer has net income of £45,100 consisting only of gross dividend income, his taxable income would be £38,625 after deducting the PA of £6,475. His tax liability would be £4,138 (£37,400 × 10% + £1,225 × 32.5%) but he would be entitled to a tax credit based on the taxable dividend of only £3,863 (£38,625 × 10%) – not the whole £4,510.

This is not the case for savings income where the full tax credit is available.

Example 4

Carol has a salary of £5,540 and received building society interest of £12,800 and a UK dividend of £22,140. How much tax is payable by Carol?

Example 5

Jackie, has the following income and outgoings.

	£
Salary (tax deducted under PAYE £3,950)	26,240
UK dividend received (net)	2,000
Building society interest received (net)	14,800
Gift Aid donation (net amount paid)	640

What is Jackie's tax payable for 2010/11?

---

6 Other income

6.1 Income from non-discretionary trusts

As we saw earlier **income from discretionary trusts comes with a 50% tax credit and is always taxed as non savings income**, regardless of the type of income received by the trust.

Income from non-discretionary trusts (ie interest in possession trusts), however, retains its original nature when the beneficiary receives it and is taxed at the rates relevant to the type of income received by the trust, ie at 10%, 20%, 40%, 50%, 32½% or 42½%.

The trustees give the beneficiary a 'Statement of income from Trusts' (Form R185 (Trust Income)) which shows the net income (ie after tax has been taken off) and the tax deducted which the beneficiary can use to complete his tax return.

6.2 Accrued income scheme

The Accrued Income Scheme (AIS) applies on the disposal of interest-bearing securities (Treasury stock (gilts) and company loan stock) to ensure that the buyer and the seller are only taxed on the interest relating to the period of time that they have actually owned the securities.

The AIS does not apply to shares.

Interest on securities (sometimes called the 'coupon') **is generally paid twice a year**. For example, if an individual owns '£5,000 5% loan stock', paying interest on 15 March and 15 September each year, the interest taxable in 2010/11 will be:

- £125 (£5,000 × 5% × 6/12) received on 15 September 2010, and
- £125 received on 15 March 2011.

As we saw earlier, interest is usually taxed on the receipts basis. However on a disposal of securities, the AIS allocates the interest on a straight line time basis between the buyer and the seller. The seller is taxed on the interest for the period that has 'accrued' up to the date of disposal, while the buyer is taxed on the income that accrues from the date they purchase the stock.

If an individual sells securities 'cum interest', this means that the buyer receives the next interest payment on the six monthly date, even if he has not owned the securities for that whole six months. The buyer will be taxed on the interest received but will receive relief for the interest relating to the period of time that he did not own the securities.

Illustration 2

An investor purchases £10,000 of 6% loan stock 'cum interest' on 1 July 2010, which pays interest on 1 June and 1 December each year. He will receive the next interest payment of £300 (6% × £10,000 ÷ 2) due on 1 December 2010, which relates to the period since the last payment (1.6.10) until the payment date (1.12.10).

The interest received of £300 is chargeable to tax but, as he has only owned the stock for five months (1.7.10 – 1.12.10), he will receive relief of £50 ($^1/_6$ × £300) for the one month (June) that he didn't own it so will only actually be taxed on interest of £250 (£300 – £50).

The seller will be taxed on that one month's worth of interest (£50) even though he did not own the securities on 1 December 2010. It is taxable as **miscellaneous income** (see below).

Example 6

Ralph purchases £10,000 5% Treasury Stock cum interest on 1 February 2010 and sells it cum interest on 1 April 2011. Interest is paid on the stock on 1 May and 1 November each year.

How much is taxable on Ralph in 2010/11 and 2011/12?

If an individual sells securities 'ex interest' (ie without the interest), he receives, and is taxed on, the next interest payment on the six monthly date, even though he no longer owns the stock. He will receive relief for the interest relating to the period of time that he did not own the securities, while the buyer will be taxed on 'miscellaneous' income (see below) equal to the interest relating to the period he owns the stock.

The rules **do not apply in a number of situations, for example where an individual has not held securities exceeding £5,000** (nominal value) in the current or previous year.

6.3 Life assurance policies

6.3.1 Qualifying policies

There is no income tax charge on the maturity or encashment of a qualifying life assurance policy.

A policy is qualifying if:

(a) The policy secures a capital sum on death, earlier disability, or a date not before the tenth anniversary of taking out the policy

(b) The premiums are reasonably even and are payable annually or at shorter intervals

(c) At least a certain capital sum is assured, broadly 75% of the premiums payable.

Gifts worth up to £30 that are commonly offered to induce people to take out policies do not make a policy 'non-qualifying'.

Any profit (the excess of proceeds over total premiums paid) **on maturity or encashment of the policy is free of tax so long as premiums have been paid for a minimum of one of the following.**

(a)   **Life of the assured**
(b)   **10 years and**
(c)   **3/4 of the term.**

6.3.2 Non-qualifying policies

Non-qualifying policies include **single premium bonds, investment bonds** or **property bonds**. A lump sum is invested in a life fund, a small part of which buys life cover and the balance is invested. During the term of the policy any investment gains and income are taxed only in the hands of the insurance company.

Withdrawals of up to 5% of the premium per year (on a cumulative basis) **are allowed with no immediate tax liability.** So, in 2010/11 an investor who purchased a £30,000 single premium bond in 2004 can effect a partial surrender for £9,000 (6 years × 5% × £30,000) tax free.

The overall gain on the policy on a **chargeable event** (eg encashment, sale or death of the investor) **is taxed as savings income and comes with a basic rate tax credit (20%)**. Top slicing relief (see below) may apply.

When the policy is finally encashed, any tax free withdrawals are added to the amount received on encashment to determine the overall tax liability. There is no starting rate or basic rate liability. In addition, any tax at the higher or additional rate can be reduced by using the following *top slicing* rules:

Step 1   Calculate the overall profit from the policy.

(proceeds on encashment *plus* early withdrawals *less* initial premium).

Step 2   Divide the overall profit by the number of complete years since the policy was taken out

Step 3   Calculate the increase in the taxpayer's total tax liability that arises from adding the slice found in Step 2 to his other sources of income. This slice is taxed as the top slice of income above all other income, *including dividend income and termination payments*. Remember that the slice is only liable to tax at the higher or additional rate.

Step 4   Multiply the increase found in Step 3 by the number of years used in Step 2 to find the tax payable.

If, before final encashment, withdrawals exceed the permitted limit, the excess is taxable immediately at the higher or additional rate. Again, top slicing applies. The slice is found by dividing the excess by the number of years since the policy was taken out (or, if appropriate, since the last excess occurred). In calculating the tax on final encashment, the excess(es) are excluded from the calculation of the overall profit since they have already been taxed.

Example 7

An investor took out a single premium policy on 31 October 2004 for £15,000. He withdrew 4% of the premium in each of the next five years and he encashed the policy on 30 June 2010 receiving £20,000. In 2010/11 his other income (all non savings) was £36,500 after deducting his personal allowance.

Calculate the amount of tax payable in respect of the single premium policy.

TQT
Tax Qualification Training

6.4 Miscellaneous income

Income that is not categorised as from a specific source, eg savings, property or earnings, is taxed as 'miscellaneous income'. An example of miscellaneous income is income received by a child but taxed on the parent (see Chapter 1) and certain interest taxed under the Accrued Income Scheme (see above).

Chapter roundup

- Some interest income is received gross and some net. Interest received net (typically bank and building society interest) must be grossed up by 100/80 for inclusion in the income tax computation.

- Dividends from UK companies are deemed to be received net of a 10% tax credit. They must be grossed up by 100/90 for inclusion in the tax computation.

- We categorise income into different types: non savings, savings and dividends. Each type of income suffers different rates of tax depending on whether the income falls into the starting, basic, higher or additional rate band. Non savings income is taxed first (at 20%, 40% then 50%) then savings income (at 10%, 20%, 40% then 50%) and finally dividend income (at 10%, 32.5% and 42.5%).

- The 10% band for savings income is only available if taxable non savings income does not exceed £2,440.

- Income from discretionary trusts is always taxed as non-savings income. Income from interest in possession trusts is taxed at the beneficiary's tax rates, depending on the type of income.

- The accrued income scheme applies on the disposal of interest-bearing securities to ensure that the buyer and seller are only taxed on the interest relating to their period of ownership

- There is no income tax charge on the maturity/encashment of a qualifying life assurance policy

- The gain arising on a non-qualifying life assurance policy is taxed as savings income and comes with a basic rate tax credit. Tax at the higher or additional rate can be reduced by using top slicing relief,

- Some income does not fall into a specific category and is taxed as miscellaneous income.

Quiz

1. How will the following sources of interest be taxed?
   (a) NS&I Easy Access savings account interest
   (b) Current account interest from Lloyds Bank
   (c) Interest on $3\frac{1}{2}$% War Loan
   (d) Interest on NS&I Certificates

2. Glenda is age 70 and has a state pension (received gross) and a small amount of building society interest each year. What advice would you give her on tax recovery?

3. On 31 December 2010, an individual receives a UK dividend of £832. Calculate the amount that will be shown in the income tax computation.

4. Doreen, aged 30, has the following sources of income in 2010/11:

Income from employment (PAYE suffered £2,105)	£17,000
Income from rented properties	£3,500
Interest received on NS&I Easy Access savings account	£3,800
UK dividends received	£6,500

   Calculate her tax payable for the year.

5. Alison, aged 45, has the following sources of income in 2010/11:

Income from employment (PAYE suffered £14,430)	£61,250
Income from rented properties	£30,000
Interest received on high rate savings bank account	£3,000
UK dividends received	£9,000

   Calculate her tax payable for the year.

1. (a) Received gross and taxable in full as savings income.
    (b) Bank interest is received net of 20% tax and the gross amount is taxable savings income.
    (c) Interest on 3½% War Loan, as with most UK government stocks, is received gross.
    (d) Exempt.

2. She is clearly a non-taxpayer so should lodge a form R85 with the building society to be paid her interest gross. This is more efficient from a cash flow perspective than making a claim for repayment of tax which would be required if the interest continued to be paid net.

3. £924 (ie £832 × 100/90)

4.

	Non savings income	Savings income	Dividend income
	£	£	£
Employment income	17,000		
Property income	3,500		
NS&I interest (received gross)		3,800	
Dividends £6,500 × 100/90			7,222
Net income	20,500	3,800	7,222
Less: PA	(6,475)		
Taxable income	14,025	3,800	7,222

Tax:	£
14,025 @ 20%	2,805
3,800 @ 20%	760
7,222 @ 10%	722
Tax liability	4,287
Less: tax suffered at source	
tax credit on dividends	(722)
PAYE	(2,105)
Tax payable	1,460

5.

	Non savings income	Savings income	Dividends
	£	£	£
Employment income	61,250		
Property income	30,000		
Bank interest £3,000 × 100/80		3,750	
Dividends £9,000 × 100/90			10,000
Net income	91,250	3,750	10,000
Less: PA (W)	(3,975)		
Taxable income	87,275	3,750	10,000

Tax:	£
37,400 @ 20%	7,480
49,875 @ 40%	19,950
3,750 @ 40%	1,500
10,000 @ 32.5%	3,250
Tax liability	32,180
Less: tax suffered at source	
tax credit on dividends	(1,000)
tax credit on interest	(750)
PAYE	(14,430)
Tax payable	16,000

Working	£	£
Basic PA		6,475
Total income £(91,250 + 3,750 + 10,000)	105,000	
Less: limit	(100,000)	
	5,000	
Restriction (£5,000 ÷ 2)		(2,500)
Available PA		3,975

Solution to Example 1

	Non savings income £	Savings income £	Dividends £
Net income	11,200	2,000	3,000
Less: PA	(6,475)	–	–
Taxable income	4,725	2,000	3,000

Income tax:	£
£	
4,725 × 20% (non-savings income taxed first)	945
2,000 × 20% (savings income taxed second)	400
3,000 × 10% (UK dividends taxed last (top slice))	300
9,725	
Tax liability	1,645

The £2,000 savings income falls within the basic rate band so is taxed at 20%. The £3,000 dividend income also falls within the basic rate band and is taxed at 10%.

Note that the non-savings income exceeds the savings income starting rate band of £2,440. All of the savings income is therefore taxed at the basic rate.

Albert has tax credits of £700 (£2,000 × 20% + £3,000 × 10%) which can be offset against his tax liability leaving tax payable of £945 (1,645 – 700) most of which, if not all, will have been collected under PAYE.

Solution to Example 2

(a) Property income £25,185

	Non savings income £	Savings income £	Dividends £
Property income	25,185		
Interest (× 100/80)		10,000	
Dividends (× 100/90)			12,000
Less: PA	(6,475)	–	–
Taxable income	18,710	10,000	12,000

Income tax:	
£	£
18,710 × 20%	3,742
10,000 × 20% (savings income)	2,000
8,690× 10% (UK dividend income in BR band)	869
37,400	
3,310 × 32.5% (UK dividend income in HR band)	1,076
40,710	
Tax liability	7,687

UK dividend income in the basic rate band is taxed at 10%. The 32.5% rate applies where it exceeds the higher rate threshold. Barry's tax credits of £3,200 (£10,000 × 20% + £12,000 × 10%) reduce the liability to tax payable of £4,487 (£7,687 – £3,200).

(b) Property income £135,000

	Non savings income £	Savings income £	Dividends £
Property income	135,000		
Interest (× 100/80)		10,000	
Dividends (× 100/90)			12,000
Less: PA (total income > £112,950)	(NIL)	–	–
Taxable income	135,000	10,000	12,000

Income tax:

£		£
37,400 × 20%		7,480
97,600 × 40% (non savings income in HR band)		39,040
10,000 × 40% (savings income in HR band)		4,000
5,000 × 32.5% (dividend income in HR band)		1,625
150,000		
7,000 × 42.5% (UK dividend income at AR)		2,975
Tax liability		55,120

Non savings and savings income in the higher rate band is taxed at 40%. Dividend income in the higher rate band is taxed at 32.5% and the additional rate of tax (ie in excess of the higher rate band) for dividends is 42.5%. Barry's tax credits of £3,200 (£10,000 × 20% + £12,000 × 10%) reduce the tax liability to £51,920 (£55,120 – £3,200).

Solution to Example 3

	Non savings income £	Savings income £	Dividends £
Property income	1,500		
Interest (× 100/80)		10,000	
Dividends (× 100/90)			12,000
Less: PA	(1,500)	(4,975)	–
Taxable income	Nil	5,025	12,000

Income tax:

£		£
2,440 × 10%		244
2,585 × 20% (savings income)		517
12,000 × 10% (UK dividend income in BR band)		1,200
17,025		
Tax liability		1,961

Bertha's non savings income is below £2,440 so the starting rate band is available. Her tax credits of £3,200 (£10,000 × 20% + £12,000 × 10%) reduce the liability to tax *repayable* (ie a refund) of £1,239 (£1,961 – £3,200).

Solution to Example 4

	Non savings income £	Savings income £	Dividends £
Employment income	5,540		
Interest (× 100/80)		16,000	
Dividends (× 100/90)			24,600
Less: PA	(5,540)	(935)	–
Taxable income	Nil	15,065	24,600

Income tax:

£		£
2,440 × 10%		244
12,625 × 20%		2,525
22,335 × 10%		2,233
37,400		
2,265 × 32.5%		736
39,665		
Tax liability		5,738
Less: tax deducted at source:		
On dividends (£24,600 @ 10%)		(2,460)
On interest (£16,000 @ 20%)		(3,200)
Tax payable		78

Solution to Example 5

	Non savings income £	Savings income £	Dividends £
Employment income	26,240		
Building society interest (BSI) £14,800 × 100/80		18,500	
UK dividends £2,000 × 100/90			2,222
Net income	26,240	18,500	2,222
Less: PA	(6,475)		
Taxable income	19,765	18,500	2,222

Income tax		£	£
Basic rate band	Non savings income = £19,765 × 20%		3,953
	Savings income		
	£(37,400 – 19,765) = £17,635 × 20%		3,527
	£800 × 20% (note)		160
Higher rate	£(18,500 – 17,635 – 800) = £65 × 40%		26
	Dividends £2,222 × 32.5%		722
Tax liability			8,388
Less: Tax suffered on dividends £(2,222 × 10%)		222	
Tax suffered – PAYE		3,950	
Tax suffered on BSI £(18,500 × 20%)		3,700	(7,872)
Tax payable			516

Note. The basic rate band is extended by the gross amount of the Gift Aid payment ie by £800 (£640 × $^{100}/_{80}$).

Solution to Example 6

2010/11

Ralph purchases the stock on 1 February 2010 'cum interest', which means that he receives the next interest payment due on 1 May 2010. He will obtain relief for the three months that he did not own the stock.

		£
1.5.10	Interest: 5% × £10,000 × ½	250
	Less: accrued income relief (1 Nov 09 – 1 Feb 10)	
	£250 × $^3/_6$	(125)
		125
1.11.10	Interest (owned for the whole 6 months)	250
	Interest	375

2011/12

Ralph sells the stock on 1 April 2011 'cum interest', which means that the purchaser receives the next interest payment due on 1 May 2011. However, as Ralph owned the stock from 1 November 2010 to 1 April 2011 he will be taxable on that five months' worth of interest in 2011/12. As he does not own the stock on 1 May 2011 he cannot be taxed on it as interest. Instead it is taxable as 'miscellaneous' income.

1.5.11	Accrued income (1 Nov 10 – 1 Apr 11)	
	£250 × $^5/_6$	£208

Solution to Example 7

	£
Proceeds on encashment	20,000
Add: withdrawals within 5% limit: 5 × 4% × £15,000	3,000
	23,000
Less: initial premium	(15,000)
Overall profit	8,000

The profit is taxed as savings income and comes with a basic rate tax credit. Tax is only payable at the higher and additional rate. If the profit is taxed in full in 2010/11, it is taxed as the top slice of income and therefore £7,100 (£36,500 + £8,000 – £37,400) is taxed at the higher rate. Using the top slicing rules the tax payable is reduced and is calculated as follows:

Number of complete years = 5. One slice = £8,000/5 = £1,600
Tax liability in respect of the policy:

	£
Total income: £36,500 + £1,600	38,100
Less: basic rate band	(37,400)
Slice taxed at higher rates	700
Tax @ 20% (40% – 20% credit)	140
£140 × 5 years	700

Note. No tax is payable on the slice (£1,600 – £700) that falls within the basic rate band.

Now try the following questions

Short Form Questions:

2.1 – 2.9 inclusive

Long Form Questions:

2.1	Mr Poor
2.2	Jonty
2.3	Fred
2.4	Fiona
2.5	Jane Bradbury
2.6	George and Mildred Roper
2.7	Lauren

3

The purpose of this chapter is to help you to:

- understand the rules for the taxation of income from land and buildings
- set off property losses correctly
- calculate the amount of a short lease premium taxable as income
- identify a furnished holiday letting property
- understand when 'the rent a room' scheme applies
- understand the tax position of landlords living outside the UK
- be aware of the rules for Real Estate Investment Trusts (REITs)

References: ITTOIA 2005 unless otherwise stated

1 Introduction

All lettings in the UK by an individual landlord are treated as a single business with the profit or loss computed for a tax year on normal business accounting principles – ie **rents and expenses included on an accruals basis. Profits and losses on individual properties are automatically set off**.

Property income is always taxed as non-savings income.

Exam focus point

This is a core area of the syllabus. It appears within the personal income tax computation and can be set either as a long written or computational question.

A UK resident landlord will be taxable on property income from property within and outside the UK.

In this chapter we consider the rules for taxing UK property income.

Now look at the following chapters in the ATT Manual 'Essential Law for the Taxation Technician'.

- Chapter 14 – Introduction to property Law
- Chapter 15 – Land Law in England, Wales and Northern Ireland*
- Chapter 16 – Dealings in land in England, Wales and Northern Ireland*

*You need only study Land Law in Scotland if you are intending to answer the paper under Scots law. Note that there is a Scots Law Supplement covering Land law of Scotland and Dealings in Land under Scots law, which is available from the Association.

2 UK property income

2.1 Calculating property income

The property income taxable on individuals is based on the annual profits arising from the 'business' including:

(a) Rent charges

(b) Part of the premium on the grant of a short lease (see below).

A person receiving rental income is taxed on the full amount of the profits **accrued in the tax year**.

2.2 Allowable property expenses

Expenses are allowed (ie are deductible) if they are wholly and exclusively incurred for the 'business' of letting. Expenses such as advertising, accountancy and insurance are allowed but depreciation is not (capital allowances or 'wear & tear' allowances (see below) are given instead).

Capital expenditure on properties let, eg cost of building an extension, **is not deductible** when computing the assessable property income.

Bad debts are allowed on business principles, so if a rent payment appears unlikely, the landlord can provide for it in his letting accounts at the end of the tax year.

Capital allowances are not allowed on furniture used in a residential dwelling. Instead, HMRC gives relief for such capital expenditure on a renewals basis. The original cost and the cost of any improvements are not relieved but the cost of replacing furniture to the same standard is allowed as an expense.

As this can be cumbersome to administer **for furnished lettings there is a concession whereby a 'wear and tear allowance' is given instead**. This allowance is equal to:

10% × [rents – (water rates & council tax if paid by the landlord)]

and is allowed as a deduction in place of claiming relief for the replacement of furniture.

The cost of repairing or maintaining furniture and fittings is also allowed whether the renewals basis or the wear and tear allowance is claimed.

Where there is a business of letting, the landlord can set off the running expenses incurred on empty properties (eg properties under repair between lets), against property income generally.

If property normally let furnished is occupied at some time by the owner, the allowable deduction for repairs, insurance, council tax and so on is restricted to a proportion based on the period that the property is available for letting. For example, if HMRC accepted that letting took place throughout the year and was occupied by the owner for 4 weeks and by tenants for 30 weeks, 48/52 of the expenses would be allowed. Expenses specific to the letting such as advertising would, however, be allowed in full.

Both loan (ie mortgage) interest and overdraft interest are deductible in computing property income, provided the related borrowing was applied wholly and exclusively for the purposes of the letting business.

Example 1

Natalie rents out a furnished investment property for the whole of 2010/11 for £1,200 a month, payable on the first day of the month, in advance. The tenants do not pay the rent for April 2011 until 15 April 2011.

During the year she had the following expenses in connection with letting the property:

	£
Mortgage interest	7,200
Repairs and maintenance	565
Water rates	275
Painting and decorating	1,350
Insurance	(see below)
Gardening and cleaning	175

For the year ended 31 December 2010 Natalie paid landlord's insurance premiums totalling £685. For the year ended 31 December 2011 this increased to £755. Council tax of £1,650 is paid by the tenants.

Natalie claims the wear and tear allowance.

Calculate Natalie's property income assessment for 2010/11.

2.3 Capital allowances

Capital allowances (ie the tax equivalent of accounting depreciation) may be claimed on plant and machinery (P&M) used for the maintenance or repair of the properties or plant let as part of the building (eg lawn mowers).

As explained above, capital allowances are not available in respect of furniture and instead the renewals basis or the wear and tear allowance is available.

The Landlord's Energy Savings Allowance of up to £1,500 per property is also available to landlords who incur capital expenditure on energy savings items, eg insulation and draught proofing in a dwelling house.

3 Property losses

Where there is an overall loss:

(a)   The **loss is carried forward and set against UK property income** in subsequent years

(b)   Losses resulting from capital allowances can be set against the taxpayer's general income for the year of the loss and the following tax year.

The loss relief at (a) above is automatic and no claim is required. Losses under (b) above must be claimed within 12 months from the self assessment filing date for the year of the loss (ie by 31 January 2013 for a 2010/11 loss).

Where a property is let on non-commercial terms (eg to a relative at a nominal or 'peppercorn' rent), and a loss arises in respect of that property, this loss is not pooled with profits/losses on other rental properties. It may only be offset against future rental profits on that same lease to that same tenant. As such, it is unlikely that this loss will ever be fully relieved.

TQT
Tax Qualification Training

4 Premiums on leases

4.1 Basic principle

A 'lease' is a right to use an asset (in this case a property) for a specified period of time. Any amount paid up front by the lessee (the tenant) to the lessor (landlord) for the use of a property is referred to as a 'premium' and is treated as a capital receipt. There are usually therefore no income tax implications for a premium as it is a capital sum.

However, when a premium is received on the *grant* (that is, by a landlord to a tenant) of a short lease (50 years or less), part of the premium is treated as rent and is taxed as property income in the year of grant.

4.2 Amount taxed as income

The premium taxed as property income is the whole premium less 2% of the premium for each complete year of the lease, except the first year. This is expressed as the formula: [s.277(4)]

$$P \times \frac{50-Y}{50}\text{, where P = the premium and Y = the number of years on the lease minus 1 year}$$

The balance (ie the capital element) is subject to capital gains tax (see later in this Text).

This rule does not apply on the *assignment* (ie sale) of a lease (one tenant selling his interest in the property to another), nor to the grant of a lease of more than 50 years, which is usually only subject to capital gains tax.

Example 2

Samantha granted a lease to Carrie on 1 March 2011 for a duration of 12 years. Carrie paid Samantha a premium of £42,000. Show Samantha's property income for 2010/11.

4.3 Premiums for granting subleases

A tenant may sublet the property and charge a premium on the grant of the lease to the subtenant. This premium is taxed as property income in the normal way, except that where the tenant originally paid a premium for his own original or head lease, relief is given, computed as:

$$\text{Premium taxable as property income for head lease} \times \frac{\text{duration of sub-lease}}{\text{duration of head lease}}$$

Example 3

Clive granted a lease to Derek on 1 March 1996 for a period of 40 years. Derek paid a premium of £16,000. On 1 June 2010 Derek granted a sublease to Eric for a period of ten years. Eric paid a premium of £30,000. Calculate the amount assessable as property income for 2010/11 in respect of the premium received by Derek.

---

5 Furnished holiday lettings (FHLs)

Income from commercial lettings of furnished holiday accommodation in the UK and other parts of the European Economic Area (EEA)is taxed as property income but, provided certain conditions are satisfied, is treated as normal trade profits so that:

(a)   **Relief for losses is available as if they were trading losses**, including the facility to set losses against general income.

(b)   The profits are treated as earned income so the **income qualifies as relevant earnings** for pension purposes (see later in this Text).

(c)   **Capital allowances are available as for traders**. This applies to furnishings etc used in a dwelling. This replaces the wear and tear allowance.

(d)   Capital gains tax entrepreneurs' relief, rollover relief, and relief for gifts of business assets, are available (see later in this Text).

Exam focus point

Do not assume that just because a property is let furnished that it is furnished holiday accommodation. Read the question carefully to see whether it satisfies the following conditions.

The property must satisfy the following conditions: [s.325]

(a)   It is **available for commercial letting to the public for at least 140 days** in a year and

(b)   It must be **let for at least 70 days** in the year. If two or more properties each pass the 140 day test separately, then they need only pass the 70 day test on average.

A landlord may choose to leave particular properties out of the averaging computation if they would pull the average down to below 70 days.

(c)   During the year, not more than 155 days may fall into periods where the property is in the same occupation for a continuous period exceeding 31 days ('longer term' occupation).

Where the taxpayer also has other letting income, he is treated as running a 'business of letting' and a 'business of furnished holiday letting' and the two are computed separately.

Exam focus point

Examiner's report – Personal Taxation (old syllabus)

November 2006 – Question 5

The main areas where marks were lost were in the explanation of income tax and capital gains tax in connection with the holiday home. Several candidates did not mention the beneficial treatment as a business and simply described the taxation of rental property.

6 The rent a room scheme

If an individual lets a room or rooms in his main residence (ie to a lodger), then a special exemption may apply.

If gross rents (ie before deducting expenses) **are less than the limit of £4,250 per property a year, the rents are wholly exempt from income tax** and expenses and capital allowances are ignored. However, the taxpayer may claim to ignore the exemption, for example to generate a loss by taking into account both rent and expenses.

This limit is halved if any other person (including the owner's spouse) also received income from renting accommodation in the property while the property was the owner's main residence.

TQT
Tax Qualification Training

If gross rents exceed the limit, the taxpayer will be taxed in the ordinary way, ignoring the rent a room scheme, unless he elects for the 'alternative basis'. If he so elects, he will be taxable on gross receipts less £4,250 (or £2,125 if the limit is halved), with no deductions for expenses or capital allowances.

An election to ignore the exemption or an election for the alternative basis must be made on or before the anniversary of 31 January following the end of the tax year concerned. An election to ignore the exemption applies only for the year for which it is made, but an election for the alternative basis remains in force until it is withdrawn or until a year in which gross rents do not exceed the limit.

7 Rent paid to a non-resident landlord

Under the **Non Resident Landlord Scheme** (NRLS) the agent for the property (or where there is no agent, the tenant) must **deduct basic rate tax at source before rent is paid** over to a non-UK resident landlord of a UK property. [s.971 ITA 2007]

Any higher or additional rate tax that is payable is dealt with by the non-resident landlord under self assessment.

Rent can be paid gross to the non-resident landlord by agreement with HMRC under the NRLS, as long as the landlord's UK tax affairs are up to date and he undertakes to include tax from property income in the payments on account which he makes under self assessment.

8 Real Estate Investment Trusts (REITs)

A REIT is a listed company (AIM does *not* count for this purpose) owning, managing and earning rental income from commercial or residential property.

REITs can elect for their property income (and gains) to be exempt from corporation tax and must withhold basic rate (20%) tax from distributions paid to shareholders (who cannot own more than 10% of a REIT's shares) out of these profits. These distributions are taxed as property income on the investor, not as dividends.

Distributions by REITs out of other income (ie not property income or gains) are taxed as dividends in the normal way.

Illustration

Sue has a holding of shares in The Property Business which is a REIT. During 2010/11 she received a dividend from her investment of £6,400. She also has a salary of £31,000 and interest income (gross) of £1,000 in the year.

Sue's tax liability for 2010/11 is as follows:

	Non savings income £	Savings income £	Total £
Salary	31,000		
Dividend from REIT – Property income £6,400 × 100/80	8,000		
Interest		1,000	
Net income	39,000	1,000	40,000
PA	(6,475)		(6,475)
	32,525	1,000	33,525

Non savings income £32,525 @ 20%	6,505
Savings income £1,000 @ 20%	200
Tax liability	6,705

Note. Dividends from REITs are taxed as property income not as company dividends. Basic rate tax (20%) is deducted at source from such distributions.

Chapter roundup

- UK property income is calculated as accrued rental income less accrued revenue expenses for each property.

- Profits and losses of individual properties are pooled to arrive at the UK property income assessment for the individual

- The renewals basis or a 10% wear and tear allowance is available in respect of furniture for furnished properties.

- Losses on UK properties must be carried forward and set against future UK property profits.

- An element of the premium received by a landlord on the grant of a short lease is taxable as UK property income.

- If a property meets various conditions it may be classified as a Furnished Holiday Let (FHL).

- Income/losses from FHLs are treated as trading income/losses.

- If an individual rents out a room in their main residence and charges their tenant less than £4,250 pa, this amount is not taxable.

- Dividends from REITs are taxed as property income not as company dividends. Basic rate tax (20%) is deducted at source from such distributions.

Quiz

1. David buys a property for letting on 1 August 2010 and grants a tenancy to Ethel from 1 December 2010 at £3,600 pa payable quarterly in advance. How much is taxable in 2010/11?

2. Catherine rents out a furnished property for £16,000 pa and pays the water rates of £320 and council tax of £780 on the property. Calculate the amount of wear and tear allowance she can claim.

3. John pays buildings insurance premiums for 12 months in advance on 1 October each year to cover all his letting properties. He pays £4,800 in 2009 and £5,200 in 2010. How much is deductible from his property income in 2010/11?

4. Debbie lets a flat to her widowed mother for £600 pa when a market rent would be £3,600 pa. Debbie pays all the letting expenses which amount to £1,800 for 2010/11. Explain what relief is available for the loss incurred.

5. Paul grants a lease for 10 years to Graham for a premium of £20,000. How much is assessable as property income and when will it be assessed?

6. Fred has let three holiday bungalows during 2010/11 making a net loss. Explain briefly the difference in the treatment of this loss if the lettings meet the conditions required for furnished holiday lettings.

7. What is the main income tax advantage of a profitable 'furnished holiday letting' business?

8. What is the income threshold for 'rent a room' relief?

Solutions to Quiz

1. Rent accrued 1.12.10 – 5.4.11 ie $^4/_{12} \times$ £3,600 = £1,200.

2. Wear and tear allowance against rents:

   10% × £(16,000 – 320 – 780) = £1,490

3. Insurance premiums accrued in 2010/11

	£
$^6/_{12} \times$ £4,800	2,400
$^6/_{12} \times$ £5,200	2,600
	5,000

4. A loss of £1,200 would arise (£600 – £1,800). This can only be offset against profits made on the same property with the same tenant (ie her mother).

5. Property income £20,000 × ((50 – 9)/50)   £16,400

   Assessable in the year the lease is granted.

6. Property losses are generally carried forward against future property income. However if they arise from a FHL they are allowed as if they were trading losses and can be set off against other income.

7. FHL income qualifies as relevant earnings which gives scope to make higher pension contributions (see later in this Text).

8. £4,250 a year.

Solution to chapter examples

Solution to Example 1

	£	£
Rental income (amount accrued – late payment irrelevant)		14,400
Less: Expenses:		
Loan interest	7,200	
Repairs and maintenance	565	
Water rates	275	
Painting and decorating	1,350	
Insurance ([9/12 × £685] + [3/12 × £755])	703	
Gardening and cleaning	175	
Wear & tear allowance (10% × [14,400 – 275])	1,413	
Total expenses		(11,681)
Property income		2,719

Note. The council tax is paid by the tenants so does not affect the calculation.

Solution to Example 2

	£
Assessable as property income: £42,000 × ((50 – 11)/50)	32,760

Solution to Example 3

	£
Assessable as property income: £30,000 × ((50 – 9)/50)	24,600
Less: allowance for premium paid to Clive	
(£16,000 × ((50 – 39)/50)) × 10/40	(880)
Amount assessable	23,720

Short Form Questions:

3.1 – 3.10 inclusive

Long Form Questions:

3.1	Randall
3.2	Corelli

3: Income from UK land and buildings | Part A Personal Income Tax

TQT
Tax Qualification Training

Tax efficient investments

The purpose of this chapter is to help you to:

- identify specific tax free investments

- set out and apply the rules for Individual Savings Accounts, the Enterprise Investment Scheme and Venture Capital Trusts

- Identify and apply the anti avoidance rules for pre-owned assets

References: ITA 2007 unless otherwise stated

1 Introduction

1.1 Tax-free investments

The following investments are tax free:

(a)   NS&I Savings Certificates (including indexed-linked issues) (see below)
(b)   Save As You Earn (SAYE) (building society, bank, or NS&I) schemes (see later in this Text)
(c)   Premium Bond winnings
(d)   Income from Individual Savings Accounts (ISAs) (see below)
(e)   Dividends from Venture Capital Trusts (VCTs) (see below)

1.2 NS&I Savings Certificates

These are attractive particularly to higher and additional rate taxpayers as **the accumulated interest paid at the end of the period of investment is totally free from income tax and capital gains tax (CGT)**. There is a maximum holding permitted of £15,000.

NS&I Index-Linked Certificates are also popular as they provide protection from inflation. The maximum holding is again £15,000. In both instances, the limits apply to each spouse/partner in a civil partnership.

2 Individual Savings Accounts (ISAs)

2.1 Introduction

ISAs are available to individuals **aged over 18** who are **resident and ordinarily resident in the UK. Investment is permitted in cash and shares**.

The main features of ISAs are as follows.

(a)   There is an **annual subscription limit of £10,200, of which no more than £5,100 can be in cash**

(b)   There is **no statutory lock in period** or minimum subscription

(c)   There is **no lifetime limit**

(d)   The account is **completely free of tax** on both income and capital growth

(e)   ISAs are offered and operated by HMRC approved account managers who must agree to operate accounts in accordance with the ISA regulations.

Individuals under 18 but over 16 are allowed to subscribe up to £5,100 pa in a cash only ISA account.

Once the maximum amount has been subscribed for in any type of ISA for a year, it is not possible to make further investments even after a withdrawal is subsequently made.

2.2 Types of ISA

There are two types of ISA account:

(a)   **Cash**, including all the kinds of bank and building society accounts as well as NS&I products, supermarket savings accounts and similar, and

(b)   **Stocks and shares**, including shares obtained from savings-related share option schemes (transferred into the shares component at market value) but not shares acquired on a public offer or a demutualisation.

Individuals over 18 can invest in two ISA accounts each year, one cash and one stocks and shares, so long as they keep within the investment limits.

Illustration 1

James, age 35, wants advice on how much to invest in an ISA in 2010/11.

(a)   If he puts £5,100 into a cash account he can invest a maximum of £5,100 in a stocks and shares account.
(b)   If he puts £2,000 into a cash account he can invest a maximum of £8,200 in a stocks and shares account.
(c)   If he does not invest in a cash account he can put the full £10,200 in a stocks and shares account.

2.3 Tax exemption

Income and capital gains are tax free within an ISA account, even if the investor makes a withdrawal from the account.

An investor cannot put any more money into an existing ISA account if he becomes non-resident or not ordinarily resident (see later in this Text). The investor can, however, still keep the account open and is still entitled to the benefits. If the investor later resumes his UK residence and ordinary residence, he can continue to put money in again.

3 The Enterprise Investment Scheme (EIS)

3.1 Introduction

The Enterprise Investment Scheme (EIS) is intended to encourage investment in the **ordinary shares** of **unquoted trading companies** by offering income tax and capital gains tax (CGT) reliefs and exemptions where certain conditions are satisfied.

The EIS income tax rules are discussed below. The CGT rules are covered later in this Text.

3.2 The relief

When an individual subscribes for eligible shares in a qualifying company, the **amount subscribed is treated as a tax reduction (see earlier in this Text), saving income tax at 20%.** [s.158]

The maximum total investment that can qualify for this income tax relief in a tax year is £500,000.

If an investment is less than £500 no relief is available (unless subscription is made by an approved EIS fund, which pools the contributions of several investors).

Relief is usually given on an actual basis: a 2010/11 investment will attract relief against the tax liability for 2010/11.

However, a **taxpayer can claim to carry back his investment**, up to the usual limit of £500,000, to the previous year. [s.158(4)]

Dividends from EIS shares are taxable under the normal rules.

3.3 Withdrawal of relief

If an individual disposes of shares (by sale or gift other than a gift to a spouse or civil partner) **within three years of their issue, the tax reduction obtained may be wholly or partly withdrawn.** [s.209 and s.210]

If the shares are given away (other than to the investor's spouse or civil partner) **within the three years, all of the tax reduction is withdrawn.**

On a sale within the three years, the tax reduction to be withdrawn is:

$$\text{Consideration obtained} \times \frac{\text{Tax reduction obtained on issue}}{\text{Issue price of shares}}$$

However, the withdrawal cannot exceed the tax reduction originally obtained.

A transfer of shares between spouses/civil partners does not give rise to a withdrawal of the tax reduction. The reduction obtained remains associated with the shares, and if the recipient partner disposes of the shares outside the marriage/civil partnership within three years of their issue, it is withdrawn by an assessment on the recipient spouse/ partner.

The death of a shareholder is not treated as a disposal.

If shares are disposed of after three years from issue, the following consequences ensue:

(a)   **The tax reduction is not withdrawn**

(b)   **If there is a gain for CGT purposes, it is exempt**

(c)   **Any loss for CGT purposes is restricted by reducing the issue price, ie the cost, by the tax reduction not withdrawn (but not so as to create a gain).**

When shares issued under the EIS are sold at arm's length at a loss at any time (within or outside the first three years), and the EIS relief is not wholly withdrawn, the **loss may be set against general income (ie in the same way as a trading loss)**, of the current and/or previous year. [s.131]

Example 1

In May 2010, David subscribes £34,000 for shares in an EIS company. David's tax liability for 2010/11 (before tax reductions) is £5,000, reduced to nil by the EIS relief.

In May 2012, David sells half of the shares for £12,000. The other half are sold for £25,000 in June 2013, giving rise to a gain of £8,000.

(a)   How much of the tax reduction is withdrawn on the first sale?
(b)   How is the gain on the second sale treated?

3.4 The conditions for relief

Exam focus point

Most of the information below on EIS is contained in the legislation, in ss.156-234 ITA 2007. There is no need for you to learn rules and conditions that can easily be looked up. Learn where to find them and make sure you would be able to apply them given a particular scenario in the examination.

3.4.1 Conditions to be satisfied by the investor

A **qualifying individual is one who is not connected with the company** at any time in the period from two years before the issue (or from incorporation if later) to three years after the issue. An individual is connected with the company in any of the following circumstances: [s.166-170]

(a)   He (either alone or with his associates) holds **more than 30%** of the ordinary shares or can exercise more than 30% of the voting rights in the company or any subsidiary

(b)   He is an **employee or a non-qualifying director** of the company or of a subsidiary, or of a partner of the company or of a subsidiary. **A qualifying director who is also an employee is not treated as connected under this rule**.

(c)   On a winding up of the company or any subsidiary, he (either alone or with his associates) would be entitled to more than 30% of the assets

(d)   He is a **partner** of the company or of any subsidiary

Associates include business partners, spouses, partners in a civil partnership, parents or remoter forebears and children or remoter issue.

A **qualifying director is, broadly, one who only receives reasonable remuneration (including any benefits) from the company**. [s.169]

The investor does not need to be UK resident or ordinarily resident (see later in this Text) although he must have income which is taxable in the UK in order to benefit from the relief.

3.5 Conditions to be satisfied by the company

3.5.1 Qualifying company

A **qualifying company** is a company which satisfies all of the following conditions: [s.180]

(a)   It exists wholly to carry on one or more qualifying trades (see below) throughout the 3 year period commencing with the issue of the shares

(b)   At any time in the 3-year period when trade or research and development is being carried on, it is carried on **wholly or mainly in the UK**

(c)   The company must be **unquoted** at the time the EIS shares are issued and no arrangements must exist at that time for the company to cease to be unquoted

(d) **It does not control any other company** (except for qualifying 90% subsidiaries) **and it is not under the control of another company**

(e) The **assets of the company** must not exceed £7 million immediately before and £8 million immediately after the issue

(f) The company must have **fewer than 50 full time equivalent employees** and must have **raised less than £2 million** in venture capital funds in the previous 12 months

3.5.2 Qualifying trade

A **qualifying trade is one carried on commercially with a view to profit**. The following activities are excluded. [s.192]

(a) Dealing in commodities, futures, shares, securities, other financial instruments or land

(b) Dealing in goods other than in an ordinary trade of wholesale or retail distribution

(c) Financial activities such as banking, hire purchase and insurance

(d) Leasing, apart from chartering of ships (other than oil rigs and pleasure craft) for up to 12 months at a time

(e) The receipt of royalties or licence fees, except in respect of a company's research and development or by a film production company

(f) The provision of legal and accountancy services

(g) Property development

(h) Farming or market gardening

(i) Holding or managing woodlands or any forestry activity

(j) Operating or managing hotels

(k) Operating or managing residential care homes or nursing homes

(l) Providing certain services for another business [s.199]

(m) Shipbuilding

(n) Coal and steel production.

3.5.3 Qualifying shares

The shares must be newly issued, fully paid up ordinary shares which carry no preferential rights to dividends, assets or redemption in the three years from the date of issue. [s.173]

They must be issued to raise money for the purpose of a **qualifying business activity**, which can be to carry on a qualifying trade (see above) *or* carry out research and development intended to lead to such a trade *or* to hold shares and securities in companies carrying out qualifying trades or research and development. [s.174]

3.5.4 Use of funds

The company must use the money raised from the share subscription for the purpose of the qualifying business activity generally within two years of the date of the share issue, or within two years of commencement of a qualifying activity if later. [s.175]

4 Venture Capital Trusts (VCTs)

4.1 Introduction

Certain income tax and capital gains tax advantages are available to individuals who invest in a Venture Capital Trust (VCT). These tax advantages are intended to encourage investment in unquoted trading companies (broadly EIS type companies) through a listed VCT company, so spreading the investment risk.

4.2 Tax reduction on investment

An **individual** who is at **least 18 years of age** who subscribes for **new eligible shares in a Venture Capital Trust** (VCT) can claim income tax relief in respect of his investment. The amount of income tax relief available to such an individual is the lower of: [s.263]

(a)   **30% of the amount subscribed for eligible shares in VCTs in the year up to a maximum investment of £200,000** per tax year, and

(b)   The individual's income tax liability for the year.

The tax relief is given as a tax reduction in the income tax computation (see earlier in this Text).

4.3 Relief on distributions

Distributions (ie dividends) received by an individual in respect of ordinary shares in a VCT are exempt from income tax, provided:

(a)   The company was a VCT when the individual acquired his shares, and

(b)   The dividend is paid out of profits which accrued to the company in an accounting period ending after its approval as a VCT, and

(c)   **The shares in respect of which the dividend is paid were not acquired by the investor in excess of the permitted maximum £200,000** investment for any tax year. [s.709 ITTOIA 2005]

The relief on dividends is available to individuals at least 18 years old on the first £200,000 of ordinary shares **acquired** in each tax year at a time when the company was a VCT. This includes shares acquired by purchase on the Stock Exchange (or by gift, or in any other manner). **It is not necessary for the individual to have subscribed for new VCT shares**.

The 30% tax relief given on the investment, however, is only given on the first £200,000 of new VCT ordinary shares **subscribed** for in each tax year. [s.261]

Illustration 2

Miss Davis bought existing ordinary shares in VCT1 with a value of £30,000 on 1 May 2010. On 1 December 2010 she subscribed £400,000 for new ordinary shares in VCT2.

1.   The VCT1 shares will qualify for relief on distributions only as she did not subscribe for these shares and therefore they do not qualify.

2.   The first £200,000 of the £400,000 invested in VCT2 shares will qualify for the 30% relief on investment as these shares were subscribed for. Only £170,000 of the investment will qualify for relief on distributions.

4.4 Withdrawal of relief

VCT income tax relief is withdrawn if the investor disposes of his shares in the VCT within five years of their issue. A disposal by gift or sale at a profit results in a withdrawal of the full relief.

A disposal by sale for less than the cost of the shares (ie at a loss) results in a clawback of relief equal to the proceeds received, multiplied by 30%.

The death of the investor or a disposal to a spouse/civil partner does not result in any withdrawal of relief.

VCT income tax relief is also withdrawn if the VCT loses its approved status within five years after issuing eligible shares to the investor. In such circumstances the investor's full income tax relief is withdrawn. [s.266]

Withdrawals of VCT income tax relief are made by way of an assessment for the year in which the relief was originally given. [s.270]

Investors are required to give notice to an officer of HMRC within 60 days if an event occurs which gives rise to withdrawal of relief. [s.271]

Exam focus point

Again, it is worth highlighting the relevant sections of the legislation on VCTs. Also note the similarities and differences between EIS and VCT investments.

Examiner's report – Personal Taxation

November 2009 –Part II LFQ 3

The most common incorrect answer from...candidates would be to confuse the VCT and EIS reliefs (the rates and holding periods)...

4.5 Conditions for relief

VCTs are companies, that are not close companies, that are approved by HMRC. The legislation should primarily be relied on in this area but an outline of the conditions is given below: [s.274]

(a)   **The VCT's ordinary shares must be quoted on the Stock Exchange**

(b)   Its **income has been derived wholly or mainly from shares** or securities

(c)   It **has not retained more than 15% of this income**, ie it must distribute 85% of such income and 100% of any other income. However, this distribution requirement is waived if the amount required to satisfy the 15% rule is less than £10,000 per 12 month accounting period

(d)   **Not more than 15% of the company's investments is in a company other than another VCT** or a company that would qualify as a VCT if it were quoted

(e)   In each accounting period **at least 70% of its investments are in shares in qualifying holdings** (broadly holdings in unquoted companies carrying on qualifying trades in the UK).

(f)   **At least 30% of the company's qualifying holdings has been or will be represented by holdings of eligible shares**

(g)   The company must have **fewer than 50 full time equivalent employees** and must have **raised less than £2 million** in venture capital funds in the previous 12 months

HMRC will specify the date from which a VCT is approved. This cannot be earlier than the date on which application for approval was made by the company.

Approval may be withdrawn where a VCT ceases to satisfy the above conditions or fails to satisfy such conditions within the above time periods. A notice of withdrawal of approval normally has effect from the time it is given.

The money raised from the issue of shares must be used for the purposes of its qualifying trade within two years. [s.293]

The value of the relevant company's assets must not exceed £7 million immediately before the share issue and £8 million immediately afterwards. [s.297]

4.6 Qualifying trades

All trades (including research and development from which it is intended that a trade will be derived) **are qualifying trades except for the following prohibited activities**: [s.303]

(a)   Dealing in land, in commodities, shares, securities or other financial instruments
(b)   Dealing in goods, otherwise than in the course of an ordinary trade of wholesale or retail distribution
(c)   Banking, insurance, money-lending, debt-factoring, hire-purchase financing or other financial activities
(d)   Leasing
(e)   Receiving royalties or licence fees
(f)   Providing legal or accountancy services
(g)   Property development
(h)   Farming or market gardening
(i)   Holding or managing woodlands or any forestry activity
(j)   Operating or managing hotels
(k)   Operating or managing residential care homes or nursing homes
(l)   Providing certain services for another business [s.310]
(m)   Shipbuilding
(n)   Coal and steel production

5 Pre-owned asset tax

5.1 Introduction

An income tax charge, the 'pre owned asset tax' (POAT), may apply where, for example, a person makes a gift of cash and subsequently benefits from that cash usually in the form of an asset, in circumstances where the inheritance tax (IHT) gift with reservation rules do not apply.

Exam focus point

The IHT gift with reservation rules are outside the scope of the Personal Taxation paper syllabus. You do not need to know them to be able to attempt a POAT calculation in the examination.

The POAT broadly applies to **land (including buildings) and chattels. There is no charge if the total taxable amount does not exceed £5,000.**

5.2 Land

The rules apply where an individual occupies land and he had either:

(a)   Previously owned the land but had disposed of it, or

(b)   Provided consideration used by another person in acquiring the land.

The taxable amount is the **annual value of the land** less any amount paid by the individual for the use of the land. **Payment of full rent will reduce the taxable amount to nil**.

5.3 Chattels

The rules apply where an individual possesses a chattel (ie an item of personal property) and he had either:

(a)   Previously owned the chattel but had disposed of it, or

(b)   Provided consideration used by another person in acquiring the chattel.

The taxable amount is the **value of the chattel multiplied by the official rate of interest**, which will be given in the exam, less any amount paid by the individual for the use of the chattel.

5.4 Exclusions

The rules do **not** apply to:

(a)   Arm's length disposals to an unconnected person

(b)   Disposals to connected persons made as if at arm's length (the definition of connected persons (see later in this Text) is extended by including as 'relatives' uncles, aunts, nephews and nieces)

There is no charge if the land or chattel is treated as a gift with reservation for IHT purposes.

5.5 Inheritance tax (IHT) election

An individual caught by the rules can elect to disapply this income tax charge by 31 January following the tax year in which the charge arises. The property will instead be within the gift with reservation rules for IHT purposes.

Example 2

Joe gifted £400,000 cash to his son, Tony, in June 2005. Tony bought a house with the money in September 2008. Joe moved into the property, which has an annual rental value of £6,000, shortly after. What is the pre-owned asset tax charge for Joe, who is a higher rate taxpayer?

Example 3

Joe also gifted £400,000 cash to his daughter, Caroline, in June 2005. Caroline bought a picture worth £250,000 with the money. The picture hangs in Joe's reception room. What is the pre owned asset tax charge for Joe, assuming the official interest rate is 4%?

Chapter roundup

- Certain investments (eg NS&I certificates) are completely tax free.

- ISAs are available to individuals over 18 (over 16 for cash investments) who are resident and ordinarily resident in the UK.

- ISAs can exist as cash or shares accounts.

- There is no income tax on interest or dividends, nor capital gains tax on disposal of shares from the ISA.

- Certain income tax and capital gains tax advantages are available to individuals who invest in EIS and VCTs.

- EIS relief applies where an individual subscribes for new ordinary shares in a qualifying company. Qualifying companies are in general unquoted trading companies where the trade is not a 'secure' one ('secure' being dealing in land, finance etc).

- EIS relief allows 20% of the investment as a tax reduction. The maximum investment qualifying for relief is £500,000.

- Under certain specific circumstances EIS relief can be clawed back (ie withdrawn) by HMRC.

- A VCT company must meet a number of conditions for approval for VCT relief to be available including that the VCT must be a listed company whose income must derive wholly or mainly from shares and securities.

- The VCT investor will receive a tax reduction for 30% of the amount subscribed up to £200,000 of new VCT ordinary shares subscribed for in each tax year. This relief is withdrawn if the investor disposes of his shares in the VCT within five years of their issue.

- VCT dividends on the first £200,000 of VCT ordinary shares acquired (by subscription or purchase) are exempt from income tax.

- There is an income tax charge, the pre-owned asset tax, on benefits received by former owners of property.

Quiz

1. Mr and Mrs Daniels have two sons, Jason aged 17 and Paul aged 19. Who may invest in an ISA?

2. Which of the following individuals cannot obtain EIS income tax relief?

   (a) An individual who, together with his associates, controls 26% of the voting power in the company
   (b) An unpaid (non-executive) director of the company
   (c) The managing director's secretary.

Solutions to Quiz

1. Both of them, but Jason may only subscribe to a cash account as he is under 18.

2. (a) Is fine because he owns ≤ 30%.
   (b) Is fine as a 'qualifying director'.
   (c) Employees are not entitled to relief.

Solutions to chapter examples

Solution to Example 1

(a) The sale is within three years of the subscription for the shares, so the income tax relief is proportionately withdrawn. The tax reduction obtained on the shares sold after two years was £5,000/2 = £2,500. The issue price was £34,000/2 = £17,000. The amount of relief withdrawn is £12,000 × £2,500/£17,000 = £1,765

(b) The full gain of £8.000 is exempt as the shares have been held for more than three years.

Solution to Example 2

Income tax charge: £6,000 @ 40%   £2,400

Solution to Example 3

Notional interest: £250,000 @ 4%   £10,000
Income tax charge: £10,000 @ 40%   £4,000

Now try the following questions

Short Form Questions:

4.1 – 4.4 inclusive

Long Form Question:

4.1	Enterprise Investment Scheme

The purpose of this chapter is to help you to:

- explain the scope of the charge to income tax on employment income

- identify and calculate the benefits taxable on all employees

- calculate the benefits taxable only on employees paid £8,500 or more pa and directors

- identify tax free benefits available to all employees

- identify the payments and expenses that can be deducted from employment income

- apply the special provisions taxing payments on termination of employment

References: ITEPA 2003 unless otherwise stated

1 Basis of employment income

1.1 Assessable income

Remuneration from an office or employment is taxed as employment income. Employment income is divided into:

(a)   General earnings, and
(b)   Specific employment income

General earnings include:

(a)   Any salary, wages or fee
(b)   Any benefits.

Specific employment income includes:

(a)   Payments made on termination of employment
(b)   Income from acquisition of shares derived from employment
(c)   Pension income received from an unregistered pension scheme.

Pensions and annuities paid in the UK, whether provided by the State, a registered occupational pension scheme or a personal pension scheme are taxed simply as 'pension income'.

Various social security benefits are taxed as 'Social Security income' (see earlier in this Text).

1.2 The receipts basis

General earnings are assessed as income for the year in which they are received. The date of receipt is the earliest of:

(a)   The date of **payment** (or payment on account), or

(b)   The date when a person becomes **entitled** to the payment, or

(c)   In the case of directors only, the earliest of:

    (i)   The date the earnings are credited in the company's records or accounts, or

    (ii)   The end of a period of account if earnings for that period are determined before the period ends, or

    (iii)   The date earnings are determined if the amount is not determined until after the period of account ends.

Taxable benefits (eg company cars) are generally treated as received when they are provided to the employee. If an employer provides a benefit to an employee's family member, the benefit will be taxable on that employee.

Example 1

A director of a company is entitled under his employment contract to a salary of £24,000 pa payable monthly on the last day of each month in equal amounts. Additionally he is entitled to a performance related bonus calculated on each half year's profits. The company prepares accounts to 31 December each year.

His bonus for the six months to 30 June 2009 of £8,000 is determined on 1 November 2009, credited to his account on 1 January 2010 and paid to him with his January salary. His bonus of £11,500 for the six months to 31 December 2009 is not determined until agreed by the shareholders at the AGM on 30 April 2010. It is then entered into the company's records and paid with his May salary.

You are required to calculate his taxable employment income for 2009/10 and 2010/11.

If remuneration is received after the employee has ceased to work for that employer it is still taxable, regardless of whether the office or employment is still held at the date of receipt.

Pensions and any taxable social security benefits are not assessed on the receipts basis but on the basis of the amount accruing in the tax year.

Now look at Chapter 7, 'Working relationships and the law', in the ATT publication 'Essential Law for the Taxation Technician'.

2 Taxable benefits assessable on all employees

2.1 The general rules

The general rule for benefits received by excluded employees (ie paid less than £8,500 pa) is that they are **only taxable** if they can be turned into money. The value of such benefits can be thought of as the **'second-hand value'**.

The general rule for non-excluded employees is that the taxable value of the benefit is the cost to the employer of providing the benefit.

For both excluded and non-excluded employees there are now many specific rules, which override the general rules.

The following specific rules for the provision of vouchers, living accommodation and mileage allowances apply to *all* employees regardless of the level of their earnings.

Certain benefits are only taxed on employees earning £8,500 or more and directors (ie non-excluded employees). The specific rules for how to calculate these taxable benefits are set out below.

Any amounts received by an employee in respect of benefits (or expenses – see below) from their employer usually form part of a director's or employee's earnings and must be **reported on Form P11D** (*Expenses and benefits*) or Form 9D for excluded employees.

2.2 Vouchers

If an employee receives

(a)   Non-cash vouchers (eg book tokens), or

(b)   Credit tokens (eg a credit card)

he will be **assessable on the *cost to the employer of providing* the benefit**, unless the benefit itself is exempt (see below).

If an employee receives a cash voucher, he is assessable on the sum of money for which the voucher is capable of being exchanged. He is assessed in the year he receives the voucher.

2.3 Accommodation [ss.104 – 107]

2.3.1 Basic charge

The value of the accommodation benefit provided to any employee (including employees paid £8,500+ and directors) **is the annual value of that property** (given in the exam). If the premises are rented rather than owned by the company, then the benefit to the employee is the higher of:

(a)   The rent actually paid by the employer, including a proportion of any premium paid in respect of a lease of ten years or less, entered into (or extended) on or after 22 April 2009, and

(b)   The annual value.

The amount of lease premium to include in (a) above is broadly the lease premium divided by the number of years of the lease. [s.105A]

The amount taxable on the employee will be reduced by any contribution he makes for the use of the property and any element of business use.

Example 2

Tony is provided with a company flat.

Annual value	£300
Rent paid by the company	£3,380
Amount paid by Tony to the company for the use of the flat	£520

You are required to show Tony's assessable benefit.

2.3.2 Job related accommodation

The employee will not be taxable if the accommodation is provided in one of the following circumstances.

(a)   Residence in the accommodation is **necessary** for the proper performance of the employee's duties (eg a caretaker), or

(b)   Accommodation is provided for the better performance of the employee's duties and the employment is of a kind in which it is **customary** for accommodation to be provided (eg a vicar or policeman), or

(c)   The accommodation is provided as part of special **security** arrangements in force because of a special threat to the employee's security (eg the Prime Minister).

TQT
Tax Qualification Training

2.3.3 Expensive accommodation

Where the cost of the living accommodation exceeds £75,000, an additional benefit will be chargeable which is found by applying the following formula: [s.104]

$$ORI \times (C - £75,000)$$

ORI is the official rate of interest at the start of the tax year, C is the 'cost of providing' the living accommodation. The cost is the aggregate of the cost of purchase and the cost of any improvements made before the relevant tax year. It is therefore *not* possible to avoid the charge by purchasing a property requiring substantial repairs and 'doing it up'. The cost is the net cost, after taking account of any amounts paid by the employee.

If the accommodation was acquired by the employer more than six years before it was first provided to the employee and its original cost, plus improvements, exceeded £75,000, the 'cost of providing' is increased (or reduced if appropriate) **to its market value when first provided to that employee.** Note that regardless of current market value, an additional charge cannot apply if the *original* cost plus improvements is under £75,000.

Where any contribution paid by the employee for the use of the property exceeds its annual value, the excess may be deducted from the additional expensive accommodation benefit.

Example 3

Simon is provided with a house by his employer (not job related accommodation). It was originally made available to him on 1 July 2007, although the company had acquired the house at a cost of £125,000 on 1 April 2004.

On 1 September 2009, £8,000 was spent on extending the property.

For 2010/11, the annual value of the house is £1,400. Simon pays £3,000 for the use of the house to his employer.

You are required to calculate his total benefit for 2010/11 in respect of the house. The official rate of interest is 4%.

2.4 Mileage allowances

Where employers pay mileage allowances to their employees to use their own cars for business travel the employees are taxed on any amounts in excess of the HMRC authorised mileage rates.

The tax-free limits are 40p a mile for the first 10,000 business miles and 25p a mile thereafter and are shown in the Association's tables available in the exam.

Any amount paid in excess of the limit is taxable on the employee. If the employer pays less than the authorised rates the employee can claim a deduction from their employment income for the shortfall.

The rates take into account depreciation, running expenses etc and the employee cannot claim a deduction for any loan taken out to purchase the car or any capital allowances on the cost of the car.

Any amount paid to the employee for mileage other than on the employer's business (eg for home to office mileage) is always taxable in full.

Example 4

Owen drives 14,000 business miles in his own car. Calculate the taxable benefit or allowable deduction assuming:

(a)   He is reimbursed 40p a mile
(b)   He is reimbursed 25p a mile
(c)   No reimbursement is made.

The employer is only required to report the taxable profit (if any) and the employee will only claim for the shortfall (if any).

Employers can pay employees using their own cars up to 5p a mile tax free for taking fellow employees as passengers on business journeys. There is no tax relief where employees receive either no payment from the employer or less than 5p a mile.

Employers can also pay a tax free mileage allowance to employees using motorcycles and bicycles in the course of their employment as follows:

Motorcycles   24p
Bicycles   20p

These generous rates are intended to encourage the use of more environmentally friendly transport. There is no reduction in the rates for over 10,000 miles (although, in the case of bicycles, this is not likely to be a practical point!)

Exam focus point

Examiner's report – Personal Taxation (old syllabus)

Nov 2001 – Question 1

Some candidates confused the mileage allowance calculation and deducted the excess of the allowance paid over the … Authorised Mileage allowance from the salary as an expense.

Many candidates were confused over the correct way to calculate the accommodation benefits. The most common error was to restrict the amount of the benefit by one half (on the basis that he spent only half his time in each property?) …

---

3 Benefits assessable on employees paid £8,500 or more and directors

3.1 Employees paid £8,500 or more and directors

'Emoluments', or **earnings, for the £8,500 pa test include salary, commissions, fees, reimbursed expenses and also benefits assessable on employees paid £8,500+ pa/directors**. In other words, one must *initially assume* that a particular employee is paid £8,500 pa or more in order to determine whether or not he really is in that category.

You may find it useful to learn the following proforma:

	£
Employment income (net of occupational pension contributions)	X
Reimbursed expenses	X
Benefits as if were paid £8,500 pa or more	X
TEST HERE	X
Less: allowable deductions	(X)
Assessment if the taxpayer is paid £8,500 pa or more	X

The £8,500 is pro-rated where the employment is held for less than the full tax year.

The term 'director' refers to any person who acts as a director or any person in accordance with whose instructions the directors are accustomed to act (other than a professional adviser).

A full-time working director, or a director of a non-profit making company or charity, and who, with associates, controls not more than 5% of the voting rights of the company is excluded unless he earns £8,500 pa or more.

3.2 The general rule

The value of a benefit is the cost to the employer *of providing* that benefit. So, for example, private medical insurance is caught, even though there is no resale value. There are, however, special rules for a number of specific benefits.

A **benefit arises if it is provided 'by reason of the employment' so there is no need for the employer to provide it directly**. In addition the rules apply if benefits are provided to members of an individual's family or household.

Where **in-house benefits** are provided, the case of *Pepper v Hart (1992)* established that the cost of **providing the benefit is the marginal (ie additional) cost** and not the average cost. This case involved employees of a public school paying reduced fees for their own children, calculated to cover the extra cost to the school eg food and laundry for the employee's child. They successfully argued that there was no cost to the employer as they had reimbursed the marginal costs. HMRC had wanted to value the benefit by averaging the total school costs over the total number of pupils.

This marginal cost basis is relevant to a wide range of employments and can apply, for example, where employees of transport undertakings (eg British Airways) are allowed to take up unsold seats free or at below the full price.

Exam focus point

Preparation of an income tax computation is a common long form question that can often test the position of a higher paid employee with several benefits. You will be required to calculate the cash value of these benefits using the rules detailed in this chapter. Use a separate working for each benefit.

3.3 Expenses connected with living accommodation

The following expenses are only assessable on non-excluded employees, or directors.

(a)   Heating, lighting or cleaning the premises
(b)   Repairing, maintaining or decorating them
(c)   Providing furniture etc normal for domestic occupation (annual value taken as 20% of cost – see below).

Unless the accommodation qualifies as 'job related' (see above) the full cost of additional services (excluding structural repairs) is assessable. If the accommodation is 'job related', however, the value of additional services is restricted to a maximum of 10% of 'net earnings'. For this purpose, net earnings are all amounts taxable as employment income (*excluding* the additional benefits (a) – (c) above) less any allowable expenses. [s.315]

If the employer pays the council tax due in respect of the property this will also be assessable *unless* the employee is in job related accommodation.

Example 5

Mr Quinton is employed as a security guard earning £12,000 in 2010/11. In order to carry out his duties properly he is required to live in a house adjacent to his employer's premises and this is accepted by HMRC as job related accommodation. The house cost £70,000 two years ago. The annual value of the house is £650.

In the year the company pays an electricity bill of £250, a gas bill of £200, a gardener's bill of £150 and redecoration costs of £1,000. Mr Quinton makes a monthly contribution of £50 for his accommodation. He drives a company car on which the assessable benefit is £2,990 (see below).

You are required to calculate the amount assessable as employment income for 2010/11.

Exam focus point

Examiner's report – Personal Taxation (old syllabus)

Nov 2004 – Question 1

Answers were generally well laid out and easy to follow. The main areas in which candidates did not do well were the calculation of the accommodation benefit and in particular the expenses paid by the employer ...

3.4 The car benefit rules

Special rules apply for taxing car benefits enjoyed by employees paid £8,500 pa or more and directors. [s.121]

(a) The tax charge arises whether the car is provided by the employer or by some other person.

(b) **The taxable benefit is a percentage, determined by the level of the car's carbon dioxide (CO_2) emissions** (see below) × **the car's list price.**

(c) The **list price** of the car is the sum of the following items:

(i)   The list price of the car for a single retail sale in the UK at the time of first registration, including delivery charges and the cost of standard accessories. **Discounts are not taken into account.**

(ii) The price (including fitting) of all optional accessories added when the car was first provided to the employee, excluding mobile telephones, equipment needed by a disabled employee, and equipment for the car to run on road fuel gas.

(iii) The price (including fitting) of all optional accessories fitted later and costing at least £100 each, with exclusions as in (ii). Such accessories affect the taxable benefit from and including the year of assessment in which they are fitted. Accessories that merely replace existing accessories and are not superior to the ones replaced are ignored.

(d) There is a special rule for classic cars. If the car is at least 15 years old (from the time of first registration) at the *end* of the tax year, and its market value at the end of the year is over £15,000 and greater than the price found under (c), that market value (including accessories) is used instead of the price.

(e) **If the employee makes a capital contribution** towards the cost of the car or accessories this is **deducted from the list price** for calculating the benefit, subject to a **maximum deduction of £5,000.**

(f) **The maximum list price after deducting the employee's capital contribution is £80,000. This price cap is being abolished from 6 April 2011.**

(g) **The percentage used in the benefit calculation depends on the CO_2 emissions of the car as follows:**

Emissions	Car benefit percentage
0g/km	0%
1 – 75g/km	5%
76 – 120g/km	10%
121 – 130g/km	15%
131 – 230g/km	15% + 1% for every 5g/km in excess of 130g/km
230g/km and over	35% (maximum)

There is a 3% supplement for diesel cars (maximum is still 35%).

Exam focus point

Examiner's report – Personal Taxation (old syllabus)

Nov 2006 – Question 1

Some candidates lost a mark in the car benefit calculation as they deducted the employee's contribution from the cost price of the car.

Example 6

Nigel Issan is provided with a diesel car which had a list price of £22,000 when it was first registered. The car has CO_2 emissions of 193g/km.

You are required to calculate Nigel's car benefit for 2010/11.

(h) **The benefit is reduced on a time basis where a car is first made available or ceases to be made available during the year** or is incapable of being used for a continuous period of not less than 30 days (for example because it is being repaired). If a car is unavailable for less than 30 days and a replacement car of similar quality is provided, the replacement car is ignored and treated as being the usual car.

Exam focus point

Note that where *any* benefit is only available for part of the tax year, the taxable benefit must be time apportioned. Look carefully at the dates given in the question.

(i) **The benefit is reduced by any payment the user is required to make for the private use of the car** (as distinct from a capital contribution to the cost of the car). However, the benefit cannot become negative to create a deduction from the employee's income. **Payments for insuring the car do not count.**

Example 7

Vicky Olvo starts her employment on 6 January 2011 and is immediately provided with a new petrol car with a list price of £25,000. The car was more expensive than her employer would have provided and she therefore made a capital contribution of £6,200. The employer was able to buy the car at a discount and paid only £23,000. Vicky contributed £100 a month for being able to use the car privately. CO_2 emissions are 257g/km per the car's registration document.

You are required to calculate her car benefit for 2010/11.

(j) **Pool cars are exempt.** A car only qualifies as a pool car if *all* the following conditions are satisfied: [s.167]

   (i)   It is used by more than one director or employee and is not ordinarily used by any one of them to the exclusion of the others.

   (ii)   Any private use is merely incidental to business use.

   (iii) It is not normally kept overnight at or near the residence of an employee.

(k) Where an employee has sacrificed salary to obtain private use of a car, the taxable benefit will be the higher of salary foregone and the benefit calculated above.

(l) Employers must make quarterly returns containing details of cars provided to employees on form P46 (car). These returns are made for income tax quarters (ending on 5 July, 5 October, 5 January and 5 April), and must be made within 28 days of the end of each quarter.

(m) **The benefit calculated above covers all expenditure by the employer on repairs, servicing, insurance, road fund licence and cleaning.** It does not cover the cost of a chauffeur. Where a chauffeur is provided for both business and private mileage, an agreed proportion of the employer's associated costs would be assessable on the employee.

(n) A car telephone is exempt (see below).

(o) No benefit arises on the provision of a car parking space at or near work (see below).

3.5 The fuel benefit rules

Where fuel for private motoring is provided to an employee paid £8,500 pa or more or a director with a company car, he will be assessed on a fuel benefit in addition to the car benefit above.

The fuel benefit charge is based on the same percentage as is used to calculate the car benefit × the base figure. The base figure for 2010/11 is £18,000 and is shown in the Association's tax tables. [s.150]

There is no taxable benefit if either all the fuel was provided for business travel or the employee reimburses all of the cost of private fuel.

Any reduction for non-availability of a company car also applies to the fuel benefit. If the car is available for x months but fuel is only supplied for private use for y months ($y < x$) the fuel charge is still $^x/_{12}$ of the full charge.

The taxable fuel benefit only applies to company cars. If fuel is provided for an employee's own car, the normal rule of 'cost of providing' applies.

Example 8

An employee was provided with a new petrol car costing £15,000 (the list price) on 1 June 2010. During 2010/11 the employer spent £900 on insurance, repairs and vehicle licence. The firm paid for all petrol (£2,300) without reimbursement. The employee was required to pay the firm £25 per month for the private use of the car.

The car has CO_2 emissions of 130g/km.

You are required to calculate the total assessable benefit for 2010/11 in respect of the car and fuel.

3.6 Company vans

An annual scale charge of £3,000 applies for unrestricted private use of company vans. A further £550 charge applies for the provision of private fuel. [s.157]

This charge only applies to employees who use a company van for significant private journeys other than journeys between home and work.

The charge is pro-rated if the van is only provided for part of the year or if it is incapable of being used for 30 or more consecutive days. The charge is also reduced by any employee contributions.

3.7 Private use of employer's assets

The taxable value of the private use of an employer's assets (other than cars, vans and accommodation) **is:**

20% × the market value of the asset when first used by the employee. [s.205]

If the asset is leased by the employer and the lease charge is greater than the 20% benefit, that lease charge will be the taxable benefit.

If that asset is subsequently acquired by the employee, the assessable benefit on the acquisition is the greater of:

(a)   **The current market value of the asset,** and

(b)   **Market value when first provided less any amounts already assessed as a benefit (at 20%) in respect of use of the asset.**

This rule prevents tax free benefits arising on fast depreciating items by the employee purchasing them at a much reduced second hand value.

Illustration

A suit costing £200 is bought by an employer for use by an employee on 6 April 2009. On 6 April 2010 the suit is purchased by the employee for £15, its market value then being £25.

The benefit assessable in 2009/10 will be 20% × £200   £40

The benefit assessable in 2010/11 will be the greater of:

		£	£
(a)	Market value at acquisition by employee	25	
(b)	Original market value	200	
	Less: assessed in respect of use .	(40)	
		160	
	ie		160
	Less: price paid by employee		(15)
	Benefit		145

If the employee does not buy the asset he will continue to be assessed on 20% × the original value each year (even if use continues for more than five years). However, it remains tax efficient for assets like suits, which need replacing every two or three years, to be purchased by the employer rather than by the employee out of net income.

As the provision of a bicycle for home to work travel is a tax free benefit (see below) if an employee buys a bicycle that they have previously used, the tax charge is always based on the market value when they buy it.

3.8 Taxable cheap loans

3.8.1 Basic rule

Loans to employees, directors and their families give rise to taxable benefits equal to:

(a)   **Any amounts written off, and**
(b)   **The excess of the interest based on the official rate over any interest actually charged.** [s.175]

There is no taxable benefit if the total balance on all loans to the employee did not exceed £5,000 at any time in the year. If the £5,000 threshold is exceeded, a benefit arises on interest on the whole loan, not just on the excess of the loan over £5,000. [s.180]

When a loan is written off there is no £5,000 threshold so writing off a loan of £1 would give rise to a £1 benefit.

3.8.2 Calculating the interest benefit

There are two methods of calculating the amount of the benefit.

(a) **The normal 'averaging method'** takes the average of the amount of loan outstanding at the beginning and end of the tax year (or the dates on which the loan was made and repaid in the tax year) and applies the official rate of interest to it. [s.182]

(b) **The alternative method calculates interest on a daily basis on the actual amount outstanding.** [s.183]

The normal 'averaging' method applies automatically unless an election is made by the taxpayer or HMRC who normally only make the election where it appears that the 'averaging' method is being deliberately exploited.

Different loans to the same employee are usually treated separately.

Example 9

At 6 April 2010 a cheap loan of £30,000 was outstanding to a director, who repaid £20,000 on 6 December 2010. The remaining balance of £10,000 was outstanding at 5 April 2011. Interest paid during the year was £250.

What is the benefit under both methods for 2010/11, assuming the official rate of interest was 4% throughout the year?

3.8.3 Exceptions

The following categories of cheap loan can be ignored:

(a) Loans made on **ordinary commercial terms** [s.176]

(b) Loans **qualifying for tax relief** (eg loan to buy shares in a close company or to buy a property for letting). Any interest the employee actually pays is relieved as normal (eg as a deduction from total income or as an expense deductible from property income).

   If the loan only partly qualifies for tax relief (eg a loan to buy computer equipment used partly for business purposes and partly privately) it is not exempt. [s.184]

   Instead the full cash equivalent of the loan should be included as part of the employee's employment income (and reported on form P11D). The employee must then claim any tax relief due on his self assessment tax return.

   In effect, only the private element of the loan interest paid is a taxable benefit. [s.178]

Example 10

Anna, who is single, has an annual salary of £35,000 and a loan from her employer of £24,000 at 1.25% interest to buy a holiday cottage which Anna uses herself and lets to tenants. The net rents (before interest relief) are £4,500 and 15% of general expenses have been disallowed to reflect Anna's occupation.

The official rate of interest is 4%.

What is Anna's tax liability for 2010/11?

---

4 Tax-free benefits – summary

There is a fairly long list of benefits which are *non-taxable* on *all* employees, including:

(a) Accommodation and subsistence:

   (i) **Job related accommodation** (see above)

   (ii) **Meals in a staff canteen**, provided that they are available to all employees on broadly similar terms

   (iii) The first 15p per working day of luncheon vouchers

   (iv) Personal incidental expenses of up to £5 per night for employees working away from home in the UK, or £10 per night if working abroad which would otherwise be taxable (eg laundry, newspapers, telephone calls home)

   However, where more than one night is spent away, the exemption works on an aggregate basis, eg for four nights the overall limit is £20

   (v) Subsistence costs for 'site based employees' (see below)

(b) Travel:

   (i) **Provision of a car parking space at or near the place of work**

   (ii) **Mileage allowances for cars etc within the HMRC Authorised mileage rates** (see above)

   (iii) Payment for additional transport costs or the cost of overnight accommodation in a case where public transport is disrupted by industrial action

   (iv) Payment for a taxi or hired car for an employee who is occasionally required to work late (after 9pm), in circumstances where either public transport has ceased or it would be unreasonable to expect the employee to use it. If such arrangements occur frequently (more than 60 times a year) or regularly (eg every Friday), then *no* exemption is available

   (v) Reimbursement to a director or employee of costs necessarily incurred in travelling to another company in the same group of which he is a director

   (vi) **Home to site travel costs for 'site based employees'**

   (vii) Provision of works buses with a seating capacity of 9 or more which are used mainly to bring employees to and from work

   (viii) The payment of general subsidies to public bus services used by employees to travel to work, regardless of whether the employees pay the same fare as other members of the public or any fare at all

   (ix) Provision of bicycles and cycling safety equipment made available for employees mainly to travel between home and work

   (x) Provision of workplace parking for bicycles and motorcycles

   (xi) Provision of alternative transport to get car sharers home when exceptional circumstances, such as a domestic emergency, mean that the normal car sharing arrangements unavoidably break down

   (xii) Tax free breakfasts on official 'cycle to work' days

(c) **Education and training**:

    (i)   Payments of up to £15,480 per academic year made by an employer to an employee for attendance at a full-time training course (including a sandwich course) at a university, college, school or similar establishment

    (ii)   Payments made in respect of a past or present employee for the costs of a qualifying training or retraining course – full time, day release or block release

(d) **Removal expenses**:

Up to £8,000 of removal expenses borne by the employer where the employee has to move house on first taking up the employment or on a transfer within the organisation. 'Removal expenses' include for this purpose the reimbursement of interest on a bridging loan, usual professional fees, costs of finding a new home, and replacement of curtains and carpets

(e) **Entertainment**:

    (i)   **The provision of a Christmas party or alternative function, provided that the cost is no more than £150 per head per annum**

    (ii)   The provision of entertainment by a person who is neither the employer, nor connected with them

(f) **Childcare**:

    (i)   **Childcare facilities available to all employees either on the employer's premises or on other premises where the employer is responsible for the financing and management of the facilities**

    (ii)   £55 per week of qualifying childcare costs paid by employers either directly to an employee, or to officially registered or approved childcare providers, including those in the employee's home (eg nannies)

(g) **Health**:

    (i)   **Overseas medical expenses** incurred while working abroad as part of the duties of the employment, and the cost of insuring against such expenses

    (ii)   Provision of eyesight tests, and spectacles, contact lenses etc, where required by health and safety at work legislation. The exemption is available if tests/appliances are made available to all relevant employees

    (iii)   One health screening or medical check up per tax year

(h) **Home-working**:

A **tax free allowance of up to £3 per week** is payable to employees to cover the additional household costs of working some or all of the time at home. No record keeping is required for the flat-rate £3 per week allowance. For payments above that figure, evidence is required that the payment is wholly in respect of additional household expenses incurred by the employee in carrying out his duties at home

(i) **Miscellaneous**:

    (i)   **Non-cash long service awards – for service in excess of 20 years, £50 per year of service is tax-free**

    (ii)   Staff uniforms

    (iii)   Awards under a formally constituted staff suggestion scheme

    (iv)   Gifts (other than cash) received by reason of the employment from someone other than the employer, provided that they amount to less than £250 in a tax year from a particular source

    (v)   Assets or services provided to improve an employee's personal physical security from a threat arising out of his employment

    (vi)   **Workplace sports or recreational facilities provided by employers for use by their staff generally**. This does not apply where the employer pays or reimburses an employee's subscription to a sports club nor where the facilities are only available to limited groups of employees

    (vii)   Air miles and car fuel coupons obtained in the course of business travel

Tax Qualification Training

(viii) Liabilities and indemnities insurance premiums for directors and employees; expenditure in discharging an employee's liabilities incurred in his capacity as employee; costs of proceedings relating to such matters (any costs paid by an employee qualify for tax relief)

(ix) **Private use of one mobile phone**; other mobile phones are a taxable benefit

(x) Use of shower facilities and changing room on employers' premises available to all employees

(xi) **Cheap loans under £5,000** (see above)

(xii) Vouchers provided for any exempt benefit

Exam focus point

The above list is not exhaustive, but provides a reasonably comprehensive summary of the tax free benefits of which you need to be aware. The main ones are in bold.

---

5 Allowable deductions

5.1 Introduction

Three types of expenditure made by employees are deductible from employment income:

(a) **Contributions** (within certain limits) **to a registered occupational pension scheme**

(b) **Subscriptions to professional bodies**, if relevant to the duties, and

(c) **Donations to charity** (of any amount) **under an approved payroll deduction scheme**. These may also be referred to as a 'Payroll giving scheme' or a 'Give as You Earn scheme'.

In such a scheme, the employee authorises the employer to deduct the donations from their employment income and pay them over to a government-approved payroll giving agency which then pays the money on to a specified charity or charities.

The employee obtains income tax relief for the donations via the PAYE system. The donations are deducted from the employee's taxable pay to which PAYE is applied. The employee therefore obtains income tax relief at both basic and higher rates depending on the level of his employment income. There is no limit on the amount of donations on which the employee can obtain tax relief under the scheme.

Other claims for deductions are hard to obtain. When they are available, they fall into the following categories:

(a) **Qualifying travel expenses** (see below)

(b) Other **expenses incurred *wholly, exclusively and necessarily in* the performance of the duties**

(c) **Capital allowances on plant and machinery *necessarily* provided for use *in* the performance of the duties**. Note that the plant cannot include the employee's own transport as the depreciation is already factored into the HMRC Authorised mileage rates (see above).

Note that the word **'necessarily'** is particularly restrictive. Trading expenses for a company, sole trader or partner have to satisfy only a 'wholly and exclusively' test and are, therefore, much more likely to be allowable. This partly explains why taxpayers prefer to be self employed rather than employed.

5.2 Travel expenses

Expenditure 'in the performance of' duties does not include expenditure incurred in order to get into a position to perform duties. **Thus travel to work (ie commuting) is not usually allowable**.

However, a deduction for commuting costs is available to employees with no permanent workplace. This includes 'site based employees' and those intending to spend less than 24 months at a temporary workplace.

A deduction is also available for **accommodation and subsistence** if an overnight stay is necessary.

5.3 Other expenses

5.3.1 Reimbursed expenses

Where an employee incurs an expense that is reimbursed by his employer, he must include the full expense as taxable earnings and deduct any amount incurred **wholly, exclusively and necessarily** in the performance of his duties.

An employer can obtain a 'dispensation' (notice of nil liability) from HMRC relieving them from reporting employees' expenses payments on form P11D. HMRC will issue a dispensation if the employees would ordinarily receive a tax deduction for the expenses (eg salesmen's travel expenses) and the payments are properly controlled. Employees do not have to include any expenses covered by the dispensation on their tax returns.

5.3.2 Round sum allowances

Where an employee is provided with a round sum allowance (ie a lump sum) to cover future expenses, he must include the full allowance as a taxable emolument and take a deduction for any amounts spent that would be deductible from trade profits for his employer on a **'wholly and exclusively'** basis.

A dispensation is not available for round sum allowances.

Example 11

Daniel earns £50,000 pa. He is given a £1,000 round sum allowance to cover his expenses for 2010/11.

He spends it as follows:

	£
Business travel	600
Staff entertaining	180
Client entertaining	150
Unaccounted	70
	1,000

Daniel has no other taxable benefits.

What is Daniel's employment income for 2010/11?

---

6 Payments on termination of employment

6.1 Introduction

Payments on termination of employment fall into one of three categories for taxation purposes:

(a)   **Entirely exempt**
(b)   **Partially exempt**
(c)   **Entirely chargeable**.

6.2 Exempt payments

The **following types of payment** on termination of employment are **exempt**. [ss.406-410]

(a)   A payment **on death**

(b)   A payment on account of **injury or disability**

(c)   A lump sum payment **from or to a registered pension scheme**

(d)   **Legal costs** recovered by the employee from the employer following legal action to recover compensation for loss of employment.

6.3 Fully taxable payments

Any termination payment not falling within (a) to (d) above but which is made *in return for services* **will be fully taxable under normal employment income rules**.

The question of whether a payment is made in return for services can be a complex one, but generally, if the **contract of employment provides for payment** to be made on termination of employment, the **payment will be in return for services**. If the contract is silent on this point but a payment is made, **it will be taken to be in return for services if there was a reasonable expectation** that such a sum would be paid. Accordingly, these payments made in return for services are taxed in full as part of the individual's employment income 'general earnings'.

Payments made in return for the employee promising, for example, not to work in a particular area **following the termination of his employment (a 'restrictive covenant')** are always **taxable in full**.

6.4 Partially taxable payments

Other 'termination' (or redundancy) payments, such as compensation for loss of office, are not taxable under the normal employment income rules as general earnings because they are not in return for services. They are, however, taxable as 'specific employment income' and the first £30,000 of such payments is free of income tax. [ss.401 – 403]

Redundancy payments (including statutory redundancy) are exempt from tax as earnings but like other termination payments are taxable under s.402 and the first £30,000 is exempt. [s.309]

Any benefits (eg the provision of a company car) which would be assessable had the employment continued, are taxed in the year in which the benefit is received or enjoyed. The £30,000 exemption is set against cash payments in priority to non-cash payments. [s.404]

The cost of outplacement (eg counselling) services incurred by the employer for the employee's benefit is exempt and does not reduce the £30,000 exempt amount.

HMRC may treat termination payments made on or around the time of an employee's retirement as arising from an unregistered pension scheme and so are fully taxable, with no £30,000 exemption. HMRC have indicated that a man of middle years moving on to further full-time employment is obviously not retiring but that they are likely to apply this rule to a man of older years who has no other full-time employment in prospect.

Example 12

Paula, 37, is made redundant on 10 October 2010 and her termination package includes the following:

	£
Compensation payment	50,000
Payment to registered pension scheme	5,000
Company car (market value)	12,000
Statutory redundancy	6,000
	73,000

Calculate the amount assessable as employment income in 2010/11.

6.5 Payments in lieu of notice (PILONS)

The tax treatment of a payment made in lieu of the employee working their notice period (a PILON) largely depends on whether the PILON is provided for in the employee's contract.

(a) **Contractual PILONs**

Where an employee's contract contains a provision that enables a PILON to be made, it is usually fully taxable. However, if the contract simply provides for a **notice period with no further qualification**, then any payment made instead of requiring the employee to work that notice is treated as **liquidated damages for breach of contract** and will come within the £30,000 exemption. [Hunter v Dewhurst (1932)].

TQT
Tax Qualification Training

(b)   Discretionary PILONs

(i)   Where the contract term gives the employer discretion **to make a PILON and the employer exercises that discretion, the payment is usually taxable in full**. [EMI Group Electronics Ltd v Coldicott (1999)]

(ii)   However, **if the employer decides not to exercise their discretion but makes a payment to terminate the contract early instead, this will be treated as a breach of contract.** The payment will be treated as compensation arising from the termination of employment (ie damages), rather than from the employment relationship. **The first £30,000 will be tax free.** [Cerberus Software v Rowley (2001)]

(iii)   Where a PILON is an **automatic response** by the employer, ie it is the employer's custom, habit or **practice or there is an expectation** (not merely a hope, but an 'enforceable contractual certainty') of **receiving it on the part of the employee, the payment may be taxable in full as earnings**. However, if the employer follows a procedure for making a **genuine 'critical assessment'** for each payment, for example using an internal written procedure to assess what payment is to be made to each employee and identifying adjustments typical of a damages payment, the payment will be treated as damages (for constructive dismissal in the Clinton case). [Clinton v HMRC (2009); EIM12977]

(c)   Non-contractual PILONs

If there is no contractual term covering the PILON the payment may still be taxable in full if:

(i)   The employer offers a PILON to the employee **in advance of terminating the employment and the employee agrees to take it. This will be treated as a variation of the contract** and the payment will be taxable in full. [SCA Packaging v HMRC (2007)]

(ii)   There is no contractual term but the PILON is an **automatic response** by the employer (see above). In this case it may be treated as an **integral part of the employer/employee relationship** and assessable in full. [EIM12977]

6.6 Termination payments after foreign service

Payments received on termination of an employment which included an element of foreign service may be exempt from tax. Complete exemption is given where the foreign service element is 'substantial'.

For the purposes of this exemption, the employee's period of service is treated as including a substantial element of foreign service where the foreign service comprises: [s.413]

(a)   Three-quarters of the whole period of service, or

(b)   The last 10 years, where the whole period of service is in excess of 10 years, or

(c)   Half of the total period of service, including any 10 out of the last 20 years, where the total period of service exceeds 20 years.

If part of the termination payment is still taxable *after* all other exemptions (eg the £30,000 exemption for compensation payments) and there has been foreign service during the period of employment, a **fraction of the otherwise taxable payment can be deducted** equal to: [s.414]

$$\frac{\text{period of foreign service}}{\text{total service}}$$

- Employment income includes general earnings and certain other receipts. Pensions and certain social security benefits are also charged to tax under ITEPA 2003.

- Earnings are assessable in the tax year in which they are received. Earnings are not only wages or salary but also certain benefits and reimbursed expenses.

- The provision of living accommodation (unless it is job related accommodation), credit cards, cash or non-cash vouchers and mileage allowances in excess of the authorised mileage rates gives rise to an assessable benefit for *all* employees.

- The living accommodation benefit is based on the annual value of the property. An additional benefit arises where the cost of the property, or in certain circumstances the market value at the date it is first occupied, exceeds £75,000.

- Relief is given to employees for the cost of using their own vehicle or bicycle for work if any mileage allowance paid is less than the authorised rates. Any excess is taxable.

- To determine whether an employee is a non-excluded employee (ie the £8,500 threshold is exceeded) all reimbursed expenses and benefits are included, but no deduction for expenses or payments (other than occupational pension contributions and charitable donations) are taken into account.

- A director is only treated as an excluded employee if, in addition to receiving earnings of less than £8,500, he both works full-time for the company and controls 5% or less of the ordinary share capital.

- The general rule for valuing benefits for excluded employees is the second-hand value, ie the amount of money into which it can be converted.

- The general rule for valuing benefits for employees earning £8,500+ and directors is the employer's cost of provision, unless special rules apply.

- The benefits that are only chargeable on employees paid £8,500+ and on directors are:
  - Expenses in connection with living accommodation
  - The provision of a company car and private fuel
  - The provision of a company van with significant private use
  - Use of assets owned by the employer and
  - Taxable cheap loans.

- Some benefits are exempt for all employees (eg workplace parking).

- Only occupational pension contributions, subscriptions to professional bodies, charitable donations under an approved payroll deduction scheme and expenses incurred 'wholly, exclusively and necessarily' in the performance of the employee's duties can be deducted from employment income.

- Employees can only claim a deduction for commuting costs if they are site based employees or have a temporary workplace (<24 months).

- Certain payments made on the termination of employment are completely exempt, eg on death of the employee.

- The first £30,000 of non-contractual termination payments, including statutory redundancy payments, is tax-free.

Quiz

1. Describe the basis of assessment for employment income.

2. An employee is provided with a flat by his employer (not job related accommodation). The annual value of the flat is £400; rent paid by the employer amounts to £3,900 per annum.

   How much is included in the employee's earnings in respect of this benefit?

3. The additional charge on 'expensive' accommodation (costing more than £75,000) applies only to employees paid £8,500+ pa and directors. True/False?

4. Megan, an employee, received the following in 2010/11:

	£
Salary	5,560
Company car (benefit)	2,310
Reimbursed expenses (of which 75% are deductible)	880

   Is Megan 'an employee paid £8,500 or more'?

5. Buster is the Managing Director of Buster Braces Ltd and is supplied with a Bentley (3 litre, petrol engine) which cost £82,000 in 2008. It has CO_2 emissions of 190g/km. He was disqualified for dangerous driving so is supplied with a chauffeur at the company's expense (full salary costs for 2010/11 – £13,500). The car is fitted with a telephone which Buster uses both for business and privately. All running costs are borne by the company. Buster did 12,000 miles in 2010/11, of which 3,000 miles were for business. What is the total taxable benefit?

6. A video recorder costing £500 was made available to Gordon by his employer on 6 April 2009. On 6 April 2010, Gordon bought the recorder for £150, when its market value was £325. What assessable benefit arises in 2010/11 if Gordon's annual salary is £15,000?

7. The first £5,000 of an interest free loan is exempt from tax. True/False?

8. How much of a termination payment, brought within the charge to employment income by virtue only of s.402 ITEPA 2003, is exempt from tax?

9. Is a taxable fuel benefit reduced by any reimbursement by the employee of the cost of fuel provided for private mileage?

TQT
Tax Qualification Training

1. Employment income is assessed on the receipts basis, ie on amounts received during the tax year, regardless of when it is earned.

2. £3,900, being the higher of the annual value and rent actually paid.

3. False. Only those in occupation of 'job related' accommodation can avoid the additional charge.

4. Yes

		£
Emoluments:	Salary	5,560
	Car benefit	2,310
	Reimbursed expenses	880
	TEST HERE (>£8,500)	8,750
	Less: allowable expenses (£880 × 75%)	(660)
	Employment income	8,090

5.

	£
Car benefit (W)	21,600
Fuel benefit (£18,000 × 27%)	4,860
Telephone benefit	nil
Chauffeur £13,500 × $\dfrac{9,000}{12,000}$	10,125
Total benefit	36,585

Working

	£
Maximum value £80,000 × 27%	21,600

$(15\% + ((190 - 130) \times 1/5) = 27\%)$

6. Benefit is based on the higher of:

		£	£
(a)	Current MV		325
(b)	Original MV	500	
	Less: already assessed (in 2009/10)		
	£500 × 20%	(100)	
			400

ie £400

The assessable benefit after deduction of the amount paid (£150) is £250.

7. False – only if the loan does not exceed £5,000 is it exempt.

8. £30,000.

9. Not unless the employer is fully reimbursed, in which case the fuel benefit is nil.

Solutions to chapter examples

Solution to Example 1

	£
2009/10	
Basic salary paid 30 April 2009 to 31 March 2010 inclusive	24,000
Bonus for six months to 30 June 2009 – determined before the end of the period of account ∴ 'received' on 31.12.09	8,000
Employment income 2009/10	<u>32,000</u>
2010/11	
Basic salary (30 April 2010 to 31 March 2011 inclusive)	24,000
Bonus for six months to 31 December 2009 – not determined until the AGM and payable subsequently therefore 'received' 30 April 2010	11,500
Employment income 2010/11	<u>35,500</u>

Solution to Example 2

		£
Benefit: greater of		
– annual value	£300	
– rent paid	£3,380	3,380
Less: reimbursed to the company		(520)
Taxable benefit		<u>2,860</u>

Solution to Example 3

Basic charge:

	£
Annual value	1,400
Less: contribution	(1,400)
	<u>nil</u>

Additional charge:

	£	£
Cost including improvements £(125,000 + 8,000)	133,000	
Less:	(75,000)	
Excess	<u>58,000</u>	
£58,000 × 4%		2,320
Less: balance of contribution £(3,000 – 1,400)		(1,600)
Taxable benefit		<u>720</u>

Solution to Example 4

		£
Authorised mileage rates:	10,000 × 40p	4,000
	4,000 × 25p	1,000
		<u>5,000</u>

		£
(a)	Taxable benefit: (40p × 14,000 =) £5,600 – £5,000	£600
(b)	Deduction: £(14,000 × 25p =) £3,500 – £5,000	£(1,500)
(c)	Deduction:	£(5,000)

Solution to Example 5

	£	£
Salary		12,000
Car benefit		2,990
Net earnings		14,990
Accommodation benefit:		
Annual value – exempt (job related)	nil	
Additional services:		
Electricity	250	
Gas	200	
Gardener	150	
Redecorations	1,000	
	1,600	
Restricted to 10% of £14,990	1,499	
Less: employee's contribution (12 × £50)	(600)	899
Employment income		15,889

Solution to Example 6

Car benefit £22,000 × 30% (15% + ((190 − 130) × 1/5) + 3%)	£6,600

Note that 193 g/km is rounded down to 190 g/km to be exactly divisible by 5.

Solution to Example 7

	£
List price (N1)	25,000
Less: capital contribution (maximum)	(5,000)
	20,000
£20,000 × 35% (N2)	7,000
3/12 × £7,000 (N3)	1,750
Less: contribution to running costs (£100 × 3)	(300)
Car benefit	1,450

Notes

(1) The discounted price is irrelevant
(2) 15% + ((255 − 130) × 1/5) = 40% restricted to 35% max
(3) Only available for 3 months in the year (6 January – 5 April)

Solution to Example 8

Car was available for 10 months.

	£
List price £15,000 × 15% (CO_2 emissions between 121 and 134g/km)	2,250
£2,250 × $^{10}/_{12}$	1,875
Less contribution (10 × £25)	(250)
	1,625
Fuel benefit £18,000 × 15% × $^{10}/_{12}$	2,250
Total taxable benefit	3,875

If the contribution of £25 per month had been towards the petrol, the benefit assessable would have been £(1,875 + 2,250) = £4,125. If the cost of private petrol were fully reimbursed by the employee then there would have been no fuel benefit at all.

Solution to Example 9

Averaging method

£

$$4\% \times \frac{(30,000 + 10,000)}{2}$$ 800

Less: interest paid (250)
Taxable benefit 550

Alternative method

£

£30,000 $\times \dfrac{8}{12}$ (6 April 2010 – 5 December 2010) $\times 4\%$ 800

£10,000 $\times \dfrac{4}{12}$ (6 December 2010 – 5 April 2011) $\times 4\%$ 133

933

Less: interest paid (250)
Taxable benefit 683

The taxpayer will use the average method but HMRC can elect for the alternative method if it wishes.

Solution to Example 10

	£
Salary	35,000
Cheap taxable loan: £24,000 × (4 – 1.25 =) 2.75% × 15% (personal use)	99
Employment Income	35,099
Property income: (£4,500 – [£24,000 × 1.25% × 85%])	4,245
Net income	39,344
Less: Personal allowance	(6,475)
Taxable income	32,869

Income tax
£32,869 × 20% 6,574

Solution to Example 11

	£	£
Salary and round sum allowance – employment income		51,000
Less: expense deduction:		
Round sum allowance	1,000	
Less: Disallowed expenditure for the employer		
Client entertaining	(150)	
Unaccounted	(70)	
		(780)
		50,220

Note. Client entertaining is never deductible as a trading expense for the employer.

Solution to Example 12

	£
Compensation payment	50,000
Payment to registered pension scheme – exempt	–
Company car	12,000
Statutory redundancy	6,000
	68,000
Less: exemption	(30,000)
Assessable	38,000

Short Form Questions:

5.1 – 5.23 inclusive

Long Form Questions:

5.1	Mr Thomas
5.2	Alf
5.3	Mr Bjork
5.4	HiTech computers
5.5	Grovelands
5.6	Mr Morris

TQT
Tax Qualification Training

6

The purpose of this chapter is to help you to:

- understand the tax charges for employees receiving shares directly from their employer

- calculate the tax charge for employees receiving shares under an unapproved share option scheme

- identify the various approved employee share schemes and understand when there may be a tax charge

- understand when there may be an NIC tax charge in connection with a share scheme

- identify the base cost of share scheme shares for CGT purposes

References: ITEPA 2003 unless otherwise stated

Share remuneration

1 Introduction to share schemes

Share schemes are an important element in the remuneration package of not only key executives but the workforce as a whole. They can provide both a reward for contributions made to the company's success and an incentive to maintain and improve its performance. The legislation provides for beneficial tax treatment for various schemes approved by HMRC.

Share schemes fall into two main categories:

(a) **Schemes where shares are allocated or transferred directly to employees or directors, and**
(b) **Schemes which provide for the granting of share options.**

A share option is a right to buy shares in the future at a price fixed at the time the option is granted. Assuming that the market price of the shares either is or will in the future be above the option price, an employee will then be able to acquire shares at a discount to their full value at the time the option is exercised. The employee does not have to exercise the option (ie buy the shares) if the shares have gone down in value.

2 Free or cheap shares given directly to employees

2.1 General provision

If an **employer (former, current or prospective) gives shares or securities to an employee or director in the employer company** ('Employment Related Securities') **at below their market value there is an income tax charge (and possibly a National Insurance Contribution charge – see below) at the date of acquisition. This is based on the difference between market value and the amount paid (if any) for the shares.**

2.2 Restricted shares [ss.422-432]

2.2.1 Charge on acquisition

If shares (or securities) are subject to restrictions that depress their value, and they are acquired for less than their actual market value, taking account of the restrictions, **there will be an income tax charge on acquisition,** as above, based on that market value less any consideration paid.

Restrictions include the **risk or forfeiture** (eg the employee must give the shares back if he does not complete a minimum period of service with the employer) and **restrictions on the freedom to dispose of the shares** (eg the employee is not allowed to sell the shares for three years).

Illustration 1

Shares worth £5 are gifted to an employee subject to restrictions that stop the employee selling their shares to anyone, at any time, except purchasers approved by the company. The restrictions reduce the value of the shares to £3.

The restrictions last for more than five years, so in this case the employee will pay income tax on £3, ie the restricted value.

However, **if the shares are restricted by a risk of forfeiture and the forfeiture period lasts less than 5 years, there is no income tax charge at acquisition** (but see below for employee elections).

2.2.2 Charge on lifting of restrictions

There is also an income tax charge (a post acquisition charge) when the restrictions are lifted or varied, or when, prior to this, the restricted shares are sold. The amount charged to tax as employment income at that time is the **proportion of value that escaped tax on acquisition as a result of the restrictions, plus that same proportion of any growth in value since acquisition.**

Illustration 2

Following on the illustration above, let's assume the employee sells the shares for £9 when the whole company is sold (so the restrictions no longer apply).

On acquisition the amount of untaxed value due to the restrictions was 40% (ie (£5–£3)/£5).

On disposal the employee will pay income tax on:

The untaxed part of the value at acquisition: 40% × £5	2.00
Plus 40% of the growth in value since acquisition £40% × (£9 – £5)	1.60
Total charged to income tax	£3.60

Note that this is the same as 40% of the proceeds on sale (40% × £9 = £3.60).

2.2.3 Income tax elections

Instead of paying income tax on a chargeable event (ie on acquisition or the lifting of restrictions), the employee and employer can elect up front to pay tax on the unrestricted market value of the shares at acquisition. This avoids the risk of a substantial income tax charge arising in the future because of a large increase in the share value.

Instead any growth in value will be subject to capital gains tax (CGT), which is generally chargeable at a lower rate than income tax and various reliefs may be available to reduce the tax liability (see later in this Text). However, this may mean that the employee pays more tax than finally proves necessary if the value of the shares does not increase as expected, as any 'overpaid' tax cannot be refunded.

Illustration 3

Shares worth £5 are gifted to an employee subject to restrictions that stop the employee selling their shares to anyone except purchasers approved by the company. The restrictions reduce the value of the shares to £3. The employee and employer jointly elect for the employee to be taxed on the unrestricted market value of the shares.

The employee will pay income tax on £5 in the tax year of acquisition, ie the unrestricted value.

We saw above that if a risk of forfeiture lasts less than 5 years there is no income tax charge on acquisition. However, it is possible for the employee and employer to make an election to ignore this income tax exemption and instead be charged up front. Any future growth in value of the shares will then be subject to CGT rather than income tax with the same advantages as described above.

Both elections must be made within 14 days of the transaction. This short time period is designed to stop taxpayers monitoring the share value to decide whether to make an election.

2.3 Conversion of convertible shares

Where shares (or securities) are acquired that are convertible into other shares (or securities) the value of the right to convert is disregarded at acquisition.

Instead **income tax is charged on the gain arising from the conversion**. So, if ordinary shares are converted into preference shares the charge is made on the difference in market value between the two types of shares at that date (not any gain arising since acquisition).

3 Unapproved share option schemes

An unapproved option is simply an option that has not been granted under a scheme approved by HMRC.

There is no income tax (or NIC) at the date the employer grants the unapproved option.

When the employee *exercises* the option (ie buys the shares at the price set out in the option), there is an income tax charge (and possibly an NIC charge – see below) on the difference between the market value of the shares at the time of the exercise of the option and the cost of the shares (plus the cost of the option if the employee had to pay the employer for the option at the date of grant).

Example 1

On 1 December 2010 James exercised options under an unapproved share option scheme run by his employer and acquired 1,000 shares at the option price of £3 per share. The market value at that date was £5 per share.

Calculate the amount assessable to income tax in respect of the exercise of the options.

The base cost of the shares for capital gains tax (CGT) purposes is the market value at the date of the exercise.

4 Approved share schemes

4.1 Introduction

There are four types of approved share scheme:

(a)   Share incentive plans (SIP)
(b)   Savings related share option schemes (Save As You Earn or 'SAYE')
(c)   Company share option plans (CSOP)
(d)   Enterprise Management Incentive schemes (EMI).

4.2 Share incentive plans (SIPs)

4.2.1 How the SIP works [Sch 2]

A share incentive plan (SIP) is a tax efficient way for employees to own shares in their employer company. **Employees can buy shares out of their pre-tax remuneration and there is usually no income tax (or NIC) when the employee takes the shares out of the plan.**

The scheme is operated by creating a trust ('the plan') that acquires shares in the employer company using funds from that company. The trustees then award the shares to the employees in accordance with the employer's instructions and hold the shares within the plan on behalf of the individual employees.

4.2.2 SIP shares

There are four ways in which an employee can obtain plan shares (all shares are held within the plan): [s.64 Part 8, Sch 2]

(a)   An employer can give up to £3,000 worth of shares (**'free shares'**) per tax year to an employee.

(b)   An employee can be allowed to buy shares (**'partnership shares'**) out of pre-tax remuneration up to a value of the lower of £1,500 per year and 10% of salary.

(c)   An employer can match the partnership shares bought by the employee by giving him up to 2 free shares (**'matching shares'**) for every partnership share purchased.

(d)   An employee can use up to £1,500 of his dividends from the existing plan shares each year to reinvest in further plan shares (**'dividend shares'**).

The employer company must offer all employees (even part time) the opportunity to participate in the scheme. The company can specify a minimum employment period before an employee is allowed to participate but this must not be longer than 12 months.

Employers must award 'free' shares to employees on similar terms (eg based on level of remuneration or length of service). **The employer can make the award conditional on the meeting of performance targets** by the employee or his team. There must be no deliberate weighting of rewards in favour of directors and more highly paid employees.

4.2.3 Tax advantages of a SIP

The tax advantages are summarised in the table below as follows:

	Free shares	Partnership shares	Matching shares	Dividend shares
Tax on award	None	None – tax relief for salary used to buy shares	None	None
Tax on removal of shares from plan within 3 years of award	On market value when taken out	On market value when taken out	On market value when taken out	Original dividend taxable but in year when shares taken out of plan if removed within holding period
Tax on removal between 3 and 5 year of award	On lower of: – value at award, and – value on removal	On lower of: – salary used to buy shares, and – value on removal	On lower of: – value at award, and – value on removal	None
Tax on removal after 5 years	None	None	None	None

If no income tax is due when the employee removes the shares from the plan after five years, **there is also no NIC charge** (see later in this Text).

4.2.4 Capital gains tax aspects of SIPs

The base cost of the SIP shares for capital gains tax (CGT) purposes (see later in this Text) **is the market value at the date the employee takes them out of the plan (ie on removal). So, when the employee sells the shares they are liable to CGT on any increase in value arising between taking them out of the plan and the date of sale.**

The employee can avoid CGT by keeping the shares in the plan until just before they plan to sell them.

Exam focus point

Examiner's report – Personal Taxation

November 2008 – Part II LFQ 3

Part A1 was rarely answered well with candidates making vague comments about tax being due and most missing the distinction between shares being within the plan for less than 3 years as opposed to between 3 and 5 years. For Part A3 few candidates realised that the base cost was uplifted to market value on withdrawal from the SIP.

4.3 Savings related share option schemes (SAYE)

4.3.1 How the SAYE scheme works [Sch 3]

The savings related share option scheme (or 'Save As You Earn' (SAYE) scheme) allows an **employee or director to save a fixed amount** of between £5 (company cannot set the minimum at more than £10) and £250 per month **for a three or five year contract**, in a contractual savings scheme set up by their employer. Seven year contracts are available but no additional contributions may be made after 5 years.

At the beginning of the savings period, the employer grants the employee an option to buy shares in the employer company when the savings period ends, at a price set in the option.

At the end of the contractual period, the employee can withdraw his contributions, together with a tax free bonus dependent on the length of the contract. **He can choose to use this money to buy the shares at the option price (ie 'exercise' the option), or simply take the money.**

4.3.2 Tax advantages of the SAYE scheme

There is usually no income tax (or NIC) on the grant or exercise of a SAYE option.

However, **if at the date of the grant of the option the company set the exercise price (ie the purchase price of the shares when the savings period ends) at less than 80% of the market value at that time, there is an income tax charge (and possibly an NIC charge – see below) at the date of exercise** (ie when the employee buys the shares).

The income tax charge is based on the difference between the market value of the shares at the date of the grant of the option and the price the employee actually pays (ie the discount at the date of *grant*).

4.3.3 Capital gains tax aspects of the SAYE scheme

The base cost of the shares for capital gains tax (CGT) purposes is the amount the employee pays for the shares (ie the exercise price). So, when the employee sells the shares they are liable to CGT on any increase in value between that price and the value on the date of sale.

Exam focus point

Examiner's report – Personal Taxation

November 2008 – Part II LFQ 3

For Part C7 too many candidates spent too long writing about the general rules surrounding a SAYE scheme rather than answering the specific questions asked...there was often uncertainty as to what the base cost was for the CGT computation on the disposal of the shares that were acquired under the scheme.

4.4 Approved company share option plans (CSOP)

4.4.1 How the CSOP works [Sch 4]

Just as with an unapproved scheme, in an approved company share option plan (CSOP) the employer company simply 'grants' an option to the employee to buy shares in the future at a price set at the date of grant. However, there are certain tax advantages as the scheme must satisfy a number of conditions to be 'approved' by HMRC.

The CSOP is not linked to, and is more flexible than, the SAYE scheme (see above). **It does not need to be made available to all employees,** ie the employer can reward key employees by granting them CSOP options.

In order to be approved, and benefit from the tax advantages of the plan (see below) **the options must satisfy certain conditions:**

(a) **The maximum value of shares any one employee can have under option at any time is £30,000.**

(b) **The employee must not be able to exercise the option (ie buy the shares) less than 3 years from the date of grant.**

(c) **The exercise price for the shares must be broadly equal to their market value at the date the option is granted.**

4.4.2 Tax advantages of the CSOP scheme

There is no income tax or NIC on either the grant or exercise of a CSOP option, even if the employee pays much less for the shares than they are worth when he buys them (ie when he 'exercises' his option).

4.4.3 Capital gains tax aspects of the CSOP scheme

The base cost of the shares for capital gains tax (CGT) purposes is the amount the employee pays for the shares (ie the exercise price). So, when the employee sells the shares they are liable to CGT on any increase in value between that price and the value on the date of sale

In practice, the cost of exercising the option is usually funded from the sale proceeds.

Example 2

On 1 December 2010 Patrick exercised options under an approved share option scheme run by his employer and acquired 1,000 shares at the option price of £3 per share. The market value at that date was £5 per share.

Calculate the income tax charge assuming Patrick is a higher rate taxpayer.

Example 3

Last year, Cathy's employer granted her an option over 10,000 shares under its approved company share option scheme. At that date the market value of the shares was £2 per share.

Her employer is about to grant a further option to Cathy under the same scheme, up to the maximum permitted value.

Calculate the maximum market value of shares over which Cathy's employer can grant the options, assuming the current market value of the shares is £1.25.

4.5 Enterprise management incentives (EMIs)

4.5.1 How the EMI works [Sch 5]

The EMI scheme enables small trading companies to attract and retain high calibre staff. There are similarities with the approved company share option plans (CSOP) (see above) but the reliefs are more carefully targeted and the conditions harder to satisfy.

Under an EMI scheme a **trading company** with **gross assets not exceeding £30 million** can award **key employees** with **share options worth up to £120,000 each** at the time the option is granted. The maximum value of options which may be granted at any time under an EMI scheme is £3 million.

The scheme is administratively simple to operate. There is no approval procedure to follow. Instead, the company enters into a share option agreement with each employee separately and notifies the details to HMRC within 92 days.

The company must comply with certain further conditions. Principally it must be carrying on a trade which would qualify under the EIS rules (see earlier in this Text).

The scheme is restricted to companies with fewer than 250 full time equivalent employees.

4.5.2 Tax advantages of the EMI

There is no income tax (or NIC) on the grant of an EMI option.

There is no income tax (or NIC) when the options are exercised if the exercise price was set at a price at least equal to the market value of the shares at the date of grant.

However, **if the options were granted at a discount to the market value at the date of grant there is an income tax charge (and possibly an NIC charge – see below) when the options are exercised on the lower of:**

(a)   **The discount** (ie the difference between the market value of the shares at the date of grant and the price paid for the shares (the 'exercise' price)), and

(b)   **The difference between the market value of the shares at the date of exercise and the exercise price.**

4.5.3 Capital gains tax aspects of the EMI

The base cost of the shares for capital gains tax (CGT) purposes depends on whether or not income tax was paid at the date of exercise.

If no income tax was paid when the option was exercised, the base cost of the shares is the amount the employee paid for the shares (ie the exercise price).

If, on the other hand, income tax *was* paid when the option was exercised, the base cost is the market value of the shares at the date of exercise (ie the exercise price plus the amount subject to income tax).

5 National insurance contributions (NIC) and share schemes

If there is an income tax charge in respect of acquiring shares through a share scheme, Class 1 National insurance contributions (NIC) (see later in this Text) may also be due, but only if the shares are 'readily convertible assets', ie they can be sold on a stock exchange.

The NIC charge follows the income tax charge so there is never an NIC (or income tax) charge on the grant or exercise of options under an approved Company share option plan (CSOP).

There may, however, be an NIC charge (if the shares are readily convertible assets):

(a)   On the **exercise of an unapproved share option**.

(b)   On the **exercise of an Enterprise management incentive (EMI) option** if, at the date of grant, the exercise price was set at lower than market value.

(c)   On the **withdrawal of shares from a Share Incentive Plan (SIP)** within the five year holding period.

(d)   On the exercise of a SAYE option if, at the date of grant, the exercise price was set at less than 80% of the market value.

(e)   On the **receipt of free or cheap shares** provided directly by the employer.

Chapter roundup

- Where shares are obtained in an employer company at below their market value there will usually be an income tax charge.

- There is no charge to income tax when share options are granted under an unapproved share option scheme. However, gains realised on the *exercise* of an unapproved share option are subject to income tax, based on the market value of the shares acquired less the cost of the shares and the option.

- A SIP allows employees to acquire shares in their employer company whilst avoiding income tax, NIC and capital gains tax. Employees can obtain free shares from the employer, purchase partnership shares from pre-tax salary, the employer can match the partnership shares, and dividends can be reinvested in further shares.

- A SAYE scheme is an option scheme that must be available to all employees and be linked to a contractual savings scheme, which the employee can use to buy shares on exercising the option. There is no income tax or NIC on grant. However there will be a charge on exercise if the exercise price was set at less than 80% of the market value of the shares at the date of grant.

- Under the CSOP scheme there is no charge to income tax or NIC when the options are granted or when the options are exercised.

- Under an EMI scheme options over shares worth up to £120,000 per employee may be granted, up to a maximum of £3 million. There is no income tax or NIC charge on the grant of the option, and a charge will only arise on exercise if the exercise price was set at less than the market value of the shares at the time the options were granted.

- If income tax is payable in respect of a share scheme Class 1 NIC may also be due but only if the shares are readily convertible assets.

Quiz

1. Emma, Fiona and Gillian all participate in their employer's approved share incentive plan. On 1 June 2008 they were each awarded free shares worth £3,000.

   Assume they withdraw their shares as follows.

	Date withdrawn	Value when withdrawn £
Emma	1 May 2011	3,500
Fiona	1 July 2011	3,650
Gillian	1 July 2013	4,000

   Which withdrawals will suffer an income tax charge and on what value? Give your reasons.

2. On 1 November 2010, Dean exercised options in a share option scheme run by his employer and acquired 2,000 shares at the exercise price of £4 per share. The market value at that date was £6 per share.

   Calculate the income tax liability as a result of the above assuming Dean is a higher rate taxpayer and

   (a) The scheme has HMRC approval, or
   (b) The scheme is unapproved.

Solutions to Quiz

1. Emma: charge on £3,500 (market value when taken out)
   Withdrawal within 3 years

   Fiona: charge on £3,000 (lower of value on award and on withdrawal)
   Withdrawal 3 – 5 years

   Gillian: no charge
   Withdrawal after 5 years

2. (a) No IT due on exercise of shares in an approved scheme

   (b) Income tax on exercise

	£
MV of shares at exercise (£6 × 2,000)	12,000
Less exercise price (£4 × 2,000)	(8,000)
	4,000

   IT due @ 40% = 1,600

Solution to chapter examples

Solution to Example 1

	£
Market value at exercise (£5 × 1,000)	5,000
Exercise price (ie price paid by James) (£3 × 1,000)	(3,000)
Amount subject to income tax	2,000

Solution to Example 2

£Nil. This is an approved scheme so there are no income tax charges.

Contrast this with James's position in the previous example.

Solution to Example 3

	£
Maximum value for options	30,000
Less: value of existing option: 10,000 × £2	(20,000)
Maximum remaining value	10,000
£10,000 ÷ £1.25	8,000

The option can therefore be granted over 8,000 shares.

Now try the following questions

Short Form Questions:

6.1 – 6.3 inclusive

Long Form Question:

6.1	Sue

National insurance contributions

The purpose of this chapter is to help you to:

- identify payments liable to Class 1 NIC

- detail the charges to Class 1A and 1B NIC

- consider the position of non-employed persons: Class 3 NIC

- describe the circumstances in which liability to Class and Class 4 contributions arises

- understand when annual maxima calculations are necessary and when NIC deferment is possible

References: SSC&BA 1992 unless otherwise stated

Exam focus point

The topics in this chapter are examinable at the principle level. Candidates are expected to have an awareness of NIC and the main thrust of the NIC provisions without necessarily knowing the details of those provisions.

1 An overview of the NIC system

The Treasury maintains a National Insurance Fund to provide 'contributory benefits' such as the State retirement pension, jobseeker's allowance, various bereavement benefits, incapacity benefit and certain sickness and maternity benefits.

Collection is administered by the National Insurance Contributions Office (NICO), which is an Executive Office of the HMRC.

However, most of the actual collection is made by HMRC, either as part of the process of self assessment or through the Pay As You Earn (PAYE) system.

There are four main Classes of NIC (Classes 1A and 1B are a subset of Class 1 NICs) as follows:

Class 1   Payable in respect of the 'earnings' of employed earners. The employee makes 'primary' contributions and the employer makes 'secondary' contributions.

Class 1A   Payable by employers only on (most) taxable benefits provided to employees (other than excluded employees) unless already caught under Class 1 or Class 1B.

Class 1B   Payable by employers on the grossed-up value of earnings included in a PAYE settlement (an arrangement entered into with HMRC for the employer to settle the employee's tax liability on small and irregular benefits).

Class 2   Payable weekly by the self employed based on their accounting profits, unless these are below a small earnings threshold.

Class 3   Paid voluntarily by those not paying Class 1, 2, or 4, to preserve rights to contributory benefits.

Class 4   Payable by the self employed based on their taxable profits.

2 Class 1 contributions

2.1 Employed earners

Employees (including directors) and their employers pay Class 1 NI contributions.

Both *primary* (employee's) and *secondary* (employer's) Class 1 contributions are payable where the employed earner:

(a)   **Is aged 16** or over, and
(b)   Is paid an amount equal to or greater than the current earnings threshold (see below).

Only secondary contributions (ie employer's only) are payable if the employed earner has reached pensionable age (currently 65 for men, 60 for women rising to 65 by 2020).

2.2 Earnings for NIC

Earnings include an employee's gross cash pay, eg salary, bonus, commission, tips and expenses.

If a reimbursed expense has a business purpose it is not treated as earnings. For example, if an employee is reimbursed for business travel or for staying in a hotel on the employer's business this is not normally 'earnings'.

The NIC treatment broadly follows the income tax treatment, so if a payment is taxable for income tax purposes it is usually part of earnings for Class 1 NIC purposes.

Earnings does not usually include taxable benefits, eg company cars, but does include non-cash vouchers, any non-business credit card charges and the settlement of an employee's personal liabilities (eg telephone bills). **Instead there is usually a Class 1A NIC charge on taxable benefits** – see below.

In addition, 'earnings' can include employment income from share schemes if there is also an income tax charge (see earlier in this Text).

Example 1

Justin earns an annual salary of £40,000.

During 2010/11 his employment income also included the following:

Bonus (received June 2010)	£5,000
Company car (taxable benefit figure)	£2,100
Company car petrol (taxable benefit figure)	£2,535
Car parking space at work (cost to employer)	£875
Reimbursed expenses (£575 spent for private purposes)	£1,275

How much of Justin's employment income will be treated as earnings for Class 1 NIC purposes?

2.3 Types of Class 1 contributions

2.3.1 Primary contributions

Employed earners whose earnings exceed the earnings threshold £5,715 (£110 per week for 2010/11), must pay a percentage of their earnings above that threshold as primary Class 1 NIC.

Any earnings between the earnings threshold and the upper earnings limit £43,875 (£844 per week) are chargeable at 11%, and earnings above the upper earnings limit are chargeable at 1%. [s.6]; [s.8]

From **6 April 2011** the Class 1 primary rate paid will increase to **12%** and the additional rate above the upper earnings limit will increase to **2%**.

Note that the earnings threshold (£5,715) is not the same as the income tax personal allowance (£6,475) for 2010/11.

2.3.2 Secondary contributions

Employers are required to pay secondary Class 1 NIC. This is 12.8% of earnings above the earnings threshold. There is no reduction in the rate for earnings above the upper earnings limit. [s.7]; [s.9]

From **6 April 2011** the Class 1 secondary rate will increase to **13.8%**.

2.4 Rates of Class 1 contributions

The weekly, monthly and annual earnings threshold (ET) and upper earnings limit (UEL) and the rates of NIC are shown in the Associations' tax tables.

In summary, the weekly rates for Class 1 primary contributions are:

Earnings	Primary contributions
Below £110 per week	Nil
Between £110 and £844 per week	11% on the amount above £110
Above £844 per week	11% on the amount between £110 and £844 and 1% on the amount above £844

Illustration 1

The primary Class 1 NIC due in 2010/11 for the following employees is:

	Primary contributions
Employee 1 £60 per week	Nil
Employee 2 £328 per week £(328 – 110) × 11%	£24
Employee 3 £950 per week £(844 – 110) × 11% (maximum) £(950 – 844) × 1%	£81 1 £82

In summary, the weekly rates for Class 1 secondary contributions are:

Earnings	Secondary contributions
Below £110 per week	Nil
Over £110 per week	12.8% on the amount above £110

Illustration 2

Employee 1 £60 per week	Secondary Contributions Nil
Employee 2 £328 per week	£(328 – 110) × 12.8% = £28
Employee 3 £950 per week	£(950 – 110) × 12.8% = £108

An employee who earns below the earnings threshold (ET) but above the lower earnings limit (LEL) (£97 per week for 2010/11) qualifies for contributory benefits even though they do not pay NIC.

2.5 Contracting out of S2P

When an individual retires and has paid sufficient NIC throughout their working life they become entitled to receive the basic state pension and the state second pension scheme (S2P). An individual may, however, decide to leave the S2P during their working life if they have a personal pension or are a member of their employer's occupational scheme (see later in this Text). This is known as 'contracting out'.

If the individual 'contracts out', he and his employer will continue to pay the standard rates of Class 1 NIC (see above) but, at the end of the tax year, HMRC will pay a rebate on earnings between the lower earnings limit (LEL) and the earnings threshold (ET). **A lower rate of NIC is then payable up to the upper accruals point (UAP).** Above the UAP the standard NIC rates apply.

For example for 2010/11 an employee in a contracted out scheme would pay 9.4% rather than the usual 11% on earnings between the ET and UAP. They would then pay at the usual 11% rate on earnings between the UAP and the upper earnings limit (UEL) and at 1% on earnings above the UEL.

The employer also pays reduced rates of NIC in a contracted out scheme on earnings between the ET and the UAP. The reduced rate of NIC depends on whether the scheme is **salary related (COSRS) (ie defined benefit scheme) where the reduced rate is 9.1% or a money purchase (COMPS) (ie defined contribution scheme) where it is 11.4%.**

TQT
Tax Qualification Training

3 Class 1A NIC

3.1 Background

Employers are liable for Class 1A contributions on most benefits provided to directors and employees with earnings over £8,500 pa. [s.10]

Class 1A NICs are payable by **employers only**, not by employees.

3.2 Payment of Class 1A NIC

Payments are collected annually on 19 July following the tax year. Class 1A contributions for 2010/11 are payable on 19 July 2011 (22 July 2011 for electronic payments).

3.3 Scope of Class 1A NIC

An employer must pay Class 1A NICs on all benefits except those which are exempt from income tax (such as a mobile telephone) and those which are liable to Class 1 NICs (such as non-cash vouchers).

The NIC treatment broadly follows the income tax treatment, so if a benefit is taxable for income tax purposes it is usually liable to Class 1A NIC.

Class 1A NICs are **not payable on benefits received by excluded employees (ie earnings < £8,500)**.

Example 2

How much of Justin's (Example 1) employment income is liable to Class 1A NICs? Who must pay the liability?

3.4 Computation of Class 1A NIC liability

The Class 1A NIC liability is calculated as **12.8% of the amount of the benefit as measured for income tax purposes.** This will be as shown on the annual return form P11D.

However, not all items included on the P11D are liable to Class 1A NICs. In particular remember that if the employer provides vouchers or settles an employee's personal liability (eg telephone bill) these 'benefits' are subject to Class 1 primary and secondary contributions rather than Class 1A (see above).

From **6 April 2011** the rate will increase to **13.8%**.

Illustration 3

Adrian, an employee with an annual salary of £40,000, received the following benefits and expenses during 2010/11 as calculated for earnings purposes.

	£
Car benefit	6,600
Car fuel benefit	4,200
Cheap loan	800
Private medical insurance (employer's scheme)	560
High Street store vouchers	40
Payment of professional subscription*	200
Membership of local golf club (contracted for by employer)	600
Travelling expenses*	1,000

*Adrian was entitled to claim a full income tax deduction for these expenses.

The Class 1A NIC liability for 2010/11 is calculated as follows:

Benefits liable to Class 1A NICs:

	£
Car benefit	6,600
Car fuel benefit	4,200
Cheap loan	800
Private medical insurance	560
Membership of local golf club	600
	12,760

Class 1A NIC liability £12,760 × 12.8% = £1,633

Note. The vouchers are subject to Class 1 NIC, not Class 1A NIC. The medical insurance and golf club membership are subject to Class 1A because the employer contracted for these. If the employee had contracted for the benefits and then claimed reimbursement from his employer, this would have been subject to Class 1 primary and secondary NIC instead as a reimbursement of an employee liability.

4 Class 1B NIC

PAYE settlement agreements (PSAs) enable employers to account for income tax on a number of minor employee benefits and expenses payments in one lump sum. The object is to save having to account separately for such items, keeping separate records and entering them individually on forms P11D or P9D.

Where an employer has a PSA with HMRC, he will be liable to Class 1B contributions on the amount of the earnings in the PSA which would otherwise be chargeable to Class 1 or Class 1A NICs, together with the total amount of income tax payable under the PSA.

Class 1B contributions are chargeable at 12.8% and this amount is **payable by the employer on 19 October** (22 October for electronic payments) following the year covered by the PSA.

From 6 April 2011 the rate will increase to 13.8%.

5 Class 3 NIC

Class 3 is a voluntary contribution usually paid by individuals who do not already pay any of the other classes of NIC. For 2010/11 the weekly rate is £12.05. Class 3 contributions can only be made to create entitlement to a limited range of benefits (eg the retirement pension and bereavement benefits).

6 Classes 2 and 4 NIC

6.1 Class 2 NIC

Self employed persons may have to pay both Class 2 and Class 4 contributions. [ss.11 & 15]

Class 2 is a flat rate contribution of £2.40 per week for 2010/11. Class 2 contributions are not required if the taxpayer has small earnings (£5,075 for 2010/11). This is based on the accounts profit for the tax year rather than the tax adjusted trading profit figure shown in the income tax computation. [s.11(4)]

Class 2 liability is normally collected by NICO by monthly bank direct debit or by quarterly billing, in arrears.

6.2 Class 4 NIC

Class 4 is an earnings related contribution. Unlike other NI contributions it is payable at the same time as the income tax liability on the relevant profits under self assessment. So, the **payments on account due on 31 January and 31 July each include an amount equal to half the Class 4 NIC payable for the previous year with any balancing adjustment due on 31 January following** (see later in this Text).

The Class 4 contribution for **2010/11 is calculated as a flat rate of 8% on trade profits between the lower profits limit (£5,715) and the upper profits limit (£43,875), plus a further 1% on all trade profits above this.**

Illustration 4

Brent has taxable trade profits for 2010/11 of £50,000. His Class 4 NIC liability would be as follows:

	£
£(50,000 – 43,875) @ 1%	61
£(43,875 – 5,715) @ 8%	<u>3,053</u>
Total Class 4 NIC	<u>3,114</u>

From 6 April 2011 the above rates will increase to 9% for profits between the lower and upper profits limits and 2% for profits above the upper profits limit.

7 Maximum contributions and deferral

7.1 General principles

National insurance contributions are payable by an individual in respect of **each employment and self employment**.

Where an individual has **more than one employment or is employed and also in self employment it is possible that he could pay more national insurance** than someone earning the same total income from only one employment/self employment.

To ensure this does not occur there is a maximum amount of contributions payable, known as the 'annual maxima', for both combined Class 1 and Class 2 contributions or two or more Class 1 contributions and combined Classes 1, 2 and 4 contributions.

7.2 Deferment of payment

7.2.1 Introduction

Where the employee expects that the annual maxima limit will (or may be) exceeded for a particular tax year, NICO may agree to defer payment of one or more class of contribution until the precise liability can be determined.

7.2.2 Two or more employments

Where an individual has more than one employment and believes that, even if deferment is granted, he **will still pay Class 1 contributions equal to at least 52 weekly contributions on earnings at the upper earnings limit, he may apply to NICO not to collect primary Class 1 contributions at the main rate** (ie at 11%) in respect of at least one of his employments.

If NICO grants deferment the employee **must still pay Class 1 contributions at the additional rate** (ie at 1%) on earnings above the primary earnings threshold.

At the end of the tax year if maximum contributions have been paid, the earnings in respect of which deferment was granted are **formally excepted from liability at the main rate**. If they have not been paid (because the earner's expectations were false), the shortfall is collected directly from the individual.

7.2.3 Employment and self employment

Where an individual is both employed and self employed in a tax year, deferment of both Class 2 and Class 4 contributions may be granted.

Class 2 contributions may be deferred if the individual can show that his primary Class 1 contributions will equal or exceed the combined Class 1 and Class 2 annual maximum.

In addition, main rate Class 4 contributions (ie at 8%) may be deferred where it is likely that the individual will have no (or low) Class 4 contributions in a particular tax year. However, in this case, additional rate (ie 1%) Class 4 contributions must continue to be paid on all profits above the lower profit limit.

Chapter roundup

- Employees and employers both pay Class 1 contributions on the employee's 'earnings', but at different rates.

- Lower NIC rates are payable if the individual contracts out of S2P.

- Class 1A contributions are payable by employers where a taxable benefit is provided to a director or £8,500 + employee.

- Class 1B contributions are payable by employers when a PSA is in place.

- Self employed persons pay flat rate weekly Class 2 contributions if their accounts profit exceeds a lower limit.

- They must also pay Class 4 contributions, at the same time as they pay their income tax, based on their taxable trade profits.

- The 'annual maxima' rules for combined Class 1 and Class 2 contributions and combined Classes 1, 2 and 4 contributions prevent those who either hold more than one employment or who are both employed and self employed from paying excessive contributions. Deferment of payment may be granted in appropriate circumstances.

Quiz

1. Ursula's employer provided her with living accommodation (not job related) during 2010/11. The taxable benefit is £2,200. She also had the use of a company credit card which she used solely for business purposes. During 2010/11 the credit card bill came to £14,500. What class of NIC is payable for each of the benefits and who is responsible for paying the liability?

2. Only employers pay Class 1A and Class 1B NICs? True/ False.

3. What classes of NIC do self employed individuals pay?

1.   The living accommodation benefit is liable to Class 1A NIC. This is payable by Ursula's employer.

      The credit card bill would usually be liable to Class 1 NIC, payable by both Ursula and her employer. However, all her expenditure was for business purposes so the NIC liability is £Nil.

2.   True. Employees do not pay Class 1A or 1B NIC.

3.   Self employed individuals pay Class 2 and Class 4 NIC.

Solutions to chapter examples

Solution to Example 1

Justin's Class 1 NIC earnings are as follows:

	£
Salary	40,000
Bonus	5,000
Non-business expenses	575
Total earnings	45,575

Taxable benefits (the company car and fuel) are not earnings for Class 1 NIC purposes. They are however subject to Class 1A NIC payable by the employer only. The car parking space is not subject to any NIC as it is not taxable for income tax purposes – it is an exempt benefit.

The business element of the reimbursed expenses is not part of earnings as it is an allowable deduction from employment income for income tax purposes.

Solution to Example 2

Liable to Class 1A NIC:	£
Company car benefit	2,100
Fuel benefit	2,535
Car parking space (exempt)	Nil
Total	4,635

The employer alone pays the Class 1A NIC liability.

> Now try the following questions:

Short Form Questions:

Q7.1 – Q7.3 inclusive

Long Form Question:

Q7.1	Mr Howe

chapter

8

Pensions

The purpose of this chapter is to help you to:

- understand the tax treatment of pensions

- calculate and explain the tax relief available for pension contributions

- understand the tax consequences of taking funds out of a pension at retirement age

References: FA 2004 unless otherwise stated

1 Introduction

1.1 Types of pension

An employer may set up an occupational pension scheme for its employees. The scheme may either require contributions from employees or be 'non contributory'. The employer may use the services of an insurance company (an insured scheme) or may set up a totally self administered pension fund.

In all other cases **any individual with or without earnings, or even without any taxable income, can pay into a personal pension**. An employee can obtain tax relief on contributions to both their employer's occupational pension scheme and a personal pension scheme, subject to the rules below.

The same set of tax rules apply to all personal and employer provided pensions.

1.2 Taxation of the pension fund

The premiums (ie contributions) go into a fund that is invested and is ultimately used to provide a pension.

Income and gains within the pension are not liable to tax. It might help to think of a pension fund as a tax free wrapper around any investments within the fund.

1.3 State pension

Individuals can also provide for a pension by contributing to the State pension scheme through their National Insurance Contributions (NICs). The State scheme has no impact on income tax during an individual's working career.

2 Contributions

2.1 Introduction

An individual can contribute to any number of pension schemes, out of both income or capital, and to both occupational and personal schemes, and will obtain tax relief so long as he stays within the contribution limits (see below).

The payments can even be made on behalf of another (eg a parent for a child, or a husband for a wife).

There are two main restrictions on the amount of contributions that attract tax relief that can be made into a pension scheme: the annual allowance and the lifetime allowance.

2.2 Annual allowance

The '**annual allowance**' is effectively the maximum amount that can be paid into a pension tax free each year during the pension input period. The annual allowance for 2010/11 is £255,000 and is given to you in the Association's tax tables.

The **pension input period** is normally the period of 12 months commencing on the date of the first contribution to the scheme and each anniversary thereafter. The end date of the pension input period will determine the tax year that the excess value will be tested against the annual allowance.

If more than this allowance is paid into the pension there is a tax charge of 40% on the excess that must be included on the individual's self assessment tax return.

The annual allowance charge does not apply in the year benefits are taken (see below).

A significant reduction in the annual allowance is expected from 6 April 2011 to restrict tax relief for pension contributions made by individuals with an annual income of £150,000 or more.

From 22 April 2009 'anti-forestalling' provisions apply to prevent high income individuals from increasing their pension contributions in excess of their normal pattern before the new allowance comes into force. These anti-forestalling provisions are **not** examinable in the Personal Taxation paper.

2.3 Lifetime allowance

The '**lifetime allowance**' is the maximum amount that can be accumulated in a pension during lifetime, without incurring tax charges. The lifetime allowance for 2010/11 is £1.8 million and is given to you in the Association's tax tables.

If this amount is exceeded there is a tax charge when benefits are taken from the fund. If the benefit is taken as a lump sum the charge on the excess is 55%, otherwise the income tax charge is 25%. The tax charge is added to the taxpayer's tax liability which has been calculated on their income to arrive at their total tax liability for the year (see earlier in this Text).

3 Tax relief

3.1 Amount of tax relief

Each year, tax relief is available to an individual for pension contributions up to the higher of:

(a)   **100% of relevant earnings (salary and other earned income) subject to the 'annual allowance' (see above), and**

(b)   **£3,600**.

3.2 Obtaining tax relief

3.2.1 Occupational pension schemes

Occupational pension scheme contributions may be made gross. The gross amount of the contributions is deducted from employment income on the face of the income tax computation.

Employers usually operate net pay arrangements ie they deduct gross pension contributions from the employee's earnings before operating PAYE. The individual therefore obtains basic, higher and additional rate tax relief, if appropriate, at source.

Contributions paid by the employer are deductible for the employer in calculating their taxable profits. These **employer's contributions are not taxable benefits for the employee. They are added to the employee's own contributions when determining if the annual allowance has been exceeded.**

Provision can be made for a tax free lump sum to be paid on the employee's retirement or death in service.

An employee who feels that his employer's scheme is inadequate may make additional voluntary contributions (AVCs), either to the employer's scheme or to a separate scheme operated by an insurance company (freestanding AVCs). These are deductible from the employee's taxable pay, but only to the extent that they, plus any contributions by the employee to the employer's scheme, do not exceed the maximum amount that qualifies for tax relief (see above).

Freestanding AVCs are paid net of basic rate tax.

3.2.2 Personal pension schemes

All contributions made to personal pension schemes are paid net of basic rate tax. The pension company then recovers the basic rate tax from HMRC. So, for every £80 contributed in a tax year, the government will contribute a further £20. In this way all taxpayers obtain basic rate tax relief.

Tax relief at higher rates is obtained by increasing a taxpayer's basic rate and higher rate tax bands by the amount of the gross contribution (like we did with Gift Aid – see earlier in this Text).

Even those with no or little income can contribute up to £3,600 to a personal pension scheme each year.

Exam focus point

Do not confuse the way in which tax relief is obtained for the two different types of pensions. Personal pension scheme contributions are paid **net** and relief is given at source and by extending the basic rate and higher rate bands of higher and additional rate taxpayers. Occupational pension scheme contributions are usually made **gross**, out of pre-tax salary, so relief is given immediately at the employee's highest tax rate.

Example 1

Darren has self employment earnings of £610,000 for the 2010/11 tax year and makes gross contributions of £21,500 each month to his registered personal pension scheme during the year. He has made the same level of contributions for the past five years.

Required

(a) State the maximum amount of gross pension contributions for which Darren will be entitled to tax relief and the actual amount he will have paid into the pension during the year.

(b) Explain how tax relief is given for contributions to personal pension schemes and calculate his income tax liability for 2010/11.

Exam focus point

Examiner's report – Personal Taxation (old syllabus)

May 2004 – Question 2

There were many good answers to this question. The main reason for candidates not gaining marks was lack of detail in the answer. The first part on the rules regarding self assessment was generally better answered than the part on tax relief for payments into a pension plan.

4 Drawing a pension

4.1 Pension age

Employees can draw part of their pension from a company scheme whilst they are still working full or part time for the same employer so long as they have reached the requisite age. From 2010 the minimum age for receiving a pension rises from 50 to 55.

For men the state pension age is 65. For women it will rise gradually from 60 to 65 between 2010 and 2020.

4.2 Tax free lump sum

Individuals can usually take a tax free lump sum of as much as 25% of their pension fund, subject to a maximum of 25% × the lifetime allowance.

The tax free lump sum is not available once the investor reaches age 75.

4.3 Balance of the pension fund

There are a number of alternative ways of taking the balance of the pension fund:

(a)   Take a scheme pension – secure for life
(b)   Buy an annuity – providing a regular income for life
(c)   Draw income directly from the pension (an unsecured pension) up to **age 77 (75 if he turned 75 before 22 June 2010)**
(d)   Draw income directly from the pension as an 'alternatively secured pension' (ASV) up to **age 77.**

Drawing income means that regular income may be withdrawn from the pension fund while the fund remains invested.

An **alternatively secured pension** (ASV) allows an investor to draw an income from the pension fund without buying a lifetime annuity.

4.4 Taxation of pension income

Apart from the tax free lump sum (above) all other income taken from a pension (including the state pension) is **taxed as non savings income.**

Chapter roundup

- Employees can contribute to their employer's occupational pension scheme and/or a personal pension. Other individuals can only contribute to a personal pension.

- Income and gains within a pension are tax free. The pension is effectively a tax free wrapper.

- Contributions can be made on behalf of another person and out of income or capital.

- The 'annual allowance' is the maximum amount that can be paid into a pension tax free each year. In 2010/11 this is £255,000. Contributions in excess of the annual allowance are taxed on the individual taxpayer at 40%.

- The 'lifetime allowance' is the maximum amount that can be accumulated in a pension during lifetime. In 2010/11 this is £1.8m.

- Tax relief for pension contributions made by individuals is given on the higher of 100% of relevant earnings and £3,600.

- Occupational pension scheme contributions are paid gross. Tax relief, at basic, higher and additional rates, is obtained by deducting the contributions from taxable employment income.

- Contributions paid by employers are deductible for the employer and a tax free benefit for the employee. They count towards the annual and lifetime allowances.

- Additional voluntary contributions (AVCs) can be made either to the employer scheme or separate scheme.

- Basic rate tax relief on personal pension schemes is given at source. The contributions are paid into the scheme net of basic rate tax and HMRC pay the additional 20% to the scheme. Higher and additional rate tax relief is given by extending the basic and higher rate tax bands.

- When drawing a pension a lump sum of up to 25% × the fund is available. There is flexibility regarding how to take the balance of the pension.

- The pension on retirement is treated as non savings income of the taxpayer.

Quiz

1. What is the maximum amount that can be contributed by an individual to a pension for which tax relief is available?

2. What is the lifetime allowance for 2010/11?

1. The higher of:

   £3,600 and 100% × relevant earnings.

2. £1,800,000.

Solution to chapter example

Solution to Example 1

(a) As Darren's earnings are £610,000, all of the contributions of £258,000 (£21,500 × 12) qualify for tax relief.

   He will have paid £206,400 (£258,000 less 20% basic rate tax) to the pension company.

(b) Basic rate tax relief has been given at source. Higher and additional rate tax relief will be given by extending Darren's basic and higher rate tax bands for 2010/11 to £295,400 (£37,400 + £258,000) and £408,000 (£150,000 + £258,000) respectively.

   However, there will be tax charge at the rate of 40% on the excess of his contributions above the annual allowance of £255,000.

   His income tax liability for the tax year 2010/11 is:

	£
Trading profit	610,000
Less: personal allowance (income > £112,950)	(NIL)
Taxable income	610,000
Income tax:	
£295,400 at 20%	59,080
£112,600 at 40%	45,040
£202,000 at 50%	101,000
	205,120
Add: excess contribution charge	
£3,000 (£258,000 − £255,000) at 40%	1,200
Tax liability	206,320

Now try the following questions

Short Form Questions:

8.1 – 8.6 inclusive

Long Form Questions:

8.1	Mr Matthews (Pilot Paper)
8.2	Ed & Joan
8.3	Dwaine Pipe

The purpose of this chapter is to help you to:

- define the terms residence, ordinary residence and domicile and explain their significance

- outline the scope and basis of assessment of overseas income

- calculate double taxation relief

References: ITTOIA 2005 unless otherwise stated

Overseas aspects of income tax

1 Residence, ordinary residence and domicile

1.1 Introduction

In Chapter 1 of this Study Text we saw that a taxpayer's *residence, ordinary residence* and *domicile* had important consequences in establishing the treatment of his UK and overseas income. The rules are now set out in detail.

Exam focus point

The broad definitions of residence, ordinary residence and domicile which follow are derived from statute, case law and HMRC practice. HMRC publish a booklet (HMRC6) from which the definitions and tables below are taken (latest version available from HMRC's website). **The guidance in this booklet is binding** in relation to any individual falling clearly within its terms.

1.2 Residence

1.2.1 Introduction

The terms residence (and ordinary residence – see below) are not defined by statute. The courts have generally given the expression its common sense meaning, stressing that residence is a question of fact which is rightly decided by the Tribunal.

Each individual's residence status is determined by the facts of his particular case and is not simply a question of the number of days he spends in the UK. [HMRC6 Para 1.2]

Generally, a person coming to the UK permanently or for a period of at least three years, is treated as resident (and ordinarily resident) in the UK from the date of arrival.

1.2.2 Test of residence

A person is resident in the UK for a given tax year if, in that tax year, he is present in the UK for a period, or periods, totalling 183 days or more (ie more than six months). There are no exceptions to this.

Any day where an individual is present in the UK at midnight is counted for residency purposes. [s.831(1A) ITA 2007]

If an individual spends less than six months in the UK, he may be treated as UK resident if he makes regular visits to the UK averaging 91 days or more (ie more than three months) over a period of four tax years (see 'Coming to the UK' below).

However, the number of days that an individual is present in the UK is only one of the factors taken into account when deciding his residence status. If he is present in the UK for less than 91 days, other factors that might also make an individual resident include location of family and property, and business and social ties in the UK. [R v Gaines-Cooper (2010)]

1.2.3 Splitting the tax year

Each tax year must be looked at as a whole: a person is resident either for none or for all of the tax year, depending on the circumstances. So a person who comes to the UK on 1 July 2010 will technically be treated as resident for the whole 2010/11 tax year as they will be here for more than 183 days

By concession, however, a person can split the tax year into resident and non resident parts for income tax purposes if he: [ESC A11]

(a)   Comes to **take up permanent residency**, or

(b)   Comes to **stay for at least two years**, or

(c)   Leaves the UK for **permanent residence abroad**, or

(d)   Leaves to take up **employment abroad which covers at least a whole tax year**, subject to certain conditions (see below).

1.3 Ordinary residence

1.3.1 What is ordinary residence?

'Ordinary' residence implies a greater degree of permanence than mere residence. **A person is ordinarily resident if his residence in the UK is typical for him, and not just casual.**

An individual will be treated as ordinarily resident in the UK if he has come to the UK voluntarily for a 'settled purpose' and his presence in the UK forms part of the regular and habitual mode of his life for the moment, for example by coming to live and work in the UK for a period of three years or more.

If an individual has come to the UK voluntarily and for a settled purpose he will be ordinarily resident from the date that he first arrives in the UK. In addition, if the individual owns or acquires accommodation on a long term lease in the year that he arrives in the UK, this may indicate an intention to stay for several years, and he may be treated as ordinarily resident from his arrival.

1.3.2 Consequences of being not ordinarily resident

Individuals who are not ordinarily resident may be taxed on their income on the 'remittance basis' (see below).

1.4 Coming to the UK

1.4.1 General principles

A person whose home has previously been abroad and who comes to the UK to take up permanent residence here, or who intends to stay for at least three years from the outset, is regarded as resident and ordinarily resident from the date of his arrival.

Otherwise, the position largely depends upon whether the person is a short or long term visitor.

Up until 1 June 2010, the individual should complete **Form P86** if they have come to the UK for the first time or after a period of absence. This helps HMRC to decide on the correct residence treatment, allocate a PAYE code (see later in this Text) and, if relevant, review their domicile position (see below). The form does not need to be completed from 1 June 2010.

1.4.2 Short term visitors

Individuals who make one off visits to the UK lasting less than six months are neither resident nor ordinarily resident in the UK.

However, as we saw above, even where an individual is in the UK for less than six months he may be treated as resident and ordinarily resident if he makes regular visits averaging 91 days or more (ie more than three months) over a four year period.

The position is as follows:

(a)   If he did not know that he would be making this level of visits, he will be resident and ordinarily resident from the start of the next (ie fifth) tax year.

(b)   If he knew that he would be making this level of visits from the outset, he will be resident and ordinarily resident from the start of the tax year of his first visit.

(c)   If he realises that will be making this level of visits after starting to visit the UK, he will be resident and ordinarily resident from the start of the tax year in which he makes the realisation.

Example 1

Charles is resident in Jersey. Over the last four years he has made average visits of 93 days per year to the UK.

When, if at all, will he be treated as ordinarily resident in the UK assuming he:

(a)   Never intended to make such regular visits to the UK?
(b)   Decided on 17 June 2009 that he would be making regular visits to the UK?

1.4.3 Long term visitors

Where an individual does not originally intend to stay in the UK for at least three years, but has come for at least two years, he will be treated as being resident, but not ordinarily resident, in the UK from the start of the tax year of arrival. [HMRC6 paras 7.7.1 & 7.7.2]

An individual will, however, be treated as ordinarily resident in the following circumstances: [HMRC6 paras 7.7.4 & 7.8]

(a) Once he has **been in the UK for three years from his arrival date, he will usually be treated as ordinarily resident from 6 April of the tax year in which the third anniversary falls.** However, **HMRC will determine whether before that date the individual had a 'settled' purpose for living in the UK**, in which case he will be treated as ordinarily resident from the tax year he became so 'settled'. [Tuczka v HMRC (2010)]

For example, if Carlos arrives on 1 July 2010 and is still in the UK on 1 July 2013 he will be ordinarily resident from 6 April 2013. However, if he has remained in the UK to take up a full-time, non-temporary employment position he may be considered ordinarily resident sooner.

(b) If **he subsequently decides to stay in the UK for at least three years from his original arrival date, he will be treated as ordinarily resident from the start of the tax year in which he makes that decision.**

For example, if Pedro arrives on 1 July 2010 and decides on 1 September 2011 to stay until 31 December 2013, he will be ordinarily resident from 6 April 2011. If instead he makes the decision to stay on 1 September 2010, he will be ordinarily resident from 6 April 2010, the year of arrival.

(c) **If he buys or acquires accommodation on a lease of at least three years** he will be treated as ordinarily resident from 6 April in the tax year of acquisition. However, if he disposes of the accommodation and leaves the UK within three years of arrival he will not be treated as ordinarily resident simply because of the existence of the property.

For example, if Hans arrives in the UK on 1 October 2010 intending only to stay for 30 months, he will become ordinarily resident from 6 April 2013 if he is still in the UK on 1 October 2013 (see (a) above). If he buys a house in the UK in December 2011 he will be treated as ordinarily resident from 6 April 2011. If he sells the house and leaves the UK before 1 October 2013 he will not be treated as ordinarily resident for the duration of his stay.

1.5 Leaving the UK

1.5.1 General principles

A person who has been ordinarily resident in the UK is treated as remaining resident and ordinarily resident if he goes abroad for short periods (usually less than one year) only, for example, a holiday or business trip.

The individual should complete and submit Form P85 so that HMRC can advise them whether they need to complete a UK tax return after they have left the country.

1.5.2 Leaving the UK permanently or indefinitely

If a person leaves the UK permanently or indefinitely (ie for at least three years) he will become not resident and not ordinarily resident in the UK from the day after his departure if he physically leaves the UK for a stated purpose (eg work abroad or permanent emigration).

If the individual's visits to the UK, after his departure, average 91 days or more each tax year, he will remain UK resident and ordinarily resident, and in some cases will remain resident even if the number of days spent in the UK falls below 91 days.

1.5.3 Working abroad

A person who goes abroad on a full time contract of employment for a complete tax year, whose interim visits to the UK do not make him resident, can split the tax year for income tax purposes (see above).

In these circumstances the individual does not have to make a 'clean break' from (ie sever social, economic and financial ties with) the UK.

The above applies equally to an individual who leaves the UK to work abroad as a self employed person.

Where the individual is accompanied, or later joined, by his spouse (or civil partner) who is not in full time employment, but who is also abroad for a complete tax year and does not exceed the UK visit limits, the spouse/civil partner can also, by concession, split the tax year for income tax purposes. [ESC A78]

1.6 Domicile

1.6.1 General principles

Whether someone is domiciled is only important if they have income (or gains) from an overseas source during the tax year. [HMRC6 para 4.1]

A person is domiciled in the country in which he has his *permanent home*. Domicile is distinct from nationality or residence. A person may be resident in more than one country, but at any given time he can only be domiciled in one.

There are three types of domicile for income tax purposes, which are explored in detail below. [HMRC6 para 4.3]

1.6.2 Domicile of origin

A person acquires a *domicile of origin* at birth, determined as follows:

(a)   **A legitimate child born during the father's lifetime takes the father's domicile at the date** of the child's birth

(b)   **An illegitimate or posthumous (born after its father's death) child takes the mother's domicile** at the date of the child's birth.

It is difficult to displace a domicile of origin.

1.6.3 Domicile of dependency

Until an individual reaches age 16 his domicile will follow that of the person on whom he is legally dependent (usually his father). If the domicile of that person changes, he will automatically acquire the same domicile, in place of the domicile of origin.

1.6.4 Domicile of choice

An individual can acquire a new domicile at the age of 16. He can do this by showing that he has left his current country of domicile and has settled in another country.

No formal steps are necessary to acquire a domicile of choice, but the individual must provide strong evidence that they intend to live in the other country permanently or indefinitely. The question will be determined in the overall review of the circumstances of the case. **Relevant factors include intentions, permanent residence, family, social and business interests, ownership of property and the individual's Will** and the ultimate resting place, for example, the reservation of a grave plot. **The onus of proof is on the individual alleging that he has acquired a domicile of choice**.

Example 2

Cedric, who has lived in Wales all his life, is now aged 44. He plans to spend the next 20 years in France, selling his house in Wales and transferring all of his assets to France. He will then return to Wales to retire. When will he become non-UK domiciled?

1.6.5 Consequences of domicile status

If an individual is resident, ordinarily resident but not domiciled in the UK he is taxable on UK income on an arising basis as normal.

If he has overseas income he is taxable on an arising basis *unless* he makes a claim to be taxed on the 'remittance' basis (or it applies automatically), ie only when he brings the foreign income into the UK (see below). [s.809B(2)(a) ITA 2007]

If the remittance basis applies, foreign dividends and foreign interest are not treated as dividend or savings income, ie the income is always taxed as non savings income at 20%, 40% and 50%.

2 Taxation of income

2.1 Effect of residence and domicile status

Generally, **UK residents** are **liable to UK income tax on their worldwide income (ie all UK and foreign income)** while **non-residents are liable to UK income tax only on income arising in the UK,** ie income received during the tax year.

A non-UK resident's income tax liability on their UK income is broadly limited to any tax deducted at source. So, where interest is received gross (eg NS&I accounts), the interest is not taxed but if the interest is received net (eg bank interest), the tax liability is limited to the basic rate tax deducted at source. [s.811 ITA 2007]

UK residents who are either not domiciled or not ordinarily resident in the UK may be taxable on their foreign income on the remittance basis (see below), ie only to the extent that such income is brought (either actually or effectively) into the UK.

The diagram below provides a broad summary of how an individual is taxed, based on his residence, ordinary residence and domicile status. The detail for specific types of income is covered below.

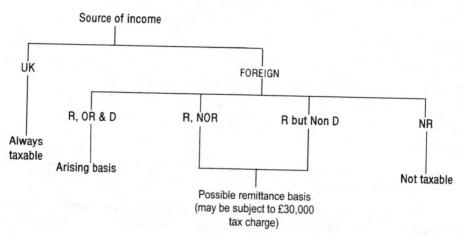

2.2 Taxation of UK income

2.2.1 UK property income

Income from UK property is always taxable in the UK, regardless of the residence position of the recipient landlord. It can never be 'disregarded' income (see below).

The rules for the Non Resident Landlord Scheme (NRLS) were covered earlier in this Text.

2.2.2 UK investment income

A non-UK resident's tax liability is limited to the income tax deducted from 'disregarded income' or the tax credit it carries. [s.811 ITA 2007]

'Disregarded income' includes UK savings and dividend income but does not include trading, employment or rental income.

Bank and Building society interest can be received gross (and so will have no UK tax liability) if the recipient is not ordinarily resident in the UK (for the whole tax year) and makes a not ordinarily resident (NOR) declaration on Form R105.

Interest that arises on UK government 'Free of Tax to Residents Abroad' (FOTRA) securities (ie UK Treasury Stock) is not taxable if received by an individual who is either not resident in the UK, or is resident but not ordinarily resident in the UK.

If income tax is limited in this way the personal and married couples' allowances are not available. If the level of income that cannot be disregarded is high, it may be more tax efficient for the individual to claim personal allowances and include their entire UK income in their tax computation.

UK businesses and public bodies are required to provide details of payments of interest and other savings income to residents of EU member states. [EU directive 2003/48/EC]

2.3 Taxation of foreign income

2.3.1 What is foreign income

Foreign income is income arising outside the UK and includes:

(a)   Interest from foreign savings accounts
(b)   Dividends from overseas companies
(c)   Rent from property abroad, and
(d)   Foreign pension income.

Exam focus point

The detail for employment income from duties carried on abroad and partnership or trade profits from a business carried on and controlled wholly outside the UK are not in the ATT Personal Taxation paper syllabus.

2.3.2 Arising basis

For UK residents, tax is chargeable on 'the full amount of the income arising' in the tax year, that is, regardless of whether the income has been or will be received in the UK.

2.3.3 Foreign property income

UK income tax applies to any income arising to a UK resident from land or property situated in the UK or overseas.

The income tax treatment of income from property situated outside the UK is computed using the same rules as for UK property income (see earlier in this Text).

The remittance basis may apply to non-UK domiciled or not ordinarily resident individuals (see earlier in this Text).

All income arising from overseas property – even if in different countries – is treated as derived from a single business which is separate and distinct from any UK property income. Therefore, there is no possibility of obtaining relief for a UK property loss against overseas rental income, or vice versa.

Losses arising from the letting of overseas property may be used in the same way as for a UK property business, ie

(a)   Carried forward for offset against future property business profits, or
(b)   Set against general income in the year of the loss in restricted circumstances (see earlier in this Text).

2.3.4 Overseas savings and dividend income

Foreign dividends are taxed in a similar way to UK dividends, ie at 10% in the basic rate band and at the higher and additional rates of 32.5% and 42.5% respectively.

A **10% non-refundable tax credit is available to individuals receiving dividends from non UK resident companies** if the overseas country is a 'qualifying territory' (ie has a double taxation agreement with the UK that contains a non-discrimination provision). [ss.397A & 397AA]

The gross amount of foreign dividend received in the UK (ie including any foreign tax) must be included in the UK income tax computation, grossed up at 100/90 (see further below).

Foreign investment income (ie dividends and interest, whether bank interest or interest from securities) is taxed on an arising basis as either dividend or savings income depending on its source, unless the remittance basis applies in which case it is taxed as non savings income, ie the income is always taxed as non savings income at 20%, 40% and 50%.

2.3.5 Foreign pension income

Foreign pension income is taxable on UK residents. However, **only 90% of the amount arising is taxed if the individual is UK domiciled and ordinarily resident, ie an individual not eligible for remittance basis. The full amount of the pension remitted to the UK is taxable if the individual is taxed on the remittance basis.** [s.575(2) ITEPA 2003]

3 Remittance basis

3.1 Availability of the remittance basis

The remittance basis for foreign income can be claimed by persons who are either:

(a)   **Non-UK domiciled**, or

(b)   **Not ordinarily resident in the UK**.

3.2 Automatic application of the remittance basis

A non-UK domiciled or not ordinarily resident individual is automatically taxed on the remittance basis where:

(a)   He has **unremitted income and gains below £2,000**, or [s.809D ITA 2007]

(b)   He: [s.809E ITA 2007]

    (i)   **Has either no UK income or gains, or only has taxed UK investment income of £100 or less**

    (ii)   **Makes no remittances** of foreign income or gains during the tax year, and

    (iii)   **Either**

        –   **Has been resident in the UK for not more than six out of the last nine years**, or
        –   **Is under 18 throughout the year**.

The individual does not need to submit a self assessment tax return to be able to use the remittance basis. He must, however, **notify HMRC if he wishes the arising basis to apply instead.** [ss.809D(1B) & 809E(1) ITA 2007]

3.3 Claiming to use the remittance basis

In all other cases, a non-UK domiciled or not ordinarily resident individual must make a claim to use the remittance basis and is known **as a 'remittance basis user' (RBU).**

RBUs do not receive the personal or blind person's allowance, or the married couples' allowance tax reduction.

A claim must be made each year that the individual wishes to be taxed on the remittance basis. If the individual does not make a claim, the arising basis applies to their foreign income.

3.4 Additional remittance basis charge

3.4.1 General principles

Where an individual makes a remittance basis claim (ie is a RBU), he must also pay an additional tax charge for every year he chooses to be taxed on the remittance basis if he:

(a)   Is **over the age of 18**, *and*

(b)   Has been **resident in the UK for at least seven out of the last nine tax years**.

This 'remittance basis charge' (RBC) of £30,000 is in addition to the tax due on remitted income (and gains).

3.4.2 Nominated income

The individual must 'nominate' unremitted income (or gains), which is effectively subject to UK tax in the year on an arising basis, to create the £30,000 charge.

If the amount nominated is insufficient to generate the £30,000 charge, additional income is deemed to have been nominated to make up the shortfall.

When the individual remits nominated income (not including any deemed nominated income) to the UK in the future it should not be taxed again. However, if they do have any other unremitted foreign income at that time complex re-characterisation rules apply. [ss.809I & 809J ITA 2007]

Example 3

Sophia, age 32, has been UK resident for the last ten years, but is not UK domiciled. She receives overseas bank interest of £250,000 (gross) during the tax year but only remits £50,000 to the UK. She has no other unremitted income or gains and makes a remittance basis claim for the year. She is a higher rate taxpayer.

You are required to calculate Sophia's income tax liability. Ignore double tax relief.

3.4.3 Practical and tax planning issues

If, in a particular year, it would be more beneficial for the individual to pay tax on their worldwide income and gains than to pay the RBC, he **may choose not to claim the remittance basis.**

Funds remitted to the UK, directly to HMRC, to pay the £30,000 charge are treated as if they had not been remitted to the UK.

3.5 When is income remitted to the UK?

An 'actual' remittance takes place where actual monies are brought into the UK. Remittances of capital are not taxed as income. For this reason it is essential that RBUs keep foreign income and capital in separate bank accounts, and remit only from the capital account.

A remittance can also occur in certain other situations, for example when assets representing the monies are brought into the UK. **This is known as a 'constructive' remittance.**

Constructive remittances include:

(a)   **Alienation**, ie where the individual gifts the income to relatives outside the UK who then remit it to the UK so that the individual or his close family can benefit from the money.

(b)   **Buying assets outside the UK with untaxed foreign money** and bringing them into the UK. There is an exemption for certain items such as personal effects (eg jewellery) and assets that are only in the UK to be repaired. [809X ITA 2007]

(c)   **If income is not remitted until after a source has ceased it will be taxable if the individual was taxed on the remittance basis in the year the income arose**, even if they are not taxable on the remittance basis in the year the remittance is made.

(d)   **Paying loan interest, whether inside or outside the UK, on an overseas mortgage taken out to purchase a residential UK property.**

3.6 Temporary non-residents

If an individual is 'temporarily non-resident', ie is non resident for less than five complete tax years, and was resident for at least four out of the seven years before departure, **any remittances of income arising in or before the year of departure, made whilst non-resident, are treated as made in the year of return.** [s.832A]

Illustration

Damien left the UK to become resident overseas on 12 May 2008, having been UK resident for the previous ten years. HMRC confirmed his residence status as 'not resident'.

During 2010/11 he made a remittance of £10,000 of foreign income. He returned to the UK on 4 June 2012.

Damien was not resident when the income was remitted to the UK, so it would not have been taxed during 2010/11.

However, he was only temporarily non-resident, as he had been resident for at least four out of the seven years before his departure and returned to the UK within five tax years. He will therefore be taxable on the income remitted in the year of his return to the UK, ie in 2012/13.

3.7 Remittance basis charge summary flowchart

Do I need to pay the Remittance Basis Charge (RBC)?

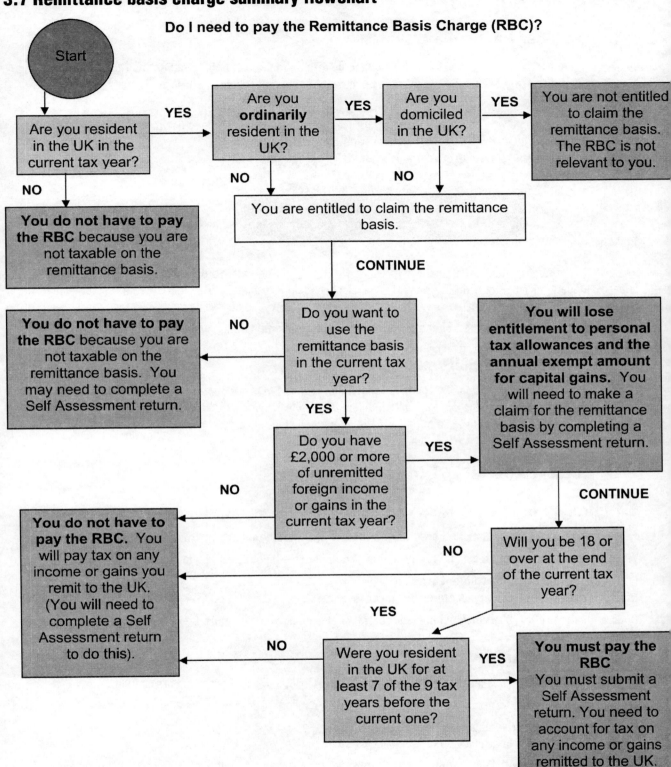

Note: The flowchart is a broad guide to help you decide if you need to pay the RBC. You have a choice each year about whether to claim the remittance basis. If, in a particular year, it would be more beneficial for you to pay tax on your worldwide income and gains than to pay the RBC, you may choose not to claim the remittance basis.

4 Personal allowances

4.1 Allowances for non-UK residents

In general, non-UK residents are liable to tax on income arising in the UK, but are not entitled to allowances. However, certain people are entitled to allowances despite being non-resident. These are:

(a)   Individuals resident in the Isle of Man or the Channel Islands
(b)   Former residents who have left the country for their own or a family member's health reasons
(c)   Current or former Crown servants and their widows or widowers
(d)   Employees in the service of any territory under Her Majesty's protection
(e)   Missionaries
(f)   European Economic Area (EEA) nationals. [s.278 ICTA 1988]

From 6 April 2010 Commonwealth citizens can qualify for a personal allowance if broadly they are already entitled to them under one of the categories listed above. [Sch 1 FA 2009]

The EEA covers Austria, Belgium, Bulgaria, Cyprus, Czech Republic, Denmark, Estonia, Finland, France, Germany, Greece, Hungary, Iceland, Ireland (Eire), Italy, Latvia, Liechtenstein, Lithuania, Luxembourg, Malta, Netherlands, Norway, Poland, Portugal, Romania, Slovakia, Slovenia, Spain and Sweden as well as the United Kingdom.

Non-residents who can claim personal allowances may use them against any income chargeable to UK tax.

4.2 Allowances for remittance basis users

If a not ordinarily resident or non-UK domiciled individual claims the remittance basis for their income, they are not entitled to a personal allowance or to the married couples' allowance. Individuals to whom the remittance basis automatically applies (see above) do not lose these allowances (see above).

5 Double taxation relief (DTR)

5.1 Introduction

As we have seen, **UK tax applies to the worldwide income of UK residents and the UK income of non-residents**.

When other countries adopt the same approach it is clear that some **income may be taxed twice**:

(a)   **Firstly in the country where it arises**
(b)   **Secondly in the country where the taxpayer is resident.**

Double taxation relief (DTR) may avoid the problem, or at least diminish its impact.

5.2 Double taxation agreements

Typical provisions of double taxation agreements based on the OECD Model Agreement are as follows:

(a)   **Total exemption** from tax is given in the country where income arises in the hands of, for example:
    (i)   Visiting diplomats
    (ii)   Teachers on exchange programmes

(b)   **Preferential rates of withholding tax** are applied to, for example, payments of rent, interest and dividends. The usual rate is frequently replaced by 15% or less

(c)   DTR is given to taxpayers in their country of residence by way of a **credit for tax suffered in the country where income arises**

(d)   There are **exchange of information clauses** so that tax evaders can be chased internationally

(e)   There are rules to determine a person's residence and to prevent dual residence (tie-breaker clauses)

(f)   There are clauses which render certain profits taxable in only one rather than both of the contracting states

(g)   There is a non-discrimination clause so that a country does not tax foreigners more heavily than its own nationals.

5.3 Unilateral relief

If no relief is available under a double taxation agreement, UK legislation provides for unilateral (ie one way) relief. This is also known as credit relief.

Foreign income must be included gross (ie inclusive of foreign tax) in the UK tax computation. A deduction is then available for the lower of:

(a)   **The UK tax**
(b)   **The foreign tax.**

The maximum double taxation relief (DTR) available for overseas dividends is limited to the UK tax paid less the dividend tax credit, ie for a higher rate taxpayer in 2010/11 the maximum DTR is 22.5% of the gross dividends and for an additional rate taxpayer is 32.5%.

Example 4

Tim, a UK resident higher rate taxpayer, received a dividend of £12,000 from Haki Inc, a US resident company during 2010/11. The dividend was paid net of 20% withholding tax. The USA is a qualifying territory for UK tax purposes.

You are required to calculate Tim's higher rate tax liability, after DTR, in respect of the dividend.

The UK tax on the foreign income is the difference between:

(a)   The UK tax before DTR on all income including the foreign income
(b)   The UK tax on all income except the foreign income.

In both (a) and (b), we take account of tax reductions.

Exam focus point

Examiner's report – Personal Taxation

May 2007 – Part II SFQ 1

Many candidates did not appreciate the restriction on double tax relief.

Example 5

Jane is resident, ordinarily resident and domiciled in the UK. She has the following income for 2010/11.

	£
UK salary	36,352
Interest on foreign debenture (net of foreign tax at 5%)	5,700
Foreign rents (net of foreign tax at 60%)	1,500

Assuming that maximum DTR is claimed, show her UK tax liability.

5.4 Expense relief

Where there is no point in claiming credit relief as above, perhaps because trading losses have eliminated any liability to UK tax, **the taxpayer may elect for expense relief instead**. No credit is given against the UK tax liability for foreign tax suffered, instead only the income *after* foreign taxes is brought into the tax computation.

5.5 Other matters

If foreign taxes are not relieved in the year in which the income is taxable in the UK, no relief can be obtained in any earlier or later year.

Credit relief, whether under a treaty or unilateral, is ignored when working out the tax which remains to be reduced by tax reductions.

Taxpayers who have claimed relief against their UK tax bill for taxes paid abroad must notify HMRC in writing of any changes to the foreign liabilities if these changes result in the DTR claimed becoming excessive. This rule applies to all taxes not just income tax.

Exam focus point

Examiner's report – Personal Taxation (old syllabus)

May 2000 – Question 5

This was the least popular question to answer, and although there were a few good answers, the majority were confused over the difference living abroad would make to the UK tax liability of Mr and Mrs Little. Very few explained the basis of determining the UK residence status of an individual or the taxation of rental income for an overseas landlord. Most candidates explained the position regarding personal allowances correctly, and the taxation of foreign income on returning to the UK.

However, several candidates wasted time explaining the potential capital gains tax liability on the rental properties when this was not required by the question.

Chapter roundup

- An individual is resident in the UK if he is present in the UK for 183 days in the tax year, or visits the UK for an *average* of 91 days or more a year for each *of four* consecutive tax years. He can also be treated as resident in the UK if he spends less than 91 days there but has strong ties (eg family, property).

- A person is *ordinarily resident* in the UK if residence in the UK is typical for him, and not just casual, ie he is habitually resident in the UK.

- Usually an individual is resident or not resident for a complete tax year, but HMRC will split a tax year in the following circumstances:
    - Permanent emigration
    - Permanent immigration
    - Arriving for at least two years
    - Going abroad under a full-time contract of employment lasting a complete tax year (and interim visits are less than 183 days/91 days on average).

- Those coming to the UK to take up permanent residence, or who intend to stay for at least three years from the outset, are regarded as resident and ordinarily resident in the UK from the date of arrival.

- Those coming to the UK for at least two years are resident for the entire period. They are not ordinarily resident until at least three years have passed, unless they intended the visit to last three or more years from the outset or have since settled in the UK.

- Domicile indicates one's permanent home:

  - *Domicile of origin:* usually an individual's father's domicile is his first domicile.

  - *Domicile of dependence:* a minor child (< 16) changes his domicile if the person on whom he is dependent (usually his father) changes his domicile.

  - *Domicile of choice:* an adult can change his domicile if he severs ties with his previous country and settles in another country. This can be difficult to establish.

- An individual who is UK resident, ordinarily resident and UK domiciled is liable to UK income tax on his worldwide income (ie UK and overseas) on an arising basis.

- A UK resident individual who is not UK domiciled and/or not ordinarily resident is liable to UK income tax on:

  - UK income – arising basis
  - Overseas income – arising basis unless claims remittance basis (or it applies automatically)

- An individual who is not UK resident is only liable to UK income tax on income arising in the UK.

- There is no further tax liability on interest and dividend income for a non resident, as it is restricted to the amount of the tax credit. If UK interest is paid gross to a non resident, it is tax free.

- Income from UK property is always taxable in the UK, even on landlords who are not UK resident.

- UK residents are taxed on income from property situated overseas. Overseas property income is calculated using the same rules as for UK property income. Losses on UK property income cannot be set against profit on overseas property income or vice versa.

- An individual claiming the remittance basis who is over 18 *and* who has been UK resident in seven out of the previous nine tax years is subject to a £30,000 additional tax charge.

- Double tax relief (DTR) is available where income is taxed both in the UK and in another country.

Quiz

1. Meredith, age 37, is domiciled in the state of New York, but has been resident and ordinarily resident in the UK since 2007. To what extent is Meredith charged to UK income tax on rental income from letting a property in New York?

2. Hector, who is resident, ordinarily resident and domiciled in the UK, receives a pension of £8,000 per annum from his former employer, a Canadian company based in Montreal. Hector used to work in Montreal.

   To what extent is Hector charged to UK income tax on the pension?

Solutions to Quiz

1. Meredith can make a claim to use the remittance basis so that she is only taxed on rental income she remits to the UK. She will not need to pay the additional £30,000 annual remittance basis charge in 2010/11 as Meredith has not been resident in the UK for seven out of the nine previous years.

2. Hector is taxed on an arising basis, but only on 90% (ie £7,200) of the amount.

Solutions to chapter examples

Solution to Example 1

Charles is not present for at least 183 days in any of the years so, on basic principles, he is not UK resident.

However, as he has spent 91 days or more on average in the UK, the position is as follows:

(a) As Charles never intended to make this level of visits he is likely to be treated as UK resident and ordinarily resident from 6 April 2011 (year five).

(b) As Charles decided to make this level of visits during the 2009/10 tax year, he is likely to be treated as UK resident and ordinarily resident from 6 April 2009.

Note. An individual can be treated as UK resident and ordinarily resident sooner if he has strong ties to the UK or has clearly 'settled' there.

Solution to Example 2

Cedric will not become non-UK domiciled, because he intends to return to the UK.

Solution to Example 3

Sophia is taxable on the remitted income as she has made a remittance basis claim. In addition, as she is over 18 and has been resident in the UK for at least 7 out of the last 9 years she is also subject to the £30,000 remittance basis charge.

She can nominate up to (£30,000 ÷ 40% =) £75,000 of her unremitted income of the year for the charge. If she nominates a lower amount, the shortfall will be deemed to be nominated. She can bring any actual (not deemed) nominated income into the UK in the future without triggering a tax charge.

She does not receive a personal allowance because she is a remittance basis user.

	£
Tax on remitted income: £50,000 × 40%	20,000
Add: remittance basis charge	30,000
Total income tax due	50,000

Solution to Example 4

	£	£
Gross foreign dividend: £12,000 × 100/80	15,000	
Add: UK tax credit £15,000 × 10/90	1,667	
Taxable foreign dividend (ie £12,000 × 100/80 × 100/90)		16,667
Tax @ 32.5%		5,417
Less DTR – lower of:		
(i) Foreign tax: £15,000 × 20%	3,000	
(ii) UK tax: £5,417 – £1,667 (ie £16,667 × 22.5%)	3,750	
ie		(3,000)
Less 10% UK tax credit		(1,667)
Tax due		750

Solution to Example 5

	Non savings £	Savings £	Total £
Salary	36,352		
Overseas interest £5,700 × 100/95		6,000	
Overseas rents £1,500 × 100/40	3,750		
Net income	40,102	6,000	46,102
Less personal allowance	(6,475)		(6,475)
Taxable income	33,627	6,000	39,627

	£
Non-savings income	
£33,627 × 20%	6,725
Savings income	
£3,773 × 20%	755
2,227 × 40%	891
Tax liability	8,371
Less: Double taxation relief:	
Rents (see below)	1,196
Interest (see below)	300
	(1,496)
Tax due	6,875

Since the rents are taxed more highly overseas, these should be regarded as the top slice of UK taxable income. Taxable income excluding the rents is £35,877 and the UK tax on this is:

	£
£35,877 × 20%	7,175

The UK tax on the rents is £1,196 (£8,371 – 7,175). Since foreign tax of £2,250 (60% of £3,750) is greater, the DTR is the smaller figure of £1,196. Foreign interest was taxed abroad at the rate of 5% (£300). Since the UK rate is clearly higher (taxed at 20%) the DTR given is limited to £300.

Now try the following questions

Short Form Questions:

9.1 – 9.3 inclusive

Long Form Question:

9.1	Ricardo Garcia

Part A Personal Income Tax | **9: Overseas aspects of income tax**

TQT
Tax Qualification Training

Personal Taxation

Part B:
Capital Gains Tax

- identify the basic charging provision and basis of assessment to CGT
- identify chargeable persons, occasions and assets
- identify exempt assets
- outline the rules for payment of CGT
- identify the overseas aspects of CGT

References: TCGA 1992 unless otherwise stated

Outline of CGT

1 The charge to tax

1.1 Basic charging provision

Capital gains tax (CGT) is charged on the total amount of chargeable gains made by a chargeable person in a tax year after deducting:

(a)   Any **allowable capital losses of the same tax year**, and

(b)   Any **allowable capital losses brought forward from earlier years**

Gains and losses of the same tax year are netted off. If gains exceed losses, there is a net chargeable gain for the tax year. If losses exceed gains, there is a **net allowable loss** (see later in this Text).

1.2 Basis of assessment

UK resident or ordinarily resident individuals are liable to CGT on the disposal of assets situated anywhere in the world.

Non-UK domiciled individuals with foreign gains may be taxable on the remittance basis (see below). **Not ordinarily resident individuals are always taxable on their UK and foreign gains on an arising basis.**

The concepts of residence, ordinary residence and domicile have the same meaning as for income tax purposes.

1.3 Annual exempt amount

Each individual is allowed to make an amount of gains each tax year that is not taxable. This 'annual exempt amount' is £10,100 for 2010/11. It is deducted from net chargeable gains to give the taxable gain for the tax year.

Non-UK domiciled individuals who claim to be taxed on a remittance basis are not entitled to an annual exempt amount.

1.4 Rates of CGT

This section is new.

1.4.1 Pre-23 June 2010 disposals

Gains arising on disposals taking place before 23 June 2010 are taxed separately from income at a flat rate of 18%.

Example 1

Carol makes a chargeable gain, before the annual exempt amount, of £25,000 on a disposal in May 2010. How much CGT is payable by her on this gain assuming she has taxable income of £44,000.

1.4.2 Disposals on or after 23 June 2010

Gains arising on disposals taking place **on or after 23 June 2010 are taxed as the 'top slice' of income**. If the gains fall **within the individual's basic rate band, after taking his income into account, they are taxed at 18%.** Gains falling above the **basic rate band are taxed at 28%.**

Pre-23 June 2010 gains are not taken into account when establishing the CGT rate(s).

An individual may deduct capital losses (see later in this Text) and the annual exempt amount in a way that minimises his CGT liability.

Example 2

Cheryl has taxable income of £27,400 in 2010/11. The basic rate band is £37,400.

She realises a gain on the sale of an asset in May 2010 of £15,000, and a further gain of £35,000 on a disposal in January 2011. Cheryl has no capital losses in 2010/11.

What is Cheryl's CGT position?

Exam focus point

A lower CGT rate of 10% applies to gains qualifying for 'entrepreneurs' relief'. Entrepreneurs' relief is **not** examinable in the Personal Taxation paper.

2 Chargeable persons, disposals and assets

2.1 Persons chargeable to CGT

The following are examples of **persons chargeable to CGT**:

(a)   Individuals
(b)   Partners (who are individually responsible for their share of partnership gains)
(c)   Trustees.

The following are examples of **persons exempt from CGT**:

(a)   Charities using gains for charitable purposes
(b)   Registered pension funds
(c)   Persons who are both not resident and not ordinarily resident in the UK

2.2 Disposals chargeable to CGT

A **chargeable disposal** includes:

(a)   A **sale** of an asset or part of an asset
(b)   A **gift** of all or part of an asset
(c)   The **receipt of insurance proceeds** on the loss or destruction of an asset

A **chargeable disposal occurs on the date of contract**, which may in some circumstances differ from the date of actual transfer. Where the contract is conditional, the date of disposal is taken as the date on which the condition is satisfied. However, when a capital sum is received under (c) above, the disposal takes place on the day the sum is *received*.

Where a disposal involves an acquisition by someone else ((a) or (b) above), the date of acquisition for the recipient of the asset is the same as the date of disposal.

The following are not treated as disposals:

(a)   **Passing of assets on death** (the heirs inherit assets as if they bought them at death for their then market value ('probate value'), but there is no disposal for the deceased on the death)

(b)   Transfers of assets as security for a loan or mortgage.

Gifts to charities and housing associations are generally not chargeable to CGT.

Exam focus point

Examiner's report – Personal Taxation (old syllabus)

November 2004 – Question 5

This question was fairly popular but there were few good answers. Many candidates did not appear to know that the gift of an asset to the charity was not chargeable to capital gains tax and could be used as a deduction from income. Several stated that it would qualify for gift relief....

2.3 Assets chargeable to CGT

All forms of property, wherever in the world they are situated, are chargeable assets for CGT purposes unless they are specifically designated as non-chargeable in the legislation.

Gains on disposal of the following assets are **exempt**:

(a)   Motor vehicles suitable for private use

(b)   NS&I certificates, premium bonds and SAYE deposits

(c)   Foreign currency for private use

(d)   Betting and lottery winnings

(e)   Medals etc awarded for bravery (unless purchased)

(f)   Damages for personal or professional injury

(g)   Life assurance policies (exempt in the hands of the original beneficial owner)

(h)   Works of art, scientific collections etc provided they are of national importance and are given for national purposes (breach of any conditions imposed will nullify the CGT exemption)

(i)   Principal (or main) private residence

(j)   Gilt edged securities (ie Treasury stock) and qualifying corporate bonds (loan stock)

(k)   Wasting chattels (tangible movable property with a life of 50 years or less, eg a racehorse)

(l)   Debts other than debts on a security

(m)   Pension and annuity rights

(n)   Investments held in an individual savings account (ISA).

3 Administration of CGT

CGT is chargeable for tax years, like income tax. Any gains arising in the year from 6 April 2010 to 5 April 2011 are charged in 2010/11.

There is one payment of CGT due on 31 January after the end of the tax year, ie 31 January 2012 for 2010/11. There are no payments on account for CGT.

It may also be possible to pay CGT in instalments (see later in this Text).

4 The overseas aspects of CGT

4.1 Liability to CGT

Individuals are liable to CGT on the disposal of assets situated anywhere in the world if they are resident or ordinarily resident in the UK at any point in the year in which the gain is made.

By concession, individuals who arrive in or leave the UK during the year may be able to split the tax year for CGT purposes ie they are charged to CGT only in respect of disposals made after the date of arrival or before the date of departure.

The concession does not apply if the individual was resident or ordinarily resident:

(a)   At any time in the five tax years before the tax year of arrival, or

(b)   For at least four out of seven tax years before the tax year of departure.

4.2 Individuals with non-UK domiciles

If a person is UK resident or ordinarily resident but is not UK domiciled, they may be able to use the remittance basis of taxation either automatically or by making a claim. Where a non UK domiciled individual makes a remittance basis claim it applies to both their foreign income and foreign gains. The remittance basis was covered in detail earlier in this Text.

If the remittance basis applies, the individual's gains on the disposal of assets located overseas (see below) are only chargeable to CGT when the gains are *remitted* (ie brought in) to the UK.

If a non-UK domiciled individual over the age of 18 makes a claim to use the remittance basis (ie it does not apply automatically) and he has been UK resident for seven out of the previous nine tax years, he must also pay the £30,000 remittance basis charge (RBU). This is the RBU that we covered earlier in this Text and is not an additional charge specifically in relation to capital gains.

There are **special rules for capital losses** made by non-UK domiciled individuals. These are covered in the next chapter.

Not ordinarily resident individuals are always taxable on their UK and foreign gains on an arising basis (even if they are able to use the remittance basis for their foreign *income*).

4.3 Non-UK residents

Normally a disposal of assets situated in the UK is not a chargeable event if the vendor is not resident and not ordinarily resident in the UK at the time of disposal. However, a liability to CGT may arise if the person is carrying on a trade, profession or vocation in the UK through a permanent establishment and an asset which has been used for the purpose of the permanent establishment is either disposed of or removed from the UK.

A charge will also arise if the UK trade, profession or vocation ceases. In this case, and in the case of removal of assets from the UK, there is a deemed disposal of assets at their market value.

> ### Exam focus point
>
> **Examiner's report – Personal Taxation**
>
> **May 2008 – Part I SFQ 6**
>
> ...part (b) caused problems for a small minority of candidates who thought that all disposals of UK assets would be chargeable, irrespective of the residence of the taxpayer.

4.4 Temporary non-residents

Temporary non-residents may be taxable on gains realised whilst they are abroad if:

(a)   **They are outside the UK for less than five years between the year of departure and the year of return.**

(b)   **They were UK resident or ordinarily resident for four out of the seven years immediately preceding the year of departure**.

Net gains realised in the year of departure are taxed in that year (this applies whether the absence is temporary or permanent under general principles). **Subsequent gains/losses are chargeable/allowable in the year of return as if they were gains/losses of that year.**

Gains on assets acquired in the non-resident period are not included in the above charge nor are gains which are already chargeable because they arise on a permanent establishment's assets (see above).

4.5 Double taxation relief (DTR)

If a gain on the disposal of an overseas asset is taxed both overseas and in the UK, DTR will be available.

The DTR applies in the same way as for income tax, ie relief is given for the lower of the UK and overseas tax. However, the annual exempt amount is deducted pro rata from gains on different assets to give the taxable gain in each case.

Example 3

Geraldine who is UK resident and ordinarily resident, makes a gain on a UK asset of £20,000 in July 2010 and on a non-UK asset of £10,000 in October 2010. She paid foreign tax of £3,000 on the non-UK asset. She has taxable income of £17,000 in the year. Calculate the DTR available.

4.6 Location of assets

For CGT purposes assets are located as follows:

(a)	Immovable property	–	where physically located
(b)	Tangible movable property (chattels)	–	where physically located at time of disposal
(c)	A debt	–	where the creditor is resident
(d)	Government securities	–	within country of that government
(e)	Shares and securities	–	in a UK incorporated company are located in the UK other shares/securities are located where registered
(f)	Goodwill of a business	–	where business is carried on
(g)	Patents	–	where registered

Chapter roundup

- CGT is charged on 'chargeable gains' that arise when a 'chargeable person' makes a 'chargeable disposal' of a 'chargeable asset'.

- Individuals are entitled to an annual exempt amount for each tax year.

- Taxable gains from disposals taking place before 23 June 2010 are taxed at 18%.

- The rate of CGT on taxable gains arising from disposals taking place on or after 23 June 2010 depends on the individual's taxable income. Any gains falling within any remaining basic rate band are taxed at 18%. Gains in excess of the basic rate band are taxed at 28%.

- A disposal occurs not only when there is a sale of an asset but also when there is a gift or a capital sum is received (eg insurance money received when an asset is damaged or destroyed).

- Certain assets, such as cars, are exempt from CGT.

- CGT is due on 31 January following the tax year. On certain occasions the CGT may be paid by instalments.

- CGT is charged on persons who are resident or ordinarily resident in the UK and persons only temporarily abroad. A tax year may be split into resident and non-resident parts by concession but the concession is denied in certain circumstances.

- A UK resident and/or ordinarily resident person is chargeable to CGT on disposals of their worldwide assets.

- UK resident and/or ordinarily resident persons who are not UK domiciled may be able to use the remittance basis (either automatically or by making a claim) so that foreign gains are taxed only when they are remitted to the UK.

- Individuals who make a claim to use the remittance basis must also pay the £30,000 remittance basis charge on unremitted foreign income and gains if they are over 18 and have been UK resident for 7 of the last 9 tax years.

- Double taxation relief may be available to reduce the tax liability when the same gain is taxed in two countries.

Quiz

1. Martha has chargeable gains (before the annual exempt amount) of £28,400, all arising from disposals that took place in August 2010. Calculate her CGT liability for 2010/11 assuming she has total income (before the personal allowance) of £42,500.

2. Which of the following constitute chargeable disposals for CGT?

    (a) A gift of shares
    (b) A sale of 2 acres of land out of a plot of 10 acres
    (c) The demolition of a building.

3. Which of the following are chargeable assets for CGT purposes?

    (a) Proceeds from backing the winner of the Grand National
    (b) Damages awarded in an action for libel
    (c) A diamond necklace
    (d) A vintage Rolls Royce.

4. By what date is CGT is due for 2010/11?

5. In which country are the following assets situated?

    (a) A villa in Portugal
    (b) Securities issued by the government of Italy, purchased through a UK agent
    (c) Shares in a company which is UK resident for tax purposes but which is incorporated in and has its share register maintained in Jersey, Channel Islands
    (d) A diamond necklace owned by a UK resident but which is kept in the vaults of a French bank.

TQT
Tax Qualification Training

1.

		£
Martha – 2010/11		
Chargeable gains		28,400
Less: annual exempt amount		(10,100)
Taxable gain		18,300
CGT:		
£37,400 – (£42,500 – £6,475) = £ 1,375 @ 18%		247
£18,300 – £1,375 = £16,925 @ 28%		4,739
Total CGT		4,986

2.   All of them.

3.   (c) only – (a), (b) and (d) are exempt assets.

4.   31 January 2012

5.   (a)   Portugal
      (b)   Italy
      (c)   Jersey
      (d)   France

Solutions to chapter examples

Solution to Example 1

	£
Chargeable gains (pre-23.6.10)	25,000
Less: annual exempt amount	(10,100)
Taxable gains	14,900
Tax: £14,900 × 18% (ignore taxable income)	2,682

Solution to Example 2

	£	£
Pre-23.6.10 gain		
£15,000 @ 18%		2,700
Post-22.6.10 gain		
Chargeable gain	35,000	
Less: Annual exempt amount *(Note)*	(10,100)	
Taxable gain	24,900	
CGT payable:		
Basic rate band remaining = £37,400 – £27,400 = £10,000		
£10,000 @ 18%	1,800	
£24,900 – £10,000 = £14,900 @ 28%	4,172	
		5,972
Total CGT		8,672

Note. Cheryl can set her annual exempt amount against the later gain as a higher CGT rate applies.

TQT
Tax Qualification Training

Solution to Example 3

The annual exempt amount is split:

UK asset $\dfrac{20,000}{30,000} \times £10,100 = £6,733$, giving a taxable gain of <u>£13,267</u>

Non-UK asset $\dfrac{10,000}{30,000} \times £10,100 = £3,367$ giving a taxable gain of <u>£6,633</u>

	£
UK CGT on overseas asset is:	
£6,633 @ 18% (all within the BR band)	<u>1,194</u>
DTR is the lower of £1,194 and £3,000 ie	<u>1,194</u>

Now try the following questions

Short Form Questions:

10.1 – 10.4 inclusive

Long Form Questions:

10.1	Peter Jones
10.2	Simon James

The purpose of this chapter is to help you to:

- set out the basic CGT computation

- understand how to set off capital losses

- use the valuation rules for specific assets (eg shares)

- identify connected persons and understand the consequences of transfers between them

- understand the value at which transfers take place between husband and wife/civil partners

- apply the part disposal rules

- understand the tax treatment of debts and loans

References: TCGA 1992 unless otherwise stated

Computing gains and losses

1 Calculating a gain or loss

1.1 The CGT computation

A chargeable gain or allowable loss is calculated as follows:

	£
Disposal consideration (or market value)	X
Less: costs of disposal	(X)
Net proceeds	X
Less: allowable costs	(X)
Chargeable gain (allowable loss)	X/(X)

Exam focus point

In computational CGT questions, if an individual disposes of several assets in the tax year, you will need to calculate the gain/loss on each asset individually using the above proforma.

1.2 Disposal consideration

Normally, it is the actual consideration passing between the parties which is taken into account. However where the disposal is not a bargain at arm's length (ie a gift or sale at below market value) **the disposal is deemed to take place at market value.**

1.3 Costs of disposal

These may include:

(a)   Valuation fees
(b)   Estate agency fees
(c)   Advertising costs
(d)   Legal costs

These costs are deducted from gross proceeds of sale.

1.4 Other allowable costs

Allowable costs include:

(a)   **Original cost of acquisition** (or market value at the date of acquisition)
(b)   **Incidental costs of acquisition**
(c)   **Capital expenditure incurred in enhancing the asset** (see below).

1.5 Enhancement expenditure

Enhancement expenditure means capital expenditure which enhances the value of the asset and is *reflected in the state or nature of the asset at the time of disposal*. Certain costs are specifically excluded from this category as follows:

(a)   Cost of repairs and maintenance
(b)   Cost of insurance
(c)   Any expenditure which is treated as a deduction for the purposes of assessing the taxpayer to income tax, and
(d)   Any expenditure transferred out of public funds eg council grants.

Example 1

Fred bought an asset on 15 February 1984 for £5,000. Enhancement expenditure of £2,000 was incurred on 10 April 1985. Fred sold the asset for £20,500 on 20 December 2010. Incidental costs of sale were £500.

You are required to calculate his chargeable gain.

2 Capital losses

2.1 Current year losses

Losses arising in one tax year must be set against gains of that year. An individual may deduct losses (and the annual exempt amount) in a way that minimises his CGT liability.

Example 2

George has chargeable gains for 2010/11 of £10,000 from a disposal in July 2010 and allowable losses of £6,000 from a disposal in December 2010. How will he take relief for the losses?

Example 3

Martin has chargeable gains of £15,000 arising from a disposal on 15 May 2010, further gains of £18,000 from a disposal on 28 October 2010 and allowable losses of £10,000 from a disposal on 16 April 2010. Show Martin's CGT liability for 2010/11 assuming he has taxable income of £50,000.

2.2 Losses carried forward

If current year losses exceed current year gains, the excess is automatically carried forward against the first net chargeable gains arising in a future year.

Brought forward losses are used only to the extent that they reduce chargeable gains down to the annual exempt amount. No set off is made if net chargeable gains for the current year do not exceed the annual exempt amount.

Example 4

Bob makes a gain of £11,800 on 25 June 2010. He has losses brought forward of £6,000. How will Bob take relief for these losses?

Example 5

Tom makes chargeable gains of £5,000 in September 2010 and has losses brought forward from 2009/10 of £4,000. How will Tom take relief for these losses?

2.3 Losses in the year of death

The *only* (examinable) time that an individual may carry *back* capital losses is on death. Losses (in excess of gains) arising in the tax year in which an individual dies can be carried back to the previous three tax years on a LIFO basis (ie most recent year first). Losses are utilised so as to reduce chargeable gains for each of the years to an amount equal to the annual exempt amount of that year.

This will result in a repayment of CGT that has already been paid.

Example 6

Joe dies on 1 January 2011. His chargeable gains and allowable losses for recent years, before taking account of annual exempt amounts, have been as follows:

		Gain /(Loss)	Annual Exempt Amount
		£	£
2010/11	Gains	2,100	10,100
	Losses	(12,000)	
2009/10	Gains	10,300	10,100
2008/09	Gains	7,200	9,600
2007/08	Gains	19,600	9,200

You are required to show how the losses arising in 2010/11 are utilised.

2.4 Share loss relief

Relief is available for losses arising on the disposal of shares in certain unquoted trading companies (broadly EIS type companies – see earlier in this Text). [s.131 ITA 2007]

The capital loss is computed as normal but is instead **deducted from the taxpayer's general income in**:

(a)   The tax year in which the disposal takes place, and/or
(b)   The previous tax year.

A claim must be made by the anniversary of 31 January following the end of the tax year of the loss, so by 31 January 2013 for 2010/11.

The taxpayer cannot choose the amount of loss to relieve, but can choose whether to set a loss first against the current year's income and then against the previous year's income, or the other way round.

Exam focus point

Examiner's report – Personal Taxation (old syllabus)

November 2004 – Question 5

Many failed to notice that the loss on the shares in Wonder Fabrications could be set against income which therefore meant that for many candidates the answer produced a capital gains tax liability.

2.5 Losses of non-UK domiciled individuals

A non-UK domiciled individual who does not need to make a claim to use the remittance basis (ie it applies automatically) or who chooses to be taxed on an arising basis, can set capital losses from assets situated overseas ('overseas losses') against their foreign gains.

However, **if the individual has had to make a claim to use the remittance basis (see earlier in this Text) he can only obtain relief for his overseas losses if he chooses to make an irrevocable overseas losses election.** [s.16ZA]

The individual must make the election in the first year that he claims the remittance basis (even if he has no overseas gains or losses in that year). If he does not make the election none of his foreign losses will be allowable losses for as long as he remains non-UK domiciled.

Where the election is made, capital losses (both UK and overseas) must be allocated in the following order:

(a)   Against foreign chargeable gains that are remitted to the UK, then
(b)   Against foreign chargeable gains that are not remitted to the UK, then
(c)   Against UK chargeable gains.

Only losses allocated under (a) and (c) are actually offset in the CGT computation. **Losses cannot be set against remitted foreign chargeable gains that accrued in an earlier year.** This is in line with the general principle that losses cannot usually be carried back.

Where a loss is set against an unremitted gain under (b), that gain is permanently reduced by the loss.

Example 7

Sergio, 34, has been UK resident for four years but is not UK domiciled. In 2010/11 he has the following gains and losses (all disposals took place after 23 June 2010):

	£
Gains on sale of UK shares	30,000
Loss on sale of UK shares	(5,000)
Gain on sale of overseas house	10,000
Loss on sale of overseas shares	(15,000)

Sergio remits £2,000 of the overseas gain on 12 August 2010. He makes a capital losses election as this is the first year that he has had to claim the remittance basis.

Show Sergio's chargeable gains.

---

3 Valuation of assets

3.1 The basic rule

Where it is necessary to use the market value, rather than the actual consideration in the CGT computation, the value to use is **the price that the asset might reasonably be expected to fetch on a sale in the open market.**

3.2 Shares and securities

Quoted shares and securities are valued at the **lower of two figures** as quoted in The Stock Exchange Daily Official List as follows:

(a)   **'Quarter-up'** rule: add a quarter of the difference between the lower and the higher quoted prices to the lower quoted price, or

(b)   'Average rule': take the **average of highest and lowest marked bargains** (ignore marked special prices).

Example 8

Shares in A plc are quoted at 100-110p. The marked bargains for that day were 99p, 102p and 110p. What value will the shares have for CGT purposes?

Unquoted shares are much harder to value than quoted shares. Values are usually agreed with HMRC's special Shares and Assets Valuation division.

Exam focus point

You will be given the market value of unquoted shares in the examination.

3.3 Negligible value claim

If an asset becomes worthless, the owner may make a claim to treat the asset as though it had been sold and then immediately reacquired at its current market value. This will give rise to an allowable loss. This 'negligible value' claim is often used for shares. [s.24(2)]

TQT
Tax Qualification Training

The claim can be backdated up to two tax years, provided that the asset had become negligible in value at that time, eg in 2010/11 a claim can be made that an asset's value became negligible in 2008/09, which crystallises an allowable loss in 2008/09.

If the asset is subsequently sold, the base cost of the asset will be the value at the time of the negligible value claim.

Example 9

Rhona owns shares in Alf Ltd which she purchased in 1983. Following a sudden change in the company's business in the summer of 2009 the shares plummeted in value and the company went into liquidation. Rhona only learnt of the liquidation in May 2010.

For which tax year(s) may a negligible value claim be made?

3.4 Probate value

Where an individual inherits an asset on the death of another person they are treated as acquiring that asset at the market value at the date of death. This is known as the 'probate value'.

4 Connected persons

4.1 Introduction

If a transferor and transferee are 'connected' persons any transaction is treated as taking place at market value, regardless of any actual price paid.

If a loss results, it can **only be set off against gains arising in the same or future years from transactions with the** *same* **connected person** *while they remain connected*.

4.2 Definition of connected persons

An individual is connected with:

(a)   His spouse or civil partner
(b)   His relatives (brothers, sisters, ancestors and lineal descendants)
(c)   The relatives of his spouse/civil partner
(d)   The spouses of his relatives and his spouse's/civil partner's relatives
(e)   Business partners, partners' spouses/civil partners and partners' relatives
(f)   Trustees of any settlement of which the individual is the settlor.

A company is connected with another person if:

(a)   That person has control of the company, or
(b)   He and persons connected with him together have control of it.

A company is connected with another company if:

(a)   The same person has control of both companies, or
(b)   One person has control of one company and persons connected with him have control of the other.

Exam focus point

Examiner's report – Personal Taxation

November 2009 – Part I SFQ 2

There was general uncertainty as to whether the uncle and trustees were connected, and very few candidates even considered whether the company was connected.

4.3 Series of disposals to connected persons ('linked transactions')

A taxpayer might attempt to avoid tax by disposing of his property piecemeal to persons connected with him. For example, a majority holding of shares might be broken up into several minority holdings, each with a much lower value per share, and each of the shareholder's children could be given a minority holding.

To prevent the avoidance of tax in this way, **where a person disposes of assets to one or more persons, with whom he is connected, in a series of linked transactions, the disposal proceeds for each disposal will be a proportion of the value of the assets taken together**. So, in the example of the shareholding, the value of the majority holding would be apportioned between the minority holdings. **Transactions are linked if they occur within six years of each other**.

5 Married couples and civil partners

5.1 Introduction

A husband and wife (or partners in a civil partnership) are taxed as two separate people. Each has an annual exempt amount, and losses of one cannot be set against gains of the other.

Disposals between a husband and wife (or civil partners) living together do not give rise to chargeable gains or allowable losses. The disposal is said to be on a **'no gain/no loss' basis. The acquiring spouse/partner takes over the base cost of the disposing spouse/partner.**

Example 10

Jacob gave his wife Leah a painting in July 2005. Its market value was £50,000. He had acquired the painting in February 1999 for £10,000. Leah sold the painting in July 2010 for £75,000.

Calculate Leah's chargeable gain.

A couple are treated as living together unless they are separated under a court order or separation deed, or are in fact separated in circumstances which make permanent separation likely. **A transfer in the tax year of separation will therefore be treated as a no gain/no loss transfer.**

From the beginning of the next tax year, the spouses/civil partners will be connected persons until their divorce is finalised (ie when they receive the 'decree absolute'), after which time disposals will be taxed using the normal rules.

Exam focus point

Examiner's report – Personal Taxation

May 2008 – Part I SFQ 2

There was a general lack of appreciation of the distinction, for capital gains tax purposes, of the difference between separation and divorce...There was often reference to the disposals occurring at NGNL *(no gain/no loss)* but, at the same time, the proceeds being deemed to be the market value.

5.2 Jointly owned assets

Where an asset is jointly owned, the spouses/civil partners' actual interests determine the tax treatment, so if there is evidence that a wife's share is 60%, then 60% of any gain or loss will be attributed to her. **If there is no evidence of the actual interests, HMRC accept that the asset is held in equal shares.**

Where an income tax declaration has been made (see Chapter 1) stating how income from the asset is to be shared for income tax purposes, there is a presumption that the same split will apply for CGT purposes.

5.3 Tax planning issues

If a spouse who is making other substantial gains wishes to dispose of an asset standing at a gain and the other spouse has his/her CGT annual exempt amount available, **the asset could first be transferred, at no gain/no loss, to the spouse with the annual exempt amount who can then sell the asset.** The transfer must have 'no strings attached' to be effective for tax purposes.

6 Part disposals

6.1 General rules

The disposal of part of a chargeable asset is a chargeable event for CGT purposes. The chargeable gain (or allowable loss) is computed by **deducting only a fraction of the original cost of the whole asset.** The fraction is:

$$\frac{A}{A+B} = \frac{\text{value of the part disposed of}}{\text{value of the part disposed of} + \text{market value of the remainder}}$$

The balance of the cost is used when the rest of the asset is sold.

Example 11

Mr Heal possesses a set of four Chippendale chairs (treated as a single asset for CGT purposes) which originally cost him £27,000 in March 1984. He sold one of the chairs at auction in July 2010 for £20,000, before auction expenses of 10%. The market value of the three remaining chairs together is £46,000.

You are required to calculate Mr Heal's chargeable gain.

6.2 Small part disposals of land [s.242]

If the consideration on the part disposal of land is small *and* the total consideration in that tax year from all disposals of land do not exceed £20,000, the taxpayer may claim for there not to be a part disposal and instead to deduct the 'small' sale proceeds from the base cost of the land rather than calculate the gain on the part disposal.

'Small' is defined as not more than 20% of the total market value of the land (A + B) immediately before the disposal.

Exam focus point

Examiner's report – Personal Taxation

May 2008 – Part II LFQ 2

Approximately half of candidates identified the application of the small part disposal rules with the majority of incorrect answers referring to claiming Principal Private Residence relief.

Example 12

Tony sells 2 acres of land out of a plot of 20 acres for £10,000 in 2000/01 (his only disposal that tax year). The market value of the 20 acre plot was £80,000 immediately prior to the sale. The remaining 18 acres are sold in August 2010 for £100,000.

Date of acquisition:	30 April 1983
Original cost:	£45,000
Date of part disposal:	30 April 2000
Date of final disposal:	30 August 2010

Assume a claim was made in respect of the part disposal under s.242 TCGA 1992.

You are required to show the adjustment to Tony's base cost on the sale in 2000/01 and his chargeable gain in 2010/11.

Exam focus point

Attempt the following example on your own before looking at the solution. Use the steps below:

Step 1 **Calculate the chargeable gain on each asset as a separate working.**

Step 2 Prepare a **summary table** and aggregate the gains calculated in Step 1. This should be the first page of your answer and should clearly reference in your workings from Step 1 above.

Step 3 If there are any **losses** available for offset, these **should be deducted – current year capital losses first, then capital losses brought forward against the gains that will be taxed at the highest CGT rate.**

Step 4 **Deduct the annual exempt amount, again from the gains that will be taxed at the highest CGT rate,** to arrive at the taxable gain.

Step 5 **Calculate the CGT payable at 18%** (all gains before 23 June 2010 and gains on or after that date that fall within the individual's basic rate band) **or 28%** (for gains that are in excess of the basic rate band).

Example 13

Brian made the following disposals:

(1)   On 23 May 2010 he sold a warehouse used in his trade at auction for £70,000 (gross). The auction house charged him a commission of 10% on the sale. The warehouse had cost him £10,000 in May 1983.

(2)   On 2 November 2010 he sold a tenanted cottage for £258,200 before costs of sale, which amounted to £1,200. He had inherited the cottage, which was one of a pair, on the death of his grandfather in October 1983. They were valued as a pair for probate purposes at £254,000. The value of the cottage retained by him was estimated at £222,500 when he sold the other one.

He has losses brought forward of £35,000 at 6 April 2010. His taxable income for the year was £52,000.

You are required to compute his capital gains tax liability.

7 Debts and loans

7.1 Debts

7.1.1 Introduction

Debts are specifically included in the definition of chargeable assets.

7.1.2 Ordinary debts

The original creditor (ie lender) does not make a chargeable gain or an allowable loss on a disposal of the original debt (unless it is a debt on a security – see below).

If someone purchases the debt from the original lender and then disposes of it, he will be liable to tax on any gain or entitled to an allowable loss. The satisfaction (ie payment) of a debt is treated as a disposal.

However, if the debt was acquired from the original lender and is disposed of at a loss by someone connected with that lender, the loss is not allowable.

Illustration

Fred lends £10,000 to Tom. Fred assigns (ie sells) the debt to Harry for £9,000. Tom repays the full amount lent to Harry.

Whether or not Harry is connected with Fred, Harry has made a disposal and realised a gain of £1,000.

7.2 Debt on a security

A 'debt on a security' is not necessarily a 'secured' debt (ie its payment is not secured on another asset, for example a mortgage is secured on the property over which it is given).

To be a debt on a security it must be:

- **Capable of being held as an investment**
- **Marketable** (ie be capable of being realised at a profit)
- **From an institution** (not from an individual)
- **Evidenced in writing**
- **Loan stock** (ie a loan to a company).

Exam focus point

If the original lender disposes of a debt on a security there will be a chargeable gain or an allowable loss because they are generally commercial investments. In all other ways a debt on a security is treated in the same way as an ordinary loan.

7.3 Loans to traders

7.3.1 Introduction

Although the original lender is not usually entitled to an allowable loss when a debt becomes irrecoverable, relief is available for certain loans to traders, and for guarantees in respect of such loans.

The lender must claim the relief.

7.3.2 Qualifying loans

A qualifying loan must satisfy the following conditions: [s.253(1)]

(a) **The money lent is used by the borrower wholly for the purposes of a trade (not involving lending money) carried on by him**, including furnished holiday lettings, *and*

(b) **The borrower is resident in the UK, *and***

(c) **The debt is *not* a debt on a security**.

The lender can make a claim for loss relief if:

- The loan capital (ie principal) has become irrecoverable, and
- He has not assigned the right to recover the amount, and
- The lender and the borrower were **not spouses** or civil partners either when, or after, the loan was made.

The date of the 'disposal' is the date of the claim, although the lender can specify an earlier time (not more than two years before the beginning of the tax year in which the claim is made) so long as the above conditions were satisfied at that earlier time.

Chapter roundup

- CGT is a tax on the increase in value of assets between acquisition and disposal.

- Disposal proceeds are actual money received or market value, if an asset is gifted or sold for less than its market value.

- Allowable expenditure includes the acquisition cost, enhancement expenditure and incidental costs of acquisition or disposal.

- Chargeable gains and losses arising in a tax year are netted off.

- Excess allowable losses must be carried forward and set against chargeable gains arising in a subsequent year to bring the chargeable gain down to the level of the annual exempt amount.

- Losses incurred in the year of death can be carried back against gains arising in the preceding three years on a LIFO basis.

- Losses on unquoted shares may be set against general income.

- If an individual makes an election in the first year that he is entitled to make a remittance basis claim he can obtain relief for losses on foreign assets. Otherwise he will never be able to use his foreign capital losses.

- A loss arising on a transaction between connected persons may only be set off in restricted circumstances.

- Shares are valued at the lower of the quarter-up and average bargain values.

- No gain/no loss disposals effectively transfer base costs between spouses and civil partners.

- For a part disposal, allowable expenditure is apportioned between the part disposed of and the part retained using the formula: $\dfrac{A}{A+B} \times \text{cost}$.

- In the case of a 'small' part disposal of land the taxpayer may elect that no part disposal takes place. Instead allowable expenditure is reduced by the 'small' disposal proceeds. 'Small' means the disposal proceeds do not exceed 20% of A + B and the proceeds from the part disposal (and from all land disposals in the tax year) do not exceed £20,000.

- Only the disposal of a debt on a security gives rise to a gain or loss to the original lender. Usually there is no chargeable gain or allowable loss unless the lender purchased the debt.

- In certain cases a taxpayer can claim an allowable capital loss for irrecoverable loans made to traders.

1. Yvette buys a 2% shareholding in Blanche Ltd, a trading company on 9 August 2002 for £125,000. She sells the shares on 12 December 2010 for £160,000. Show her taxable gain after the annual exempt amount.

2. Philip has chargeable gains of £13,200 and allowable losses of £2,300 in 2010/11. Losses brought forward at 6 April 2010 are £7,000. What amount is chargeable to CGT in 2010/11? What are the losses carried forward?

3. Losses arising in the year in which an individual dies are set first against gains arising in the year of death. Any excess losses may then be carried back and set against gains of the four preceding years, using gains of a more recent year before those of an earlier year. True/False?

4. Compute the CGT value of the following shares in quoted companies:

    (a) Z plc – quoted prices : 250p to 260p
         marked bargains : 248p, 254p and 262p

    (b) Y plc – quoted prices : 402p to 420p
         marked bargains : 380p (special), 390p and 410p

5. With which of the following persons is Joe connected for CGT purposes?

    (a) His son Eddie
    (b) His cousin Frank
    (c) A company, Joe Ltd, of which he owns 95% of the ordinary share capital and voting power
    (d) His brother Ray's wife

6. Richard, a higher rate taxpayer, sells 4 acres of land in May 2010 out of a plot of 10 acres for £38,000. Costs of disposal amount to £3,000. The 10 acre plot cost £41,500 in 1987. The market value of the 6 acres remaining is £48,000.

    Compute his capital gains tax liability.

1.

	£
Proceeds	160,000
Less: cost	(125,000)
Chargeable gain	35,000
Less: annual exempt amount	(10,100)
Taxable gain	24,900

2.

	£
Gains in year	13,200
Losses in year	(2,300)
	10,900
Losses brought forward (£10,900 – 10,100)	(800)
	10,100
Annual exempt amount	(10,100)
Chargeable amount	£ nil

Losses carried forward at 5 April 2011
£(7,000 – 800) = £6,200.

3. False – the carry back period is three years only.

4. (a) Z plc : lower of

     (i) $250p + ((260-250p)/4) = 252.5p$

     (ii) $\dfrac{248 + 262}{2} = 255p$

     ie 252.5p per share

   (b) Y plc : lower of

     (i) $402p + ((420 - 402p)/4) = 406.5p$

     (ii) $\dfrac{390 + 410}{2} = 400p$

     ie 400p per share

5. Joe is connected with all except (b), his cousin.

6.

	£
Proceeds	38,000
Less: costs of disposal	(3,000)
	35,000
Less: allowable cost : $£41,500 \times \dfrac{38,000}{38,000 + 48,000}$	(18,337)
Chargeable gain	16,663
Less: Annual exempt amount	(10,100)
Taxable gain	6,563
CGT @ 18% (pre-23.6.10 disposal)	1,181

Solutions to chapter examples

Solution to Example 1

The computation of the chargeable gain will be as follows:

	£
Disposal proceeds	20,500
Less: incidental costs of sale	(500)
Net proceeds	20,000
Less: allowable costs £(5,000 + 2,000)	(7,000)
Chargeable gain	13,000

Solution to Example 2

As the losses are *current year* losses they must be fully relieved against the £10,000 of gains to produce net gains of £4,000, despite the fact that net gains are now below the annual exempt amount, part of which will be wasted.

Solution to Example 3

Martin will set the loss and the annual exempt amount against the gains that are taxed at the highest CGT rate, ie first against the post-22.6.10 gains which are taxed at 28% (as there is no basic rate band left) and then against the pre-23.6.10 gains which are taxed at 18%.

	Pre-23.6.10 £	Post-22.6.10 £
Chargeable gains	15,000	18,000
Less: current year loss		(10,000)
Net gains	15,000	8,000
Less: annual exempt amount	(2,100)	(8,000)
Taxable gain	12,900	NIL
CGT @ 18%	£2,322	

Solution to Example 4

Bob's loss relief can be restricted to £1,700 so as to leave net gains of:

£(11,800 − 1,700) = £10,100

which will be exactly covered by his annual exempt amount for 2010/11.

The remaining £4,300 of loss relief (ie £6,000 − £1,700) is carried forward to 2011/12.

Solution to Example 5

His gains of £5,000 are covered by his annual exempt amount for 2010/11. He can therefore carry forward all of his losses to 2011/12.

Solution to Example 6

Loss relief is:

	£	Gains £	Losses £
2010/11			
Gains	2,100		
Less: losses	(12,000)		
Loss available for c/b			9,900
2009/10			
Gains	10,300		
Less: loss c/b	(200)	10,100	(200)
Less: AE		(10,100)	
Taxable gain		nil	
Loss available for c/b			9,700
2008/09			
Gains		7,200	
Less: AE (part)		(7,200)	
Taxable gain		nil	

2007/08

Gains	19,600	
Less: loss c/b	(9,700)	(9,700)
	9,900	
Less: AE	(9,200)	
Taxable gain	700	
Unrelieved loss		nil

This will generate a repayment of any CGT that may have been paid in the earlier years.

Solution to Example 7

As Sergio makes an overseas loss election he can set his overseas and UK losses against his gains. The losses must be offset in a particular order:

		£
(i)	Remitted overseas gain	2,000
	Less: losses (W)	(2,000)
	Chargeable gain	Nil
(ii)	Unremitted overseas gain (£10,000 – £2,000)	8,000
	Less: losses (W)	(8,000)
	Reduced permanently to:	Nil
(iii)	UK gain	30,000
	Less: losses (W)	(10,000)
	Chargeable gain	20,000
	Total chargeable gains ((i) £nil + (iii) £20,000)	£20,000

Working

	£
2010/11 capital losses £(15,000 + 5,000)	20,000
Less: set against (i)	(2,000)
Less: set against (ii)	(8,000)
Less: set against (iii)	(10,000)
Loss c/f	Nil

The annual exempt amount is not available to reduce either the UK or overseas gains as Sergio has claimed to use the remittance basis.

However, Sergio does not have to pay the remittance basis charge as he has not been UK resident for at least seven out of the last nine years.

Solution to Example 8

The valuation of the shares in A plc for CGT purposes will be the lower of:

(a) $100 + 1/4 (110 - 100) = 102.5$, and

(b) $\dfrac{110 + 99}{2} = 104.5$

The market value for CGT will therefore be 102.5p (ie £1.025).

Solution to Example 9

For 2009/10 or a later year until the liquidation is complete. Although Rhona discovers the information in 2010/11 and usually a negligible value claim can be backdated two years, the shares were not of negligible value in 2008/09. So 2009/10 is the earliest year for the claim.

Solution to Example 10

The transfer from Jacob to Leah is automatically at no gain no loss.

	£
The base cost for Leah is:	
Original cost to Jacob	10,000

Note. The market value of the painting at transfer is irrelevant.

When Leah sells the painting, a gain will arise:

	£
Proceeds	75,000
Cost (as above)	(10,000)
Chargeable gain	65,000

Solution to Example 11

	£
Disposal proceeds	20,000
Less: incidental costs of sale	(2,000)
Net proceeds	18,000
Less: cost (W)	(8,182)
Chargeable gain	9,818

Working

The cost of the single chair being sold is: $\dfrac{A}{A+B} \times \text{cost}$

$$\frac{20,000}{20,000+46,000} \times £27,000 = \underline{£8,182}$$

Solution to Example 12

		£
(a)	*No part disposal:* adjustment to cost instead	
	Original cost	45,000
	Proceeds from part disposal (small as < 20% × £80,000 and < £20,000)	(10,000)
	Allowable cost c/f	35,000
(b)	*Subsequent disposal*	£
	Proceeds	100,000
	Less: allowable cost (above)	(35,000)
	Chargeable gain	65,000

Solution to Example 13

Summary

		Pre-23.6.10	Post-22.6.10
		£	£
Chargeable gains:	Warehouse (W1)	53,000	
	Cottage (W2)		120,568
Less: loss b/f			(35,000)
Net gains		59,563	85,568
Less: annual exempt amount			(10,100)
Taxable gain		59,563	75,468
CGT @ 18%/ 28% (no BR band left)		10,721	21,131
Total CGT		31,852	

Workings

		£
(1)	*Warehouse – pre-23.6.10*	
	Proceeds (net) £(70,000 – 7,000)	63,000
	Cost	(10,000)
	Chargeable gain	53,000

(2) *Cottage – post-22.6.10*   £
     Proceeds   258,200
     Less selling costs   (1,200)
     Net proceeds   257,000

     Cost: $\dfrac{258,200}{258,200+222,500} \times £254,000$ (136,432)

     Chargeable gain   120,568

Now try the following questions

Short Form Questions:

11.1 – 11.10 inclusive

Long Form Questions:

11.1	Dorrit
11.2	Harbottle

- understand the need for and apply the matching rules

- calculate the share pool holding

- calculate the gain where a reorganisation of share capital takes place

- identify gilts and qualifying corporate bonds (QCBs)

- calculate the gain where a reorganisation involves QCBs

References: TCGA 1992 unless otherwise stated

Shares and securities

1 The need for special rules

Shares present special problems when computing gains or losses on their disposal. Suppose that a taxpayer buys some quoted shares in X plc on the following dates:

		Cost £
5 May 1983	100 shares	150
17 January 1985	100 shares	375
2 May 1998	100 shares	1,000

On 15 June 2010, he sells 220 of his shares for £3,300. To determine his chargeable gain, we need to be able to work out which shares out of his three original holdings were actually sold. Since one share is identical to any other, it is not possible to work this out by reference to factual evidence.

As a result, it has been necessary to devise 'matching rules'. These allow us to **identify which shares have been sold and so work out what the allowable cost (and the gain) on disposal should be**. These rules are considered in detail below.

2 Share matching rules

For individuals, the matching of shares sold is in the following order:

(a)   Shares acquired on the **same day** (average cost)
(b)   Shares acquired in the **following thirty days** on a FIFO (first in, first out) basis
(c)   Shares from the share pool (average cost) which contains all shares acquired prior to the disposal date.

Example 1

George bought the following shares in Red plc:

Date	No.	Cost £
1.5.06	9,000	18,000
20.2.11	2,000	5,000
12.3.11	5,000	12,000

He sold 10,000 shares on 20 February 2011 for £30,000.

Show George's gain on sale.

3 The share pool [s.104]

3.1 The composition of the share pool

The share pool contains all shares of the *same* class in the *same* company that were acquired before the disposal date.

The share pool is also referred to as the 's.104 pool' or 's.104 holding', indicating where in TCGA1992 the relevant legislation can be found.

3.2 The calculation of the share pool value

In order to compute the value of the share pool, **two columns are required showing**:

(a)   The **number of shares**
(b)   The aggregated **cost** of the shares.

Example 2

Oliver bought 1,000 shares in Judith plc for £2,750 in August 1982, another 1,000 for £3,250 in December 1984 and 2,000 more shares in July 1986 at a cost of £4,000.

On 9 July 2010 Oliver disposed of 3,000 shares for £18,000.

Compute the chargeable gain on disposal.

4 Reorganisations

4.1 Introduction

There are several circumstances where a company will reorganise its share capital including:

(a)   Bonus issues (or scrip issues): quoted and unquoted shares
(b)   Rights issues: quoted and unquoted shares
(c)   Capital distributions: quoted and unquoted shares
(d)   Reorganisations of quoted shares
(e)   Takeovers: quoted and unquoted shares

The effects of such transactions on an individual is that his existing, original holding is in some way altered. The problem so far as CGT is concerned is usually how to apportion the original base cost between the original shareholding and whatever the shareholding is after the reorganisation.

4.2 Bonus issues

Bonus shares are free shares, issued at no cost, to existing shareholders. When a company (quoted or unquoted) issues bonus shares, the **size of the shareholder's original holding is increased but there is no need to adjust the original cost**.

The bonus issue shares are treated as having been acquired at the date of each original acquisition of the underlying shares. The normal matching rules then apply.

Example 3

Show how the disposal of the ordinary shares of X plc would be matched assuming the following transactions had taken place:

6.4.83   Purchase of 800 shares
6.4.88   Purchase of 600 shares
6.5.99   Purchase of 1,000 shares
1.7.10   Bonus issue of 1 for 4
6.7.10   Sale of 2,200 shares.
15.7.10   Purchase of 200 shares

4.3 Rights issues

4.3.1 Effect of a rights issue

The difference between a bonus issue and a rights issue is that in a **rights issue the new shares are paid for so we must adjust the original cost**.

Example 4

Julia had the following transactions in the shares of T Ltd:

July 1983	purchased 1,500 for	£3,750
July 1988	purchased 1,000 for	£3,000
May 1999	purchased 2,000 for	£8,000
June 2000	takes up 1 for 4 rights issue at £4.20 per share	
October 2010	sells 5,625 for	£50,400

Compute the chargeable gain or allowable loss arising.

4.3.2 Sale of rights nil paid

Where the shareholder does not take up his rights to buy new shares but instead sells that right to a third party, the proceeds received from the third party are treated as a capital distribution (see below) and the **proceeds are dealt with under the part disposal rules** (see the previous Chapter) where A = the proceeds received and B = the MV of the existing shareholding.

However, if the proceeds are 'small' (ie less than the higher of £3,000 or 5% of the value of the shares (A+B) at the time of the rights issue), there is no part disposal and instead the 'small' proceeds can be deducted from the cost.

Alternatively, if the proceeds from the sale of the rights are greater than the full original cost of the shares, an election can be made to use the full cost of the shares in calculating the gain. The base cost carried forward will then be nil.

4.4 Capital distributions

For CGT purposes, a capital distribution (such as a payment received on a liquidation) is a repayment of share capital. The way in which the distribution is dealt with depends on the size of the distribution.

The normal rule is that the **distribution will be treated as a part disposal of the asset** where A = the capital distribution received and B = the MV of the shareholding after the distribution.

If, however, the **distribution is 'small', defined as less than the higher of £3,000 or 5% of the value of the shares (A+B)**, there is no part disposal and instead the **'small' distribution proceeds can be deducted from the cost**.

Example 5

Barr holds 1,000 shares in Woodleigh plc for which he paid £10,000 in October 1986. The company is now in liquidation and in July 2010 the liquidator made a distribution of £4 per share.

Show how this will be treated if the market value of the shares after the distribution is either:

(a)   £61,000, or
(b)   £80,000 and in December 2010 Barr received a final distribution of £90,000.

Where the proceeds from a distribution are greater than the full original cost of the shares, the taxpayer may elect to have the **full cost** set against the part disposal proceeds. Therefore on a later disposal of the shares, allowable cost will be nil.

4.5 Reorganisation of shares

A reorganisation takes place where new shares, or a mixture of new shares and securities (debentures), are issued in exchange for the original shareholding. **A reorganisation does not in itself amount to a disposal of the original shareholding. Instead the new holding is regarded simply as having been acquired on the same date and for the same consideration as the old**. The problem is how to apportion the original cost between the different types of capital issued on reorganisation.

If the new shares and/or securities are *quoted*, then the original cost is apportioned by reference to the market values of the new types of capital on the first day of quotation after the reorganisation.

Example 6

Dan owns ordinary shares in Sullivan plc, purchased as follows:

| 1983 | 2,000 | shares costing | £1,750 |
| 1985 | 3,000 | shares costing | £13,250 |

In August 2010 there was a reorganisation whereby each ordinary Sullivan plc share was exchanged for 2 'A' ordinary shares (quoted at £2 each) and 1 preference share (quoted at £1 each).

Show how the original costs will be apportioned.

Where the new holding comprises *unquoted* shares or securities, the original cost is again apportioned on the basis of the market value of those new shares or securities. However in this case it is the market value *at the date of a subsequent disposal* which is used. Therefore if the shares are sold a few at a time, a separate calculation is needed for every subsequent disposal.

Example 7

An unquoted company reorganises its share capital in August 1988, so that for every 10 ordinary shares, a shareholder receives:

| 6 | 'A' ordinary shares |
| 14 | 5% preference shares |

Samuel originally owned 10,000 ordinary shares in the company which he acquired in 1984 for £16,000. In September 2010 he sells 7,000 of his preference shares, at which time the market value of the preference shares is £1.25 each and of the 'A' ordinary shares, £3.50 each.

Compute the allowable cost to set against proceeds from the September 2010 disposal.

4.6 Takeovers

When a company is taken over and the shareholders of the old company receive shares in the new company in exchange for their old shares this is known as a **'paper for paper' takeover, and there is usually no CGT liability**. For both quoted and unquoted shares **the new holding is deemed to have been acquired on the same date and at the same cost as the *original* holding**.

If part of the takeover consideration is in cash, then a liability will arise on the proportion of the gain that the cash element bears to the overall consideration and the normal part disposal rules will apply, where A = the cash received and B = the MV of the shares received.

If the cash received is 'small', ie not more than the higher of £3,000 and 5% of the total value on the takeover (A+B), then the small distribution rules apply and the cash received will be deducted from cost for the purpose of further disposals.

These takeover rules apply where the company issuing the new shares (the acquiring company) takes over more than 25% of the ordinary share capital of the old company (the target company) or where the acquiring company makes a general offer to shareholders in the target company which would, if accepted, give the acquiring company control of the target company.

Exam focus point

Examiner's report – Personal Taxation

May 2007 – Part II LFQ 3

This question caused the biggest problems. The fact that cash received on a takeover would cause a gain was not appreciated by many candidates.

TQT
Tax Qualification Training

Example 8

Le Bon holds 10,000 £1 shares bought originally for £2 each in Duran plc, a quoted company. In May 2010 the board of Duran plc agrees to a takeover bid by Spandau plc under which shareholders in Duran plc are to receive 3 Spandau plc shares plus £1.50 cash for every 4 shares held in Duran plc. Immediately following the takeover, the shares in Spandau plc are quoted at £5 each.

Show Le Bon's chargeable gain.

Note that 'paper for paper' transactions are only treated as not giving rise to any immediate CGT liability if the transactions are entered into for *bona fide* commercial reasons and not for tax avoidance motives.

5 Reorganisations involving gilts and qualifying corporate bonds

5.1 Definition and treatment

The disposal of gilts or qualifying corporate bonds (QCBs) does not usually give rise to a chargeable gain or an allowable loss.

Gilts include Treasury Loans, Treasury Stock, Exchequer Loans, Exchequer Stock and War Loan.

A QCB is a security (ie debenture, or loan note/stock) that:

(a)   Represents a '**normal commercial loan**'. This excludes any bonds which are convertible into shares, or which carry the right to excessive interest or interest which depends on the results of the issuer's business;

(b)   Is **expressed in sterling** and for which no provision is made for conversion into or redemption in another currency.

Exam focus point

Assume that loan notes (ie loan stock/ debentures) qualify as QCBs in your exam unless told otherwise.

5.2 Tax treatment on reorganisations involving QCBs

Special rules apply when a reorganisation or takeover involves QCBs issued in exchange for shares.

When QCBs are issued, the chargeable gain which would have arisen if the shares had been sold for cash at their market value at the time of the reorganisation must be calculated. This gain is then 'frozen' (ie not charged) **until the QCB is redeemed, sold or given away**.

If the disposal is a no gain/no loss disposal to a spouse/civil partner, the gain does not become chargeable until a disposal outside the marriage/partnership.

If the reorganisation is followed by the owner's death while he still owns the QCBs, the gain never becomes chargeable.

Example 9

Mr Holland bought 10,000 shares (a 25% shareholding) in Tilbrook plc in June 1988 for £18,000. On 19 May 2010, Tilbrook plc was taken-over by Difford Group plc and Mr Holland received:

*   20,000 ordinary shares in Difford Group plc
*   £10,000 8.5% QCB loan stock in Difford Group plc
*   £10,000 cash.

At 19 May 2010, the ordinary shares in Difford Group plc were quoted at £2.50 and the QCB Loan Stock at £1.50.

Show the gains arising as a result of the above.

Chapter roundup

- Special matching rules apply to identify which shares an individual is selling out of a holding acquired at different times.

- Disposals by an individual are matched with his acquisitions in the following order:
  - Same day acquisitions (average cost)
  - Acquisitions in the next thirty days (FIFO)
  - The share pool (also known as the s.104 pool) (average cost)

- Bonus and rights issues are broadly treated as acquired at the same date as the original holding to which they relate.

- Where shares are converted into other shares, no disposal takes place, and the new shares take over the original shares' acquisition date and cost.

- On a takeover, 'paper for paper' transactions (ie shares received in exchange for other shares) are not usually chargeable disposals.

- If both cash and shares (or securities) are received on a takeover, there is a part disposal in respect of the cash element.

- Disposals of gilts and QCBs are exempt from capital gains tax. Losses are not allowable.

- If a QCB is exchanged for shares on a reorganisation, the gain is calculated at the date of the reorganisation but is frozen and not charged until a later disposal.

1. Set out the order of matching for 5,000 shares sold by an individual on 7 November 2010, if acquisitions have been made as follows:

	No of shares
30 October 1983	3,000
4 April 1984	2,000
30 September 1987	2,000
10 July 1989	1,000
7 November 2010	1,000
30 November 2010	2,000

2. A capital distribution is treated as small if it amounts to less than the higher of £X and Y% of the value of the shares. What are X and Y?

3. Reggie owns 5,000 ordinary shares in Perrin plc (a quoted company) which cost him £7,000 in 1984. Perrin plc is the subject of a takeover bid by Marwell plc (also a quoted company) which offers, in exchange for each Perrin plc ordinary share:

   2 Marwell plc £1 ordinary shares – valued at 75p each
   £1 Marwell plc loan stock – valued at 80p

   Compute the base costs for any later disposal of the new shares and loan stock owned by Reggie.

Solutions to Quiz

1. (a) 1,000 shares acquired on disposal date (7.11.10)
   (b) 2,000 shares acquired in next 30 days (30.11.10)
   (c) 2,000 (out of 8,000) shares from the share pool

2. X = 3,000, Y = 5.

3. Market value of new holdings:

		£
Ordinary shares:	5,000 × 2 × 75p	7,500
Loan stock:	5,000 × 80p	4,000
		11,500

Base cost of Perrin plc shares (£7,000) is allocated in the ratio 7,500 : 4,000, ie

Base cost of Marwell plc shares:

$$£7,000 \times \frac{7,500}{11,500} = \underline{£4,565}$$

The loan stock is (presumably) a qualifying corporate bond (QCB) so, at the date of the takeover, the gain arising in respect of the QCBs received will be frozen:

		£
Proceeds (MV)		4,000
Less: cost	$£7,000 \times \dfrac{4,000}{11,500}$	(2,435)
Frozen gain		1,565

This will crystallise when the loan stock is redeemed or sold in the future. Any actual gain arising on that redemption/ disposal will be exempt (or any loss not allowable).

Solution to Example 1

Matching:

20.2.11	2,000 shares (same day)
12.3.11	5,000 shares (next 30 days)
1.5.06	3,000 shares (share pool)
	10,000

Note. We do not need to construct a share pool as there is only one acquisition before the date of disposal.

Gains

		Gains
	£	£
20.2.11 holding		
Proceeds $\dfrac{2,000}{10,000} \times £30,000$	6,000	
Less: cost	(5,000)	1,000
12.3.11 holding		
Proceeds $\dfrac{5,000}{10,000} \times £30,000$	15,000	
Less: cost	(12,000)	3,000
Share pool		
Proceeds $\dfrac{3,000}{10,000} \times £30,000$	9,000	
Less: cost $\dfrac{3,000}{9,000} \times £18,000$	(6,000)	3,000
Total gains		7,000

Solution to Example 2

Share pool:

	No of shares	Cost
		£
August 1982	1,000	2,750
December 1984	1,000	3,250
July 1986	2,000	4,000
	4,000	10,000
Disposal: July 2010	(3,000)	
Cost: $\dfrac{3,000}{4,000} \times 10,000$		(7,500)
Pool c/f	1,000	2,500

	£
Proceeds	18,000
Cost (above)	(7,500)
Chargeable gain	10,500

Solution to Example 3

Order of matching:

(i) *Next 30 days*

		No. of shares
Purchase	15.7.10	200
Disposal	6.7.10	(200)

(ii) *Share pool*

		No. of shares
Purchase	6.4.83	800
Purchase	6.4.88	600
Purchase	6.5.99	1,000
		2,400
Bonus issue (1 for 4)		600
		3,000
Disposal	6.7.10	(2,000)
Pool c/f		1,000

Note. The bonus issue is not treated as a separate acquisition, but is matched with previous acquisitions.

Solution to Example 4

Share pool:

	No. of shares		Cost £
Purchase July 1983	1,500		3,750
Purchase July 1988	1,000		3,000
Purchase May 1999	2,000		8,000
	4,500		14,750
Rights issue (1 for 4)	1,125	× £4.20	4,725
	5,625		19,475
Disposal October 2010	(5,625)		(19,475)
	–		–

Calculate gain:

	£
Proceeds	50,400
Cost	(19,475)
Chargeable gain	30,925

Solution to Example 5

(a) The distribution of £4,000 is not small (ie it is > 5% × £65,000 (£61,000 + £4,000) = £3,250) so there is a part disposal. A = proceeds received. B = market value of the shares after the distribution

	£
Disposal proceeds	4,000
Less: cost £10,000 × $\dfrac{4,000}{61,000 + 4,000}$	(615)
Chargeable gain	3,385

(b) The first distribution is less than 5% of the value of the shares (£84,000 (£80,000 + £4,000) × 5% = £4,200). The small distribution reduces the cost used when he receives the final distribution:

	£	£
Disposal proceeds		90,000
Less: cost	10,000	
Less: small distribution	(4,000)	(6,000)
Chargeable gain		84,000

Solution to Example 6

The value of the new holding is:

	£
10,000 'A' ordinary shares at £2	20,000
5,000 preference shares at £1	5,000
	25,000

The original costs will be apportioned 20,000 : 5,000 as follows:

Share pool:

	No of shares	Cost £
Purchase 1983	2,000	1,750
Purchase 1985	3,000	13,250
	5,000	15,000

Apportioned cost:

10,000 new 'A' ordinary shares: $\dfrac{20,000}{25,000} \times £15,000 = £12,000$

5,000 new preference shares: $\dfrac{5,000}{25,000} \times £15,000 = £3,000$

Solution to Example 7

Original cost: 10,000 ordinary shares = £16,000

Market values of new holdings in September 2010:

6,000 'A' ordinary shares @ £3.50 each =	£21,000
14,000 5% preference shares @ £1.25 each =	£17,500
	£38,500

Allowable cost of shares sold:

$\dfrac{7,000}{14,000} \times \dfrac{17,500}{38,500} \times £16,000 = £3,636$

Solution to Example 8

Total value of the takeover package due to Le Bon on the takeover:

		£
Shares	3/4 × 10,000 (= 7,500) × £5	37,500
Cash	1/4 × 10,000 × £1.50	3,750
		41,250

The share for share element of the takeover does not give rise to a CGT event. The new shares in Spandau plc simply take on the acquisition date and original cost of the old shares in Duran plc.

Since the cash (£3,750) exceeds the higher of £3,000 and £2,063 (5% × £41,250), ie £3,000, it cannot be deducted from the acquisition cost. There is therefore a part disposal.

	£
Disposal proceeds (cash received)	3,750

Less: apportioned cost:

$$\frac{\text{Cash received}}{\text{Cash received} + \text{value of shares received}} \times \text{original cost}$$

$\dfrac{3,750}{3,750 + 37,500} \times 10,000 \times £2$	(1,818)
Chargeable gain	1,932

Note. The base cost of the shares is £18,182 (£20,000 − £1,818)

Solution to Example 9

Value received on takeover:

	£
Ordinary shares (20,000 × £2.50)	50,000
QCB Loan Stock (£10,000 × £1.50)	15,000
Cash	10,000
Total	75,000

TQT
Tax Qualification Training

Original cost of Tilbrook plc shares allocated as follows:

	£
Ordinary shares in Difford Group:	
$\dfrac{50,000}{75,000} \times £18,000$	12,000
QCB Loan Stock in Difford Group	
$\dfrac{15,000}{75,000} \times £18,000$	3,600
Cash	
$\dfrac{10,000}{75,000} \times £18,000$	2,400
Total	18,000

Gain on receipt of cash:

	£
Proceeds	10,000
Less: cost (above)	(2,400)
Chargeable gain	7,600

Gain on receipt of QCB:

	£
Proceeds (MV of QCB)	15,000
Less: cost (above)	(3,600)
Frozen gain	11,400

This gain is frozen until the loan stock is disposed of.

New ordinary shares:

This is a 'share for share' disposal so no gain arises. The new shares in Difford Group plc are treated as having been acquired in June 1988 for £12,000.

Now try the following questions

Short Form Questions:

12.1– 12.3 inclusive

Long Form Questions:

12.1	Julie Green (Pilot Paper)
12.2	Mr Jones
12.3	Richard Price
12.4	Eric James

TQT
Tax Qualification Training

The purpose of this chapter is to help you to:

- define the terms 'chattel' and 'wasting asset'
- calculate the gain or loss on the disposal of chattels
- understand the taxation of wasting assets that are not chattels
- understand and apply the rules for the taxation of leases

References: TCGA 1992 unless otherwise stated

Chattels and wasting assets

1 Chattels

1.1 Definition

A *chattel* is an item of tangible movable property (it can be moved, seen and touched). Chattels include antiques, stamp collections and works of art.

'Wasting' chattels are generally exempt from CGT. A *wasting* asset is one with an estimated life of 50 years or less, for example a racehorse.

All items of plant and machinery are regarded as having an estimated life of 50 years or less, so are wasting chattels and are exempt from CGT (although see below for assets used in a business).

Such wasting chattels include:

(a) Antique clocks and watches [CCH IR Int 86, Tolleys RI 88]
(b) Taxi cabs
(c) Guns
(d) Racehorses.

1.2 Gains

If a chattel is not a wasting asset, any gain arising will still be exempt from CGT if the gross proceeds and cost are both £6,000 or less.

If sale proceeds exceed £6,000, but the cost is less than £6,000, the gain is limited to:

$5/3 \times$ (gross proceeds − £6,000).

Example 1

Adam purchased a Chippendale chair on 1 June 1985 for £800. On 10 October 2010 he sold the chair at auction for £6,480 net of the auctioneer's 10% commission. Show the chargeable gain arising.

Exam focus point

Examiner's report – Personal Taxation (old syllabus)

May 2002 – Question 2

...The gain on the sale of the vase was calculated correctly in many cases but there were a few who muddled the chattel relief calculation. The vintage car was treated correctly in most cases, but there were a few who appeared to consider that because the car was 'vintage' it became chargeable. ...

1.3 Capital losses

Where a chattel is sold for less than £6,000, but cost more than £6,000, any allowable loss is restricted to that which would arise if it were sold for gross proceeds of £6,000.

Example 2

Eve purchased a manuscript on 1 July 1982 for £8,000 which she sold in October 2010 at auction for £2,800. Costs of disposal were £280. Compute the gain or loss arising.

A loss cannot be turned into a gain under this provision. If a real loss arises, but substituting £6,000 for the sale proceeds produces a theoretical gain, then there is no allowable loss or chargeable gain.

Exam focus point

The CGT treatment of non-wasting chattels may be examined in the short form or part of long form questions. The tricky bit is spotting that the asset in question is a non-wasting chattel. Look out for assets with relatively low values.

1.4 Plant and machinery

There are special rules for plant and machinery qualifying for capital allowances (CAs). They are strictly wasting chattels but they are *not* exempt from CGT. Instead the CGT treatment is as follows:

Proceeds < Cost	No allowable loss for CGT (relief already given by CAs).
Proceeds ≤ £6,000, Cost ≤ £6,000	Exempt.
Proceeds > £6,000, Cost < £6,000	Chargeable (regardless of expected useful life). Any CAs given will have been clawed back as a 'balancing charge'. Apply the non wasting chattels' restriction to the gain if appropriate.

Example 3

Suppose the asset sold by Adam in Example 1 was plant and machinery. How much is the chargeable gain?

Exam focus point

Examiner's report – Personal Taxation

November 2009 – Part I SFQ 4

Less than a handful [of candidates] knew that the antique clock is categorised as machinery and is therefore a wasting chattel. A significant minority thought that claiming capital allowances on the machinery exempted it from CGT, believing that any tax charge would be dealt with through the capital allowances calculation.

November 2009 – Part II LFQ 2

…many candidates failed to apply the chattels rules to the calculations.

2 Wasting assets (other than leases)

Special rules apply to wasting assets that are not chattels. An example of an 'intangible' wasting asset is a copyright.

The allowable expenditure in respect of a wasting asset is deemed to waste away to nothing over its predictable life on a straight line basis.

Example 4

Sarah acquires a copyright for £20,000 for use in her trade on 10 May 2001 when it has 15 years to run. On 9 August 2010 she sells the copyright for £17,500. What is her chargeable gain?

3 Leases

3.1 Introduction

A lease is the right to occupy land for a fixed period of time. **For CGT purposes a distinction is made between a long lease which has more than 50 years to run and a short lease which has 50 years or less to run.**

There are five different situations to consider:

(a) Assignment (ie sale) of a long lease
(b) Assignment of a short lease
(c) Granting (ie sub-letting) of a long lease out of a freehold or out of a long head lease

Tax Qualification Training

(d)   Granting a short lease out of a freehold or out of a long head lease

(e)   Granting a short lease out of a short head lease.

The duration of the lease is usually determined by the period specified in the lease.

3.2 Assignment of a long lease

This is the simplest case, since the assignment (sale) of a long lease is the same as a **disposal of the whole asset**. Any gain on disposal will be chargeable to CGT (subject to any private residence exemption – see later in this Text). **The gain is computed in the same way as for any other asset.**

3.3 Assignment of a short lease

A lease which has 50 years or less to run at the date of disposal is a wasting asset. As we saw above, when calculating the gain on the disposal of a wasting asset only a **certain proportion of the original cost is deductible** as the rest of it will have wasted away. In the case of short leases the proportion is determined by a table of percentages contained in Schedule 8 TCGA 1992. [para 1 Sch 8]

The allowable proportion is given by X/Y × original cost where X is the percentage relating to the number of years left for the lease to run at the date of the assignment, and Y is the percentage relating to the number of years the lease had to run when first acquired by the disposer.

The table only provides percentages for exact numbers of years. Where the duration is not an exact number of years the relevant percentage is found by **adding** one twelfth of the difference between the two years on either side of the actual duration for each extra month. Odd days of 14 or more will count as a month. These rules are also given in Schedule 8.

The percentages are reproduced in the Association's Tax Tables available to you in the examination.

Example 5

Mr A acquired a 20 year lease on 1 August 2001 for £15,000. He assigned it on 1 August 2010 for £19,000.

You are required to compute the chargeable gain.

3.4 Grant of a long lease

If the taxpayer grants a lease out of his freehold or long lease, this is treated as a part disposal. Where the lease is granted for 50 years or more, the gain on the part disposal is calculated using the usual part disposal rules. **The gain will be calculated by deducting the following proportion of the original cost from the proceeds:**

$$\text{Original cost} \times \frac{A}{A+B}$$

where **A** is the premium paid for the lease, and **B** is the value of the remainder, in this case the value of the right to get the property back on the expiry of the lease, known as the *reversionary interest*. This will be given to you in the examination.

Example 6

Mr B acquired a freehold property for £18,000 on 1 January 1983. On 1 July 2010 he granted a 60 year lease for a premium of £20,000. At the time of the grant the value of the reversion was £25,000.

You are required to compute any chargeable gain arising.

3.5 Grant of a short lease out of a freehold or long lease

If a short lease is granted out of a freehold or long head-lease, part of the premium is assessable as property income (see earlier in this Text) **and must be excluded from the CGT computation**. The proceeds figure used in the CGT computation is the 'capital element' of the premium (ie the total premium less the amount assessable as property income). We must also adjust the allowable cost and we do this by using the following formula:

$$\text{Original cost} \times \frac{a}{A + B}$$

where **a** is the capital element of the premium, **A** is the total premium, and **B** is the value of the reversionary interest.

Example 7

Assume the facts as in the previous example, except that the lease is for 30 years rather than 60.

3.6 Grant of a short lease out of a short lease

If a short lease is granted out of a short head lease, part of the premium will be assessable as property income (see earlier in this Text) which must be excluded from the CGT computation.

We do this by initially **using the full amount of the premium as the consideration for CGT purposes. The cost is then adjusted using the lease percentage table in Schedule 8. The allowable proportion is given by** $\frac{X - Y}{Z}$ **× original cost** where:

- **X** is the percentage relating to the number of years left for the lease to run at the date of grant of the sublease
- **Y** is the percentage relating to the number of years left to run at the date when the sublease expires, and
- **Z** is the percentage relating to the number of years the lease had to run when first acquired.

After calculating the gain, **deduct the amount chargeable as property income to arrive at the chargeable gain**. This deduction cannot turn a chargeable gain into an allowable loss, nor can it increase the amount of an allowable loss.

Example 8

On 1 June 2005, Amy paid a premium of £30,000 to acquire a 30 year lease on a property. On 1 June 2010, she granted a 10 year sub-lease over the whole property in return for a premium of £40,000. The rent payable under the sub-lease was the same as the rent payable under the original lease.

Calculate Amy's chargeable gain.

Chapter roundup

- Chattels are 'tangible moveable property' ie assets which can be moved, seen and touched.

- 'Wasting chattels', ie those with a predictable life of 50 years or less, are exempt from CGT unless they qualify for capital allowances (when a gain is chargeable, but a loss is not allowable).

- The following summarises the rules relating to disposals of non wasting chattels.

Proceeds	Cost	CGT implications
≤ £6,000	≤ £6,000	Exempt
> £6,000	> £6,000	Gain calculated in normal way
> £6,000	< £6,000	Gain calculated in normal way but restricted to $\frac{5}{3} \times$ (gross proceeds – £6,000)
< £6,000	> £6,000	Loss is restricted by deeming gross proceeds to be £6,000

- The cost of a wasting intangible asset (eg a copyright) wastes away over time, so only the cost remaining at the date of disposal can be deducted in the CGT computation.

- When considering the tax consequences of transactions involving leases, it is essential to ascertain whether the transaction involves the assignment (sale) of an existing lease, or the sub-letting (grant) of a lease out of a freehold or a superior lease.

- An assignment involves transferring the lease from one person to another, with the transferor entirely disposing of his interest.

- The grant of a sub-lease is treated as a part disposal of the lease. Where a lease is granted for 50 years or less part of the premium received will be subject to a charge as property income, with the balance chargeable to CGT.

- The following table summarises the different ways in which leases are treated for CGT purposes.

	Type of lease	Treatment
Assignment	Lease > 50 years	Disposal of whole asset – normal CGT computation
	Lease ≤ 50 years	Gain chargeable according to percentage table
Granting of leases	Sub-lease > 50 years	Normal part disposal rules
	Sub-lease ≤ 50 years, out of freehold or headlease > 50 years	Part disposal rules with proceeds reduced by amount charged as property income. Capital element of premium used in top line of part disposal formula.
	Sub-lease ≤ 50 years, out of head lease ≤ 50 years	Full premium used as proceeds. Adjust cost using lease percentage table. Deduct property income assessment.

Quiz

1. What is a wasting asset?

2. Robert sells his racing greyhound 'Spot' for £15,000, having bought him as a pup for £1,000 four years ago. What is the chargeable gain/allowable loss?

3. Micky sells an antique vase in August 2010 for £8,000, having acquired it in November 1997 for £5,800.

   Compute the chargeable gain.

4. Petra sells a diamond ring, which she inherited from her aunt, for £5,000. Probate value of the ring was £7,600. What is the allowable loss on sale?

5. State how your answer to Question 4 above would differ if the probate value of the ring had been £4,600.

6. Assignment of a lease with 40 years to run is the disposal of a wasting asset. True/False?

7. Danny assigns a lease on 30 November 2010 which he acquired on 31 May 2004, at which time it had exactly 30 years to run. If Danny paid £55,000 for the lease in May 2004, compute the allowable cost for the disposal on 30 November 2010.

8. Edward grants a 60 year sub-lease out of his 999 year head lease for a premium of £80,000. Edward's head lease was acquired by him two years ago at a cost of £105,000. If the value of the reversionary interest is agreed to be £40,000, how much of Edward's original cost is allowable against the premium received on the grant of the sub-lease?

9. Show how your answer to Question 8 above would differ, if the sub-lease had been for a duration of only 40 years instead of 60.

Solutions to Quiz

1. A wasting asset is one with an estimated life of not more than 50 years.

2. Nil – a greyhound is a wasting chattel so is exempt from CGT.

3.

	£
Proceeds	8,000
Less: cost	(5,800)
	2,200

The chargeable gain cannot exceed:

5/3 (£8,000 – 6,000) = £3,333

Chargeable gain (lower gain) = £2,200

4.

	£
Deemed proceeds	6,000
Less: cost (= probate value)	(7,600)
Loss	(1,600)

5. As proceeds and original cost (ie, probate value in this instance) are less than £6,000, the gain is exempt. There is therefore neither a gain nor a loss.

6. True

7. This is the sale of a short lease so we need to adjust the cost using the percentages from the table. The allowable cost is: £55,000 × $\dfrac{X}{Y}$

X: % for 23 years 6 months = 78.055 + ($^6/_{12}$ (79.622 – 78.055)) = 78.839

Y: % for 30 years = 87.330

Therefore, allowable cost = £55,000 × $\dfrac{78.839}{87.330}$ = £49,652

8. This is the grant of a long lease from a longer head lease so there is a part disposal:

Allowable cost = original cost × $\dfrac{A}{A+B}$

ie £105,000 × $\dfrac{80,000}{80,000+40,000}$ = £70,000

9. This would be the grant of a short lease from a long head lease so there we need to use a modified part disposal calculation:

Allowable cost = original cost × $\dfrac{a}{A+B}$

Where a = capital element of the premium (ie not charged as property income)

	£
Full premium	80,000
Less: amount taxed as property income (£80,000 × $\dfrac{50-39}{50}$)	(17,600)
Capital element	62,400

Allowable cost: £105,000 × $\dfrac{62,400}{80,000+40,000}$ = £54,600

Solutions to chapter examples

Solution to Example 1

	£
Gross proceeds (£6,480 × $\frac{100}{90}$)	7,200
Less: incidental costs of sale (10%)	(720)
Net proceeds	6,480
Less: cost	(800)
	5,680

Restricted to a maximum of 5/3 × £(7,200 − 6,000) = <u>£2,000</u>

Solution to Example 2

Eve has a loss that must be calculated using deemed proceeds of £6,000.

	£
Deemed disposal proceeds	6,000
Less: incidental costs of disposal	(280)
	5,720
Less: cost	(8,000)
Allowable loss	(2,280)

Solution to Example 3

Chargeable gain	<u>£2,000</u>

Exactly the same calculation as Example 1

Solution to Example 4

	£
Disposal proceeds	17,500
Less: cost	
£20,000 × $\frac{5\frac{3}{4}}{15}$	(7,667)
Chargeable gain	9,833

Note. The sale proceeds are for the time remaining in respect of the copyright (ie 5.75 years) so we match this to the cost of what is left (ie 5.75 years worth of 15 years' cost). The remainder of the cost has wasted away.

Solution to Example 5

	£
Disposal proceeds	19,000
Less: cost	
£15,000 × $\frac{11 \text{ years}}{20 \text{ years}}$ ie $\frac{50.038}{72.770}$	(10,314)
Chargeable gain	8,686

50.038 = percentage for 11 years (time left on lease at disposal on 1.8.10)

72.770 = percentage for 20 years (time on lease when purchased on 1.8.01)

Solution to Example 6

	£
Disposal proceeds (full premium)	20,000
Cost:	
£18,000 × $\frac{20,000}{20,000 + 25,000}$	(8,000)
Chargeable gain	12,000

TQT
Tax Qualification Training

Solution to Example 7

	£
Premium (A)	20,000
Less: amount taxed as property income ($£20,000 \times \dfrac{50-29}{50}$)	(8,400)
Capital element of premium (a)	11,600
Less: cost:	
$£18,000 \times \dfrac{11,600\,^*}{20,000\,^* + 25,000}$	(4,640)
Chargeable gain	6,960

*Note. the numerator (top number) of the part disposal fraction is the *capital element* of the premium (a), whilst the denominator (bottom number) is the total premium (A).

Solution to Example 8

Amy's allowable expenditure on the grant of the sub-lease is:

$£30,000 \times \dfrac{81.100 - 61.617}{87.330}$ (see working) = £6,693

The amount of the premium chargeable as property income is:

	£
Premium (full)	40,000
Less: amount taxed as property income ($£40,000 \times \dfrac{50-9}{50}$)	(32,800)
Capital element of premium	7,200

Amy's gain is therefore:

	£
Premium	40,000
Less: allowable expenditure	(6,693)
Gain	33,307
Less: chargeable as property income	(32,800)
Chargeable gain	507

Working for percentages:

61.617 = 15 years	Time left on lease when 10 year sublease ends
81.100 = 25 years	Time left on lease when sublease granted 1 June 2010
87.330 = 30 years	Time on lease when purchased on 1 June 2005

Now try the following questions

Short Form Questions:

13.1 – 13.7 inclusive

Long Form Questions:

13.1	Doug
13.2	Mr Cole
13.3	CGT Leases

Principal private residence relief

The purpose of this chapter is to help you to:

- calculate the relief available on the disposal of an individual's home

- identify an individual's PPR where he owns more than one home

- calculate the further relief available where a residence is let as residential accommodation

- understand how business use of a property impacts on the availability of PPR relief

References: TCGA 1992 unless otherwise stated

1 General principles

1.1 Overview

A gain arising on the sale of an individual's only or main private residence (principal private residence) is exempt from CGT. Any loss is not allowable. The exemption applies to both leasehold and freehold property.

1.2 Relief for actual occupation

The basic rule is that the gain is wholly exempt where the owner has occupied the whole of the residence throughout his period of ownership. Where occupation has been for only part of the period, the exempt proportion of the gain is: [s.223]

$$\text{Total gain} \times \frac{\text{period of occupation}}{\text{total period of ownership}}$$

A further proportionate restriction is made where only part of the property has been occupied as his residence, eg where part is used exclusively for business purposes.

The last 36 months of ownership is exempt in all cases if at some time the residence has been the taxpayer's main residence. [s.223(1)]

There is no exemption for a property that is acquired wholly or partly for the purpose of making a gain on a subsequent disposal. However, it is difficult for HMRC to prove such an intention.

1.3 Deemed occupation

The period of occupation is also deemed to include certain periods of absence, provided the individual had no other exempt residence at that time and the **period of absence was at some time both preceded by and followed by a period of actual occupation**.

The periods of *deemed occupation* are: [s.223(3)]

(a)   **Any period** (or periods taken together) of absence, for any reason, **up to three years**. Where the period exceeds three years, three years out of the longer period are deemed to be a period of occupation;

(b)   **Any periods** during which the owner was **required by his employment to live abroad**;

(c)   **Any period** (or periods taken together) **not exceeding four years** where the owner was:

   (i)   **Self-employed and forced to work away from home** (UK and abroad)
   (ii)   **Employed and required to work elsewhere in the UK** (overseas employment is covered by (b) above.)

The above periods apply even if the residence is let while the owner is away.

Although deemed periods of occupation must usually be preceded and followed by a period of actual occupation, the **re-occupation requirement is waived by extra-statutory concession where the individual has been required to work abroad or elsewhere in the UK (paras (b) and (c) above) and is unable to return home** because the terms of his employment require him to work elsewhere.

Also by HMRC concession, a house is treated as occupied as the owner's main residence for a period of up to 12 months (or longer if there is a good reason) if he was prevented from living in the house because it was being built or altered or because necessary steps were being taken to dispose of their previous residence.

Exam focus point

Examiner's report – Personal Taxation

November 2009 – Part I SFQ 7

...the most frequently omitted point was reference to the fact that the first period of deemed occupation only qualifies because there is actual occupation both before and after. A significant minority overlooked the requirement for there to be actual occupation after the period working overseas to enable that period to qualify for deemed occupation.

Example 1

Arnold purchased a house in July 1982 for £50,000. He lived in the house until June 1984 and then moved to a rented apartment until June 1988. He then worked abroad for ten years before returning to the UK to live in the house again in July 1998. He stayed in the house for six months before moving out to live with friends until the house was sold on 23 December 2010 for £150,000.

Calculate any chargeable gain arising on disposal.

1.4 Disposal of a garden

The exemption covers a garden and grounds up to half a hectare (slightly over one acre), but it can exceed half a hectare if the house is sufficiently large to warrant it.

Where the main residence is sold along with only part of the garden, leaving the rest of the garden to be sold separately (for development purposes) at a later date, the PPR exemption will not be available on the later sale as the garden is no longer part of the individual's main residence. HMRC has indicated that this view will only be taken if the garden has development value. [Varty v Lynes (1976)]

2 More than one residence

2.1 Election for residence to be treated as main residence

Where a person has more than one residence, he may, by notice to HMRC, nominate which is his main residence. The notice must be given within two years of the second property being used as a residence. The nomination may be varied at a later date. The individual must actually reside in both residences, at least from time to time. Any period of ownership of a residence not nominated as the main residence will be a chargeable period. An election can have effect for any period beginning not more than two years prior to the date of the election.

If no election is made then HMRC can determine, based on all the facts, whether the property is or is not the taxpayer's PPR. The taxpayer may appeal to the Tax Tribunal.

2.2 Job related accommodation

A person lives in job related accommodation (see earlier in this Text) where:

(a)   It is necessary for the proper performance of his duties; or

(b)   It is provided for the better performance of his duties and it is one of the kinds of employment in which it is customary for employers to provide accommodation; or

(c)   There is a special threat to the employee's security and use of the accommodation is part of security arrangements.

An individual living in job related accommodation will be treated as occupying any second house that he owns and where he intends, in due course, to occupy the house as his only or main residence. It is not necessary to establish any form of actual residency in such cases. The benefit of this rule also applies to self employed persons living in 'job related' accommodation (eg tenants of public houses).

2.3 Husband and wife and civil partners

Where spouses (or civil partners) live together, only one residence can qualify as the main residence for PPR relief.

By extra-statutory concession, in a case where a marriage/partnership has broken down and one partner owning or having an interest in the matrimonial home has ceased to occupy the house, the departing partner will continue to be treated as resident for CGT purposes. This is provided that the other partner has continued to reside in the home and the departing partner has not elected that some other house should be treated as his or her main residence for this period. This concession only applies where one spouse/partner disposes of his interest to the other.

3 Letting relief

Gains may also be exempt where they relate to a period while the property is let, up to a certain limit. The two main circumstances in which letting relief will apply are: [s.223(4)]

(a)   When the owner is absent and lets the property during his absence, and

(b)   When the owner lets part of the property while still occupying the rest of it. In this case the owner will get full PPR relief on the part he has occupied and letting relief on the rest of the property.

In both cases **the letting must be for *residential* use** and the last 36 months of ownership of the property will qualify for full relief even if the whole or part of the property is let during that period.

Letting relief is restricted to the lowest of:

(a) **The gain relating to the letting period** (and not already covered by the deemed occupation provisions),

(b) **The gain that is already exempt under the PPR provisions**, and

(c) **£40,000**.

Letting relief cannot turn a gain into an allowable loss, nor increase an existing loss.

Where a lodger lives as a member of the owner's family, sharing their living accommodation and eating with them, no part of the accommodation is treated as having ceased to be occupied as the owner's main residence. The question of letting relief does not therefore arise and full PPR relief would be available on disposal.

Similarly where lodgers are taken in under the 'rent a room' scheme – which gives income tax exemption on £4,250 of gross rental income (see earlier in this Text) **– it will not lead to a restriction of PPR. Again letting relief will not be relevant.**

Exam focus point

PPR relief and letting relief are regularly examined in the long form questions of Personal Taxation either computationally or in a written question. Make sure you are familiar with the deemed occupation periods and letting relief. This is all in s.223 TCGA 1992.

Example 2

Miss Coe purchased a house in May 1982 for £90,000 and used it as her main residence. She sold it on 30 September 2010 for £384,000, having let half of it from 1 January 1984 to 30 September 1988. She then lived in the whole of the property until sale.

Calculate the chargeable gain arising.

---

4 Business use

Where part of a residence is used exclusively for business purposes the gain attributable to that part will always be taxable.

Example 3

Mr Woof purchased a property for £35,000 on 1 December 1982 and began operating a veterinary practice from that date in one third of the house. He sold the house on 1 December 2010 for £130,000. He continued to operate the veterinary practice from new premises which he rented.

Compute the chargeable gain, if any, arising on disposal.

- Gains arising on the disposal of a dwelling house are exempt from CGT if the house was the individual's only or main residence throughout the period of ownership.

- Where the house is not owner-occupied throughout the period of ownership only the proportion of the gain attributable to the period of owner-occupation is exempt.

- Certain 'periods of absence' are deemed to be periods of occupation. The last 36 months of ownership are always treated as a period of occupation.

- Although gardens of up to one half hectare (possibly more) are also covered by the private residence exemption, the disposal of part of a garden, following the disposal of the house, attracts no relief.

- Where an individual owns more than one residence he may, within two years of the second being used as a residence, nominate one as his main residence.

- A married couple (or civil partners) may have only one qualifying residence.

- Where the house or part of it is let as residential accommodation, letting relief may be available up to a maximum of £40,000.

- Where part of a house is *used exclusively* for business purposes, the gain attributable to the business use portion is not eligible for PPR relief.

Quiz

1. Provided the property has at some time been the owner's principal private residence, the last .... months of ownership is always an exempt period. How many months?

2. In what circumstances is the following requirement ignored: that in order for a period of absence to be treated as deemed occupation, the taxpayer must actually occupy the property at some time *after* the period of absence?

3. Where an individual sells one of two properties which he owns, both of which he has occupied from time to time as a residence, what is the CGT position, assuming he has failed to make any election?

4. Ruth sells a house which has been partly occupied by her as her principal private residence and partly let to students as residential accommodation.

   The facts are:

   - Gain before PPR relief: £155,000.
   - Occupied solely by Ruth as her PPR from 1 July 1988 (date of purchase) to 30 June 1989
   - Occupied from 1 July 1989 to 31 December 2010 (date of sale) 20% by Ruth, 80% by students.

   Compute:

   (a) The PPR exemption, and
   (b) The chargeable gain after all exemptions and reliefs.

5. Hannah has always used one room of her house exclusively as an office – HMRC has agreed that this amounts to 10% of the whole property. If the gain on the sale of the property is £124,000, compute the chargeable gain on the assumption that Hannah owned the property from 1 July 1987 to 30 November 2010.

1. 36.

2. By concession, where the taxpayer has been absent either because he was working abroad or because he was working elsewhere in the UK, and he is prevented from re-occupying the property because the terms of his employment require him to work elsewhere.

3. HMRC will determine, based on the facts, whether the property sold is or is not the taxpayer's principal private residence. The taxpayer has a right of appeal to the Tax Tribunal.

4. Gain before relief   £155,000

    (a)   PPR exemption:

		PPR	*Let period*
(i)	1.7.88 – 30.6.89: 100% exemption	12m	
(ii)	1.7.89 – 31.12.07: 20% exemption (222m)	44m	178m
(iii)	1.1.08 – 31.12.10: 100% exemption (last 36 months)	36m	
		92m	178m

    Total ownership = 270m

    PPR exemption:

	£
$\dfrac{92}{270} \times £155,000$	52,815

    (b)   Chargeable gain:

	£
Gain before relief	155,000
Less: PPR exemption	(52,815)
Gain attributable to letting period	102,185
Less: s.223 TCGA 1992 relief – *lowest* of:	
– £40,000	
– £52,815 (PPR relief)	
– £102,185 ($\dfrac{178}{270} \times £155,000$) (relates to let period)	(40,000)
Chargeable gain	62,185

5.

	£
Gain before relief	124,000
Less: PPR exemption	
£124,000 × 90%	(111,600)
Gain after PPR	12,400

Solution to Example 1

(a)   Exempt and chargeable periods

		Exempt months	Chargeable months
(i)	July 1982 – June 1984	24	–
(ii)	July 1984 – June 1988	36	12
(iii)	July 1988 – June 1998	120	–
(iv)	July 1998 – December 1998	6	–
(v)	January 1999 – December 2007	–	108
(vi)	January 2008 – December 2010	36	–
		222	120

(b)   *Explanations*

(i)   July 1982 – June 1984

A period of actual owner occupation.

(ii)   July 1984 – June 1988

Deemed occupation for up to '3 years of absence for any reason'. The period is both preceded and followed by actual owner occupation.

(iii)   July 1988 – June 1998

Deemed occupation as the owner is required by his employment to live abroad. The period is both preceded and followed by a period of actual owner occupation.

(iv)   July 1998 – December 1998

A period of actual owner occupation.

(v)   January 1999 – December 2007

Not occupied. Deemed occupation for up to '3 years of absence for any reason' has already been used.

(vi)   January 2008 – December 2010

Covered by the final 36 months exemption.

(c)   *Calculation of the chargeable gain*

	£
Disposal proceeds	150,000
Less: cost	(50,000)
Gain before PPR relief	100,000
Less: exempt under PPR provisions	
222/(222 + 120) × £100,000	(64,912)
Chargeable gain	35,088

In this example, had Albert gone straight to live with friends in July 1998 instead of having six months occupation he would have lost not only the extra six months, but also the periods from July 1984 to June 1998, as the property was not occupied again by the owner prior to sale so these two periods of absence would lose their 'deemed occupation' status.

Solution to Example 2

	£	£
Disposal proceeds		384,000
Less: cost		(90,000)
Gain before PPR relief		294,000
Less: PPR exemption		

$$£294,000 \times \frac{284 \text{ (W1)}}{341 \text{ (W2)}}$$ (244,856)

$$£294,000 \times \frac{57 \text{ (W3)}}{341 \text{ (W2)}} \div 2$$ (24,572)

	£	£
		(269,428)
Left in charge		24,572
Less: letting relief		
lowest of:		
(a) gain relating to letting period: £24,572		
(b) PPR relief given: £269,428		(24,572)
(c) £40,000		
Chargeable gain		NIL

Workings

	Months
(W1) Period not let and fully occupied as PPR: 1.5.82 – 31.12.83	20
1.10.88 – 30.9.10	264
	284

(W2) Period of ownership: 1.5.82 – 30.9.10 = 341 months

(W3) Period let: 1.1.84 – 30.9.88   = 57 months

Note. Miss Coe cannot claim exemption for part of the period of letting under the 3 year absence rule since during this time she has a main residence which qualifies for relief (ie the rest of the house).

Solution to Example 3

	£
Disposal proceeds	130,000
Less: cost	(35,000)
Gain before PPR relief	95,000
Less: PPR exemption £95,000 × $^2/_3$	(63,333)
Chargeable gain	31,667

PPR exemption is lost on one third owing to use of that part exclusively for business purposes. Note that the exemption is restricted for business use for the *whole* period of ownership, including the last 36 months.

Now try the following questions

Short Form Questions:

14.1 – 14.3 inclusive

Long Form Questions:

14.1	Owning two homes (Pilot paper)
14.2	Peter Stamp
14.3	Mr Richman

- understand and apply the gift relief rules in appropriate situations
- understand and apply the rules for EIS deferral relief
- understand the tax treatment when insurance money (ie compensation) is received when an asset is damaged or destroyed

References: TCGA 1992 unless otherwise stated

Other CGT reliefs

1 Introduction to CGT reliefs

In this section we consider CGT reliefs that are available to 'defer' gains arising on the disposal of certain assets.

We have already considered Principal Private Residence relief, which exempts or reduces the gain arising on the sale of a taxpayer's main residence. In this chapter we consider the circumstances in which a chargeable gain may be deferred. When a gain is deferred it is transferred, usually to another asset, until some later date.

In this chapter we consider gift relief, Enterprise Investment Scheme (EIS) deferral relief and the CGT position when compensation is received when an asset is damaged or destroyed.

In all cases the gain on disposal of the asset is calculated in the normal way and then the appropriate relief is applied to defer the gain.

2 Gift relief

2.1 General principle

If an individual makes a gift to another individual gift relief may be available. The transferor's gain, calculated using proceeds equal to market value, is reduced by the relief and the transferee acquires the asset at that market value less the transferor's deferred gain. [s.165]

A partial claim is not allowed, for example, to ensure sufficient gains remain to be covered by losses or the annual exempt amount.

The transferor and transferee, who must be resident or ordinarily resident in the UK, must make a joint claim for the relief within four years of the end of the tax year. So, for a gift in 2010/11 the claim must be made by 5 April 2015.

2.2 Assets attracting gift relief

The relief only applies if the gifted property is: [s.165 (2)]

(a)   An **asset used in a trade**, profession of vocation carried on by:

   (i)   The transferor, or

   (ii) The transferor's personal company (a company in which 5% or more of the voting rights are controlled by the individual), or

   (iii) A trading company owned by a holding company which is his personal company,

or

(b)   **Shares or securities of a trading company** (or the holding company of a trading group) where:

   (i)   The shares are **not quoted** on a recognised stock exchange, or

   (ii) The **company** (or holding company) **is the transferor's personal company** (ie transferor can exercise at least 5% of the voting rights).

      The fraction CBA/CA must be used to calculate the eligible gain – see below.

Gift relief is also available where *any* asset is gifted to a trust (other than to a disabled person's trust) as there is also an inheritance tax (IHT) charge. [s.260(2)]

Exam focus point

Trusts are outside the scope of the Personal Taxation syllabus and so are not covered further.

2.3 Gifts of shares

When an individual makes a gift of shares, we use the matching rules as normal (see earlier in this Text) to calculate the gain.

If they are shares in the individual's personal company (ie he can exercise at least 5% of the voting rights) only the gain relating to the proportion of the chargeable business assets of the company can qualify for gift relief.

It is necessary to apportion the gain in the ratio of total chargeable business assets (CBAs) to total chargeable assets (CAs) (ie the fraction $^{CBA}/_{CA}$) using the market value of the assets at the date of disposal of the shares (often given in the form of a balance sheet extract).

A CA is any asset chargeable to capital gains tax. Assets that are exempt from CGT (eg cash, stock, debtors, motor cars and items of plant and machinery with cost and value of less than £6,000) are ignored.

A CBA is a chargeable asset used in the trade or the business. Shares and other assets held as investments, such as rental property, cannot be CBAs.

The gain attributable to the value of chargeable non-business assets will not attract gift relief so this element always remains chargeable.

If the shares are in a holding company, the apportionment is made by reference to the chargeable assets of the whole trading group.

Example 1

On 6 August 2010 Henry gifts his 8% shareholding in a trading company to his brother resulting in a gain of £60,000. The market value of the shares was £150,000. The market value of the company's total chargeable assets at the time of the sale amounted to £40,000 of which the market value of total chargeable business assets was £30,000.

You are required to calculate the chargeable gain arising to Henry and the base cost of the shares for his brother, assuming all available reliefs are claimed.

Example 2

Mr McGregor owns 10% of the shares of an unquoted trading company. On 1 January 2011, the company's net assets were:

	£
Plant*	50,000
Factory	1,050,000
Investments	500,000
Net current assets	300,000
	1,900,000

* made up of items with a market value of more than £6,000 each.

Mr McGregor bought the shares in 1983 for £200,000 and gave them to his son on 1 January 2011 when their market value was £950,000.

You are required to calculate the chargeable gain.

Gift relief is **not available on gifts of shares to companies**.

Exam focus point

The CBA/CA rule only applies to gains on the disposal of personal company shares. The individual can claim to defer the whole gain if it is not his personal company.

Examiner's report – Personal Taxation

November 2009 – Part I SFQ 3

Most candidates were aware of the need to do a CBA/CA calculation, albeit many included motor cars and debtors as both CAs and CBAs. Most knew to apply the resulting restriction to the gain, although some applied it just to the cost in the gain calculation. Every single candidate who got the calculation correct also knew that a joint election was required.

2.4 Gifts of business assets with non-business use

If an individual makes a gift of a business asset, the amount of the gain that can be deferred is reduced if the asset has not been used in the transferor's trade (or that of his personal company) **throughout his period of ownership**. The reduction is pro rata on a time basis.

If the asset is a building, part of which was used for a non business purpose during the period of ownership, a 'just and reasonable' restriction will apply.

TQT
Tax Qualification Training

Example 3

Keith gives a factory to his son realising a chargeable gain of £50,000. He has owned the factory for 8 years and has used it in his trade for 5 years. For the other 3 years it was let as a warehouse.

You are required to calculate what part of the gain is eligible for gift relief and what part is immediately chargeable.

Remember, in the case of a gift of shares (see above), the deferred gain is restricted if the company owns non-business chargeable assets at the date of the gift.

2.5 Sales at an undervalue

If the disposal involves actual consideration which is less than the market value (ie a sale at an undervalue rather than an outright gift), then **the gain that can be held over (ie deferred) is the gain *less* the excess of the actual consideration over allowable costs.** This excess is immediately taxable.

Exam focus point

Gift relief is an extremely examinable topic both computationally and in written questions. Make sure you know which assets qualify for the relief (see s.165) and how much gain can be deferred in both the case of an outright gift and a sale at undervalue.

Example 4

On 1 August 2010 Angelo sold shares in his personal trading company valued at £200,000 to his son Michael for £50,000. Angelo had originally purchased the shares in July 1983 for £30,000. Michael sold the shares for £195,000 in October 2011. Angelo and Michael jointly elect for relief under s.165 TCGA 1992.

You are required to compute any chargeable gains arising assuming the rates for 2010/11 continue to apply for later years.

2.6 Relief before FA 1989

Gift relief used to be available for the transfer of *all* assets before 14 March 1989. So, paintings, quoted shares and non business property assets generally could qualify for gift relief.

It is important to know that gift relief applied generally before 14 March 1989 as the recipient of such a gift will still have to use a base cost reduced by the deferred gain when calculating a gain on a future disposal.

2.7 Anti-avoidance: the emigrating donee

Consider the situation where a gift relief claim is made but then the recipient emigrates. When they eventually sell the asset there will be no UK CGT, as they are not resident or ordinarily resident, so the deferred gain never becomes chargeable.

Anti-avoidance rules apply to ensure that this deferred gain will eventually crystallise so **where the recipient becomes not resident and not ordinarily resident in the UK, the deferred gain will be assessed on them immediately before they become not resident and not ordinarily resident.** This rule only applies **if the recipient leaves the UK within six tax years of the end of the year of the gift.**

Where the recipient disposes of the asset before ceasing to be resident and ordinarily resident, the deferred gain crystallises so there is no charge on emigration. A disposal to the recipient's spouse/civil partner before emigration, however, does not count, unless the spouse/civil partner then disposes of the asset to a third party.

If the tax payable by the recipient has not been paid within a year of the due date, HMRC may collect it from the transferor instead. The transferor has the right to recover the tax from the recipient.

If the recipient ceases to be resident because he takes up full time employment abroad, then, provided residence in the UK is resumed within three years and the asset is not disposed of in the meantime, the deferred gain will not be taxed in the way described above.

3 EIS CGT deferral relief

3.1 General provisions

If an individual makes a gain on the disposal of *any* asset, the gain may be deferred (ie delayed) if the individual subscribes for Enterprise Investment Scheme (EIS) shares. [Sch 5B]

The EIS shares do not need to qualify for the EIS income tax reduction (see earlier in this Text) **for this deferral relief to be available.** So the investor can be 'connected' with the company (ie he can own more than 30% of the shares and can be an employee) and he can invest more than the maximum allowed under the income tax rules (£500,000 for 2010/11).

3.2 Amount of relief

For every £1 invested in EIS shares, the investor can defer £1 of gain.

He can defer up to the full amount he subscribes for his shares, although he can specify a lower amount in his claim to take into account the availability of losses and the annual exempt amount.

The gain is deferred and is 'frozen' until, usually, the EIS shares are sold (see below).

Example 5

Robert made a gain of £196,000 on the disposal of a holiday cottage in 2010/11. He subscribed for some shares in a company which qualified under the EIS rules. How much should Robert claim to defer if:

(a)   The shares cost £200,000 and Robert wants to take the maximum deferral relief possible?
(b)   The shares cost £170,000 and Robert wants to take the maximum deferral relief possible?
(c)   The shares cost £200,000 and Robert has no other chargeable gains?

3.3 Conditions

3.3.1 The gain to be deferred

The gain must either arise on:

(a)   **The disposal of an asset or**
(b)   **On a gain, previously 'frozen' under these rules, crystallising (ie coming back into charge).**

3.3.2 The investor

The investor must be **UK resident or ordinarily resident when he makes the gain and also when he subscribes for the EIS shares.**

3.3.3 The company

The company must be a qualifying company under the EIS income tax rules (broadly an unlisted company carrying on a qualifying trade) (see earlier in this Text).

3.3.4 The shares

The investor must subscribe for the shares directly from the company (and not just purchase them on the open market) wholly in cash.

The shares must: [Sch 5B para 1A]

(a)   Be **new ordinary shares**, fully paid up
(b)   Not be redeemable before the termination date (generally three years after their issue)
(c)   Not have preferential rights to dividends or assets on a winding up within that period.
(d)   Be subscribed and issued for genuine commercial purposes (not for the avoidance of tax)
(e)   Be issued to raise money for a qualifying business activity.

Deferral relief will be withdrawn if the money raised is not used for the qualifying business activity within two years of the issue of the shares.

3.3.5 Time for investment

The investor must subscribe for the shares within the period of one year before and three years after the gain to be deferred accrues.

3.3.6 The claim

The claim must be made by 31 January nearly six years after the end of the tax year in which the deferred gain arose (ie by 31 January 2017 for 2010/11 gains). [Sch 5B Para 6]

3.4 Taxing the deferred gain

3.4.1 Chargeable events

The deferred gain will crystallise (ie come back into charge) if:

(a)   **The investor disposes of the shares to anyone, except to his spouse or civil partner**

(b)   **The investor's spouse or civil partner disposes of the shares, and they had acquired the shares from the investor**

(c)   **The investor becomes non resident within the three years following issue of the shares (the 'relevant period'),** unless he is employed full time abroad for up to three years and keeps the shares until he returns to the UK

(d)   **The investor's spouse or civil partner becomes non resident** within the relevant period (except as in (c) above), if they acquired the shares from the investor

(e)   **The shares cease being 'eligible shares'**, eg the company ceases to be a qualifying company or the money subscribed is not used for a qualifying business activity. However, if a company becomes listed this does not result in the gain coming back in charge unless there were arrangements in place at the outset for it to become listed.

The deferred gain becomes chargeable in the year of the event, not the year when it originally arose (if different). The gain is charged on the person holding the shares at that date, whether the investor or his spouse or civil partner if the shares have been passed to them.

4 Compensation and insurance monies

4.1 Destroyed assets

If an asset is destroyed or lost (and not merely damaged) **any insurance monies (ie compensation) received will be chargeable to CGT. However, if the proceeds are used to replace the asset within twelve months any gain can be deducted from the cost of the replacement asset.** If only part of the proceeds are used, the gain immediately chargeable is limited to the amount not spent. The rest of the gain is then deducted from the cost of the replacement.

The date of disposal is the date that the compensation is received and not the date that the asset was lost or destroyed. [s.23(4)]

Example 6

Alison bought a painting in January 1987 for £10,000. It was destroyed in a fire in May 2010 and she received £80,000 from the insurance company two months later. In March 2011 she bought another painting for £75,000 and made a claim under s.23(4) TCGA 1992.

Show Alison's CGT position in respect of the above.

4.2 Damaged assets

If an asset is damaged and insurance money (compensation) is received as a result, there is a part disposal, where A is the insurance money received and B is the value of the damaged asset. The taxpayer can avoid a part disposal computation by electing for the insurance money to be deducted from the cost of the asset ('rolled over') **so long as the asset is non wasting and:**

(a)   Not more than the higher of £3,000 or 5% of the insurance money is *not* used in restoring the asset; or

(b)   The insurance money is less than the higher of £3,000 or 5% of the value of the asset (ie is 'small').

If (a) and (b) do not apply there will be a part disposal calculation, although the taxpayer can elect for this to apply only to the part of the proceeds not used in the restoration. In this case B (in the part disposal formula) is the value of the restored asset. The allowable cost will include the costs of restoration (enhancement expenditure).

Again, the date of disposal is the date that the compensation is received and not the date that the asset was damaged.

Example 7

Mr Jones bought a building which cost £40,000 on 15 August 1990. On 10 September 2010 it was damaged in a fire and, as a result, £33,000 insurance proceeds were received. Of this £20,000 was used to restore the building; the market value of the building immediately after restoration was £62,000.

You are required to calculate the chargeable gain arising on disposal and the base cost of the building for future computations assuming Mr Jones elects for there to be a part disposal only in respect of the money not spent on restoring the building.

- Gift relief applies to gifts and sales at an undervalue of business assets, including certain shares.

- The transferor's gain is effectively transferred to the donee because the base cost of the asset for the donee is reduced by the deferred gain (ie the gift relief claimed).

- On a sale at an undervalue any real profit (ie actual consideration less original cost) remains chargeable. The balance of the gain can be deferred.

- Gift relief is restricted where there has been non-business use of an asset or where shares in the transferor's personal company are gifted and there are non-business chargeable assets (ie investments) held by the company.

- The emigration of the recipient of the gift within six years will result in the crystallisation of the chargeable gain. An exception is made for individuals employed abroad on a temporary basis.

- A gain on disposal of any asset may be deferred if the individual reinvests the amount of the gain in shares in a qualifying EIS company.

- Relief is given on a £1 for £1 basis (although it is possible to specify a smaller amount in the claim to preserve losses or the annual exempt amount)

- There are detailed conditions to be satisfied regarding the shares, the investor and the EIS company.

- If an asset is destroyed or lost a gain is calculated when insurance money is received, unless the money is spent replacing the asset within 12 months.

- If an asset is damaged there is a part disposal when insurance money is received, unless the money is spent restoring the asset. If only part of the money is spent the gain can be deferred.

Quiz

1. The gift relief election for gifts between individuals must be made jointly by the transferor and the transferee. True/False?

2. In what circumstances may the gain on a gift of a business asset between individuals be *fully* (as opposed to only partially) deferred?

3. On 15 May 2010 Philippa makes a gain on the sale of a painting of £60,000. Philippa makes no other disposals during 2010/11 and has capital losses brought forward of £12,000. What is the minimum investment she must make in qualifying EIS shares in order to reduce her gain to nil?

4. Where an asset is completely destroyed there is a part disposal of the asset. True/False?

Solutions to Quiz

1. True.

2. (a) There is no actual consideration, or there is a sale at an undervalue and the actual consideration is less than the transferor's base cost.

   (b) The whole of the asset has been used throughout the transferor's period of ownership in the transferor's (or his personal company's) trade.

3. Philippa can claim EIS deferral relief if she invests in qualifying EIS shares. To reduce her taxable gains to nil she must make a minimum investment of:

   £(60,000 – 12,000 – 10,100) = £37,900.

   Her gains computation would be as follows:

	£
Gain before relief	60,000
Less: EIS deferral relief (ie amount spent on subscribing for EIS shares)	(37,900)
	22,100
Less: capital losses b/f	(12,000)
	10,100
Less: annual exempt amount	(10,100)
Taxable gain	–

4. False. There is a part disposal if the asset is only damaged.

Solutions to chapter examples

Solution to Example 1

	£
Total gain (on shares)	60,000

Proportion relating to chargeable business assets eligible for relief:

$$£60,000 \times \frac{30,000}{40,000} = £45,000$$

Less: gift relief	(45,000)
Chargeable gain relating to other chargeable non-business assets	15,000

Base cost of shares for Henry's brother:

	£
Market value at date of gift	150,000
Less: gain deferred by gift relief	(45,000)
Cost c/f	105,000

Solution to Example 2

Total chargeable business assets are:

	£
Plant	50,000
Factory	1,050,000
	1,100,000

Total chargeable assets are:

	£
Plant	50,000
Factory	1,050,000
Investments	500,000
	1,600,000

Gain on sale of shares

	£
Disposal proceeds (use market value)	950,000
Less: cost	(200,000)
Gain before gift relief	750,000

Eligible for relief:

$$£750,000 \times \frac{1,100,000}{1,600,000} = £515,625$$

Less: gift relief	(515,625)
Chargeable gain	234,375

Solution to Example 3

	£
Total gain	50,000
Less: $^3/_8$ of £50,000 for letting	(18,750)
Gain eligible for gift relief	31,250
Chargeable gain £(50,000 − 31,250)	£18,750

Solution to Example 4

		£
(a)	*Angelo's CGT position:*	
	Disposal proceeds (market value)	200,000
	Less: cost	(30,000)
	Gain before relief	170,000
	Less: gain deferred:	
	Gain less: actual proceeds *less* cost (remains chargeable now)	
	£170,000 – £(50,000 – 30,000)	(150,000)
	Chargeable gain £(50,000 – 30,000)	20,000

		£
(b)	*Michael's CGT position:*	
	Disposal proceeds	195,000
	Less: base cost = MV at gift *less* gain deferred	
	£(200,000 – 150,000)	(50,000)
	Chargeable gain	145,000

Solution to Example 5

(a) £196,000. The cost of the shares exceeds the gain, so the whole gain can be deferred.

(b) £170,000. The cost of the shares is less than the gain, so the claim is restricted to the amount subscribed for the shares. The rest of the gain (£26,000) is chargeable (unless he subscribes for more EIS shares).

(c) Robert should claim to defer £185,900. This is calculated as follows (*hint:* work backwards!):

	£
Gain before relief	196,000
Less: EIS deferral relief	(185,900)
Chargeable gain	10,100
Less: annual exempt amount	(10,100)
Taxable gain	nil

Solution to Example 6

	£
Gain on destruction of original painting ('disposal' date is **July** 2010 (Note))	
Proceeds	80,000
Less: cost	(10,000)
	70,000
Less: gain deferred balancing figure ie £(70,000 – 5,000)	(65,000)
Chargeable gain*	5,000

* Proceeds not reinvested (ie £80,000 – £75,000)

	£
Base cost of new painting:	
Price paid	75,000
Less: gain deferred	(65,000)
Revised base cost c/f	10,000

Note. The date of disposal is important as this determines the CGT rate(s).

Solution to Example 7

			£
Chargeable gain			
Compensation received			33,000
Less: used in restoration			(20,000)
Consideration for part disposal			13,000
Allowable cost:			
$(40,000 + 20,000) \times \dfrac{13,000}{13,000 + 62,000}$			(10,400)
Chargeable gain			2,600

	£	£
Base cost of restored building		
Original cost	40,000	
Cost of restoration	20,000	
		60,000
Less: Insurance money not used in part disposal computation	20,000	
Cost used in part disposal computation	10,400	
		(30,400)
Base cost c/f		29,600

Now try the following questions

Short Form Questions:

15.1 – 15.8 inclusive

Long Form Questions:

15.1	Fran & Anna
15.2	Joe Bloggs
15.3	P J Laval
15.4	Simon
15.5	Emily
15.6	Peter
15.7	Sarah Stone

Personal Taxation

Part C: Administration

The purpose of this chapter is to help you to:

- understand when an individual must notify HMRC of their liability to income tax and capital gains tax

- understand the tax return, penalties for late filing and the need to retain records

- understand the penalties for making incorrect returns

- explain how an individual pays his income tax and CGT liabilities including when he can pay CGT by instalments

- explain how interest is charged/paid on underpaid/overpaid tax

- understand HMRC's powers to obtain information, enquire into returns, determine assessments and make discovery assessments

- understand when a taxpayer has a right of appeal and explain the procedure at an appeal hearing

References: ICTA 1988 unless otherwise stated

Administration of income tax and CGT

1 Introduction

Personal tax compliance for income tax and capital gains tax (CGT) is administered through the self assessment system. The major burden is placed on the taxpayer and his advisers.

References in this section to income tax include (where appropriate) Class 4 National Insurance Contributions (NIC).

2 Notification of liability to income tax and CGT

2.1 Who must notify?

Individuals who are chargeable to income tax or CGT for any tax year and **who have not received a notice to file a tax return must notify their chargeability** to HMRC **within six months from the end of the tax year**, ie by 5 October 2011 for 2010/11. [s.7(1) & (2) TMA 1970]

If a person has no chargeable gains and is not liable to higher rate tax he does not need to notify HMRC if all his income: [s.7(3)-(7)]

(a)   Is subject to Pay As You Earn (PAYE) (ie is employment income)
(b)   Has had (or is treated as having had) income tax deducted at source, or
(c)   Is UK dividend income.

2.2 Penalties for failure to notify chargeability

2.2.1 Introduction

From 1 April 2010 one set of rules applies to certain taxes, including income tax and capital gains tax, for failures to notify chargeability to tax that result in a loss of tax. So, these rules apply to a taxpayer becoming chargeable to tax in 2010/11, who must notify chargeability by 5 October 2011. [Sch 41 FA 2008]

The rules apply to **failures by either the taxpayer or his tax adviser**, unless the taxpayer can show that he took all reasonable steps to avoid the failure.

2.2.2 Amount of penalty

Penalties are **behaviour related**, increasing for more serious failures, and are **based on the 'potential lost revenue' (PLR)**.

For income tax and CGT purposes the PLR is **the amount of tax due in respect of the relevant tax year which is still outstanding on 31 January following the tax year (31 January 2012 for 2010/11).**

Reductions are available for disclosure, with higher reductions if the disclosure is unprompted.

The minimum and maximum penalties are as follows:

Behaviour	Maximum penalty	Minimum penalty with unprompted disclosure		Minimum penalty with prompted disclosure	
Deliberate and concealed	100%	30%		50%	
Deliberate but not concealed	70%	20%		35%	
		≥12m	<12m	≥12m	<12m
Any other case	30%	10%	Nil	20%	10%

Where the failure to notify is not deliberate the 30% penalty is reduced depending, not just on the level of disclosure but also the **amount of time that has elapsed since the tax first became unpaid**. For example where there is unprompted disclosure if HMRC become aware of the failure to notify chargeability less than 12 months after the date when tax becomes unpaid because of the failure the penalty can be reduced to £nil. If the period is 12 months or more the penalty can only be reduced to 10%.

The penalties may also be reduced at HMRC's discretion in 'special circumstances'. Inability to pay is not a 'special circumstance'.

If tax related penalties are also imposed for late filing of the tax return or late payment of tax (see below), the penalty for late notification is reduced correspondingly.

2.2.3 Disclosure

The minimum penalties shown above presume that the maximum reductions for disclosure apply. In practice, however, the reductions given are up to the HMRC officer involved and could result in a higher penalty being payable.

Making disclosure to HMRC includes:

- **Informing** HMRC of the failure
- Providing HMRC with reasonable **help in quantifying** the amount of tax unpaid
- Allowing HMRC **access to records** to check the amount of unpaid tax.

Disclosure is **unprompted** if at the time it is made the taxpayer had **no reason to believe that HMRC had or were about to discover the failure.**

The reduction in the penalty depends on the **quality of disclosure**. HMRC have indicated as a guide that they weight the elements of disclosure as **informing (30%), helping (40%) and giving access (30%).**

2.2.4 Reasonable excuse

Where the taxpayer's failure is not classed as deliberate, there is no penalty if he can show he has a 'reasonable excuse'. Reasonable excuse does not include having insufficient money to pay the penalty. [para 20(2) Sch 41 FA 2008]

2.2.5 Appeals

Taxpayers have a right of appeal against penalty decisions to the First-tier Tribunal, which may confirm, substitute or cancel the penalty (see below).

3 Self assessment tax returns

3.1 The tax return

3.1.1 The SA100 tax return

The tax return (the SA100) is a six page form, together with supplementary pages for particular sources of income. Taxpayers receive the supplementary pages they need depending on their known sources of income, together with a Tax Return Guide and various notes relating to the supplementary pages.

Where a taxpayer filed their previous year's return electronically he may be sent a notice to file a return, rather than the official HMRC return form.

3.1.2 Short tax return

Individuals with simple tax affairs can submit a 'short tax return', which is four pages long with supplementary capital gains pages if required. The return cannot be self selected, is not available online, and cannot be ordered from HMRC's Orderline. HMRC automatically issues the return to certain taxpayers, who have relatively simple tax affairs, such as employees, pensioners, and landlords with small amounts of property income, based on information on the previous year's tax return.

The individual must have only standard investment income.

Tax does not have to be calculated on the form, although a simple 'rough guide' working sheet is available for the taxpayer's own information.

If the taxpayer wishes to complete an online return they must use the normal tax return (SA100).

3.1.3 Three line accounts

Owners of small businesses, including **property letting businesses, may include simplified 'three line' accounts** (ie income *less* expenses = net profit) on their tax return. **The turnover of the business, or gross rents from property, must be less than £70,000 pa (£68,000 pa for 2009/10).**

The taxpayer must keep records (see below) whether producing detailed or three line accounts. Where a business's turnover falls below the limit for several years, HMRC may start an enquiry (see below) to ensure that turnover has been correctly stated.

> ### Exam focus point
>
> The limit of £70,000 (below which landlords need only submit three line accounts) is equivalent to the VAT threshold, which is given in the Association's tax tables. Find it.

3.2 Filing the tax return

3.2.1 Filing deadlines

A self assessment return is usually issued in April following the tax year concerned, For example, HMRC will send out the 2010/11 return to taxpayers in April 2011.

The filing date for a tax return depends on the type of return filed as follows:

Type of return	Filing date
Paper return	Later of **31 October following the end of the tax year**, ie for 2010/11 this will be 31 October 2011, and 3 months after date of issue (or 2 months if the taxpayer wishes HMRC to calculate his tax liability for him).
Electronic return	Later of **31 January following the end of the tax year**, ie for 2010/11 this will be 31 January 2012, and 3 months after the date of issue.

3.2.2 Penalties for late filing

Finance Act 2009 created a new penalty regime for the late filing of tax returns which is being implemented over a number of years to allow for changes to HMRC systems. It applies to all the main taxes **including income tax and capital gains tax**.

Exam focus point

ATT has confirmed that only the provisions of the new penalty regime are examinable in the 2011 exams even where they have not yet been implemented.

The penalties for **late filing of an individual's self assessment return** are as follows: [Sch 55 FA 2009]

- **Immediate £100 penalty**, regardless of whether or not the tax has been paid

- **Daily penalties of £10 per day** if the return is more than 3 months late (maximum 90 days)

- Where **delay is > 6 months but less than 12 months**: 5% × **tax due**

- **Where delay is > 12 months:**

    - 70% × tax due where withholding of information is deliberate but not concealed
    - 100% × tax due where withholding of information is deliberate and concealed
    - 5% × tax due in other cases (in addition to 5% due at 6 months date)

The tax based penalties above are all subject to a minimum of £300 and can be reduced for disclosure, with higher reductions if the disclosure is unprompted, as follows:

Behaviour	Maximum penalty	Minimum penalty with unprompted disclosure	Minimum penalty with prompted disclosure
Deliberate and concealed	100%	30%	50%
Deliberate, not concealed	70%	20%	35%
Other cases	5%	30%	50%

3.3 Keeping records

3.3.1 Introduction

A common framework for record keeping applies for income tax, capital gains tax and PAYE (along with corporation tax and VAT). [Sch 37 FA 2008]

This one set of high level rules apply across the taxes but the detailed rules for the individual taxes remain unchanged.

Taxpayers must keep all records used in making and delivering a correct tax return. These taxpayer records are critical to HMRC's information powers described below.

3.3.2 Which records must be kept?

Under the common framework the general rule is that taxpayers must keep **'information'** (rather than records), that shows that they have prepared a **complete and correct tax return**.

The specific rules for income tax and capital gains tax taxable are that individuals must keep **'adequate' business and accounting records**.

'Adequate' means keeping records to be sure that the right profit, loss, tax declaration or claim is made.

Taxpayers can usually keep copies of original documents except where the documents show domestic or foreign tax deducted or creditable. In this case the originals (eg dividend or interest certificates) must be kept.

3.3.3 Time limits for keeping records

The time period for keeping records depends on whether or not the taxpayer is in business. [s.12B] [IR booklet SA/BK3]

Records must be retained until the later of:

(a)   (i)   **5 years after 31 January following the tax year where the taxpayer is in business** (as a sole trader or partner or property letting), otherwise

     (ii)   **1 year after 31 January** following the tax year, or

(b)   Provided notice to deliver a return was given before the date in (a):

     (i)   The time after which enquiries by HMRC into the return could no longer be started (see below), or
     (ii)   The date any such enquiries had been completed.

The common framework allows HMRC the flexibility to shorten the periods for which records need to be retained.

3.3.4 Record keeping penalties

The maximum (mitigable) penalty for each failure to keep and retain records is generally £3,000 per tax year. [s.12B(5)]

3.4 Incorrect returns

3.4.1 Corrections and amendments

HMRC can amend a taxpayer's return to correct any obvious errors or mistakes in the return within nine months of receiving the tax return. [s.9ZB]

From 1 April 2010 HMRC's powers to correct a return are extended to correct 'anything else in the return that the officer has reason to believe is incorrect in the light of information available to the officer'. [s.119 FA2008]

The taxpayer can amend his tax return within 12 months of the 31 January filing deadline whether he has filed a paper or online return (ie by 31 January 2013 for the 2010/11 return). [s.9ZA]

3.4.2 Penalties for incorrect returns or documents

One penalty regime applies to all incorrect returns in respect of all of the main taxes including income tax and capital gains tax returns. [FA 2007 Sch 24]

The regime applies to the **submission of inaccurate returns or documents and the failure to notify HMRC where an under assessment is made.**

The amount of the penalty is a **percentage of the 'potential lost revenue'** (PLR) as a result of the inaccuracy or under assessment and **depends on the behaviour of the taxpayer** as follows:

Behaviour	Penalty
Mistake	No penalty
Careless (failure to take reasonable care)	30% of PLR
Deliberate understatement (but not concealed)	70% of PLR
Deliberate understatement with concealment	100% of PLR

The PLR is normally **the amount of tax lost.**

Like the penalties for failure to notify (see above) these standard penalties can be reduced if the taxpayer tells HMRC about the inaccuracy or under assessment or helps it to calculate or correct the error.

The amount of the reduction depends on whether the disclosure is prompted. An unprompted disclosure is where the taxpayer makes disclosure when he has no reason to believe that HMRC have or are about to discover the inaccuracy.

The minimum penalties are as follows:

Penalty	Minimum penalty	
	Unprompted	Prompted
Careless (maximum 30% penalty)	0%	15%
Deliberate understatement (maximum 70% penalty)	20%	35%
Deliberate understatement with concealment (maximum 100% penalty)	30%	50%

4 Taxpayer claims

4.1 Claims for relief

4.1.1 General principles

Generally any claims and elections that can be made in a tax return must be made in this way if HMRC issues a return. Claims for any relief, allowance or repayment of tax must be quantified at the time the claim is made. [s.42]

A claim may be made after the time limit for amending the tax return has expired.

4.1.2 Time limits [Sch 39 FA 2008]

There are new time limits for making claims which apply across the main taxes (including income tax and capital gains tax) from 1 April 2010.

The general time limit, where legislation does not state a specific date, is four years after the end of the tax year. For example, for capital gains tax purposes the legislation specifies a time limit for making a claim for EIS deferral relief of the fifth anniversary of 31 January following the end of the tax year of the disposal.

The legislation however does not specify a date for submitting a gift relief claim for CGT purposes and therefore the general time limit of four years after the end of the tax year applies.

4.2 Claims for recovery of overpaid tax (overpayment relief)

This section is new.

From 1 April 2010 there are new aligned rules for taxpayers to reclaim overpayments of **IT, CGT and CT.** [Sch 52 FA 2009]

> ### Exam focus point
>
> ATT has confirmed that only the new rules, as set out below, are examinable.

A claim may be made for tax to be repaid or an assessment discharged where:

(a)   An **amount of tax has been paid** which the **taxpayer believes was not due,** or

(b)   An **assessment or determination has been raised** but the taxpayer believes the tax is not due.

The claim must be made no later than **four years** after the end of the tax year.

The **taxpayer is responsible for determining the amount of their claim** and HMRC has the right to open an enquiry into the relevant period covered by the return, or to make either a discovery assessment or determination which may otherwise be out of date.

HMRC will **not allow a claim in certain circumstances,** which include the following: [Sch 1AB for IT & CGT].

(a)   The amount of tax paid is excessive because:

   (i)   **Of a mistake in a claim, election or notice or a mistake in making or failing to make an election, claim or notice**

   (ii)   **Of a mistake in relation to a capital allowances claim**

   (iii)   It was **calculated in accordance with practice generally prevailing** at the time

(b)   The taxpayer ought previously have been **aware of the mistake to have made a claim within the time limit**

(c)   The case has already been the **subject of a tribunal or court hearing**

(d)   The taxpayer can seek relief by other steps under tax legislation.

5 Payment of income tax and capital gains tax

5.1 Introduction

In general, taxpayers make three payments of income tax and, where relevant, one payment of capital gains tax for each tax year. The pattern of payments is usually:

31 January in the tax year:	**1st payment on account of income tax**
31 July after the tax year:	**2nd payment on account of income tax**
31 January after the tax year:	**Final payment to settle the income tax liability for the year, and**
	Payment of any CGT liability

HMRC issue payslips/demand notes in a credit card type 'Statement of Account' format, but there is no statutory obligation for them to do so and the onus is on the taxpayer to pay the correct amount of tax on the due date.

Statements of account are normally issued shortly before a payment is due, when a payment is made, and at intervals so long as any tax remains outstanding. Copies of statements of account are normally only issued to agents in June and December, unless the client authorises all statements to be sent to the agent.

5.2 Payments on account

Payments on account (POAs) are usually required where the taxpayer's tax (and Class 4 NICs but not Class 2 NICs or capital gains tax) due for the previous year exceeded the amount of income tax deducted at source (including PAYE deductions and tax credits on dividends). **This excess is known as 'the relevant amount'.**

The POAs are each equal to 50% of the relevant amount for the previous year, and are due by 31 January in the tax year and the following 31 July. [s.59A(2)]

Example 1

Gordon is a self employed builder who paid tax for 2010/11 as follows:

		£
Total amount of income tax liability		9,200
This included:	Tax deducted on savings income	3,200
He also paid:	Class 4 NIC	2,206
	Class 2 NIC	125
	Capital gains tax	4,800

How much are the payments on account for 2011/12?

POAs are not required if the relevant amount falls below £1,000 or if the relevant amount is less than 20% of the total liability. [s.59A(1)]

5.3 Claims to reduce payments on account

Where a taxpayer's liability in the year is expected to be lower than in the previous year (for example if he has sold a rental property) **he can claim to reduce his POAs:**

(a)   **To a stated amount, or** [s.59A(4)]

(b)   **To nil.** [s.59A(3)]

The claim must state the reason why the taxpayer believes his tax liability will be lower, or nil.

If the taxpayer's eventual liability is higher than that estimated he will have reduced the POA too far. Although the POA will not be adjusted, there will be an interest charge on underpayment (see below).

There may be a penalty based on the difference between the expected and actual POAs if the claim was made fraudulently or negligently. This penalty is usually only charged if there are repeated excessive claims. [s.59A(6)]

5.4 Balancing payment of income tax and capital gains tax

The balance of any income tax due for a tax year (after deducting POAs and tax deducted at source), together with any capital gains tax liability for that year, is payable on the 31 January following the tax year. [s.59B(1), (2) & (4)]

Example 2

Giles had made payments on account for 2010/11 of £6,500 each on 31 January 2011 and 31 July 2011, based on his 2009/10 liability. He then calculates his total income tax and Class 4 NIC liability for 2010/11 at £18,000 of which £2,750 had been deducted at source. In addition he calculates that his CGT liability for disposals in 2010/11 is £5,120.

What is the final payment due for 2010/11?

TQT
Tax Qualification Training

5.5 Payment of CGT by instalments

If the proceeds for a disposal are received in instalments, the general rule is that the whole gain is chargeable up front as normal. However, **if the proceeds are receivable in instalments over a period exceeding eighteen months, the taxpayer may elect for the CGT to be spread** over the *shorter* of: [s.280 TCGA 1992]

(a)   The period of instalments, and
(b)   Eight years.

There is also an instalment option for CGT due on gifts which do not qualify for gift relief (see earlier in this Text) **where the gifted assets are:** [s.281 TCGA 1992]

(a)   **Land**
(b)   **Shares or securities (quoted or unquoted) out of a controlling holding, or**
(c)   **Unquoted shares or securities**.

The person paying the tax can elect, in writing, to HMRC for the option to pay in ten equal yearly instalments. The first payment is payable on the normal due date.

The outstanding balance bears interest which is added for payment to each instalment.

The taxpayer may pay off the outstanding instalments (plus accrued interest) at any time. **The outstanding balance and accrued interest become immediately payable if the asset gifted is sold.**

6 Interest and penalties for late payment

6.1 Interest

6.1.1 Introduction

The Finance Act 2009 introduced **a single harmonised interest regime which applies to most taxes including income tax (and PAYE) and capital gains tax.** [ss.101–105, Sch 53 & 54 FA 2009]

Exam focus point

Implementation of the new regime is taking place over a number of years. However **ATT has confirmed that only the new harmonised interest regime is examinable in the 2011 examinations.**

6.1.2 Interest rates

Under the new regime:

(a)   There is **one rate of interest for late payments of tax and one for repayments of tax.**
(b)   The rates are automatically based on the Bank of England base rate, as follows:
    (i)   Interest on late payments of tax: base rate + 2.5%
    (ii)   Interest on overpayments of tax: base rate – 1%, minimum 0.5%.

6.1.3 Late payment interest

Late payment interest is charged on **any amount payable to HMRC from the late payment interest start date (normally, the date on which the tax becomes due and payable) until the date of payment.** [s.101(4) FA 2009]

For example, if tax is due for payment on 31 January 2012 but the tax is not paid until 14 March 2012, interest will be calculated from 31 January to 13 March 2012 (ie exclude the actual date of payment).

6.1.4 Interest on reduced payments on account

Where a taxpayer makes a claim to reduce his payments on account and there is still a final payment to be made interest is charged as if each of the POAs had been the lower of:

(a) The reduced amount, plus 50% of the final income tax liability, and

(b) The amount which would have been payable had no claim for reduction been made.

Illustration

Herbert's payments on account for 2010/11 based on his income tax liability for 2009/10 were £4,500 each. However, when he submitted his 2009/10 income tax return in January 2011 he made a claim to reduce the payments on account for 2010/11 to £3,500 each. The first payment on account was made on 29 January 2011, and the second on 12 August 2011.

Herbert filed his 2010/11 tax return in December 2011. The return showed that his tax liabilities for 2010/11 (before deducting payments on account) were income tax £10,000 and capital gains tax £2,500. Herbert paid the balance of tax due of £5,500 on 19 February 2012.

Herbert has made an excessive claim to reduce his payments on account, and will therefore be charged interest on the reduction. The payments on account should have been £4,500 each based on the 2009/10 liability. This is lower than the reduced POA plus 50% of the final balancing payment of £5,000 (£3,500 + (50% × (£10,000 – £7,000))). Herbert will be liable to interest as follows:

- First payment on account

    - on £3,500 – nil – paid on time
    - on £1,000 from due date of 31 January 2011 to day before payment, 18 February 2012 *(Note)*

- Second payment on account

    - on £3,500 from due date of 31 July 2011 to day before payment of £3,500, 11 August 2011
    - on £1,000 from due date of 31 July 2011 to day before payment, 18 February 2012

- Balancing payment of income tax and capital gains tax

    - on £3,500 from due date of 31 January 2012 to day before payment, 18 February 2012

Note Remember to exclude the actual date of payment from the calculation.

6.1.5 Repayment interest

Tax will be repaid when claimed unless a greater payment of tax is due in the following 30 days, in which case it will be **set off** against that payment.

Repayment interest will be received from HMRC on overpayments of:

(a) **POAs**

(b) **Payments of income tax and capital gains tax, including tax deducted at source or tax credits on dividends, and**

(c) **Penalties.**

Interest is paid from the later of the date that the tax was paid to HMRC and the due date for payment of the tax, to the date the tax is repaid. [Para 2 Sch 54 FA 2009]

Income tax deducted at source for a tax year and tax credits are treated as if they were paid on 31 January following the tax year.

6.2 Penalties for late self assessment tax payments

The Finance Act 2009 created a standardised penalty regime for the late filing of returns (see above) **and late payment of tax**. It applies to all the main taxes including income tax and capital gains tax.

The penalty for late payment of income tax or capital gains tax is generally 5% of tax unpaid on the penalty date, which is 30 days after the payment due date.

Further 5% penalties are charged where the tax still remains **unpaid five and eleven months after the above penalty date.** This gives a maximum penalty of 15% × the unpaid tax.

Late payment penalties can be suspended where the taxpayer agrees a time to pay arrangement (where a tax debt is paid over time) with HMRC, unless they abuse the arrangement.

7 HMRC's powers

7.1 Introduction

HMRC has one set of powers covering most of the taxes, including income tax and capital gains tax to ensure taxpayers comply with their obligations, pay the right amount of tax at the right time and claim the correct reliefs and allowances. [Sch 36 FA 2008]

These powers allow HMRC to make compliance checks by:

- Asking taxpayers and third parties for **information and documents**.
- **Visiting business premises** to inspect the premises, assets and records.

These compliance checks enable HMRC to make cross-tax checks using one set of rules.

The Tax Tribunal deals with the exercise of the above powers and also taxpayer appeals. This Tribunal is made up of the First-tier Tribunal and Upper Tribunal (see further below).

7.2 Information powers

7.2.1 General provisions

HMRC usually informally request information and documents from taxpayers in connection with their tax affairs. If, however, a taxpayer does not co-operate fully, **HMRC can use its statutory powers to request information and documents from taxpayers and even third parties via a written 'information notice'.**

7.2.2 Taxpayer notices

HMRC can only issue a taxpayer notice if the information and documents requested are **'reasonably required'** for the **purpose of checking the taxpayer's tax position.**

A taxpayer notice may be issued either with or without the approval of the First-tier Tribunal. An authorised HMRC officer must agree before the request is referred to the First-tier Tribunal.

HMRC can request both statutory records and supplementary information, such as appointment diaries, notes of board meetings, correspondence and contracts.

The taxpayer (or third party – see below) must provide the information or document requested by the information notice within such period as is reasonably specified within the notice.

7.2.3 Third party notices

An information notice issued to a third party must usually be issued with either the agreement of the taxpayer or the approval of the First-tier Tribunal.

An authorised HMRC officer must agree before the request is referred to the First-tier Tribunal.

The taxpayer to whom the notice relates must receive a summary of the reasons for the third party notice unless the Tribunal believes it would prejudice the assessment or collection of tax.

As above, **the request must be relevant to establishing the taxpayer's correct tax position.**

Tax advisers and auditors cannot be asked to provide information connected with their functions. For example, a tax adviser does not have to provide access to his working papers used in the preparation of the taxpayer's return.

In addition, HMRC cannot ask a tax adviser to provide communications between himself and either the taxpayer or his other advisers.

These exceptions do not apply in certain situations, for example, to explanatory material provided to a client in relation to a document already supplied to HMRC.

7.2.4 Deliberate wrongdoing by tax agents

Draft legislation currently under consultation will allow HMRC access to a tax agent's working papers and to impose penalties on tax agents who engage in deliberate wrongdoing.

7.2.5 Right of appeal

The recipient of an information notice has a right of appeal against the information notice unless the First-tier Tribunal has approved the issue of the notice

There is no right of appeal if the information or documents relate to records the person must keep for tax purposes (statutory records).

7.2.6 Restrictions on information powers

HMRC can only request information that is in the person's possession.

HMRC cannot request information that:

- Relates to any pending tax appeal.
- Constitutes journalistic material.
- Is legally privileged.
- Is over six years old (except with the approval of an authorised HMRC officer).
- Relates to someone who died over four years earlier.

In addition, HMRC cannot issue a notice to check the taxpayer's tax position if a return has already been made for a period unless:

- The return is the subject of an ongoing self assessment enquiry, (see below)
- HMRC believes there has been a loss of tax, or
- It relates to PAYE (as there is no enquiry framework for this).

TQT
Tax Qualification Training

7.2.7 Computer records

HMRC's powers to request and inspect documents explicitly include documents held on a computer or recorded electronically in any way. [s.114 FA 2008]

An 'authorised' person, who may be an HMRC officer or, in exceptional circumstances, a specialist from outside HMRC, can obtain access to a computer, and any other apparatus or material, which has been used in connection with a 'relevant document'.

Anyone obstructing HMRC in the exercise of its powers or failing to comply within a reasonable time may be charged a penalty of £300.

7.3 Inspection powers

7.3.1 Power to visit business premises

An authorised officer of HMRC can enter the business premises of a taxpayer whose liability is being checked, or of certain third parties, and inspect the premises, assets used in the business and business documents. The power does not extend to any part of the premises used solely as a dwelling. [Sch 36 FA 2008]

If an information notice has been issued, the documents required in that notice can be inspected at the same time.

The inspection must be reasonably required for the purposes of checking the taxpayer's tax position.

From 1 April 2010 HMRC can inspect premises for the purpose of valuing them if this is necessary to check a person's income tax liability. HMRC can also inspect premises and any other property on the premises for the purpose of valuing, measuring or determining their character if necessary to check a person's CGT liability. The inspection must be agreed to by the occupier of the premises or the Tribunal.

HMRC can even exercise its powers before a return is received where, for example, it believes that a taxpayer:

- Did not notify chargeability to tax.
- Did not register for VAT if required.
- Is operating in the informal economy.

7.3.2 Carrying out inspections

HMRC will usually agree a time for the inspection with the taxpayer.

However, an authorised HMRC officer can carry out the inspection at 'any reasonable time' if either:

(a) **The taxpayer receives at least seven days' written notice**, or

(b) The inspection is carried out by, or with the approval of, an authorised HMRC officer. In this case, the HMRC officer carrying out the inspection **must provide a notice, in writing, to someone present at the premises (usually the occupier), or, if there is no one present, leave the notice in a prominent place on the premises.**

HMRC has issued Compliance Checks (CC) **factsheets** covering such unannounced visits, which are likely to be undertaken where, for example, there is a strong risk that the taxpayer would move the business or remove stock or other assets. [CC/FS4 & CC/FS5]

7.3.3 Right of appeal

There is no right of appeal against an inspection notice.

The occupier of the premises can refuse entry and prevent the inspection from being completed but may then be subject to penalties (see below).

Tax Qualification Training

7.4 Information power penalties

7.4.1 When can a penalty be charged?

A penalty may be charged for:

(1) **Failure to comply or obstruction**, or [para 39 Sch 36 FA 2008]
(2) **Providing inaccurate information and documents**. [para 40A Sch 36 FA 2008]

7.4.2 Failure to comply or obstruction

A penalty may be charged where a person: [para 39 Sch 36 FA 2008]

(a) **Fails to comply with an information notice**, or
(b) **Deliberately obstructs an inspection** that has been approved by the First-tier Tribunal.

Failing to comply includes concealing, destroying or otherwise disposing of documents required by an information notice.

If the document is *likely* to be the subject of an information notice, a six month time limit applies.

Concealing, destroying or otherwise disposing of documents may also be an indictable (ie criminal) offence.

7.4.3 Types of penalties

There are three types and amounts of penalty: [Sch 36 FA 2008]

Type of penalty	Amount
Basic	£300
Daily	£60 per day
Tax-related	Based on tax

A basic penalty must be assessed before either a daily or tax-related penalty can be considered.

A daily penalty applies if the failure to comply or obstruction continues after the date the basic penalty is imposed.

A **tax-related penalty may be charged, in addition to the basic penalty and any daily penalties**, when HMRC believes that a significant amount of tax is at risk. The Upper Tribunal decides the amount based on the amount of tax at risk.

The above penalties **must be paid within a 30 day time limit**.

7.4.4 Reasonable excuse

A person is not liable to a penalty if he can satisfy HMRC (or the First-tier Tribunal on appeal) that he has a reasonable excuse for:

• Failing to comply with an information notice, or
• Obstructing an inspection,

and the failure is remedied as soon as the excuse ends.

HMRC has indicated that daily penalties will not normally be assessed after the failure has been remedied.

Reasonable excuse does not usually include lack of money to pay the penalty.

7.4.5 Providing inaccurate information and documents

A penalty may be charged where: [para 40A Sch 36 FA 2008]

(a) In complying with an information notice, a person provides inaccurate information or produces an inaccurate document, and

(b)   Either:

(i)   The inaccuracy is **careless** (failed to take reasonable care) or **deliberate,** or

(ii)   The person discovers the **inaccuracy some time later and fails to take reasonable steps to inform HMRC.**

The penalty is **£3,000 per inaccuracy**.

7.4.6 Appealing against a penalty

The taxpayer may appeal to the First-tier Tribunal against:

(a)   The imposition of a penalty, and

(b)   The amount of the penalty.

The appeal must be made to HMRC in writing, within 30 days of HMRC's issue of the original penalty notice.

The taxpayer *cannot*, however, appeal against a tax-based penalty for failure to comply or obstruction.

7.5 Enquiries into returns

7.5.1 Raising an enquiry

HMRC can enquire into a return filed on time within 12 months of receiving it. [s.9A]

If the return is filed after the due filing date, HMRC has until the quarter day following the first anniversary of the actual filing date. The quarter days are 31 January, 30 April, 31 July and 31 October.

If the taxpayer has amended the return after the due filing date for the return, the enquiry 'window' extends to the quarter day following the first anniversary of the date the amendment was filed. Where the enquiry was not raised within the limit which would have applied had no amendment been filed, the enquiry will be restricted to matters contained in the amendment.

The officer does not have to have, or give, any reason for raising an enquiry. In particular the taxpayer will not be advised whether he has been selected at random for an audit. Enquiries may be full enquiries, or may be limited to a particular 'aspect' of the return.

In addition, HMRC can use its information powers (see above) to obtain information in order to **check the taxpayer's tax position before a return has been submitted.**

7.5.2 During the enquiry

In the course of the enquiry:

(a)   **HMRC may issue a written 'information notice' (see above) to require the taxpayer to produce documents, accounts or any other information required. The taxpayer has the right to appeal to the First-tier Tribunal**. [Sch 36 FA 2008]

(b)   **HMRC may amend a self-assessment if it appears that insufficient tax has been charged** and an immediate amendment is necessary to prevent a loss of tax to the Crown. This might apply if, for example, there was a possibility that the taxpayer might emigrate, or bankruptcy proceedings be commenced. [s.9C]

(c)   Amendments may be made by the taxpayer whilst an enquiry is in progress, although they will not take effect until the end of the enquiry. The contents of the amendment may be taken into account in the enquiry.

(d)   **HMRC may postpone any repayment due as shown in the return until the enquiry is complete**. HMRC has discretion to make a provisional repayment but there is no facility to appeal if the repayment is withheld.

7.5.3 Completion of the enquiry

An enquiry is not complete until HMRC issues a closure notice. The notice must either state that the return needs no amendment, or must amend the return.

Once an enquiry is complete, HMRC cannot make further enquiries. HMRC may, in limited circumstances, raise a discovery assessment if they are of the opinion that there has been a loss of tax (see below). [s.9A(3) & s.12AC(4)] [para 5(3) Sch 1A]

7.6 Determinations

HMRC may only raise enquiries if a return has been submitted.

If a taxpayer has not submitted a return by the due filing date, HMRC may make a 'determination' (ie an estimate) of the amounts liable to income tax and capital gains tax and of the tax due. This determination is treated as if it were a self assessment. This enables the officer to seek payment of tax, including payments on account for the following year and to charge interest. [s.28C]

The determination must be made within the period ending **three years after the filing date (ie 31 January following the tax year)**. It may be superseded by a self assessment made within the same period or, if later, within 12 months of the date of the determination.

7.7 Discovery assessments

If HMRC discovers that profits have been left out of a return, that any self assessment has become insufficient, or that any relief given is excessive, a 'discovery' assessment may be raised to recover the tax lost. Conditions limit the circumstances in which a discovery assessment may be made. [s.29]

If the tax lost results from an error in the taxpayer's return but the return was made in accordance with prevailing practice at the time, no discovery assessment may be made.

A discovery assessment may only be raised where a return has been made if:

(a)   The omission is brought about either **carelessly or deliberately** by the taxpayer or his agent (eg tax adviser), or

(b)   **HMRC did not have information made available to him to make him aware of the loss of tax** at the time that enquiries into the return were completed.

Information is considered to be 'made available' to HMRC if it could be reasonably inferred by the officer or if it is contained in:

(i)   The return for the relevant tax year (or preceding two tax years),
(ii)   Any claim submitted for the relevant tax year (or preceding two tax years), or
(iii)   Accounts, statements or documents accompanying the return or claim or produced in the course of the enquiry.

Tax charged on a discovery assessment is due thirty days after the issue of the assessment. [s.59B(6)]

From April 2010, the time limits for raising a discovery assessment are as follows:

*   **Ordinary time limit**   **4 years from the end of the tax year**
*   **Where the omission is careless**   **6 years from the end of the tax year**
*   **Where the omission is deliberate**   **20 years from the end of the tax year.**

8 Appeals system

8.1 Introduction

All tax appeals are heard by the Tax Chamber of the independent Tribunals.

A person has the right of appeal to a Tribunal against certain HMRC decisions or assessments. The appeal must be made in writing within 30 days of the date of the disputed HMRC letter or assessment.

Most appeals are heard by the Tax Chamber of the First-tier Tribunal. The Upper Tribunal hears more complex tax cases and appeals against the decisions of the First-tier Tribunal. Appeals to the Upper Tribunal are only available on a point of law and with either the First-tier or Upper Tribunals' permission. There is no automatic right of appeal on a point of law.

8.2 Structure of the Tribunals

The Tribunal is made up of two 'tiers': [Tribunals, Courts and Enforcement Act 2007]

(a) **The First-tier Tribunal** and
(b) **The Upper Tribunal.**

Tax cases are usually listed to be heard, in the first instance, by the Tax Chamber of the First-tier Tribunal, although a complex case (see below) may start in the Upper Tribunal, if selected by the Tribunal President.

Appeals against decisions of the First-tier Tribunal are heard by the Finance and Tax Chamber of the Upper Tribunal.

The Tribunal has its own judiciary and also its **own rules of procedure**, set by the Tribunal Procedure Committee (TPC). The functions of the Tribunals are set out in SI 2009/196 and the rules that govern the practice and procedures of the Tribunals are set out in SI 2009/273.

It receives administrative support from the Tribunals Service, an executive agency of the Ministry of Justice.

8.3 Appeal procedure

8.3.1 Internal reviews

For direct taxes, appeals must first be made to HMRC, which will assign a 'caseworker'.

For indirect taxes, appeals must be sent directly to the Tribunal Service, although the taxpayer can continue to correspond with his caseworker where, for example, there is new information.

At this stage the taxpayer may be offered, or may ask for, an **'internal review'**, which will be made by an **objective HMRC review officer not previously connected with the case**. This is a less costly and more effective way to resolve disputes informally, without the need for a Tribunal hearing. An appeal to Tribunal cannot be made until any review has ended. The taxpayer must either accept the review offer, or notify an appeal to the tribunal, within 30 days of being offered the review, otherwise the appeal will be treated as settled.

HMRC must usually **carry out the review within 45 days**, or any longer time as agreed with the taxpayer. The review officer may decide to uphold, vary or withdraw decisions.

After the review conclusion is notified, the taxpayer has **30 days to appeal to the Tribunal**.

Reviews are optional except for decisions regarding the restoration of seized goods, which continue to have a 'mandatory' review process.

8.3.2 Tribunal hearings

If there is no internal review, or the taxpayer is unhappy with the result of an internal review, the case may be heard by the Tribunal.

It will be allocated to one of **four case 'tracks'**:

(a) **Complex** cases, which the Tribunal considers will require lengthy or complex evidence or a lengthy hearing, or involve a complex or important principle or issue, or involves a large amount of money

(b)   **Standard** cases

(c)   **Basic** cases, which will usually be disposed of after a hearing, with minimal exchange of documents before the hearing, and

(d)   **Paper** cases.

A paper case is the default, and applies to straightforward matters, such as fixed filing penalties. Both parties to the case submit their representations to the Tribunal in writing, rather than in person, unless the appellant elects for an oral hearing (see procedure below). These paper 'hearings' are intended to save time and costs for all parties concerned.

A complex case can be transferred to and heard by the Upper Tribunal.

8.3.3 Proceedings

Step 1   The person wishing to make an appeal (the appellant) must **send a notice of appeal** to the Tribunal which must include:

(a)   The name and address of the appellant
(b)   The name and address of the appellant's representative (if any)
(c)   An address where documents for the appellant may be sent or delivered
(d)   Details of the decision appealed against
(e)   The result the appellant is seeking, and
(f)   The grounds for making the appeal.

The Tribunal must then give notice of the appeal to the respondent (normally HMRC).

Step 2   **The respondent must then provide a 'statement of case'** to the Tribunal and the appellant, setting out the legislative reference(s) for the appeal matter, the respondent's position in relation to the case and whether the respondent wishes for there to be a formal hearing.

This must be done:

(a)   Within 42 days in a default paper case
(b)   Within 60 days in a standard or complex case.

A statement of case is *not* required for a basic case. Instead, the respondent need only notify the appellant, as soon as possible, of any additional grounds he has for contesting the proceedings which he intends to raise at the hearing.

Step 3   *In a paper case*

The appellant may send a written reply, within 30 days of the statement of case being sent, setting out any further relevant information and requesting the case be dealt with at a hearing.

OR

Step 3   *In a standard or complex case*

Each party must provide a list of documents owned which will be relied upon at the hearing within 42 days of the statement of case being sent.

8.3.4 Decisions of the First-tier Tribunal

The Tribunal must **provide each party with a decision notice, within 28 days of their decision**, which states the Tribunal's decision and notifies the parties of any right of appeal.

A decision of the First-tier Tribunal may be appealed to the Upper Tribunal. Previously such appeals were heard by the High Court.

The party wishing to appeal must apply in writing to the Tribunal within 56 days of the Tribunal's decision.

TQT
Tax Qualification Training

8.3.5 Decisions of the Upper Tribunal

Decisions of the Upper Tribunal are binding on the Tribunals and any relevant public authorities, such as HMRC.

A decision of the Upper Tribunal may be appealed to the Court of Appeal.

The Upper Tribunal also has the power to conduct a judicial review of decisions or actions that cannot be appealed. Permission is required from either the High Court or the Upper Tribunal to bring an action for judicial review.

Decisions of the Court of Appeal may be appealed to the UK Supreme Court, which replaced the Appellate Committee of the House of Lords from 1 October 2009. Leave to appeal must be granted by the Court of Appeal or, if refused, by the Supreme Court itself.

8.4 Costs

No costs will be awarded for standard or basic cases, except where either party behaves unreasonably. Costs will usually be awarded in complex cases unless the appellant opts out of the costs regime before the hearing.

- Self assessment is the system under which taxpayers are required to complete returns and self assess their tax liabilities. Each return has working sheets to enable the taxpayer to calculate his own income tax and CGT liability. For electronic returns the taxpayer's tax liability is automatically calculated.

- An individual must advise HMRC within 6 months of the end of the tax year if he is chargeable to income tax or CGT and he has not already received a tax return.

- The taxpayer makes two POAs and then a third payment to finalise his income tax liability. The POAs are due on 31 January in the tax year and 31 July immediately following. The final payment is due on 31 January following the end of the tax year.

- Only one CGT payment is due on 31 January after the end of the tax year.

- Self assessment is enforced through a system of automatic penalties, together with rules for interest on late paid tax.

- Penalties apply for the submission of incorrect returns based on the revenue lost and the behaviour of the taxpayer.

- HMRC has wide ranging powers to inspect a taxpayer's documents and premises.

- Random enquiries are used to ensure that taxpayers are complying correctly with their obligations.

- Appeals are heard by the Tax Chamber of the First-tier Tribunal in the first instance. Appeals against decisions of the First-tier Tribunal are heard by the Finance and Tax Chamber of the Upper Tribunal.

- There is a right of appeal from the First-tier Tribunal to the Upper Tribunal on a point of law. From the Upper tribunal, there is a right of appeal to the Court of Appeal and thereafter, with leave, to the Supreme Court.

Quiz

1. When must an individual notify HMRC of a new source of income for 2010/11?

2. Brenda was issued with her 2010/11 tax return on 15 April 2011. By which date must Brenda submit the completed form?

3. John is self employed. For how long must he retain his 2010/11 business records?

4. Which taxes are subject to payment on account for an individual?

5. An individual may reduce a payment on account to £nil.

    True or False?

6. Only CGT on gifts subject to gift relief qualify for CGT instalments.

    True or False?

Solutions to Quiz

1. By 5 October 2011.
2. If Brenda submits the return online then it is due by 31 January 2012. If Brenda submits a paper return it must be submitted by 31 October 2011.
3. Until 31 January 2017 (ie 5 years after 31 January 2012).
4. Income Tax and Class 4 NIC.
5. True.
6. False.

Solutions to chapter examples

Solution to Example 1

The relevant amount is:

	£
Income tax:	
Total income tax liability for 2010/11	9,200
Less: tax deducted for 2010/11	(3,200)
	6,000
Add: Class 4 NIC	2,206
	8,206

Payments on account for 2011/12:

31 January 2012	× ½	£4,103
31 July 2012	As before	£4,103

There is no requirement to make payments on account of capital gains tax (nor Class 2 NIC).

Solution to Example 2

	£
Total income tax and Class 4 NIC liability	18,000
Less: tax deducted at source	(2,750)
Relevant amount	15,250
Less: POAs for 2010/11 (2 × £6,500)	(13,000)
Balancing payment	2,250
CGT due	5,120

Total payment due on 31 January 2012 (excluding the first payment on account for 2011/12) £2,250 + £5,120 = £7,370

Now try the following questions

Short Form Questions:

16.1 – 16.4 inclusive

- discuss other aspects of the syllabus which includes law and professional rules and guidelines

Other aspects of the syllabus

1 Introduction

Apart from taxation there are other key areas of the syllabus for candidates to study.

Throughout this text you will have seen icons highlighting law. These icons refer candidates to specific areas within the Essential Law for the Taxation Technician manual.

Exam focus point

The syllabus for law is contained at the front of the law manual 'Essential Law for the Taxation Technician'. You should look at this and ensure that you read through any areas you have not yet studied.

There are other essential publications that must be studied:

- ATT Professional Rules and Practice Guidelines (2006 version)
- Professional Conduct in Relation to Taxation
- Engagement Letters for Tax Practitioners issued on 10 March 2009.

If you visit the official ATT website at www.att.org.uk you will find these publications plus much more valuable information for students.

Exam focus point

The above publications require knowledge at the 'principles' level of the syllabus. Candidates are expected to have an awareness that a provision exists and its main thrust without necessarily knowing the details of the provision.

Throughout your studies you **must** refer to these publications whenever possible.

Exam focus point

Examiner's report – Personal Taxation

November 2009 – Part I SFQ 13

Surprisingly poorly answered – almost everybody referred to the need for there to be adequate [data protection] security, but there was often little else offered of substance.

November 2009 – Part II LFQ 3

Part 3 [on the Money Laundering Regulations] caused the most difficulty to candidates with a noticeable number of candidates failing to produce any answer at all. Those who produced an answer tended to achieve one or two marks rather than the full allocation [of 3 marks].

Now try the following questions

Short Form Questions:

17.1 – 17.11 inclusive

Personal Taxation

Question and
Answer Bank

Short form questions

1.1 Mary, a single woman aged 67, has net income of £23,680. What are the total allowances available to Mary for 2010/11?

1.2 Darren aged 70 is registered blind. His wife Edna is aged 76. Calculate the maximum allowances that Darren may deduct from his net income in 2010/11.

1.3 Keith has a salary of £110,000 in 2010/11. This is his only income during the year. What is his personal allowance for 2010/11?

1.4 In 2010/11 James has a salary of £45,580 (PAYE £8,165). He makes a Gift Aid donation to the RNLI of £560.

What is his tax payable or repayable?

1.5 Joe is aged 90 and has net income of £30,800. He is married to Jean. What allowances and tax reductions is Joe entitled to in 2010/11?

1.6 Andy's receives a salary of £180,000 in 2010/11. During the year he won £1,500 on the lottery.

What is his tax liability?

1.7 Martin Keynes is aged 16 and is at school.

He has the following income in 2010/11:

£2,000 (gross) from his Barclays bank account where he pays in earnings from his newspaper round
£375 (gross) interest from building society account set up in his name by his mother

What is his net income for the year?

1.8 William was born on 6 March 1930 and is single. In the year ended 5 April 2011 he had income of £24,600 and paid £500 (gross) under Gift Aid to the NSPCC, a UK registered charity. What is William's personal allowance for 2010/11?

1.9 John is an unmarried student. In the year to 5 April 2011 he received the following:

	Gross £	Tax deducted £
Scholarship from a charity	1,935	–
Legacy from late grandfather	12,000	–
Earnings from employment	3,700	740
Building society interest	300	60

What is the maximum tax repayment he can claim?

Exam focus point

Question 1.10 below is taken from the Pilot Paper for the Personal Taxation Certificate paper.

1.10 Simon is 14 and in full time education. During 2010/11 he received £5,000 (net) from a discretionary trust. He has no other source of income. Calculate Simon's tax position for 2010/11.

1.11 Bert Harvey, born on 8 June 1946, and his wife Betty, born on 18 June 1934, have the following income in 2010/11:

		£
Bert	Earnings	10,214
Betty	State pension	4,953
	Occupational pension	5,200

What is Bert's tax liability for 2010/11?

TQT
Tax Qualification Training

1.12 Nicholas, a 77 year old retired journalist, received the following income during the year ended 5 April 2011:

	£
Income from writing and lecturing	7,700
Net income distributed from his grandfather's discretionary trust	1,375

On 1 March 2011 Nicholas entered into a civil partnership with Paul, who is 66 years old and has net income of £5,000. Calculate Nicholas's tax payable/repayable for 2010/11.

1.13 Richard Key gifted some shares to his twin daughters, Donna and Dawn, age 17. Donna is married and presently working. Dawn is unmarried and at college. Each daughter received a dividend of £1,500 in 2010/11.

Explain who will be taxed on the dividend income received by Donna and Dawn.

1.14 Simon has a full time salary of £34,500. His wife Sarah works part-time earning £14,500 pa. They have a daughter aged 6, she is cared for by her grandmother when Sarah is working. What child tax credit for 2010/11 can they claim assuming their income was the same in 2009/10.

Exam focus point

Question 1.15 below is taken from the Pilot Paper for the Personal Taxation Certificate paper.

1.15 Anthea, aged 34, is a single parent with a daughter, Chloe, aged 7. Anthea works 20 hours a week (during school hours) as an administrator earning £17,000 in 2010/11. She has no other income. Calculate Anthea's entitlement to tax credits for 2010/11.

1.16 Gilbert, aged 5, receives £75 each year in interest income from a deposit account set up for him as a gift from his father. If he has no other income how will this be taxed? Explain your answer.

1.17 Debbie is a single parent with a child aged 5 and she works less than 30 hours a week. Her income for 2009/10 was £8,000 and for 2010/11 is £8,200. What tax credits can she claim for 2010/11?

1.18 Debbie and Johnny are married and have 3 children aged 10, 14 and 18. The eldest child is in full time education. In 2009/10 Johnny had a salary of £21,500 from his full time job. It has not changed in 2010/11. Debbie has no income. What tax credits are available for 2010/11?

1.19 Tanya, age 17, has been unable to work for the past five days due to illness. She earns an annual salary of £15,000. How much weekly statutory sick pay is she entitled to and why?

1.20 Alan is a single man, aged 76. He has income from pensions of £50,000 in 2010/11 and makes the following payments:

(a) Mortgage interest of £5,040 on a loan of £56,000 taken out to purchase his main residence.

(b) Interest of £2,610 on a loan taken out to make a loan to a close company in which he owns 10% of the ordinary share capital.

(c) Maintenance payments to his first wife of £3,000 pa under a court order dated 1 July 1995.

Calculate Alan's tax liability for 2010/11.

2.1 Ian has a salary of £27,040 and building society interest received (gross) of £20,000. Calculate Ian's tax liability for 2010/11.

2.2 Neil and Jenny have held a joint NatEast Bank account for many years. Jenny has only ever put £100 into the account. During 2010/11 interest received on the account amounted to £300. How much of the interest should be taxed on Jenny?

2.3 Christopher has received the following amounts of interest on his NS&I products:

	Year ended 5 April 2011 £
Easy Access Savings account	276
NS&I Certificates	125

He also received a tax repayment for 2009/10 to which HM Revenue & Customs added interest of £89.

Calculate Christopher's interest income for the year ended 5 April 2011?

2.4 Julian made a five year loan to Roch Ltd (unquoted debenture) and a five year loan to his next door neighbour, Bob. During 2010/11 he received interest on both of the loans.

Will the interest receipts be received gross or net? Explain your answer.

2.5 Pamela owns 1,000 £1 ordinary shares in Esher plc. The following dividends were declared:

8p per share for the year ended 31 March 2009, paid 1 June 2010
4p per share for the year ended 31 March 2010, paid 1 June 2011

What amount will Pamela enter into her tax computation for 2010/11?

2.6 Lucy received the following income in 2010/11:

		£
1.	Lloyds Bank	
	Oxford Street branch	8,680
	Guernsey branch (paid gross)	640
2.	Interest on government stock issued in May 2005	5,000

What is her taxable income for 2010/11?

2.7 Sharon received the following income in 2010/11:

	£
Bank deposit interest	2,100
Building society interest	1,800
UK dividends	2,000
	5,900

She has no other sources of income. What is the total amount of tax repayable to Sharon?

2.8 In 2010/11 Sandra has earnings of £3,929. She also received bank interest of £2,500 and dividends of £34,000. What is her tax payable or repayable assuming she has suffered income tax (via PAYE) of £785?

2.9 Anita has earnings of £125,000 (tax of £42,520 deducted via PAYE) in 2010/11. During the year she also received building society interest of £12,500 and dividends of £27,000. What is her tax payable?

Exam focus point

Questions 3.1 to 3.3 below are taken from the Pilot Paper for the Personal Taxation Certificate paper.

3.1 Ben owns a house which he lets out furnished to earn extra income.

In 2010/11 the property was let for the whole year at a rate of £1,500 per month (although he only received rental income of £16,500 as one month was paid late).

He incurred the following expenses

	£
Agent's fee (6 April 2010 – 5 April 2011)	1,800
Mortgage interest	4,200
Water rates	120
Cost of building new porch	2,500
Insurance	500

Calculate Ben's taxable property income.

3.2 Property is anything that can be owned. Although the term is often used to refer to land, it is a much wider concept and includes all assets both tangible and intangible. Explain the difference in legal terms between ownership and possession of property.

3.3 An owner of land may agree to sell it in a number of different ways. Explain the four ways in which a sale of land may take place.

3.4 Harry owns a property which is let for the ten weeks from 1 July 2010 at a rent of £160 per week. The tenants leave at the end of this period having paid only £1,300 of the total amount due. Harry writes off the outstanding debt.

The property is re-let to new tenants on 1 March 2011 for a rent of £400 per month payable in arrears. He received the first payment on 10 April.

He pays interest of £700 during the year ended 5 April 2011 on a loan to purchase the property.

What is his taxable property income for 2010/11?

3.5 John owns two properties:

Whitehouse – let at a rental of £4,000 per annum, payable quarterly in advance. The tenant was late in paying the last quarter's rent for the quarter to 5 April 2011 and John did not receive payment until 25 April 2011.

Blackhouse – let at a rent of £2,000 per annum payable quarterly in advance. Blackhouse was not let at all during 2009/10, however a tenant moved in on 30 June 2010.

What is John's taxable property income for 2010/11?

3.6 Henry owns a property which he lets for the first time on 1 July 2010 at a rent of £4,000 per annum payable monthly in advance.

The first tenants left without notice on 28 February 2011 and the property was re-let to new tenants on 4 April 2011 at a rent of £5,000 per annum payable yearly in advance.

Henry's allowable expenditure was £1,000 in the year. What is his taxable property income for 2010/11?

3.7 Polly lets out a furnished property for £8,000 per annum. She pays insurance of £300 per annum and water rates of £400 per annum. Polly claims the wear and tear allowance. What is the amount taxable as property income?

3.8 Brian rents out a room in his main residence for £5,000 per annum, allowable expenses relating to the rental were £600. What is Brian's taxable property income for 2010/11? Explain your answer.

3.9 State four of the conditions for a property to qualify as a furnished holiday let.

3.10 Personal property under English law can be divided into 'choses in action' and 'choses in possession'.

Explain what is meant by the underlined terms.

4.1 What is the maximum amount of cash and shares that an individual can invest in an ISA in 2010/11?

4.2 What are the main income tax benefits of an ISA?

4.3 Bert, a single man, has taxable non savings income of £56,840 in 2010/11 (all earnings). He invests £580,000 of cash he inherited in qualifying Enterprise Investment Scheme shares in November 2010. What is the tax reduction available to him?

4.4 Gemma has invested the following amounts in qualifying VCTs during 2010/11:

10 June 2010	VCT 1	£150,000
5 September 2010	VCT 2	£60,000

She receives dividends in 2010/11 as follows:

VCT 1	£3,000
VCT 2	£3,400

What amount of net dividends (if any) must be included in her taxable income?

Explain your answer.

Exam focus point

Question 5.1 below is taken from the Pilot Paper for the Personal Taxation Certificate paper.

5.1   Daisy, a full time employee, was made redundant by her employer in June 2010. She received the following redundancy package:

	£
Statutory redundancy pay	3,800
Ex gratia cash payment	25,000
Market value of company car – ownership transferred to Daisy	12,000
Outplacement counselling	4,500

What amount, if any, will be taxable on Daisy?

5.2   Janet is a director of Dragon Ltd. The company accounts show the following remuneration:

Year ended	Salary £	Bonus £
31 December 2010	9,000	2,400
31 December 2011	10,000	4,200

The bonus is paid on 28 February following the year end. The salary is paid evenly over the year.

What is the amount of Janet's taxable income for 2010/11?

5.3   Tina commenced employment with Harrison Electrics Ltd on 1 November 2010. She was paid a salary of £1,000 per month and from 1 January 2011, was given the use of a new Ford Escort 1400cc which has a list price of £15,000 with all private petrol paid for by the company. The emission rate is 165g/km. What are her total earnings from Harrison Electrics Ltd for 2010/11?

5.4   In 2009 Whitegate plc bought a new 3 litre car which has a list price of £14,000 for the sole use of James, one of its directors. The emission rate is 193g/km. The company pays car expenses including all the petrol but James repays to the company a nominal £0.02 per mile for petrol consumed in private motoring. What is James's taxable benefit for 2010/11?

5.5   In 2010/11 Jim, a director of a wine importing company, is paid £10,000 per annum and is given the use of a new 2 litre car which has a list price of £16,000 and an emission rate of 195g/km, plus wine which cost the company £1,000. Jim's 20 year old student daughter, Jane, also works for the company on Saturdays, is paid £15 per day and has the use of a new 1,150cc car which has a list price of £12,000 and an emission rate of 111g/km. Jim uses £600 of the wine promoting the company's products. No private petrol is paid for by the company.

What are Jim's earnings for 2010/11?

5.6   Albert, who has been employed by Roberts Tools Ltd as a salesman for several years, earned a salary of £14,800 in 2010/11 and had the use of a 2 year old Ford Escort 1100, which has a list price of £12,000. The emission rate is 150g/km. No private diesel was paid for.

Albert is also given an expense allowance of £80 each month to cover incidental costs of travelling. At the end of the tax year, he calculated that, of this, £750 would be allowable for tax purposes.

What is the amount to be entered on Albert's form P11D in respect of benefits for 2010/11?

5.7   Grasshopper Ltd has a dispensation from HMRC in respect of travel and subsistence expenses directly reimbursed to its employees.

Mr Adams commenced employment with Grasshopper Ltd on 1 January 2011 and was paid £1,000 per month. His expenses were paid as:

(1)   A round sum allowance of £100 per month payable on the 1st of the month, plus
(2)   Reimbursement of specific travel and subsistence expenses of £250 up to 5 April 2011.

Calculate the amounts to be entered on the P11D for Mr Adams for 2010/11.

5.8 Sue earns £15,000 working for Redbridge Ltd and uses the crèche provided by the company for her child. The cost to the employer is £3,000 per year.

Tara earns £12,000 working for Bluefield Ltd. Her employer pays her registered childminder's fees of £3,200 per annum.

What amounts, if any, are taxable in respect of childcare for 2010/11?

5.9 Daphne is an employee of Surbiton Ltd. The company provided her with a credit card, and during the year paid the following amounts on her behalf:

	£
Annual fee	30
Daphne's private purchases	257
Interest charge for late payment	46
	333

What is Daphne's taxable benefit for 2010/11?

5.10 Joshua is an employee of Mumbles plc, earning £12,000 per annum. He received the following benefits in the year ended 5 April 2011:

	£
Work place parking estimated value	720
Luncheon vouchers (£1 a day for 240 days a year)	240
Credit card expenditure: goods purchased for business use	272

What are Joshua's taxable benefits in 2010/11?

5.11 A company throws a staff party which cost £200 per head. What is the tax position for the employee?

5.12 Finlay, a chartered accountant, is the Finance Director of Globe Ltd, a company which is based in Derbyshire. He personally incurs the following expenses in 2010/11:

(1) Subscription to the Chartered Institute of Taxation of £220

(2) Subscription to local golf club of £250, as required by Globe Ltd in order to promote the firm's business contacts

(3) Subscription to the Naval Club in London of £200 in order to have somewhere to stay overnight when his duties necessitate an overnight stay in London.

What amount is he able to deduct from his employment income in 2010/11?

5.13 Bert earns £18,000 pa and lives in job related accommodation provided by his employer. The company pays £2,000 rent and £3,100 for household expenses in the year ended 5 April 2011. What are Bert's taxable earnings for 2010/11?

5.14 Paul was provided with two mobile phones costing £250 each and a laptop computer costing £5,000 by his employer on 5 April 2010. During 2010/11 he used his mobile phone 40% of the time for personal calls (the other was used by his daughter) and the laptop 60% of the time for non business purposes. What is Paul's taxable benefit for 2010/11?

5.15 John has a salary of £30,000 pa. He drives his own 1.5l engine car to work taking his 2 year old daughter to a crèche on the way. John's employer pays the cost of the crèche which is £200 per week. John is provided with a designated parking space at his employer's premises. This costs the employer £1,000 pa. Sometimes John has to drive to clients and his employer reimburses him for his business mileage at 60p per mile. In 2010/11 John did 5,000 business miles. Calculate John's earnings for 2010/11.

5.16 Ruth is an employee of Benson Ltd and earns a salary of £45,000 pa. Benson Ltd have loaned her £20,000 so she can redecorate her house. As at 5 April 2010 there was an outstanding balance of £15,000. On 5 January 2011 Ruth repaid a further £5,000. Ruth pays Benson Ltd interest at 3% pa on the loan. The official rate of interest throughout 2010/11 is 4%. What is Ruth's taxable benefit for 2010/11?

5.17 Jason is an employee of Saranson Ltd. The company provide him with a house near their office. Saranson Ltd bought the house in 1992 at a cost of £80,000. Jason moved in 2002 when the market value of the house was £130,000. At 6 April 2010 the market value of the house was £250,000 and the gross annual value is £5,000. Jason pays Saranson Ltd rent of £3,000 pa. Calculate Jason's taxable benefit for 2010/11 assuming the official rate of interest is 4%.

5.18 Natalie is a receptionist at Hospitality Hotel. She was provided with the use of a dinner set by the hotel on 6 October 2009. Its market value at that date was £2,000. On 6 October 2010 the hotel agreed to sell the dinner set to Natalie for £1,000, its market value at that date was £1,500. Calculate the taxable benefit for 2010/11.

5.19 Judy is an employee of Markham Ltd. She earns £25,750 pa and is provided with a company owned flat. The flat cost the company £60,000 when it was bought in 1993. Judy moved into the flat in 2000 when its market value was £100,000. The annual value of the flat is £3,000. Markham Ltd also pays for Judy's heating and lighting bills, this costs the company £400 pa. Judy is also provided with furniture for use in her flat. The market value of the furniture was £2,500 in 2000. Calculate Judy's taxable benefit for 2010/11 assuming the official rate of interest is 4%.

5.20 George was unexpectedly made redundant on 15 August 2010. His redundancy package was as follows:

	£
Payment in lieu of notice (provided for in his employment contract)	8,000
Ex gratia payment	40,000
Statutory redundancy pay	5,000

The £40,000 payment was not contractual and George did not expect it. How much of the package is taxable?

5.21 Alan receives a non-contractual termination payment of £51,000 from Duxton Ltd. He has spent 10 years out of his 30 years service with the company working abroad, his last 2 years of service being spent in the UK. How much of the termination payment will be exempt from income tax.

5.22 Charles Prosser is a company director and occupies a house owned by the company. The house was purchased in May 2003 for £400,000 and an extension was added in September 2010 at a cost of £30,000. The gross annual value of the house was £2,225. During 2010/11 Charles paid £2,725 as rent to the company. Assume that the official rate of interest for 2010/11 is 4%.

Calculate the amount taxable on Charles Prosser for 2010/11 as a benefit in respect of the provision of accommodation.

5.23 List six items that you would expect to see covered in a typical contract for consultancy services provided by an independent contractor.

Exam focus point

Question 6.1 below is taken from the Pilot Paper for the Personal Taxation Certificate paper.

6.1 Ray was granted an Enterprise Management Incentive option in July 2007 to acquire 10,000 shares for £1.50 each in Ex Ltd, his employing company. The shares were worth £2 each at the date of grant. He exercised the option in July 2010 when the share price was £4.75.

Explain the income tax consequences of the grant and exercise, assuming all the conditions for a qualifying EMI option are met.

6.2 What is the maximum value of 'free shares' and 'partnership shares' that can be allocated to an employee per annum under an all-employee share incentive plan (SIP)?

6.3 George exercises his option over 10,000 shares which he received from an unapproved share option plan. The exercise price was £11.50 each and the shares were worth £15.00 each at the date of exercise. He is a higher rate taxpayer. What is the income tax payable on exercise?

7.1 What are the classes of national insurance contributions (NICs) payable by (a) employees, and (b) self employed individuals, and on what are they based?

7.2 Explain what Class 1A NICs are based on and who pays the Class 1A liability.

7.3 Employees who are members of an occupational pension scheme may contract out of the State Second Pension Scheme.

Explain the consequences for both the employer and the employee where the scheme is contracted out.

8.1 George has the following income:

	£
Profits from his publishing business	28,000
Dividend income from shares	5,400

What is the maximum amount George can pay into his personal pension on which he is entitled to tax relief?

8.2 Norma is a housewife. She is 52 years old. Her only taxable income in 2010/11 is a dividend of £5,000.

Norma wants to take out a pension. Explain the maximum contribution that she can make for 2010/11 on which tax relief is available?

8.3 Daniel aged 30 is an employee of Smithson Ltd. His salary for 2010/11 is £52,000. The company does not have an occupational pension scheme so Daniel pays contributions into his personal pension.

In 2010/11 Daniel pays £5,000 into his pension. What is Daniel's higher rate tax liability for 2010/11?

8.4 Jeremy has earnings of £400,000 in 2010/11. Advise him of the maximum contribution he can make to a pension in the year and obtain tax relief and the tax consequences of contributing this amount.

8.5 Cindy plans to start drawing her pension in 2010/11. Her personal pension fund is worth £65,000. How much can Cindy take as a tax free lump sum?

8.6 Maxine has taxable earnings of £54,000 in 2010/11. Her employer deducts a contribution to the company's registered occupational pension scheme of £9,000 from these earnings before operating PAYE. She has no other taxable income.

Show Maxine's tax liability for 2010/11.

9.1 Wayne, age 34, is domiciled in America but has lived in London for 15 years. In 2010/11 he remits £10,000 (including overseas tax) of foreign dividends from a company resident in America and has a further £400,000 of foreign dividends which he does not remit. He is a higher rate taxpayer and has made a remittance basis claim. How much is his tax liability on his foreign dividends?

9.2 Egbert is UK resident and ordinarily resident. He worked in Germany many years ago and now receives a German pension of £10,000 each year. How much of the pension is taxable in 2010/11?

9.3 Ronald (a British citizen) goes abroad for full time employment.

State the conditions which must be satisfied for him to be treated as not resident and not ordinarily resident from the date of his departure until the date of his return.

Exam focus point

Question 10.1 below is taken from the Pilot Paper for the Personal Taxation Certificate paper.

10.1 Jenny, a higher rate taxpayer, sold a painting on 15 May 2010 realising a chargeable gain of £18,000. Calculate Jenny's capital gains tax liability for 2010/11.

10.2 Justin made a disposal on 1 June 2010 realising a chargeable gain of £32,000. He made another disposal on 14 August 2010, realising a chargeable gain of £26,000. Calculate Justin's capital gains tax liability for 2010/11 assuming he had taxable income in the year of £29,500.

10.3 What is the minimum residency requirement for an individual to be within the charge to capital gains tax?

10.4 Which of the following assets are exempt for capital gains tax purposes?

- A diamond brooch
- A thoroughbred racehorse
- A lease with an unexpired term of 25 years
- A computer used in a business
- A limousine used by a car hire company.

Exam focus point

Questions 11.1 and 11.2 below are taken from the Pilot Paper for the Personal Taxation Certificate paper.

11.1 David was left a painting in June 1989 on the death of his great aunt. Records showed she had purchased it in May 1985 for £7,200 and it was worth £11,200 on her death in 1989. David decided to sell the painting in May 2010 when it was worth £31,250. Calculate the chargeable gain on the sale of the painting.

11.2 Toby bought a plot of land in July 2001 for investment purposes for £18,000. In June 2010 a local developer offered him £125,000 for the plot. Toby decided to keep a quarter of the plot and sold the remaining site to the developer for £85,000. The plot that Toby retained was valued at £30,000. Calculate the chargeable gain arising in 2010/11.

11.3 Edwin has chargeable gains of £9,000 and allowable losses of £5,000 in 2010/11. He has allowable losses brought forward of £6,000. What are the allowable losses carried forward to 2011/12?

11.4 James has the following chargeable gains and losses arising from disposals of assets:

Tax year	2008/09 £	2009/10 £	2010/11 £
Gains	2,000	4,000	13,000
Losses	(5,000)	(2,000)	(2,000)

All assets had been owned for many years. What is the maximum allowable loss carried forward to 2011/12?

11.5 Paul invites the following people to a celebration dinner:

(1) His wife
(2) His mother-in-law
(3) His business partner
(4) The ex-wife of his business partner
(5) His uncle
(6) His step-father
(7) His band manager

Who is connected with Paul for CGT purposes?

11.6 Callum bought a freehold shop for use in his business on 13 July 2002 for £120,000. On 12 March 2005, when the shop was worth £150,000, he transferred the shop to his wife, Grace, who also used the shop in her business. On 12 May 2010, Grace sold the shop for £170,000. What is Grace's chargeable gain on the shop?

11.7 James sold assets to the following individuals, creating chargeable gains and allowable losses as shown below:

	Date of sale	Chargeable gain/ (allowable loss) £
Charles, his brother	1 March 2010	10,000
	15 June 2010	(8,200)
	29 September 2011	14,000
Sarah, his sister	2 August 2010	21,500
	1 July 2011	8,000
Mr Smith (not connected with James)	22 December 2010	9,000

Which gain will the allowable loss be set off against? Explain your reasoning.

11.8 Julie owned a field which she purchased on 13 August 1987 for £8,000. On 10 September 2010, she sold a quarter of the field for development for £30,000. The remainder of the field was then worth £10,000. What is Julie's chargeable gain?

11.9 Mattheus made gains of £17,400 and losses of £7,000 in 2010/11. He has losses brought forward of £5,000.

Calculate the losses to carry forward to 2011/12.

11.10 Kidson purchased a plot of land on 1 January 1983 for £8,000. On 31 August 2010, he sold part of the land for £45,000 but declined an offer of £50,000 for the rest.

Calculate the taxable gain arising on the sale assuming this is the only capital transaction Kidson has in 2010/11.

Exam focus point

Question 12.1 below is taken from the Pilot Paper for the Personal Taxation Certificate paper.

12.1   Andrew bought 2,000 shares in X plc for £18,000 in August 2006 and a further 1,000 shares for £10,000 in September 2006. He sold 1,500 shares for £22,500 in January 2011. Calculate his chargeable gain.

12.2   Amber had the following transactions in the shares of Zingo Ltd:

		£
19.2.83	Purchased 2,000 shares, cost	10,000
20.9.90	Purchased 1,000 shares, cost	8,000
15.11.10	Sold 1,500 shares, proceeds	22,000

What is Amber's chargeable gain for 2010/11?

12.3   Mr Smith acquired 5,000 shares in S plc in April 1985 for £5,605. In July 1999 S plc made a bonus issue of one ordinary share for every five held. In December 2010 Mr Smith sold 3,500 of his shares for £6,250. What is the chargeable gain?

13.1   Lionel purchased a Victoria Cross medal in May 1983 for £3,000 and a vintage car in June 1985 for £4,000. He sold them both to a collector in May 2010 for £14,780 and £15,500 respectively.

What, if any, are his chargeable gains for 2010/11?

13.2   Giles purchased a picture in July 1991 for £4,500 and sold it in September 2010 for £7,500 before incurring £300 expenses of sale. What is Giles' chargeable gain?

13.3   Gail sold a painting for £90 in December 2010 which had cost £6,260 in January 1983. What is Gail's allowable loss for 2010/11?

13.4   On 1 April 1990 Mr Laycole acquired a painting on the death of his father at a probate value of £3,000. He sold the painting at auction for £7,200 on 30 October 2010 incurring costs of £350. Compute the chargeable gain.

13.5   In August 2010 Miranda, a sole trader whose business is ongoing, disposed of two assets on which capital allowances have been claimed.

	Purchase Price	Disposal Proceeds
	£	£
Motor car	8,000	4,000
Machinery	5,500	7,500

Both assets were purchased in October 2005. Calculate Miranda's chargeable gain or allowable loss.

13.6   Adrienne acquired a 90 year lease on 31 March 1983 for £40,000. On 31 March 2011 she granted a sublease of 55 years for £30,000. The reversionary interest is valued at £82,500. What is Adrienne's chargeable gain?

13.7   Jerome acquired a freehold property for £30,000 in March 1991. In November 2010 he granted an 11 year lease for a premium of £10,000 at which time the reversionary interest was valued at £50,000. What is Jerome's chargeable gain?

14.1   Neil sold a house on 30 June 2010. He realised an £80,000 gain before taking account of any PPR relief. The house was originally purchased on 1 October 1983 and was occupied by Neil until 30 June 1986 at which date he purchased and moved into another residence, letting the original house until the date of sale.

What is his chargeable gain?

14.2   Robert owned a property with three storeys of equal value in Sheffield. He bought it on 30 June 1985 for £20,000. He used the top two storeys as his main residence. The ground floor was rented out to students. The ground floor has a separate access door. On 30 November 2010 Robert sold the whole property for £200,000. What is his chargeable gain?

14.3   Give two examples of periods of absence from a property which are deemed periods of occupation for the CGT principal private residence exemption.

Exam focus point

Question 15.1 below is taken from the Pilot Paper for the Personal Taxation Certificate paper.

15.1   Jeremy Brett, who had run a manufacturing business for many years, decided to reduce the size of the operation in 2010/11. He therefore gave one of the factories (which had always been used for his business) to his son John although John persuaded his father to accept £50,000 in return.

The factory had been acquired on 2 January 1983 for £42,000. It was worth £225,974 and standing at a gain of £110,000 when it was passed to John in August 2010.

Calculate Jeremy's chargeable gain, if any, for 2010/11 and state the base cost for John, on the assumption that gift relief is claimed.

15.2   On 1 May 2010 Arthur sold a business asset to his son, Hugo, for £12,000. At that time the market value of the asset was £22,000. Arthur had purchased the asset in July 1985 for £4,000.

Gift relief is claimed on the disposal. Who needs to make the claim and what is the deadline for the claim?

15.3   On 1 January 2011 Adam sold a business asset to his son, Bernard, for £12,000. At that time the market value of the asset was £22,000. Adam had purchased the asset in July 1985 for £4,000.

In 2012/13 Bernard permanently ceased to be resident in the UK. At the time he left the UK the asset had a market value of £25,000.

What chargeable gain arises as a result (assuming a joint claim for gift relief had been made in respect of the January 2011 disposal), on whom is this chargeable and in what tax year?

15.4   Robert bought an 80% holding in an unquoted trading company on 10 July 2004 for £160,000. He gave the holding to his daughter, Lauren, on 13 December 2010, when it was worth £300,000. At that date, the assets of the company were:

	£
Factory	300,000
Quoted investments	50,000
Net current assets	25,000
	375,000

What is the gain chargeable on Robert before the annual exempt amount?

15.5   In July 2010 Phil sold an asset of his farming business to his daughter Shula for £63,000 when its open market value was £95,000. Phil had bought the asset in May 1995 for £44,000. How much gift relief can be claimed by Phil and Shula?

15.6   In March 2010 Keith Pringle purchased an antique tea set for £24,000. In September 2010 the teapot was broken and he received £4,000 from the insurance company as compensation in October 2010. The remaining tea set was valued at £16,000. Calculate the gain/loss arising.

15.7   Patrice makes a gain of £600,000 in July 2010 on the sale of a flat in Brighton (not her main residence). In November 2009 she had subscribed £800,000 for shares in a qualifying EIS company and makes the maximum possible claim for EIS deferral relief. In August 2011 Patrice emigrates to Switzerland.

What chargeable gains will arise in 2010/11 and/or 2011/12?

15.8   In 1999 John invested £50,000 to acquire a 10% shareholding in Silvanus Ltd. In July 2010 he sold all his shares in this company for £800,000. John has £150,000 of capital losses brought forward as at 6 April 2010 and made no other disposals in 2010/11.

What is the minimum investment John must make in qualifying EIS shares to reduce his gain on the disposal of the Silvanus Ltd shares to nil?

Exam focus point

Question 16.1 below is taken from the Pilot Paper for the Personal Taxation Certificate paper.

16.1   A landlord is allowed to submit a simplified return in respect of rental income provided the appropriate condition is satisfied. What is the condition and what needs to be recorded on the return?

16.2   Thomas Apple received his 2010/11 tax return on 19 May 2011. Outline Thomas's options for filing this tax return.

16.3   John's income tax and CGT position for 2009/10 was as follows:

	£
Income tax liability	10,250
Tax deducted at source	(5,000)
	5,250
Class 4 NIC	1,000
CGT liability	8,200
Payments on account made for 2009/10	(5,000)
	9,450

Calculate John's payments on account for 2010/11 stating the due dates.

16.4   Gareth filed his 2010/11 tax return on 15 December 2011. He deliberately omitted an amount of overseas interest income of £6,000, that he was aware was taxable in the UK, from the return. Gareth is a higher rate taxpayer.

Explain any penalties to which Gareth will be liable.

17.1   One of your clients, Martin Edwards, pays his pension scheme contributions through you as broker and the insurance company have just sent you commission thereon of £500. What steps should you take under the ATT Professional Rules and Practice Guidelines 2006?

17.2   A prospective client has contacted you to take over from his existing adviser. He alleges that the previous adviser was incompetent and insists that you do not contact him. What should you do?

17.3   Sheila and Ken Walters, each a client of many years standing, have decided to divorce 'amicably'. They have effectively lived apart under the same roof for some time. Ken is only interested in his garden and Sheila has made the golf club her second home so they feel they should formally separate with an intention to divorce. They are both insistent that you should continue to act for them. What should you do?

17.4   What are a member's usual responsibilities in respect of due dates and interest on tax where a member undertakes tax compliance work for a client?

17.5   If a member is engaged in a fee dispute with a client he may call for arbitration from the ATT. True/ False.

17.6   Which type of fee arrangement is specifically considered within the regime for disclosure of tax avoidance schemes?

17.7   Robbie's firm is holding £20,000 of a client's money. How long can they hold the money before they should open a designated interest bearing client account?

17.8   What are the three ways in which land can be legally held?

17.9   What is the maximum number of legal owners of land?

17.10 In the case of registered land at what point does the legal title pass from the seller to the buyer?

17.11 Sara has been unfairly dismissed. What orders may the employment tribunal make in her favour?

Long form questions

1.1 Mr Daphnis

Mr Daphnis (aged 69) is married to Chloë (aged 77) and is registered blind.

Mr Daphnis's net income for 2010/11 was £24,080, made up of rental income (£14,080) and savings interest (£10,000). Chloë's only income is her pension of £4,500.

You are required to calculate Mr and Mrs Daphnis's allowances and tax reductions for 2010/11. Also give brief advice on how they could improve their joint tax position.

1.2 Mr Rich

Mr Rich earned £118,500 from his employment in 2010/11. He paid tax of £37,330 under PAYE.

He paid £12,000 (net) to Oxfam via Gift Aid in the year.

You are required to calculate his tax payable/repayable.

> The following question is taken from the Pilot Paper for the Personal Taxation Certificate paper.

1.3 Tax Credits

You have recently received the following letter from one of your clients:

21 Avon Avenue
Avonbury
Bucks

T Adviser
Corton & Co
West Street
Anytown

Dear Tom

Thank you for preparing our tax returns, which we have signed and are returning to you for submission.

On another matter, as you may know, my husband and I are expecting a baby this June. I have heard a lot on TV about child and working tax credits and wondered whether I would be entitled to any when the baby is born, particularly as I will only be working part time going forward.

I have done some research and am familiar with the rates of the allowances together with the conditions that need to be met to be entitled to them eg age, working hours etc. However, the one thing I cannot work out is how to calculate income to compare to the income limit of £6,420.

Can you explain to me how my income would be calculated for tax credit purposes or is it simply the same as taxable income for income tax purposes?

I look forward to hearing from you.

Best regards

Julie Smythe

Julie Smythe is an employee who received the following income in 2010/11:

	£
Salary	22,000
Car benefit	2,150
Medical insurance	540
Use of home entertainment system (benefit amount)	1,200

She paid her own subscription to the Institute of Personnel and Development of £150.

Her husband is a self employed designer who, after several loss-making years, made a profit in 2009/10 of £13,500 as adjusted for tax purposes and after loss relief.

They received bank interest on their joint savings account of £45 (net) and paid £10 per month to the RSPCA under the Gift Aid scheme.

You are required to write a reply to Julie Smythe addressing the definition of income for tax credit purposes.

You are NOT required to provide any calculations.

(10 marks)

2.1 **Mr Poor**

Mr Poor took early retirement in 2003 when he was 55. He now works part time. In 2010/11 his gross earnings were £6,050 (no tax deducted via PAYE). He received £900 in dividends and £800 of building society interest. He received interest on his Midwest Savings Bank account totalling £80.

You are required to calculate his tax payable/repayable.

2.2 **Jonty**

Jonty, aged 38, is a married man whose wife has no income. The following information is relevant for the year ended 5 April 2011:

(1)   His salary was £46,000 (income tax deducted via PAYE of £8,330)

(2)   His other income was:

	£
Building society interest received	80
Dividends received	63

(3)   In March 2011 Jonty closed down his NS&I investment account which he had kept for many years. Interest of £142 was credited.

(4)   He made a donation of £396 (net of basic rate tax) to Oxfam in May 2010 under Gift Aid.

(5)   Jonty won £100 on the Grand National.

(6)   He has one child aged 4 whom his wife looks after. Jonty works over 30 hours per week.

You are required to compute the tax payable by/ repayable to Jonty for 2010/11. You are also required to calculate any Child Tax Credit/Working Tax Credit available.

2.3 **Fred**

Fred (78) is married to Wilma (71). Fred received the following income in 2010/11:

	£
Rental income	16,200
Building society interest	4,400
UK Treasury Stock interest	290
UK company dividends	7,000

Wilma has no income.

You are required to calculate Fred's tax payable for 2010/11.

2.4 **Fiona**

Fiona, who is 35, lives on her own. She has been running her own business for many years. Her taxable trading profits for 2010/11 are £32,000.

During 2010/11 she received the following investment income:

	£
UK dividends	10,000
Jersey bank interest (received gross)	4,300
Premium bond winnings	13,000
Child benefit in respect of her 6 year old twins for whom she has sole custody	1,750

Fiona borrowed £24,000 on 31 March 2009 to invest in a 15% shareholding in a close company. She pays interest at 4% per annum. She repaid £10,000 of the loan when she received her Premium Bond winnings on 5 December 2010. She subscribed for £3,000 of shares in an EIS company with the remainder.

She pays an annual donation to charity of £1,600 under Gift Aid.

You are required to calculate Fiona's tax payable for 2010/11.

2.5 Jane Bradbury

Jane Bradbury is in her 30s. Her husband died last year leaving her to bring up their child now aged 2. The child attends a registered nursery for 3 days a week at a cost of £20 per day. Jane works 20 hours per week.

Jane is a partner in a small firm making children's clothes. Her profit share for 2010/11 has been agreed at £7,140.

Jane pays interest of £4,800 each year on a loan she took out in 2002 to buy into the partnership.

Jane has an investment portfolio which generated dividends of £4,950 in 2010/11. Her only other income is bank interest received on a bank account of £200.

Calculate Jane's tax repayable for 2010/11. Calculate any Child Tax Credit/Working Tax Credit due.

2.6 George and Mildred Roper

George Roper (aged 73) married Mildred (age 77) on 10 February 2011. Both have been married before. George pays his ex-wife Liz (age 77) £250 each month by way of maintenance after their divorce in 1998. Mildred's former husband Brian died in May 2006.

George's income for 2010/11 is as follows:

	£
Earnings from part time consultancy work (£905 income tax deducted via PAYE)	11,000
Pension from former employer (£520 income tax deducted via PAYE)	2,600
State pension (£97.65 per week)	5,078
UK Treasury stock interest	180
Rental income from holiday home	4,000
UK dividends received	2,115

George pays interest at 10% per annum on a loan which he had taken out to buy shares in Hi Tek Ltd. £10,000 of the loan is outstanding and he claims interest relief.

Mildred's income for 2010/11 is as follows:

	£
State pension (£97.65 per week)	5,078
Building society interest received	8,400
Distribution from discretionary trust	3,300
Interest from bank account in Guernsey (received gross)	1,215
Premium Bond winnings	400
UK dividends received	720

Mildred pays £500 each year to the NSPCC (a registered charity) under Gift Aid.

Calculate George and Mildred's tax payable/repayable for 2010/11.

2.7 Lauren

Lauren receives earnings of £23,000 (£3,705 tax deducted via PAYE).

She also received the following investment income during 2010/11:

	£
UK bank interest	22,000
UK dividends	67,500
Payment from a discretionary trust	32,000

She makes monthly payments of £100 to charity under Gift Aid.

You are required to calculate Lauren's tax payable for 2010/11.

3.1 Randall

Randall owns three unfurnished properties which are let on the following terms, all rents being payable quarterly in advance (on 31 March, 30 June, 30 September and 31 December). Randall is responsible for repairs on all properties; the rents on properties A, B and C are full rents.

A   Let at £620 a year on a 20 year lease which commenced in 2000.

B   Let at £348 a year on a lease which expired on 30 September 2010, then empty until 31 December 2010 when let at £440 a year.

C   Let at £100 a year throughout the year.

Expenditure by Randall on these properties in the year was as follows:

	A £	B £	C £
Agent's commission	20		
Advertising for tenants		76	
Repairs: while let	142		119
while empty		255	

You are required to:

(1)   **Calculate the property income assessment for Randall for 2010/11.**

(2)   **Explain the income tax implications of receiving a premium on granting a lease.**

3.2 Corelli

Corelli, aged 41, owns three properties:

A   5 Arnhem Avenue

B   17 Blenheim Road

C   27 Cannae Road.

All are let out unfurnished.

A   This was let until 30 June 2010 at an annual rental of £1,200. On 30 September 2010, it was let out to a new tenant on a 10 year lease agreement. The annual rental is £800. The tenant paid a premium of £5,000 on 30 September 2010.

B   This was let throughout 2010/11. The annual rental was £3,100. The rental due on 31 March 2011 was not received until 12 April 2011.

C   This was let from 30 June 2010 at an annual rental of £600.

All the rents are payable quarterly in advance (on 31 March, 30 June, 30 September and 31 December) and are sufficient normally to cover the landlord's outgoings.

Properties A and B were acquired in 1981; property C was purchased on 15 April 2010.

Expenditure in connection with the properties was as follows:

	A £	B £	C £
Agent's commission 1 May 2010	25	35	10
1 November 2010	25	35	10
Repairs (note)	–	100	1,800
Advertising for new tenants 10 July 2010	50	–	–

Note. The repairs in respect of property C are analysed as follows:

	£
Installation of new kitchen equipment	300
Retiling part of the roof after damage in May 2010	1,500
	1,800

Corelli's other income during 2010/11 was as follows:

	£
Dividends received	15,300
Salary (£1,995 deducted via PAYE)	16,450

(i)   **You are required to compute Corelli's income tax payable for 2010/11.**   **(7 marks)**

(ii) **You are required to explain the difference between freehold and leasehold land.**   **(5 marks)**

(Total: 12 marks)

4.1   **Enterprise Investment Scheme**

You are required to describe the income tax relief and capital gains tax exemption in respect of an investment in shares qualifying under the Enterprise Investment Scheme.

Your answer should cover the main points in brief outline only.

5.1   **Mr Thomas**

Mr Thomas is a director of a private company. His remuneration for 2010/11 was £30,000.

During the year ended 5 April 2011, the following benefits were provided to him:

(1)   Accommodation in a four bedroom house, owned by the company.

	£
Original cost 1994	80,000
Cost of extension 1998	25,000
Annual value	750

Mr Thomas moved in on 1 March 2003, at which time the house was valued at £134,375.

Expenses paid directly by the company 2010/11:

	£
Council tax	1,400
Electricity	750
Gas	250
Telephone	350
Redecoration (internal)	700
Gardener	1,500

(2)   Interest-free loan for a non-qualifying purpose – first advance 6 June 2010

		£
6.6.10	advance	10,000
6.8.10	advance	5,000
6.12.10	repaid	7,500
6.2.11	advance	4,000
6.3.11	repaid	2,500

(3)   Car   –   Mercedes, list price £21,500, purchased 1 June 2007. The emission rate is 145g/km.

–   1,600 cc Escape, list price £10,000, purchased 5 August 2010, used by Mrs Thomas. The emission rate is 119g/km.

No petrol was provided for either vehicle.

You are required to calculate Mr Thomas's taxable benefits for 2010/11.

Assume that the official rate of interest charged throughout 2010/11 was 4%.

5.2 Alf

You have been consulted by Alf, one of the directors of your company, who has no shareholding in the company, concerning the taxability of emoluments and benefits received. The following information is provided for the tax year 2010/11.

(1) Alf's salary is £96,600 (PAYE £28,570).

(2) An expenses allowance of £2,500 for 2010/11 spent as follows:

	£
Business travelling	1,800
Entertainment:	
Overseas customers	400
Overseas suppliers	100
United Kingdom customers	200

(3) Benefits for the year were as follows:

(i) The company purchased stereo equipment for Alf's personal use at a cost of £800. The company retained ownership of the equipment.

(ii) Alf had exclusive use of a new 2.5 litre petrol engined car with a list price of £15,000. The emission rate is 175g/km. No petrol was provided for private motoring.

(iii) Medical insurance was provided for £300. Alf would have had to pay £450 to take out the insurance personally.

(iv) Alf visited Saville Row for 5 tailored shirts, which were paid for by the company, on Alf's behalf at a cost of £400.

(v) Alf's other income for 2010/11 is as follows:

	£
Bank interest received	5,440
Dividends received	4,000

(vi) He pays £1,600 each year to charity under Gift Aid.

You are required to calculate the tax payable by Alf for 2010/11, giving brief explanatory notes on the treatment of his benefits and expenses.

5.3 Mr Bjork

Mr Bjork is chairman and chief executive of Peepop Ltd.

He receives a salary of £46,000 per annum and during the income tax year 2010/11 he is provided with the following benefits:

The company provided him with the use of a 2,100 cc petrol Jaguar motor car with a list price of £20,000 from 6 April 2010. The emission rate is 215g/km.

On 31 July 2010 he was involved in a serious road accident and the car was written off. He was charged with dangerous driving and the company met his legal costs of £2,000.

While he had use of the Jaguar, he contributed 50% of the cost of his private fuel.

When he resumed work on 1 October 2010, he was provided with a Mercedes car with a list price of £30,000 and the use of a chauffeur. This car is used solely for business purposes. The emission rate is 185g/km.

Throughout the year, his wife, who is not employed by the company, has been provided with the use of a 2 litre BMW car with a list price of £15,000 four years ago. The company meets all running costs and petrol bills. The emission rate is 235g/km.

He is provided with the use of video equipment which had been purchased by the company at a cost of £800.

He is given a computer by Peepop Ltd on 6 October 2010, when it has a market value of £200. He has had use of that computer since 6 October 2008 when its market value was £3,000.

You are required to compute the total amount of benefits taxable on Mr Bjork for 2010/11.

5.4 HiTech Computers

Giles has worked for HiTech Computers Plc for many years and he has recently been promoted to sales manager, receiving a £5,000 pay rise from 1 July 2010. His revised salary is £36,000. He has continued to pay contributions into his registered occupational pension of 5% of his salary and commission. He has received sales commission as follows:

Year ended 31 December 2009	£3,000 received 28 February 2010
Year ended 31 December 2010	£4,000 received 28 February 2011

As a result of his promotion, he has been provided with a flat in London, due to being required to spend increasing amounts of time in London. The company pays £5,000 annual rent on the property, which has an annual value of £2,400. He is required to contribute £100 per month towards this.

Giles still has an interest free loan from the company for the purchase of his private car. The amount outstanding was £15,000 on 6 April 2010 and £10,000 on 5 April 2011. He has a car parking space provided in London under the HiTech Computers plc building that costs the company £1,200 per annum.

Other perks that Giles receives are as follows:

(1)   Free medical insurance – the cost to the company is £385 per annum although if Giles had taken this out privately, he would have to pay £525 to cover both him and his wife.

(2)   £100 per month payment towards the provision of crèche facilities for his child who attends a registered private nursery.

(3)   A newspaper allowance of £20 per month.

You are required to calculate Giles's earnings for 2010/11, giving explanations of your treatment of the benefits.

Assume that the official rate of interest is 4% for the whole year.

5.5 Grovelands

Grovelands Ltd, an electrical company, was taken over in 2010. Freddie, a senior executive in charge of business sales did not get along with new management and his employment was terminated on 31 December 2010. The company provided him with an ex gratia payment of £84,974, of which £72,487 was paid on 31 December 2010 and £12,487 in May 2011.

Freddie's salary from Grovelands Ltd for the year to 31 December 2010 had been £129,333. He subsequently took a part time consultancy post with another company for £8,400 per annum. The salary was to be paid in equal monthly instalments in arrears. This new job started on 1 February 2011.

Grovelands Ltd had allowed Freddie the use of a home entertainment system, which was worth £5,000 when loaned to him on 1 July 2009. On his departure from the company, Freddie bought the system (now worth £1,000) for £150.

Freddie's other income and expenses for the year 2010/11 were as follows:

	£
Benefits:	
Company car (2500 cc; list price in 2009 was £22,300; approved CO_2 emissions figure 209 g/km).	
BUPA medical insurance cover (paid by Grovelands)	200
London Transport season ticket (reimbursed by Grovelands)	2,641
UK dividends – amount received	2,754
Bank interest received	1,386
Gift aid payment (net)	800

Freddie drove his company car on business for 1,200 miles (out of a total of 10,000 miles) during 2010/11. Grovelands Ltd paid directly for all the car's running expenses including petrol which amounted to £3,200 up to 31 December 2010, at which date it was returned to the company.

(i)   **You are required to compute Freddie's total income tax liability for 2010/11.**   **(15 marks)**

(ii)   **You are required to explain the meaning of summary dismissal and constructive dismissal.** **(5 marks)**

(Total: 20 marks)

5.6 Mr Morris

Mr Morris, aged 41, joined William and Sons Limited in March 2009. He negotiated a package comprising a basic annual salary of £25,175, a two litre company car (list price £14,665; CO_2 emissions 182g/km) with all private petrol provided and also health insurance costing £340 paid on his behalf by the company.

Income tax of £5,441 was deducted from his salary via PAYE in 2010/11.

Mr Morris received the following amounts from his investments in 2010/11:

	£
Building society account interest	312
UK dividends	738

He also held a joint account with his wife at Burford Bank which had been credited with £256 worth of interest in 2010/11.

Mr Morris inherited a house in Devon from his father 15 years ago. This property (which is furnished) is let out by Mr Morris, who employs a letting agent to deal with the rental. The details for 2010/11 are as follows:

6.4.10 – 31.8.10

Let to the Adams family
Gross rent per annum £8,000 payable quarterly in arrears

	£
Agent's fees	267
Repairs and maintenance	400
Gardener	100
Council tax (for 2010/11)	590
Water rates	85

1.10.10 – 5.4.11

Let to the Potter family
Gross rent per annum £12,000 payable quarterly in arrears

	£
Agent's fees	600
Repairs and maintenance (including £1,000 incurred in September 2010)	1,500
Gardener	200
Water rates	100
Cost and installation of new gas fire	435

Note. The rent due on 31 March was not actually paid until 15 April 2011.

Mr Morris claims the wear and tear allowance rather than the renewals basis.

Mr Morris also pays £156 each year to Oxfam under the gift aid scheme (he does not intend to make an election to carry back the payment to 2009/10).

You are required to calculate Mr Morris's outstanding income tax payable for 2010/11. **(10 marks)**

6.1 Sue

Sue has been a director of Porchester Ltd for three years. In order to reward her performance to the company on 1 January 2011, she was granted 5,000 ordinary share options under an approved scheme to buy shares at £4.00 at any time in the next 10 years. The market value of the shares at January 2011 was £3.96. She is planning to buy the shares in 8 years time when she estimates that the share price will have risen to £10.00. She plans to sell them shortly afterwards (assume share price at date of sale = £10.40).

You are required to:

(a) **Explain the tax consequences of the granting of the share options and the subsequent sale by Sue.**

(b) **Explain how your answer would change if the scheme was unapproved and the exercise price was £3.00.**

7.1 **Mr Howe**

Mr Howe recently started working for a new employer. His employment package for 2010/11 is as follows:

Salary	£35,000
Company car (and petrol): CO_2 emissions 135g/km – list price of:	£9,500
Interest free loan to purchase an annual travel card	£1,472
Laptop (for wholly private use)	£1,449

You are required to write notes for an upcoming meeting with Mr Howe:

(a)   **Calculating his employment income for 2010/11, and**

(b)   **Explaining what National Insurance Contributions (NICs) are due and by whom they are payable.**

You may assume that the official rate of interest is 4% throughout 2010/11.

The following question is taken from the Pilot Paper for the Personal Taxation Certificate paper.

8.1 **Mr Matthews**

Mr Matthews, an architect, changed employers at the beginning of April 2010. He was sent a tax return form for the first time in respect of 2010/11. He has therefore approached the partner that you work for to help him with his tax affairs. Although it is already mid February 2012 he has just sent in his tax return, which he has started to complete himself, for review. He has calculated his total income as follows:

Source of income	Total income £	Tax suffered £
Salary (from P60)	48,750	9,430
Medical insurance (from P11D)	375	
Allowance for business miles (own calculation)	111	
Parking in car park next to office (paid for by employer, figure from parking receipts retained and reimbursed)	720	
Building society interest received (from passbook)	320	80
Net income from Discretionary Trust (from R185 Statement of Income)	1,000	1,000
Total income	51,276	10,510

He has sent in his P60, P11D and the form R185 which agree with the above figures.

He has entered the following information on your firm's tax return questionnaire:

Date of birth: 1.10.1973

Business mileage

Drove 925 miles on business in 2010/11. Reimbursed by employer 12p per mile.

Subscriptions

Member of the Institute of Architects

Subscriptions paid by Mr Matthews: £285 paid 1 January 2010 and £295 paid 1 January 2011

Charitable donations

£10 per month paid to Dogs Trust
£15 per month paid to English Heritage

Can I get relief for these payment and if so how does it work?

Also – can you explain how a charity can benefit if I have overpaid tax?

Pension contributions

No pension provision at present

You are required to:

(1) Review Mr Matthews' calculation of income and tax suffered and produce an amended version, explaining any changes that you have made.

(6 marks)

(2) Produce notes for the partner to enable him to explain to Mr Matthews how he may be able to get relief for the charitable donations he has made, how the relief would be given and how a charity could benefit if he has overpaid tax.

(5 marks)

(3) Calculate Mr Matthews' tax payable/repayable based on your calculation of total income giving relief for the charitable donations.

(3 marks)

(4) Produce a statement outlining the tax rules concerning payments to a personal pension plan including how much Mr Matthews could contribute to a personal pension plan (based on his 2010/11 income), the tax saving that he would achieve and whether a claim can be made for relief against 2010/11 income.

(6 marks)

(Total: 20 marks)

8.2 Ed & Joan

Ed Tommy and Joan Ball both work for a design studio. They both wish to start saving for their retirement and would like to make maximum contributions to a pension. Ed is the managing director and his salary for 2010/11 is £140,000. Joan is an assistant designer and her salary for the year is £35,000. Neither Ed or Joan has any other income.

(a) Advise Ed and Joan of the maximum amount they can each contribute to a pension for 2009/10 and 2010/11.

(b) Explain the method by which Ed and Joan will be given tax relief for their pension contributions and show their income tax liability assuming the maximum pension contributions are made.

(c) Explain how they will be able to continue to contribute to their pensions if the design studio ceases trading on 5 April 2011 and they no longer have earnings.

8.3 Dwaine Pipe

Dwaine is the sales director of a small central heating and plumbing company based in the Midlands. The company draws up accounts to 31 December each year.

Dwaine's salary (paid monthly) for the year ended 31 December 2010 was set at £20,000 per annum. This was raised to £22,000 at the Board meeting on 20 January 2011. PAYE deducted in 2010/11 came to £6,000.

Dwaine also receives half yearly bonuses dependent on the performance of his sales team. These have been as follows:

Bonus period	Bonus	Awarded	Received
6 m/e 31.12.09	£3,000	31.3.10	30.4.10
6 m/e 30.6.10	£3,850	30.9.10	31.10.10
6 m/e 31.12.10	£4,250	31.3.11	30.4.11

In addition to his salary and bonus, Dwaine receives the following benefits:

1. **Company cars**

   Vauxhall Cavalier 1.6, list price £10,629, first registered on 1 March 2005. He returned the car at the end of October 2010. The emission rate is 140g/km. He was required to pay £40 per month for the private use of the Vauxhall. All diesel for business use was paid by the company.

   On 1 November 2010 he exchanged the Vauxhall for a brand new Audi A6, list price £18,500. A CD player was added at Dwaine's request at a cost of £400. The emission rate is 195g/km. Again the company paid for all petrol for business mileage.

   Dwaine was involved in an accident on Christmas Day which left the Audi in the garage until 15 January 2011. He was provided with a replacement vehicle (another Audi) which he used until his own car was returned.

2. **Mobile phone**

As Dwaine needs to be in contact with the office, he was provided with a mobile phone. The company reimbursed all Dwaine's calls at a cost of £2,400 in the year. Dwaine estimates that only 10% of these were for private reasons.

3. **Interest free home loan**

The company lent Dwaine £75,000, interest free, on 1 June 2010 to buy his flat in Birmingham. Dwaine repaid £15,000 of the loan on 1 January 2011.

4. **Nursery fees**

Dwaine's son Wayne has a place at a local approved nursery for which the company have agreed to meet the costs. These amounted to £45 per week in 2010/11.

5. **Personal pension**

The company does not have an occupational pension scheme and has therefore agreed to make contributions into Dwaine's personal pension plan. Dwaine makes payments of £150 per month – the company add an extra £100 per month.

6. **Central heating system**

Dwaine's new flat came without central heating. The company provided the materials free of charge and Dwaine fitted the system himself. The materials cost the company £800 and usually retail at £1,200 to customers.

7. **Staff suggestion scheme**

Dwaine won second prize in the scheme being a crate of champagne costing £150. His suggestion will save the company around £3,000 in costs.

8. **Round sum allowance**

Dwaine is given a general allowance of £1,000 each year. In 2010/11 he spent this as follows:

	£
Hotel bills while away on business	710
Entertaining customers	160
	870

He was unable to account for the remainder.

His other income for the year was as follows:

Interest on ISA account	£1,000
Interest received on Building Society account (joint with his wife)	£20,000
Premium bond winnings	£120

Dwaine also made a donation to Oxfam of £400 under Gift Aid.

You are required to calculate the income tax payable/(repayable) by Dwaine for the year ended 5 April 2011.

Assume an official interest rate of 4% throughout.

9.1 **Ricardo Garcia**

Ricardo Garcia is resident and domiciled in Spain.

He has recently married a British woman and will be coming to live permanently in London when he retires; he has advised you that he will continue to return to Spain for holidays.

He has a large pension from the Spanish company that he used to work for, which he will need to bring into the UK for living expenses. He will keep his Spanish bank account and his large portfolio of Spanish investments.

The house which he presently owns in Spain will be rented out.

Mr Garcia has requested that you write to him explaining the basis of taxation in the UK on his worldwide income. He does not require any calculations at this stage.

You are required to draft a letter to Mr Garcia as requested.

10.1 Peter Jones

Peter Jones' income and chargeable gains for 2010/11 were as follows:

	£
Building society income (net)	3,200
Dividends (net)	800
Rental income	5,289
Chargeable gain on disposal on 23 October 2010 (before annual exempt amount)	40,000

You are required to:

(1)   Calculate the income tax repayment due to Peter Jones for 2010/11.

(2)   Calculate the capital gains tax due for 2010/11.

10.2 Simon James

Simon James writes to you on 3 March 2011 on various matters, including the following in relation to capital gains tax:

'I recently read an article in the financial columns of a newspaper which explained the meaning of residence, ordinary residence and domicile. Unfortunately, that article did not consider the relevance of these concepts in determining taxation liabilities. I am particularly concerned with the capital gains tax implications and I should be grateful if you would explain the significance of those terms in relation to that tax.'

You are required to write a letter explaining the relevance of residence, ordinary residence and domicile in determining an individual's liability to capital gains tax.

11.1 Dorrit

Dorrit makes the following disposals of chargeable assets during 2010/11:

Date	Proceeds	Original cost
	£	£
(1) 15 May 2010	115,000	32,000
(2) 31 July 2010	45,000	62,000
(3) 24 October 2010	47,000	16,000

Dorritt has employment income of £50,000 and UK property income of £3,000.

You are required to calculate Dorrit's capital gains tax liability for 2010/11.

11.2 Harbottle

The following information relates to your clients Fred and Iris Harbottle, both aged 30, who have been married for five years.

Fred is employed full time by a firm of chartered accountants at a salary of £40,000.

Iris is not currently working as she is staying at home to look after their two young children, aged 4 and 6. She leaves them with registered childminders one afternoon a week for which she pays £20 a week.

They have each inherited a portfolio of investments, details of which are as follows:

Fred has approximately £100,000 invested in shares currently yielding £7,000 gross income.

Iris has approximately £30,000 invested in shares which yield £1,200 gross.

They intend to make disposals of their investments during January 2011 resulting in chargeable gains of £10,700 for Fred and £2,500 for Iris.

They also have a National Savings & Investments Easy Access Account in joint names which yields £2,000 each year.

You are required to:

(a) Calculate the income tax and capital gains tax liabilities of the couple for 2010/11, and   (5 marks)

(b) State what planning action the couple may take in order to reduce their 2010/11 income tax and capital gains tax liabilities.   (5 marks)

(c) Calculate the amount of Child Tax Credit and Working Tax Credit that Fred and Iris are entitled to for 2010/11.   (5 marks)

(Total 15 marks)

The following question is taken from the Pilot Paper for the Personal Taxation Certificate paper.

12.1 Julie Green

You are currently preparing the tax return of Julie Green, who runs her own marketing company. You have completed all of her return apart from the capital gains tax pages. As well as selling a painting that she had been left by her great aunt for proceeds of £25,000 (chargeable gain £12,000), she had a number of transactions in respect of her holding of Target plc shares.

The gains in respect of the Target plc shares have been calculated by your firm's new capital gains software, but as part of the review process you are required to check the calculations.

Julie Green's file records the following transactions:

Date	Event	Cost/proceeds £
1 June 1993	Purchase 50 shares	1,000
18 September 1996	Purchase 50 shares	3,800
21 May 1997	Purchase 100 shares	9,300
10 December 1997	Bonus issue 1:2	N/A
15 January 2002	Purchase 100 shares	8,200
29 June 2010	Sale 75 shares	10,150

From her tax return questionnaire you establish that on 16 August 2010 she also sold 75 shares for £8,500.

You are required to calculate the gains arising in 2010/11 in respect of the Target plc shares, producing a complete working sheet to place on the file.

12.2 Mr Jones

Mr Jones purchased 5,000 shares in XYZ plc in August 1982 for £6,250. He subsequently carried out the following transactions.

Date	Number of shares bought/(sold)	Cost (proceeds) £
September 1982	2,000	3,000
November 1985	5,000	9,500
October 1987	(3,000)	(6,500)
May 2001	1,000	3,000
July 2010	(7,000)	(31,500)

The company has 100,000 shares in issue.

You are required to calculate the chargeable gains for Mr Jones for 2010/11.

12.3 Richard Price

Richard Price works for PB plc, a large UK quoted trading company. He has acquired shares in PB plc via a company share option plan in recent years as follows:

Date	Shares Acquired	Cost
		£
15.3.90	2,000	2,000
17.12.96	4,000	10,000

In May 1999 there was a 1:5 rights issue at £5 per share which Richard took up in full.

On 4 October 2010, Richard sold 1,800 shares at £7.50 each.

Calculate the chargeable gain on the disposal.

12.4 Eric James

On 3 March 2011 Eric James sold 2,000 ordinary shares (4% shareholding) in Toucan Play plc for £9,100. These shares had been acquired as a result of a takeover on 4 June 2000 of Parrot Games plc in which Eric had held 1,000 shares. These had been acquired in January 1999 for £4,000.

The terms of the takeover were 2 ordinary shares and 4 preference shares in Toucan Play plc for every share held in Parrot Games plc. Immediately following the takeover the ordinary shares and preference shares in Toucan Play plc were valued at £4.20 and £2 respectively.

You are required to calculate the chargeable gain arising from the above transaction.

13.1 Doug

Doug sold the following items on 1 August 2010:

(1)   A Ming vase bought in January 1984 for £2,000. The sales proceeds were £8,000.

(2)   A Leonardo cartoon bought in March 1984 for £7,200 and sold for £5,500.

(3)   A lathe bought for use in his business in March 1985 which cost £4,300. The sales proceeds were £9,500. Doug had claimed capital allowances on this asset.

You are required to calculate Doug's taxable gain for 2010/11 assuming he made no other disposals in the year.

13.2 Mr Cole

Mr Cole made the following disposals in 2010/11:

1.   On 2 June 2010 he sold his 1952 vintage Ford motor car for £7,200. He had bought the car in June 2005 for £3,600 and had incurred restoration costs of £500.

2.   On 2 September 2010 he sold 5 acres of land out of a 40 acre plot for £38,000. He had acquired the whole plot (for investment purposes) for £32,000 in July 1989. The value of the remaining 35 acres was £82,000 in September 2010.

3.   On 1 November 2010 he sold an antique chest for £7,000. He had bought this in June 1999 for £4,000.

4.   On 3 December 2010 he sold a painting for £11,500, incurring costs of sale of £150. He had been left the painting by his grandfather who had paid £2,000 for it in June 1985. It was worth £4,700 when his grandfather died in August 1989.

5.   On 15 January 2011 he sold a vase for £900. He had paid £7,500 for this in August 1997 believing it to be a Shelley vase but in fact it was a reproduction.

You are required to calculate the capital gains tax payable by Mr Cole for 2010/11 assuming he has taxable income of £32,000 in the year.

(10 marks)

13.3 CGT Leases

(1)   Joe acquired an 80 year lease on a property for £38,000 on 29 July 1984. He assigned the lease on 29 July 2010 for £79,000.

(2)   As (1) except that it was a 57 year lease when it was acquired.

(3)   Harold acquired the freehold of a property for £25,000 on 1 May 1991. On 1 October 2010 he granted a 60 year lease on the premises for a premium of £30,000, the value of the reversion being £7,500.

(4)   As (3) except that the lease granted was a 20 year lease, the premium received £20,000 and the value of the reversion £17,000.

You are required to calculate the chargeable gains arising in (1) to (4) above.

The following question is taken from the Pilot Paper for the Personal Taxation Certificate paper.

14.1 Owning two homes

Your managing partner has asked you to write an article to be published on your firm's website. There have been a number of queries submitted recently concerning the Capital Gains Tax implications of owning two homes and she feels that this would be a good topic to have an article on.

She has supplied you with a case study of a typical family to refer to in the article.

Case Study

Family	Mr and Mrs Hammond; two children aged 4 and 2.	
	Current family home:	Bought 15 August 1998
	Cost	£150,000
	Occupied throughout period of ownership by Mr and Mrs Hammond	
	To be sold May 2010 Proceeds	£560,000
New acquisitions May 2010	House in country Cost	£400,000
	Flat in town Cost	£175,000

Plans   Mr Hammond to reside in flat in town Monday night – Thursday night; weekends in country house

Mrs Hammond to reside in country house.

Flat in town either:

(a)   To be sold after five years when Mr Hammond will live full time in country, or

(b)   To be let after five years and sold five years later.

House to be family home until children leave home.

You are required to draft an article:

(a)   **Explaining the key Capital Gains Tax implications arising from the above, broken down in to sections as follows:**

    (i)   **The Capital Gains Tax implications of selling the current family home.**   **(2 marks)**

    (ii)   **The Capital Gains Tax implications for Mr and Mrs Hammond of residing in two homes and any action that they should consider.**   **(5 marks)**

    (iii)   **The advice that you would give Mr and Mrs Hammond based on their circumstances and the resulting Capital Gains Tax consequences of the flat either being sold after five years or being sold after ten years, having been let for five years.**   **(7 marks)**

    (iv)   **The Capital Gains Tax consequences of the sale of the house in 20 years.**   **(1 mark)**

(b)   Answering a frequent question from couples – what is the difference between owning our house as joint tenants or owning it as tenants in common? *(Under Scots Law – what is the difference between joint property and common property?)*

(5 marks)

You should assume that the facts of the case study will be reproduced on the website.

(Total: 20 marks)

14.2   Peter Stamp

On 2 May 1983 Peter Stamp, a retired solicitor, bought a private dwelling house for £70,000, which he sold for £270,000 under a contract dated 3 July 2010. The house was situated in grounds of one half of a hectare.

He lived in this house as his only residence until 1 February 1987. It was then let for residential purposes until 1 December 1996. From that date until the date of sale the property was unoccupied.

You are required to compute the chargeable gain arising on the sale of the house.

14.3   Mr Richman

White Cottage
Plumsted
Yorkshire

4 May 2011

Dear Mr Jones,

I have recently (on 4 April 2011) sold a house, 'Red Bricks', for £370,000. The house was originally purchased on 6 April 1983 for £90,000 and was used as my principal residence until 5 April 1988. From 6 April 1988 until 5 April 1995 the house was empty while I was working abroad. I am an architect and have always been treated as self employed from when I started to practise in 1973.

On my return to the UK in April 1995 I moved back into the house. In April 1996 the house was converted (at a cost of £20,000) to a flat upstairs (which I used as my residence) and offices downstairs from which I ran my practice. I moved out of the flat at Red Bricks on 5 October 2008 and the flat was empty until the whole property was sold on 4 April 2011. The flat occupied exactly half of the property and I believe this has been agreed with HM Revenue & Customs. I continued to use the offices for my practice until shortly before the sale.

I should be grateful if you would write to me setting out how any Capital Gains Tax liability will be calculated, taking into account any reliefs due and when the tax will be payable. I have no other capital gains for 2010/11.

Yours sincerely

A Richman.

You are required to draft a letter as requested.

15.1   Fran and Anna

Fran sold a factory worth £500,000 to her friend Anna for £100,000 on 1 June 2010 and moved her business to new premises. Fran had bought the factory on 1 January 1993 for £75,000. On 1 July 2012 Anna sold the factory for £520,000.

Both Fran and Anna have elected for gift relief to apply and have used the factory for the purposes of their respective sole trades.

You are required to calculate the chargeable gains for Fran and Anna. Assume that 2010/11 tax rates and legislation continue to apply throughout.

15.2 Joe Bloggs

Joe Bloggs had the following transactions in December 2010:

(1) He sold his flat for £700,000, which he had purchased in July 1982 for £200,000. He has always used his spare bedroom, which is approximately one quarter of the total floor space, as an office and property expenses have always been apportioned accordingly.

(2) Joe sold unquoted trading company shares to his daughter for £375,000. The shares had recently been valued at £450,000. The company had no investments. He had purchased the shares for £75,000 in September 1989.

You are required to calculate the amount subject to capital gains tax for 2010/11 on the disposals in (1) and (2) above assuming all available reliefs are claimed.

15.3 P J Laval

P J Laval had the following transactions in assets during the year 2010/11.

(1) Sold his house, 'Chez Nous', for £99,000 on 14 May 2010, having bought this for £37,000 on 6 April 1982, incurring expenditure of £2,000 on an extension on 6 May 1983. The house has never been used as his only or main residence.

(2) Sold 1,400 shares in Vic plc, a quoted company, for £8,710 on 18 July 2010 having purchased 1,400 shares on 10 February 1983 at a cost of £3,500.

There was a bonus issue of 1:4 on 10 March 1984.

(3) On 31 March 2011, PJ gifted his entire holding of shares in Lavaling Ltd, his personal trading company, to his son. If he had sold his shares on that date to a third party he would have realised a capital gain of £80,000. At that date, the company's assets consisted of:

	Book value at 31.3.11 £	Market value at 31.3.11 £
Freehold property	20,000	130,000
Quoted securities	8,000	30,000
Stocks	70,000	70,000
Debtors	35,000	35,000
Cash and bank balances	21,000	21,000
	154,000	286,000

PJ has never worked for the company.

(i) **You are required to compute the amount of capital gains tax payable by PJ Laval for the 2010/11 tax year, assuming he claims all available reliefs and is an additional rate taxpayer.** **(13 marks)**

(ii) **Briefly describe the three legal estates in land: freehold, leasehold, and common hold.** **(5 marks)**

(Total: 18 marks)

15.4 Simon

You have received the following memorandum from a partner in your firm:

'To: Frances Ackland
From: Simon Evans
Date: 3 December 2010
Subject: Deferral of gains

I have just disposed of some shares in Blue plc, a quoted company. I need some advice on how I can defer the gains arising from this sale. I remember reading something in the Tax Department's newsletter about a special relief to enable me to do this. Can you give me some details?

You may like to know that I acquired the Blue plc shares in September 1988 as a gift from my father. He had originally acquired them in 1983 and we elected to defer the gain arising. You will find the details in my personal tax affairs file. I sold the Blue shares for £200,000 on 30 November 2010. I have no other assets for CGT purposes and no other spare cash other than the proceeds of the Blue shares.

I would like to use some of the proceeds of the sale to invest in a house in France, probably about £100,000. My wife and I intend to move to France in the next couple of years to restore the house. I am currently an additional rate taxpayer.

You ascertain that the deferred gain on the Blue shares was £15,000 and that they were worth £65,000 in September 1988.

You are required to write a memorandum in reply.

(10 marks)

15.5 **Emily**

Emily made the following disposals in 2010/11:

(1) **Factory**

Acquired 1 July 2003 for £150,000. Emily let out the factory rent free to her partnership business. The factory was sold for £225,000 on 10 July 2010.

(2) **Painting**

This had been acquired by Emily's husband Arthur on 1 March 1996 for £50,000. Arthur had given the painting to Emily on 1 July 2001 when it was worth £60,000. Emily sold the painting for £73,000 on 2 May 2010.

(3) **Vase**

Emily had acquired this asset on 10 August 1988 for £40,000. She sold it on 1 December 2010 for £19,000.

You are required to calculate Emily's CGT liability for 2010/11 assuming she claims all available reliefs and had taxable income for the year of £57,000.

15.6 **Peter**

Peter made the following disposals in 2010/11:

(a) He purchased a building for £200,000 on 1 January 1983 which he let commercially as offices. On 10 April 2010 he sold the building for £600,000.

(b) He held 20,000 shares (1% shareholding) in Forum Follies plc which he purchased in May 1986 for £50,000. In March 2011, Exciting Enterprises plc acquired all the share capital of Forum Follies plc. Under the terms of the takeover for every two shares previously held in Forum Follies plc shareholders received three ordinary shares in Exciting Enterprises plc plus £1 cash. Immediately after the takeover the ordinary shares in Exciting Enterprises plc were quoted at £3 each.

(c) Peter purchased shares in Dassau plc, a quoted company, as follows.

	No of shares	Cost £
December 1984	1,000	2,000
April 1987 1 for 2 rights issue		£2 per share

In November 2010 he sold 1,200 shares for £9,500.

Peter had capital losses brought forward from 2009/10 of £6,400.

You are required to calculate the CGT payable by Peter for 2009/10, assuming his taxable income in the year was £42,500, and state the due date for payment.

15.7 Sarah Stone

Sarah had the following transactions in 2010/11.

12 April 2010:

She sold all her shares in Peterson Ltd for £150,000. She had acquired the shares as follows:

Date	No	Cost £	Notes
1/3/86	50,000	25,000	Probate value from father
1/8/99	5,000	10,000	Purchased
1/10/00	1:5 rights issue	£3 per share	

15 June 2010:

She sold an antique brooch which she had purchased in September 1994 for £5,800. She received £8,000 after selling costs of £250.

19 September 2010:

She sold her stamp collection for £3,100. She had purchased it for £7,000 in June 1987.

21 January 2011:

She sold a house which she had bought as an investment property in January 1983 for £28,000. She added a loft bedroom at a cost of £10,000 in February 1984. She sold it for £75,000.

Sarah had capital losses brought forward of £15,000.

Calculate Sarah's CGT payable assuming her taxable income for the year was £64,000.

1.1 Allowances

	£
PAA (age 65 – 74)	9,490
Less: restriction (W)	(390)
	9,100

(W) Restriction = ½ £(23,680 – 22,900) = £390

1.2

	£
PAA (65 – 74)	9,490
BPA	1,890
	11,380

The MCA does not reduce net income. It is a tax reduction. He would still get an MCA due to the fact that at least one of the couple was born before 6 April 1935.

1.3

	£
PA (basic)	6,475
Less: restriction (W)	(5,000)
Restricted PA	1,475

(W) Restriction = ½ £(110,000 – 100,000) = £5,000

1.4

	£
Earnings/ net income	45,580
Less: PA	(6,475)
Taxable income	39,105

£	
38,100 × 20% (W)	7,620
1,005 × 40%	402
Tax liability	8,022
Less tax suffered: PAYE	(8,165)
Tax repayable	(143)

Working

Basic rate band extended to £37,400 + (£560 × 100/80) = £38,100

1.5 Personal allowance

	£
PAA (> 75)	9,640
Less: ½ £(30,800 – 22,900)	(3,950)
	5,690
Restrict to basic PA	6,475
MCA – tax reduction	6,965
Less: excess restriction £(3,950 – [9,640 – 6,475])	(785)
	6,180
@ 10%	618

1.6

	£
Earnings/ net income	180,000
Less: PA (> £112,950)	(NIL)
Taxable income	180,000

TQT
Tax Qualification Training

	£
37,400 × 20%	7,480
112,600 × 40%	45,040
30,000 × 50%	15,000
Tax liability	67,520

Note. Lottery winnings are exempt.

1.7 £2,000

Interest from building society account will be assessed on his mother as income > £100 gross.

1.8 Age 75 or over in the tax year

	£
Age allowance	9,640
Less: ½ (24,600 – 500 – 22,900)	(600)
	9,040

Age allowance is restricted where net income exceeds £22,900 but net income is reduced by Gift Aid donations.

1.9

	£
Earnings	3,700
Interest income	300
Net income	4,000
Less: PA	(6,475)
Taxable income	–
IT repayable:	
Earnings – PAYE	740
Interest – 20% tax credit	60
	800

Scholarship received by a full-time student is not taxable. Legacy (ie inheritance) is a capital receipt and not taxable as income.

1.10

	£
Trust income (£5,000 × 2)	10,000
Less: PA	(6,475)
	3,525
Income tax:	
£3,525 @ 20%	705
Tax deducted:	
Trust: £10,000 @ 50%	(5,000)
Tax repayable	(4,295)

1.11

	£
Bert	
Net income	10,214
PA (Bert not over 65)	(6,475)
Taxable income	3,739
Tax	
£3,739 × 20%	748
Less: tax reduction – MCA	
£6,965 × 10%	(697)
Tax liability	51

Bert receives the MCA as his wife is born before 6 April 1935

	£
1.12	
Trade profits	7,700
Discretionary trust income (£1,375 × 2)	2,750
	10,450
Less: PA	(9,640)
Taxable income	810
Tax @ 20%	162
Less: MCA (£6,965 × 2/12 × 10%)	(116)
Tax liability	46
Less: tax deducted (£2,750 × 50%)	(1,375)
Repayable	(1,329)

Income from a discretionary trust comes with 50% tax credit. MCA is given to the partner with the higher income.

1.13 Income of minor unmarried children (ie Dawn) is taxed in the hands of the parent if it derives from a parental settlement. Therefore, Richard is taxed on Dawn's income. As Donna is married, the dividend is treated as her own income.

	£
1.14	
2009/10 joint income £(34,500 + 14,500)	49,000
Less: threshold	(16,190)
	32,810
Restriction × 39%	12,796

So, per child credit of £2,300 is withdrawn.

As joint income < £50,000, Sarah is entitled to the family element of CTC ie £545.

	£
1.15	
Child Tax Credit	
Family entitlement	545
Child element	2,300
Working Tax Credit	
Basic element	1,920
Lone parent element	1,890
	6,655
Less: restriction	
£(17,000 − 6,420) × 39%	(4,126)
Total credits	2,529

1.16 Investment income of a child arising out of a gift by his parent is aggregated with the income of that parent. However where the income does not exceed £100 (gross) pa it is treated as the income of the child.

Therefore, this income would be taxed on Gilbert and would be covered by his personal allowance.

		£
1.17		
CTC:	Family	545
	Child	2,300
WTC:	Basic	1,920
	Lone parent	1,890
		6,655
Less: 39% of excess income (W)		(616)
Total credits		6,039
Working		
2009/10 income (difference < £25,000)		8,000
Threshold		(6,420)
		1,580
@ 39%		616

1.18

		£
CTC:	Family	545
	Child £(2,300 × 3)	6,900
WTC:	Basic	1,920
	Couples	1,890
	> 30 hrs	790
		12,045
Less: (W)		(5,881)
Credit		6,164

Working

Income	21,500
Threshold	(6,420)
	15,080
× 39%	5,881

1.19   As Tanya is over 16, earns more than £97 per week and has been sick for more than four consecutive days she is entitled to SSP of £79.15 per week.

1.20   Alan – 2010/11

		£
Income		50,000
Less:	Deductible payment:	
	Loan interest	(2,610)
		47,390
Less:	PA (basic – as net income > £22,900)	(6,475)
Taxable income		40,915

Tax thereon:

	£
£37,400 @ 20%	7,480
£3,515 @ 40%	1,406
	8,886
Less: Maintenance payment (Max £2,670 × 10%)	(267)
Tax liability	8,619

There is no relief for mortgage interest payments for an individual's residence.

2.1

	Non savings £	Savings £
Earnings	27,040	
BSI		20,000
Less: PA	(6,475)	
Taxable income	20,565	20,000
Tax:		
20,565 @ 20%		4,113
16,835 @ 20% (£37,400 - £20,565) (savings)		3,367
3,165 @ 40% (£20,000 – £16,835)		1,266
40,565		8,746

Note that 'tax liability' is **before** deducting tax suffered at source.

2.2 $\frac{1}{2} \times £300 \times \frac{100}{80} = £188$

As it is a joint bank account they are each entitled to half of the interest, regardless on the amount of capital contributed by each of them.

2.3

	£
Savings a/c (received gross)	276
Interest income	276

Interest on NS&I Savings Certificates and HMRC repayment interest are tax free.

2.4 Interest from loans made by an individual to an individual are received gross.

Interest paid by a company to an individual in respect of an unquoted debenture is paid under deduction of 20% income tax.

2.5 $1,000 \times 8p = £80 \times 100/90 = \underline{£89}$

Dividends are taxed on receipts basis.

2.6

	£
UK bank interest (£8,680 × 100/80)	10,850
Guernsey interest	640
Interest on government stock (paid gross)	5,000
Net income	16,490
Less: PA	(6,475)
Taxable income	10,015

2.7

	Savings income £	Dividend income £
BDI (£2,100 × 100/80)	2,625	
BSI (£1,800 × 100/80)	2,250	
Dividends (£2,000 × 100/90)		2,222
Net income	4,875	2,222
PA	(4,875)	(1,600)
Taxable income	–	622
Tax @ 10%		62
Tax credit on dividends (£622 @ 10% – **taxable** dividend)		(62)
Tax due		Nil
Less tax deducted at source on bank interest £(525 + 450)		(975)
Tax repayable		(975)

2.8

	Non savings £	Savings £	Dividends £
Earnings	3,929		
Bank interest £2,500 × $\frac{100}{80}$		3,125	
Dividend £34,000 × $\frac{100}{90}$			37,778
Net income	3,929	3,125	37,778
Less: PA	(3,929)	(2,546)	
Taxable income	–	579	37,778

Tax	£579 @ 10 % (savings)	58
	£36,821 @ 10% (dividends)	3,682
	£957 @ 32½% £(37,778 – 36,821) (dividends)	311
Tax liability		4,051
Less:	Dividend credit 10% × £37,778	(3,778)
	PAYE	(785)
	Tax on interest 20% × £3,125	(625)
Tax repayable		(1,137)

TQT
Tax Qualification Training

2.9

	Non savings £	Savings £	Dividends £
Earnings	125,000		
Bank interest £12,500 × $\frac{100}{80}$		15,625	
Dividend £27,000 × $\frac{100}{90}$			30,000
Net income	125,000	15,625	30,000
Less: PA (income > £112,950)	(NIL)		
Taxable income	125,000	15,625	30,000

Tax £37,400 @ 20 % (non savings)	7,480
£87,600 @ 40% £(125,000 – 37,400) (non savings)	35,040
£15,625 @ 40% (savings)	6,250
£ 9,375 @ 32½% £(150,000 - 125,000 – 15,625) (dividends)	3,047
£20,625 @ 42½% £(30,000 – 9,375) (dividends)	8,766
Tax liability	60,583
Less: Dividend credit 10% × £30,000	(3,000)
PAYE	(42,520)
Tax on interest 20% × £15,625	(3,125)
Tax payable	11,938

3.1

	£
Gross rents (£1,500 × 12) (accruals basis)	18,000
Less: Agent's fees	(1,800)
Interest	(4,200)
Water rates	(120)
Insurance	(500)
Wear and tear allowance (£(18,000 – 120) × 10%)	(1,788)
Property income	9,592

The cost of building the new porch is capital expenditure and cannot be deducted for income tax purposes.

3.2 In legal terms, ownership is the most extensive possessory right conferred by the law.
Owners can do with their property what they wish, eg use it, sell it, give it away or use it as security for a loan.
Possession is the exercise (or power of exercising) physical control over property.

3.3 Unconditional sale – the contract is not subject to conditions precedent or subsequent.
Conditional sale – the contract is subject to something occurring eg grant of planning permission.
By option – the contract can be triggered by the service of a notice.
By pre-emption – if the seller wants to sell he must first offer it to the person who has the pre-emption right.

3.4

	£
Rent receivable (10 × £160) + £400	2,000
Less: Bad debt £(1,600 – 1,300)	(300)
Interest	(700)
Property income	1,000

3.5

	£
Whitehouse: rent accrued in the year	4,000
Blackhouse: (9/12 × £2,000)	1,500
Property income	5,500

No bad debt relief as payment was actually received.

3.6

	£
Rents receivable (£4,000 × 8/12)	2,667
Expenses paid	(1,000)
Property income	1,667

Note. The rent receivable from the new tenants will begin to be assessed in 2011/12.

3.7		£
Income		8,000
Less:	insurance	(300)
	water rates	(400)
	wear and tear allowance: 10% × £(8,000 − 400)	(760)
Property income		6,540

3.8 Brian should elect to assess rents received over £4,250 ie £(5,000 − 4,250) = £750 under the 'rent a room' scheme, otherwise property income of £4,400 (£5,000 − £600) would be assessable.

Note. No further deduction is available for expenses where 'rent a room' relief applies.

3.9 Four from:

- Available for letting for 140 days a year
- Actually let for 70 days in a year
- Not more than 155 days in a year are periods of longer term occupation (ie let to same tenant for more than 31 continuous days).
- Situated in the UK or any other EEA state
- Furnished
- Let with a view to a profit

3.10 Personal property is divided into choses in action (property such as debts, shares, negotiable instruments and all forms of intellectual property) and choses in possession (leasehold land and buildings and personal chattels such as furniture and machinery).

4.1 Maximum overall investment – £10,200
Maximum cash investment – £5,100

4.2 There is no income tax on interest or dividends.

4.3 Tax on taxable income

£	£
37,400 × 20%	7,480
19,440 × 40%	7,776
	15,256
Less: EIS income tax reduction: £500,000 × 20% (restricted)	(15,256)
	0

It is not possible to have a tax reduction in excess of the tax on taxable income.

4.4 The first £200,000 worth of VCT investments made in a tax year will give rise to tax free dividends.

Taxable net dividends (excess over £200,000)

$$\frac{10,000}{60,000} \times £3,400 = £567$$

5.1 Daisy

	£
Statutory redundancy pay	3,800
Cash	25,000
Value of car	12,000
Outplacement counselling (exempt)	–
	40,800
Less: exemption	(30,000)
Taxable	10,800

5.2 Salary

	£	£
9/12 × £9,000	6,750	
3/12 × £10,000	2,500	9,250
Bonus received in 2010/11 (28.2.11)		2,400
		11,650

5.3

	£
Salary (5 × £1,000)	5,000
Car benefit (£15,000 × 22% × 3/12)*	825
Fuel benefit (£18,000 × 22% × 3/12)*	990
	6,815

$* \dfrac{(165-130)}{5} = 7\%$

Percentage: 15% + 7% = 22%

5.4

	£
Car (£14,000 × 27%)*	3,780
Petrol (£18,000 × 27%)	4,860
	8,640

There is no reduction in the taxable benefit for contributions made by an employee towards the cost of private petrol. Only made for full refunds (in which case the benefit would be nil).

$* \dfrac{190-130}{5} = 12\%$ (round down the emissions so it is divisible by 5)

15% + 12% = 27%

5.5 Earnings:

	£
Salary	10,000
Car (£16,000 × 28%)*	4,480
Second car (£12,000 × 10%)**	1,200
Cost of wine	1,000
Earnings	16,680
Less: expenses	(600)
	16,080

The second car is assessed on Jim because his daughter receives it by virtue of *his* employment, not hers (would you expect a company car if you just worked on Saturdays?)

$* \dfrac{195-130}{5} = 13\%$ 15% + 13% = 28%

** emissions are between 76 and 120 g/km so percentage is 10%

5.6 Form P11D:

	£
Car (£12,000 × 22%)*	2,640
Expenses allowances (12 × £80)	960
	3,600

The amount spent by Albert on allowable expenses would be claimed separately by him on his tax return. The company must report the full allowance.

$* \dfrac{150-130}{5} = 4\% + 18\% = 22\%$ (*Note.* For cars running on diesel, the minimum percentage is 18%)

5.7

	£
Round sum allowance (£100 × 4) (not covered by dispensation)	400
Specific reimbursement – covered by dispensation	–
	400

A dispensation means that the item covered by it does not have to be reported on the P11D.

5.8   Sue: Nil

        Tara: £340 (£3,200 − (52 × £55 exempt))

No taxable benefit for onsite work place nursery. First £55 of all other qualifying childcare costs are a tax free benefit.

5.9   Private purchases £257 only. She will only ever be taxable on the goods/services bought with the card.

5.10   £204 (240 × £0.85 as first 15p per day of luncheon vouchers is a tax free benefit). Workplace parking is not taxable.

5.11   Staff entertaining becomes a taxable benefit to employees if it cost the employer > £150 per head. Where the cost exceeds £150 per head the full amount becomes taxable.

Each employee here has a £200 benefit.

5.12

	£
Professional subscriptions allowed	220
Subscription for accommodation allowable	200
	420

Golf club subscription disallowed as it is not incurred wholly, exclusively and necessarily in the performance of his duties.

5.13

	£
Salary	18,000
Accommodation – not taxable as job related	–
Household expenses £3,100	
limited to 10% × £18,000	1,800
Earnings	19,800

5.14

	£	£
Mobile phone for employee – not taxable	–	
Mobile phone for family member: 20% × £250	50	
		50
Laptop – 20% × £5,000	1,000	
Less: 40% business use	(400)	600
		650

Note. If private use of laptop had been merely incidental there would be no taxable benefit.

5.15

	£	£
Salary		30,000
Benefits: Crèche		
((200 − 55) × 52)	7,540	
Parking space	–	
Business miles		
(5,000 × 60p)	3,000	
Less: authorised mileage rates (5,000 × 40p)	(2,000)	
Earnings		8,540
		38,540

5.16

	£
Average method: $\dfrac{15,000 + 10,000}{2} \times 4\%$	500
Less: interest paid 5/4/10 – 5/1/11: £15,000 × 3% × 9/12	(338)
6/1/11 – 5/4/11: £10,000 × 3% × 3/12	(75)
	87
Strict basis:	
5/4/10 − 5/1/11: £15,000 × (4% − 3%) × 9/12	112
6/1/11 − 5/4/11: £10,000 × (4% − 3%) × 3/12	25
	137

Ruth can use the average basis but HMRC can elect to use the strict basis if they wish.

5.17

	£
Gross annual value	5,000
less rent paid by Jason	(3,000)
	2,000
Additional charge (use MV as moved in > 6 yrs after purchase)	
£(130,000 – 75,000) × 4%	2,200
	4,200

5.18 Assessable benefit is the greater of

(a)

	£
Market value at acquisition	1,500
less price paid	(1,000)
	500

(b)

	£
Original market value	2,000
less assessed in respect of use (2009/10)	
$^6/_{12} \times 20\% \times £2,000$	(200)
less assessed in respect of use (2010/11) $^6/_{12} \times 20\% \times £2,000$	(200)
less price paid	(1,000)
	600

∴ Benefit is £600 plus benefit for use in 2010/11 of £200 (see above) = £800

5.19

		£
Flat:	Annual value	3,000
	Household expenses	400
	Furniture (20% × £2,500)	500
		3,900

Note. There is no additional charge for the accommodation as the original cost was less than £75,000.

5.20

	£
Payment in lieu of notice (taxable in full)	8,000
Ex gratia payment (£30,000 exemption applies)	40,000
Statutory redundancy pay (£30,000 exemption applies)	5,000
	53,000
Less: Exemption	(30,000)
Taxable	23,000

5.21

	£	£
Ex gratia (ie non contractual) payment	51,000	
Less: Exemption	(30,000)	30,000
Taxable	21,000	
Less: foreign service exemption (not 'substantial')		
$\dfrac{10}{30} \times £21,000$	(7,000)	7,000
Taxable	14,000	
Total exemption		37,000

5.22

	£
Annual value	2,225
Less: rent paid	(2,225)
	NIL
£(400,000 – 75,000) × 4%	13,000
Less: balance of rent paid (£2,725 – 2,225)	(500)
Net benefit	12,500

The calculation is based on expenditure incurred by the company *before* the tax year in question.

5.23 Any six from:
- Names of client and consultant
- Commencement date of contract
- Description of services
- Fees
- Expenses
- Confidentiality
- Non-exclusivity
- Termination

6.1 There are no income tax consequences at the date of grant.

When the option was exercised there would not normally be an income tax charge. However, as the option was granted at a discount there will be an income tax charge at the date of exercise. The amount of the discount at the date of grant is charged to income tax, giving chargeable employment income of £5,000 (10,000 × (£2.00 − £1.50)).

Note that the amount of the discount is taxed as this is lower than the difference between the market value of the shares at the date of exercise and the exercise price ie £32,500 (10,000 × (£4.75 − £1.50))

6.2 'Free shares' are the shares an employer can give to an employee – maximum £3,000 per annum.

'Partnership shares' are the shares the employee is allowed to purchase from pre-tax salary to be held in the plan – maximum is the lower of £1,500 per annum and 10% of salary.

6.3

	£
10,000 × £(15 − 11.50) =	35,000
@ 40%	14,000

7.1 Employees pay Class 1 primary NICs based on their earnings from employment, which includes cash payments such as salary and expenses and also income from certain share schemes.

Self employed individuals pay Class 2 NIC based on their accounts profit and Class 4 NIC based on their taxable profits.

7.2 Class 1A NICs are based on taxable benefits paid to P11D employees (ie directors and employees paid £8,500+). Only the employer pays Class 1A NICs.

7.3 Contracting out of the State Second Pension Scheme

Where the employee 'contracts out' they will only be entitled to the basic pension from the State and will obtain their additional pension from the employer's scheme.

Both the employee and employer are entitled to a rebate on contributions between the lower earnings limit and the earnings threshold.

The employee pays a reduced rate of Class 1 NIC of 9.4% on earnings between the earnings threshold and the upper accruals point.

The employer also pays a reduced rate of either 9.1% or 11.4% on earnings between the earnings threshold and the upper accruals point (depending on the type of occupational pension scheme).

Above the upper accruals point, the standard NIC rates apply, ie the employee pays 11% up to the upper earnings limit and 1% thereafter. The employer pays 12.8% above the upper accruals point.

8.1 Higher of: (i) 100% × earnings ie £28,000
(ii) £3,600

ie £28,000. (*Note*. Dividends are not relevant earnings for pension contribution purposes)

8.2 Norma has no relevant earnings. She may make a maximum contribution of £3,600 (gross) into a personal pension.

8.3

	£
Earnings	52,000
less PA	(6,475)
Taxable income	45,525
BRB extended to £37,400 + (£5,000 × $\frac{100}{80}$)	(43,650)
	1,875
Tax @ 40%	750

8.4 Jeremy can pay up to £400,000 into a pension in the year and obtain tax relief. He would pay 80% directly to the pension (£320,000) and the fund would reclaim the 20% (£80,000) from HMRC. However, as he would be paying more than the 2010/11 annual allowance of £255,000 into his pension, he will have to pay 40% tax on the excess (40% × £145,000 = £58,000).

8.5 Maximum tax free lump sum: 25% × £65,000 = £16,250

8.6

	£
Earnings	54,000
Less occupational pension contribution	(9,000)
Net income	45,000
Less PA	(6,475)
Taxable income	38,525

Tax

	£
£37,400 × 20%	7,480
£1,125 × 40%	450
38,525	7,930

9.1 As Wayne is taxable on the remittance basis the dividends will be treated as non savings income, rather than dividend income. He will pay tax at 40% (and not the dividend rate of 32.5%) as he is a higher rate taxpayer.

(£10,000 × 100/90) @ 40% £4,444

In addition, as he has been UK resident for 7 out of the last 9 tax years and is over the age of 18, Wayne will be subject to an additional £30,000 income tax charge. So, his total tax liability will be £34,444.

Notes

(1) Wayne will not receive a personal allowance as he has made a remittance basis claim.

(2) Even though remitted dividends are taxed as non-savings income, they must still be grossed up by 100/90 in Wayne's income tax computation (and the 10% credit is available to reduce his tax liability).

9.2 As Egbert is UK resident and ordinarily resident he is taxable on his worldwide income on an arising basis. However, only 90% of foreign pensions are taxable so he will be taxed on £9,000 (90% × £10,000).

9.3 ESC A11:

(a) Absence for employment purposes must span a complete tax year, and

(b) Interim visits to the UK do not amount to 183 days or more in any one tax year or 91 days or more on average.

10.1

	£
Chargeable gain	18,000
Less: annual exempt amount	(10,100)
	7,900
£7,900 @ 18% (disposal before 23.6.10)	1,422

10.2

	Pre-23.6.10 £	Post-22.6.10 £
Chargeable gain	32,000	26,000
Less: annual exempt amount		(10,100)
Taxable gain	32,000	15,900
CGT @ 18%/28% (W)	5,760	3,662
Total CGT	9,422	

Working – CGT on post-23.6.10 disposal

	£
Basic rate band	37,400
Less: taxable income	(29,500)
Remaining BRB	7,900
CGT on £7,900 @ 18%	1,422
Balance of gain £8,000 @ 28% £(15,900 – 7,900)	2,240
Total CGT on post-23.6.10 gain	3,662

10.3 The individual must be resident **or** ordinarily resident in the UK.

10.4 A racehorse, as wasting chattels are exempt from CGT.

The limousine, as all cars are exempt from CGT.

11.1

	£
Sale proceeds	31,250
Less probate value	(11,200)
Chargeable gain	20,050

11.2

	£
Sale proceeds	85,000
Less: cost $\dfrac{85,000}{85,000+30,000} \times 18,000$	(13,304)
Chargeable gain	£71,696

11.3

	£
Gains	9,000
Current year losses (must be set against current year gains)	(5,000)
	4,000
AE	(10,100)
	–
Losses c/f (*Note.* Losses b/f reduce chargeable gains to AE level only)	6,000

11.4

	2008/09 £	2009/10 £	2010/11 £	
Gains	2,000	4,000	13,000	
Losses	(5,000)	(2,000)	(2,000)	
	(3,000)	2,000	11,000	
c/f	3,000		(900)	c/f £2,100
			10,100	

Explanation: Losses b/f reduce gains down to AE level only.

11.5 The persons connected (for CGT purposes) to Paul are his:
- Wife
- Mother-in-law
- Business partner
- Step father

11.6

	£
Proceeds	170,000
Less: cost	(120,000)
Gain	50,000

Explanation: Transfer between spouses is on no gain/no loss basis, so Grace's base cost is £120,000.

11.7 As losses from a sale to a connected person can only be set against gains to the same connected person, the loss of £8,200 will be carried forward and set against the gain of £14,000 arising on the sale to Charles on 29 September 2011.

Note. Carry back of the loss is not allowed.

11.8

	£
Proceeds	30,000
Less: cost	
$\dfrac{30,000}{30,000+10,000} \times £8,000$	(6,000)
Chargeable gain	24,000

11.9

	£
Gains	17,400
Losses	(7,000)
	10,400
Losses b/f (10,400 − 10,100)	(300)
	10,100
Less: annual exempt amount	(10,100)
Taxable gain	Nil

Losses c/f (5,000 − 300) = £4,700

11.10

	£
Proceeds	45,000
Cost £8,000 × $\dfrac{45,000}{45,000+50,000}$	(3,789)
Chargeable gain	41,211
Less: AE	(10,100)
Taxable gain	31,111

Note. No claim is available for a 'small part' disposal as proceeds > £20,000 and > 20% of MV of land.

12.1 Share pool:

	No. of shares	Cost
		£
Purchase Aug 2006	2,000	18,000
Purchase Sept 2006	1,000	10,000
	3,000	28,000
Sale Jan 2011	(1,500)	(14,000)
c/f	1,500	14,000

Calculate gain:

	£
Proceeds	22,500
Cost	(14,000)
Chargeable gain	8,500

12.2	Share pool:	No. of shares	Cost £
	Purchase 19.2.83	2,000	10,000
	Purchase 20.9.90	1,000	8,000
		3,000	18,000
	Sale 15.11.10	(1,500)	(9,000)
	c/f	1,500	9,000

Calculate gain:

	£
Proceeds	22,000
Cost	(9,000)
Chargeable gain	13,000

12.3	Share pool:	No. of shares	Cost £
	Purchase April 85	5,000	5,605
	Bonus issue (1 for 5)	1,000	–
		6,000	5,605
	Sale Dec 2010	(3,500)	(3,270)
	c/f	2,500	2,335

Calculate gain:

	£
Proceeds	6,250
Cost	(3,270)
Chargeable gain	2,980

13.1

		£
Victoria Cross:	Proceeds	14,780
	Less: cost	(3,000)
		11,780

Chargeable gain not to exceed 5/3 × £(14,780 – 6,000) = £14,633

∴ Gain = £11,780

Vintage car: Exempt

Note. Medals are only exempt if awarded for bravery or inherited.

13.2

	£
Proceeds	7,500
Selling costs	(300)
	7,200
Less: cost	(4,500)
Gain	2,700

Chargeable gain not to exceed 5/3 × £(7,500 – 6,000) = £2,500

So, gain is £2,500.

13.3

	Cost £
Gross proceeds (deemed)	6,000
Cost	(6,260)
Allowable loss	(260)

13.4

	£
Gross proceeds	7,200
Less: Incidental costs	(350)
	6,850
Less: Acquisition cost (probate value)	(3,000)
Chargeable gain	3,850
Limited to $5/3 \times £(7,200 - 6,000)$	2,000

13.5 Motor car: exempt

Machinery:	£
Proceeds	7,500
Less: cost	(5,500)
	2,000

Restrict to $5/3 \times £(7,500 - 6,000) = £2,500$

Chargeable gain = £2,000

Note. There is never a capital loss on an item on which capital allowances have been claimed, as a balancing allowance would be given instead through the capital allowances computation.

13.6 *Grant of long lease:*

	£
Proceeds	30,000
Less cost	
$£40,000 \times \dfrac{30,000}{30,000 + 82,500}$	(10,667)
	19,333

13.7 *Grant of short lease:*

	£
Proceeds (capital element of premium)*	2,000
Cost $£30,000 \times \dfrac{2,000}{10,000 + 50,000}$	(1,000)
Chargeable gain	1,000

*	Premium	10,000
	Less: property income: $£10,000 \times [50 - (11 - 1)] \div 50$	(8,000)
	Capital element	2,000

14.1

	£
Gain	80,000
Exempt:	
1.10.83 – 30.6.86	33 months
1.7.07 – 30.6.10	36 months
	69 months
Total period	
1.10.83 – 30.6.10	321 months

		£
PPR relief: $\dfrac{69}{321} \times £80,000$		(17,196)
Gain attributable to letting		62,804
Less: letting relief		
Lowest of	(i) £40,000	
	(ii) PPR relief: £17,196	
	(iii) letting gain (1.7.86 – 30.6.07 = 252m): £62,804	(17,196)
Chargeable gain		45,608

14.2

	£
Proceeds	200,000
Less: cost	(20,000)
	180,000
Less PPR exemption $£180,000 \times 2/3$	(120,000)
Chargeable gain	60,000

Note. As the students occupy separate self-contained accommodation, the ground floor is treated as a separate residence, the gain on which is fully chargeable to CGT.

14.3 Any **two** of:

(a)   Any period employed outside the UK

(b)   Periods of up to four years working elsewhere in the UK if employed, or elsewhere in the UK *or* overseas if self employed

(c)   Up to three years for any reason

(d)   The last 3 years of ownership where the property has been the principal private residence at some time.

Note. (a) – (c) must be preceded and followed by a period of actual occupation.

15.1   *Gain chargeable on Jeremy*

	£
Excess proceeds over cost £(50,000 – 42,000)	8,000

	£
Base cost for John	
MV in August 2010	225,974
Less deferred gain £(110,000 – 8,000)	(102,000)
	123,974

15.2   The claim must be made jointly by Arthur and Hugo. The claim must be submitted before 5 April 2015 (ie 4 years after the end of the tax year of the gift).

15.3

	£
Deemed proceeds (MV)	22,000
Less: Cost	(4,000)
Gain before gift relief	18,000
Chargeable on Adam	
£(12,000 – 4,000)	(8,000)
Deferred by gift relief	10,000

The deferred gain (£10,000) is taxed on Bernard in the year he becomes non-resident (ie 2012/13).

15.4

	£
Proceeds (MV)	300,000
Less: cost	(160,000)
Gain	140,000
Gift relief (CBA/CA)	
$\dfrac{300}{300+50} \times £140,000$	(120,000)
Chargeable gain	20,000

15.5

	£
MV	95,000
Cost	(44,000)
Gain	51,000
Chargeable now £(63,000 – 44,000)	(19,000)
Gain eligible for gift relief	32,000

15.6

	£
Proceeds	4,000
Less cost: £24,000 × $\dfrac{4,000}{4,000+16,000}$	(4,800)
Loss	(800)

15.7   *2010/11*

Patrice can claim to defer the entire gain (there is no upper limit for EIS deferral relief and the amount spent on EIS shares exceeds the gain).

	£
Gain	600,000
Less EIS deferral relief	(600,000)
Chargeable gain	–

2011/12

As Patrice emigrates within 3 years, the chargeable gain of £600,000 will crystallise.

15.8 Gain on sale of Silvanus Ltd shares:

	£
Proceeds	800,000
Cost	(50,000)
Gain before EIS relief	750,000

Therefore, John's minimum EIS investment (and claim for EIS deferral relief) will be:

£(750,000 − 150,000 − 10,100) =   £589,900

16.1 Landlords can submit simplified returns for rental income when the total annual gross income from property is under £70,000 (the VAT threshold).

They are required to record three lines:

- Gross property income
- Total allowable expenses
- Net income

16.2 If Thomas files online the return must be filed and the tax due paid by 31 January 2012. If he submits a paper return he must file by 31 October 2011. Any tax due should be paid by 31 January 2012.

16.3 POA

	£
Income tax liability	10,250
Class 4 NIC	1,000
Less: tax deducted at source	(5,000)
	6,250

POAs of £3,125 are due on 31 January 2011 and 31 July 2011. Any balancing payment is due 31 January 2012.

16.4 Gareth filed an incorrect tax return. The tax lost as a result of the inaccuracy is £6,000 × 40% = £2,400.

Gareth's action was deliberate but not concealed (he has not made arrangements to conceal it for example by submitting false evidence in support of the incorrect figure). He is therefore liable to a maximum penalty of 70% × £2,400 = £1,680. This may be reduced depending on the quality of Gareth's cooperation with HMRC in correcting the error.

17.1 You should disclose this to the client. Practitioners may have a variety of financial arrangements with the client. For example, there may be an informal understanding that any commission is 'taken into account' when billing the client for services. Perhaps the fairest approach is to pay over the pension contribution on a 'no commission' basis and bill the client for the time taken in selecting and arranging his pension contract etc. Although the client then sees exactly what it is costing him he is not necessarily pleased to be billed for the work involved even though this should usually be less than the commission snipped off his pension contribution. Practitioners may also argue that higher charge-out rates would be needed if they didn't keep the commissions. The key point, however, is disclosure.

17.2 Unless the prospective client agrees to your contacting the previous adviser, you should decline to act for him. There may be exceptional circumstances where this normal rule can be overridden.

17.3 Quite possibly an amicable divorce settlement can be reached. If you believe this is likely you can continue to act for each party. It should be made clear to both spouses, however, that if a conflict of interest subsequently arises you will have to cease acting for at least one of them and this could be detrimental to both of them and to yourself.

17.4 Where a member undertakes tax compliance work for a client this will normally include responsibility for keeping the client informed of the amount of tax due for payment, the due date for payment and drawing the client's attention to the fact that interest accrues from that date.

17.5 False. The ATT will not arbitrate between a member and his client upon the amount of a disputed fee.

17.6 Contingent fees are specifically considered within the regime for disclosure of tax avoidance schemes.

17.7 It is recommended that they open an account if they hold, or expect to hold, the money for more than 30 days.

17.8   Land can be held either (i) freehold, (ii) leasehold, or (iii) commonhold.

17.9   The maximum number of legal owners of land is four.

17.10 Legal title passes from seller to buyer when contracts are exchanged.

17.11 An employment tribunal can make an order for reinstatement, re-engagement or awards of basic and/or compensatory compensation.

1.1 Mr Daphnis

MR DAPHNIS

	£
Allowances:	
Personal allowance (65 – 74)	9,490
Restricted : ½ × (24,080 – 22,900)	(590)
PA	8,900
Blind person's allowance	1,890
Tax reductions:	
Married couple's allowance (75 or over, given based on age of older spouse) (relief restricted to 10%)	6,965
MRS DAPHNIS	
PA (>75)	9,640

Some of this is being wasted as Mrs Daphnis has income of only £4,500.

Mr Daphnis's allowances have been restricted due to high net income. In order to maximise the benefit of allowances the interest generating bank account could be held in joint names, leading to a 50:50 split of interest for tax purposes.

The revised position would be:

	Mr	Mrs
Current net income	24,080	4,500
(Less) / plus 50% interest	(5,000)	5,000
Revised net income	19,080	9,500

There is now no need to restrict Mr Daphnis' allowances and Mrs Daphnis only wastes a small amount (£9,640 - £9,500) of her personal allowance.

1.2 Mr Rich

MR RICH
INCOME TAX COMPUTATION 2010/11

	Non savings income £
Earnings	118,500
Less: PA (W1)	(4,725)
Taxable income	113,775
£	
37,400 @ 20%	7,480
15,000 @ 20% (W2)	3,000
61,375 @ 40%	24,550
Tax liability	35,030
Tax suffered at source (PAYE)	(37,330)
Tax repayable	(2,300)

Workings

(1) *Personal allowance*

	£	£
Basic PA		6,475
Total income	118,500	
Less: Gift Aid (W2)	(15,000)	
Less: limit	(100,000)	
	3,500	
÷ 2		(1,750)
Restricted PA		4,725

(2)   Basic rate band extended (and total income reduced for personal allowances purposes (W1)) by gross donation, ie (£12,000 × 100/80) = £15,000

1.3   Tax Credits

Our address

Your address

Date

Dear Julie

Thank you for your letter and congratulations on your news.

The definition of income for tax credit purposes differs in a number of ways from the definition of taxable income for income tax purposes.

Firstly however, you need to be aware that you and your husband would have to make a joint claim for tax credits, as you are living together. Therefore, when calculating your entitlement to tax credits, you would need to take into account your joint income.

By following the steps that I have set out below you will be able to calculate your joint income:

(1)   Calculate your gross income from savings, investments, pensions and property.

       If, as in your case, this amounts to £300 or less it is ignored. If it exceeds £300 then only the excess over £300 is included in the calculation.

(2)   Next, include your employment income.

       This is basically the same as employment income for tax purposes and will include your salary and the taxable value of any benefits that you receive such as the company car and medical insurance. However, certain taxable benefits are excluded from the definition of employment income for tax credit purposes, eg living accommodation and more importantly in your case use of assets (other than cars). This means that the benefit in respect of the use of the home entertainment system can be excluded.

       In addition a deduction can be taken in respect of allowable employment expenses, which means that you can deduct the amount of the subscription that you paid to the Institute of Personnel and Development.

(3)   The next stage is to include your husband's income from self employment, which is simply his profits as adjusted for tax purposes.

       If in any year your husband makes a loss then this will be deducted from the total of your income as calculated above. If the amount of the loss exceeds your other income then the amount of the excess will be carried forward for tax credit purposes – you are not able to carry a loss back when calculating income for tax credit.

(4)   Finally, you can deduct the gross amount of any pension contributions that you make and also the gross amount of any Gift Aid payments, which means that your donation to the RSPCA can be deducted.

       You will note that there is no deduction for a personal allowance when calculating income for tax credit purposes.

Please let me know if you have any other questions.

Your sincerely

T Adviser

Marking scheme

	Marks
Joint income	1
Gross savings, pensions and property income	½
£300 excess	1
Employment income – salary and benefits	1
Excluded benefits	½
Applied to home entertainment system	1
Deducted for subscription	
Self-employment income (adjusted profits)	1
Deduct loss	½
Excess loss carried forward	½
Deduct pension contributions (gross)	1
Deduct gift aid payments (gross)	½
No personal allowance deducted	½
Presentation	1
Maximum	1
	10

2.1   **Mr Poor**

MR POOR
INCOME TAX COMPUTATION 2010/11

		Non savings income £	Savings income £	Dividend income £
Earnings		6,050		
Dividends received	$(£900 \times \frac{100}{90})$			1,000
Building society interest	$(£800 \times \frac{100}{80})$		1,000	
Bank deposit interest	$(£80 \times \frac{100}{80})$		100	
Net income		6,050	1,100	1,000
Less: PA		(6,050)	(425)	
Taxable income		nil	675	1,000

	£
Tax:	
£675 @ 10%	67
£1,000 @ 10%	100
Tax liability	167
Less: notional credit on dividend	(100)
	67
Less: Tax suffered at source	
Interest (£1,100 @ 20%)	(220)
Tax repayable	(153)

Notes

The personal allowance is set off against non savings income first, then against savings income.

The tax credit on the dividends can be deducted before other tax credits so as to maximise the repayment.

2.2 Jonty

INCOME TAX COMPUTATION 2010/11

	Non savings income £	Savings income £	Dividend income £
Earnings	46,000		
Building society interest £(80 × $\frac{100}{80}$)		100	
Dividends £(63 × $\frac{100}{90}$)			70
NS&I interest		142	
Net income	46,000	242	70
Less: PA	(6,475)		
Taxable income	39,525	242	70

Tax:	£
£	
37,400 @ 20%	7,480
495 @ 20% (W)	99
1,630 @ 40%	652
242 @ 40%	97
70 @ 32.5%	23
Tax liability	8,351
Less: notional credit on dividend	(7)
Less: tax suffered at source £(20 + 8,330)	(8,350)
Tax repayable	(6)

Workings

Basic rate threshold extended by gross donation ie (£396 × 100/80) = £495

Note. Betting income is exempt.

CTC/WTC

	£
CTC	
Family element	545
Child element	2,300
WTC	
Basic element	1,920
Couple's element	1,890
30 hour element	790
Maximum available credit	7,445

	£
Annual income £46,000 + (£242 + £70 − £300) − £495	45,517
Less: threshold	(6,420)
Excess Income	39,097
Maximum tax credit	7,445
Less: 39% of excess income	(15,248)
	Nil

∴ Will only receive the family element of £545 as income < £50,000 and the rest is reduced to nil.

2.3 Fred

	Non savings income £	Savings income £	Dividend income £
Property income	16,200		
Interest (£4,400 × 100/80)		5,500	
Gilt interest		290	
Dividends (£7,000 × 100/90)			7,778
Net income	16,200	5,790	7,778 Total = £29,768
Less: PAA (W)	(6,475)		
Taxable income	9,725	5,790	7,778

		£
Tax £15,515 @ 20%		3,103
£7,778 @ 10%		778
		3,881
Less: Married couples' allowance (W)		(670)
Tax liability		3,211
Less: Tax deducted:		
Dividends		(778)
Interest		(1,100)
Tax payable		1,333

Working

	£
PAA (>75)	9,640
Less: ½ £(29,768 – 22,900) = £3,434	
Max 'restriction' £(9,640 – 6,475)	(3,165)
Allowance given	6,475
Unused restriction (£3,434 – 3,165)	269
MCA	6,965
Less: unused restriction	(269)
	6,696

Tax reduction @ 10% = £670

2.4 Fiona

	Non-savings income £	Savings income £	Dividend income £
Trade profits	32,000		
UK dividends (£10,000 × 100/90)			11,111
Jersey bank interest		4,300	
Total income	32,000	4,300	11,111
Less: interest relief (W1)	(827)		
Net income	31,173	4,300	11,111
Less: personal allowance	(6,475)		
Taxable income	24,698	4,300	11,111

	£
Tax	
£(24,698 + 4,300) @ 20%	5,800
£8,402 @ 10% £(37,400 – 24,698 – 4,300)	840
£2,000 @ 10% (W2)	200
£709 @ 32½ % £(11,111 – 8,402 – 2,000)	230
	7,070
Less: EIS relief (£3,000 @ 20%)	(600)
Tax liability	6,470
Less: tax deducted on dividends	(1,111)
Tax due	5,359

Workings

1   Loan interest relief

		£
£24,000 × 4% × $^8/_{12}$		640
£14,000 × 4% × $^4/_{12}$		187
		827

2   Basic rate band extension:

Gross gift aid donation £1,600 × 100/80 = £2,000

Notes

(1)   Premium Bond winnings are tax free.

(2)   Child benefit is tax free.

(3)   The loan interest qualifies as a deductible payment (s.392 ITA 2007).

(4)   A 20% tax reduction is available on subscription for shares in a qualifying EIS company (up to a maximum subscription of £500,000).

2.5   **Jane Bradbury**

	Non savings income £	Savings income £	Dividend income £
Trade profits	7,140		
Bank interest (£200 × 100/80)		250	
Dividends (£4,950 × 100/90)			5,500
Less: Deductible payments:			
Interest relief (Notes 1 & 3)	(4,800)		
Net income	2,340	250	5,500
Less: personal allowance	(2,340)	(250)	(3,885)
Taxable income	nil	nil	1,615

	£
Tax £1,615 @ 10%	161
Less: Tax credits:	
Dividends (Note 2) (£1,615 × 10%)	(161)
Interest	(50)
Tax repayable	(50)

CTC/WTC	£
Child Tax Credit	
Family Element	545
Child Element	2,300
Working Tax Credit	
Basic element	1,920
Lone parent element	1,890
Childcare element (£60 × 52 × 80%)	2,496
Maximum credits	9,151

	£
Annual income £(7,140 + 5,750 − 300) Note 3	12,590
Less: threshold	(6,420)
Excess income	6,170

	£
Maximum tax credit	9,151
Less: 39% of excess income	(2,406)
Tax credits payable	6,475

Notes

(1) The interest on the loan to purchase an interest in a partnership is deductible (s.388 ITA 2007).

(2) The tax credit available on the dividend is 10% of the *taxable* dividend (ie the amount left after offsetting allowances).

(3) The interest relief of £4,800 is not deductible for CTC/WTC purposes.

2.6 George and Mildred Roper

GEORGE ROPER

TAX COMPUTATION 2010/11

	Non savings income £	Savings income £	Dividend income £
Earnings	11,000		
Pension income	2,600		
State pension	5,078		
Rental income	4,000		
Gilt interest		180	
UK dividends (£2,115 × 100/90)			2,350
Total income	22,678	180	2,350
Less: interest relief (£10,000 × 10%)	(1,000)		
Net income	21,678	180	2,350 = £24,208
Less: PAA (W1)	(8,836)		
Taxable income	12,842	180	2,350

	£
Tax £12,842+ 180 @ 20% (Note)	2,604
£2,350 @ 10%	235
	2,839
Less: Tax reductions:	
Maintenance relief (W2)	(267)
MCA (W1)	(116)
Tax liability	2,456
Less: tax deducted:	
Tax on dividends	(235)
PAYE £(905 + 520)	(1,425)
Tax payable	796

Note. As non savings income exceeds £2,440 the 10% starting rate band is not available for the savings income.

Workings

		£
1	Personal Age Allowance:	
	PAA (65 – 74)	9,490
	Less: ½ (£24,208 – £22,900)	(654)
	Allowance given	8,836
	Married Couples Age Allowance:	
	MCA (as Mildred ≥76)	6,965
	Tax reduction @ 10% × ²⁄₁₂ (as 10 full tax months before the wedding) =	116

Note. MCA given to George as his net income is higher than Mildred's.

		£
2	Maintenance payment £250 × 12	3,000
	Relief restricted to	2,670
	Tax reduction @ 10%	267

MILDRED ROPER
TAX COMPUTATION 2010/11

	Non savings income £	Savings income £	Dividend income £
State pension	5,078		
Building society interest (£8,400 × 100/80)		10,500	
Discretionary trust (£3,300 × 2)	6,600		
Guernsey bank interest (received gross)		1,215	
Dividends (£720 × 100/90)			800
Net income	11,678	11,715	800 Total = £24,193
Less: PAA (W1)	(9,306)		
Taxable income	2,372	11,715	800

	£
Tax: £2,372 @ 20% (non-savings)	474
£68 @ 10% (2,440 – 2,372) (savings)	7
£(11,715 – 68) @ 20%	2,329
£800 @ 10%	80
Tax liability	2,890
Less: Tax deducted:	
Dividends	(80)
Interest (£10,500 × 20%)	(2,100)
Trust income	(3,300)
Tax repayable	(2,590)

Note. Premium Bond winnings are exempt from income tax.

Workings

1   *Personal age allowance*

	£
PAA (>75)	9,640
Less: ½ £(23,568 – 22,900) (W2)	(334)
PAA given	9,306

2   *Adjusted net income*

	£
Actual net income	24,193
Less: gross donation to charity (£500 × 100/80)	(625)
Adjusted net income for age allowance purposes	23,568

Note. Do not need to extend the basic rate band as Mildred is not a higher rate taxpayer.

2.7   **Lauren**

	Non savings income £	Savings income £	Dividend income £
Earnings	23,000		
Bank interest (£22,000 × 100/80)		27,500	
UK dividends (£67,500 × 100/90)			75,000
Discretionary trust income £32,000 × 2	64,000		
Total income	87,000	27,500	75,000
Less: personal allowance (income < £112,950)	(NIL)		
Taxable income	87,000	27,500	75,000

Tax

		£
£38,900 @ 20% (W)		7,780
£48,100 @ 40% £(87,000 – 38,900)		19,240
£27,500 @ 40%		11,000
£37,000 @ 32½% £(151,500 – 38,900 – 48,100 – 27,500)		12,025
£38,000 @ 42½ % £(75,000 – 37,000)		16,150
Tax liability		66,195
Less:	Tax credit on dividends	(7,500)
	Tax paid on bank interest £27,500 × 20%	(5,500)
	Tax paid on discretionary trust income £64,000 × 50%	(32,000)
	PAYE	(3,705)
Tax due		17,490

Working

Basic and higher rate band extension: Gross Gift Aid donation £(100 × 12) × 100/80 = £1,500

- Basic rate band: £(37,400 + 1,500) = £38,900
- Higher rate band: £(150,000 + 1,500) = £151,500

Note. The difference between the basic and higher rate band is always £112,600.

3.1 Randall

(1)

	A	Property B	C
	£	£	£
Rent	620	284 (W)	100
Agent's commission	(20)		
Advertising for tenants		(76)	
Repairs	(142)	(255)	(119)
Profit/(loss)	458	(47)	(19)

	£
Profit on A	458
Less loss on B and C	(66)
Property income assessment	392

Working

	£
April – Sept ($\frac{6}{12}$ × £348)	174
Dec – March ($\frac{3}{12}$ × £440)	110
	284

(2) When a premium or similar consideration is received on the *grant* (that is, by a landlord to a tenant) of a short lease (50 years or less), part of the premium is treated as rent so is taxed as property income in the year of grant.

A formula is used to identify the amount of the premium that is taxable as property income:

$P \times \dfrac{50 - Y}{50}$ where Y = number of years on the lease minus 1 year

3.2 Corelli

TAX COMPUTATION 2010/11

(i)

	Non savings income £	Dividend income £
Earnings	16,450	
Dividends (£15,300 × $\frac{100}{90}$)		17,000
Property income (W)	6,560	
Net income	23,010	17,000
Less: PA	(6,475)	
Taxable income	16,535	17,000

		£
Tax:	£16,535 @ 20%	3,307
	£17,000 @ 10%	1,700
		5,007
Tax liability		
Less: notional credit on dividend		(1,700)
Less: PAYE		(1,995)
Tax payable		1,312

Working

Property income:

	A £	B £	C £
Income (3/12 × £1,200 + 6/12 × £800)	700		
		3,100	
(9/12 × £600)			450
Expenditure:			
Agent's commission:			
1.5.10	(25)	(35)	(10)
1.11.10	(25)	(35)	(10)
Repairs	–	(100)	(1,500)
Advertising	(50)	–	–
	600	2,930	(1,070)
Net rents			£2,460

Note. Installation of new kitchen equipment is a capital *not* a revenue expense.

Lease premium:

	£
	4,100

£5,000 × $\frac{(50-(10-1))}{50}$

Total property income: £2,460 + £4,100 = £6,560

(ii) Freehold is an absolute interest in land, which allows the freeholder to do as he wishes (subject to general law eg planning) with his land.

Leasehold is a qualified interest in land, which is limited in time. The lease normally contains a range of covenants binding on the tenant and his successors and the lease may be forfeitable if these conditions are not complied with.

Marking scheme

		Marks
(i)	Dividends	½
	Personal allowance	½
	Tax calculation	1
	Tax credits	½
	Property income	1½
	Commission	½
	Repairs	½
	Advertising	½
	Exclude capital expenditure	½
	Premium 'income'	1
		7
(ii)	Freehold – absolute interest	1
	– freedom of use	1
	Leasehold – qualified interest	1
	– covenants	1
	– forfeitable	1
		5
	Total	**12**

4.1   Enterprise Investment Scheme

The EIS is intended to encourage investment in the ordinary shares of unquoted companies. When a qualifying individual subscribes for eligible shares in a qualifying company, the amount subscribed qualifies for tax relief equal to 20% of the investment. The tax relief is given as a tax reduction in the income tax computation.

A *qualifying individual* is one who is not connected with the company at any time in the period from two years before the issue (or from incorporation if later) to three years after the issue. An individual is connected with the company if his shareholding exceeds 30%, if he is a partner of the company or if he is an employee or a non-qualifying director of the company.

A *qualifying director* is one who does not receive payment from the company apart from reasonable remuneration.

Eligible shares are newly issued ordinary shares which carry no preferential rights to dividends, assets or redemption in the three years from the date of issue.

A *qualifying company* is (broadly) an unquoted trading company. Certain trades are excluded. The company must be unquoted when the shares are issued.

The maximum total investment that can qualify in a tax year is £500,000 per individual. If an investment is less than £500 no relief is available (unless subscription is made by an approved EIS fund that pools the contributions of several investors).

Generally speaking, relief is given on an actual basis: a 2010/11 investment will attract relief against 2010/11 tax. However, a taxpayer can claim to carry back his EIS investments to the previous tax year, subject to the usual limit of £500,000.

If an individual disposes of shares (or receives value from the company, for example by taking a loan from the company) within three years of their issue, the tax reduction obtained may be wholly or partly withdrawn.

If the shares are given away or sold otherwise than at arm's length within the three years, all of the tax reduction is withdrawn.

On an arm's length sale or a receipt of value within the three years, the tax reduction to be withdrawn is:

$$\text{Consideration obtained} \times \frac{\text{Tax reduction obtained on issue}}{\text{Issue price of shares}}$$

However, the withdrawal cannot exceed the tax reduction originally obtained (which may have been less than 20% of the issue price, for example because the individual did not have enough tax to reduce).

A transfer of shares between spouses/partners in a civil partnership does not give rise to a withdrawal of the tax reduction. The reduction obtained remains associated with the shares, and if the recipient partner disposes of the shares outside the marriage/partnership within three years of their issue, it is withdrawn by an assessment on the recipient partner.

The death of a shareholder is not treated as a disposal.

If shares are disposed of after three years from issue, the following consequences ensue.

(a)   The tax reduction is not withdrawn (although earlier partial withdrawals stand).

(b)   If there is a gain for CGT purposes and EIS relief has not already been wholly withdrawn, the gain is exempt.

On a disposal before or after the expiry of the three year period, any loss for CGT purposes is restricted by reducing the issue price (but not so as to create a gain). The reduction is the tax reduction obtained and not withdrawn.

When shares issued under the EIS are sold at arm's length at a loss at any time (within or outside the first three years), and the EIS relief is not wholly withdrawn, the loss may be relieved in the same way as a trading loss.

> **Tutorial note.** The detail can be found in ss.156-257 ITA 2007.

5.1   **Mr Thomas**

TAXABLE BENEFITS – MR THOMAS – 2010/11

	£
Accommodation (W1)	3,125
Related expenses (W1)	4,950
Loan interest (W2)	317
Car 1 (W3)	3,870
Car 2 (W3)	667
Taxable benefits	12,929

Workings

1   Accommodation

	£
Annual value	750
Additional charge: 4% × £(134,375 – 75,000)	2,375
	3,125

Mr Thomas occupied the property for the first time more than 6 years after it was purchased in 1994, therefore the additional charge is based on the market value of the property when first occupied, not on cost plus alterations carried out prior to occupation.

Related expenses

	£
Household bills – electricity, gas, telephone £(750 + 250 + 350)	1,350
Council tax	1,400
Redecoration	700
Gardener	1,500
	4,950

2   *Cheap taxable loan*

Average basis: $\dfrac{(10,000 + 9,000)}{2} \times \dfrac{10}{12} \times 4\% =$ £317

Strict basis:		£
	£10,000 × 2/12 × 4%	67
	£15,000 × 4/12 × 4%	200
	£7,500 × 2/12 × 4%	50
	£11,500 × 1/12 × 4%	38
	£9,000 × 1/12 × 4%	30
		385

HMRC may insist on the strict basis, although in practice the difference should be considered insignificant.

3   Cars

Mercedes: £21,500 × 18% ($\left(\frac{145-130}{5}\right)$ = 3 + 15 = 18%) = £3,870

Escort: £10,000 × 10% (emissions between 76 and 120g/km) × 8/12 = £667

5.2 Alf

	Non savings income £	Savings income £	Dividend income £
Earnings (W1)	101,760		
Interest (£5,440 × 100/80)		6,800	
Dividends (£4,000 × 100/90)			4,444
Less: personal allowance (W2)	(973)		
Taxable income	100,787	6,800	4,444

		£
Tax:	£37,400 @ 20%	7,480
	£ 2,000 @ 20% (W3)	400
	£61,387 @ 40%	24,555
	£ 6,800 @ 40%	2,720
	£ 4,444 @ 32½%	1,444
Tax liability		36,599
Less: Tax credits:		
	Dividends	(444)
	PAYE	(28,570)
	Interest	(1,360)
Tax payable		6,225

Workings

1   Earnings

	£	£
Salary		96,600
Expenses allowance:		
Gross allowance (N1)	2,500	
Less business travel	(1,800)	
		700
		97,300
Benefits:		
Stereo equipment £(800 × 20%) (N2)	160	
Car £(15,000 × 24%) (N3)	3,600	
Medical insurance (N4)	300	
Clothing (N4)	400	
		4,460
Amount chargeable as earnings		101,760

Notes

(1)   The expenses allowance is taxable, but Alf can claim the cost of business travel as an allowable deduction. Entertainment of clients is not deductible as this would not have been deductible for his employer.

(2)   The annual value of the stereo equipment subject to tax is 20% of its cost.

(3)   The emission percentage is ([175 − 130g] ÷ 5) + 15% = 24%.

(4)   The taxable value of the medical insurance and clothing is the cost to the company of providing the benefits.

2   Personal allowance restriction

	£	£
Basic PA		6,475
Total income £(101,760 + 6,800 + 4,444)	113,004	
Less: gift aid (W3)	(2,000)	
Less: limit	(100,000)	
÷ 2		(5,502)
Restricted PA		973

3   Basic rate band extended (and income reduced for personal allowance purposes (W2)) by gross Gift Aid donation: £1,600 × 100/80 = £2,000

5.3 Mr Bjork

Mr Bjork's taxable benefits

		£
Jaguar:	car (£20,000 × 32% × $^4/_{12}$) (W1)	2,133
	petrol (£18,000 × 32% × $^4/_{12}$) (W1)	1,920
Mercedes:	no private use (all business use)	
BMW:	car (£15,000 × 35%) (W2)	5,250
	petrol (£18,000 × 35%) (W2)	6,300
Legal costs		2,000
Use of video equipment £800 × 20%		160
Use of computer £3,000 × 20% × 6/12		300
Gift of computer (W3)		1,800
Total benefits		19,863

Workings

1    $\left(\dfrac{215-130}{5}\right)$ = 17% + 15% = 32%

2    $\left(\dfrac{235-130}{5}\right)$ = 21% + 15% = 36% (35% Cap)

3   Taxable benefit is the higher of:

	£	£
(i) MV		200
(ii) MV when first provided	3,000	
Less: amounts assessed:		
2010/11 (see above)	(300)	
2009/10 £3,000 × 20%	(600)	
2008/09 £3,000 × 20% × 6/12	(300)	
		1,800

ie £1,800

5.4 HiTech Computers

EARNINGS FOR 2010/11

	£	£
Salary:		
April – June ($^3/_{12} \times$ £31,000)	7,750	
July – March ($^9/_{12} \times$ £36,000)	27,000	
		34,750
Commission – paid in year		4,000
		38,750
Accommodation (from date of promotion):		
Higher of (i) Rent paid £5,000 $\times$ $^9/_{12}$ = £3,750	3,750	
(ii) Annual value 2,400 $\times$ $^9/_{12}$ = £1,800		
Less contribution (£100 $\times$ 9 months)	(900)	
		2,850
Loan interest $\dfrac{15,000 + 10,000}{2} \times 4\%$		500
Car parking space (not taxable as near to place of work)		–
Medical insurance (cost to employer)		385
Crèche facilities (note 1)		–
Newspaper allowance £20 $\times$ 12		240
		42,725
Less: pension contribution (see later in the Text) (5% $\times$ £38,750)		(1,938)
Earnings		40,787

Note. Employers' contributions of up to £55 per week towards childcare provision are tax free therefore the £100 monthly payment is not taxable.

5.5 Grovelands

(i)   INCOME TAX LIABILITY 2010/11

	Non savings Income £	Savings Income £	Dividend Income £
Employment income – Grovelands (W1)	155,495		
Employment income – new post (2/12 $\times$ £8,400)	1,400		
Bank interest (£1,386 $\times \dfrac{100}{80}$)		1,732	
Dividends (£2,754 $\times \dfrac{100}{90}$)			3,060
Total income	156,895	1,732	3,060
Less: PA (income > £112,950)	(NIL)		
TAXABLE INCOME	156,895	1,732	3,060

TAX PAYABLE

Non savings income (excluding compensation) £113,008 (W1) + £1,400 = £114,408

	£
£37,400 @ 20%	7,480
£1,000 @ 20% (W4)	200
£76,008 @ 40%	30,403
Savings income £1,732	
£1,732 @ 40%	693
Dividends £3,060	
£3,060 @ 32.5%	994
Compensation £42,487	
£31,800 @ 40% £(151,000 – 114,408 – 1,732 – 3,060)	12,720
£10,687 @ 50% £(42,487 – 31,800)	5,343
INCOME TAX LIABILITY	57,833

Workings

(1) *Employment income – Grovelands Ltd*

	£	£
Salary (£129,333 × 9/12)		97,000
Benefits:		
Motor car (£22,300 × 30% * × 9/12)	5,017	
Car fuel (£18,000 × 30% × 9/12)	4,050	
BUPA	200	
Season ticket	2,641	
Entertainment system (W2)	4,100	
		16,008
		113,008
Termination payment (W3)	72,487	
Less: Exempt under s.403 ITEPA 2003	(30,000)	
		42,487
		155,495

* The car and fuel benefit percentage is: ([209 – 130] ÷ 5) + 15% = 30% (round down).

(2) *Entertainment system*

	£	£
6.04.10 – 31.12.10		
£5,000 @ 20% × 9/12 =		750
Transfer higher of		
(i) MV @ transfer	1,000	
or		
(ii) MV when 1st available	5,000	
Less		
– assessed 2009/10		
£5,000 @ 20% × 9/12	(750)	
– assessed 2010/11 (above)	(750)	
	3,500	3,500
Less: price paid		(150)
		4,100

(3) *Termination payment*

The compensation for loss of office payment is assessed on a receipts basis and not by reference to the year in which the employment ceased.

Termination payments are treated as the top slice of income when calculating income tax.

(4) *Gift aid payment*

Gross donation: £800 × 100/80 = £1,000.

Higher rate relief is obtained by extending the basic and higher rate bands by this gross donation to £38,400 and £151,000 respectively.

(ii) Summary dismissal occurs where an employer dismisses an employee without notice or without waiting for a fixed term contract to expire. Provided that the employee has committed an act of gross misconduct, the employer incurs no liability for breach of conduct. The employee is only entitled to receive contractual salary and benefits up to the date of termination of the employment.

Constructive dismissal arises where an employee resigns as a result of the employer breaching some essential term of the employment contract without the employee's consent. The employer in this case is liable for breach of contract.

Marking scheme

		Marks
(i)	Employment income – new post	½
	Bank interest	1
	Dividends	1
	Personal allowance	½
	Tax calculation	3
	Grovelands employment income:	
	– Salary	½
	– Car	1½
	– Fuel	1
	– BUPA	½
	– Season ticket	½
	– Entertainment system	2½
	– Termination payment and £30,000 exemption	1½
	Gift aid	1
		15
(ii)	Summary dismissal – definition	1
	– no breach	1
	– employee entitlement	1
	Constructive dismissal – definition	1
	– breach	1
		5
		20

5.6 **Mr Morris**

MR MORRIS – INCOME TAX PAYABLE FOR 2010/11

	Non savings Income £	Savings Income £	Dividend Income £
Employment income (W1)	33,681		
Building society interest ($£312 \times \frac{100}{80}$)		390	
Bank interest ($£256 \times 1/2 \times \frac{100}{80}$)		160	
Dividends ($£738 \times \frac{100}{90}$)			820
Property income (W2)	4,635		
Total income	38,316	550	820
Less: PA	(6,475)		
TAXABLE INCOME	31,841	550	820

TAX LIABILITY

	£	£
£31,841 @ 20%		6,368
£550 @ 20%		110
£820 @ 10%		82
INCOME TAX LIABILITY		6,560
Less: PAYE	5,441	
BSI	78	
Bank interest	32	
UK dividends	82	
		(5,633)
INCOME TAX PAYABLE		927

Note. As Mr Morris is a basic rate taxpayer no further relief is due for the charitable donation which does not impact on the tax calculation.

Workings

1 *Employment income*

		£
Salary		25,175
Car (£14,665 × 25%)*		3,666
Fuel (£18,000 × 25%)*		4,500
Health insurance		340
		33,681

* The car and fuel benefit percentage is: ([182 − 130g] ÷ 5) + 15% = 25% (rounded down).

2 *Property income*

	£	£
Gross rental income (5/12 × £8,000 + 6/12 × £12,000)		9,333
Less:		
Agent's fees £(267 + 600)	867	
Repairs £(400 + 1,500)	1,900	
Gardener £(100 + 200)	300	
Council tax	590	
Water rates £(85 + 100)	185	
Wear and tear allowance (£(9,333 − 590 − 185) @ 10%)	856	
		(4,698)
		4,635

The cost of the new gas fire is capital expenditure and cannot be deducted for income tax purposes.

Marking scheme

	Marks
Building society interest	½
Bank interest	½
Dividends	½
Personal allowance	½
Tax calculation	1
Tax credits	1
Salary	½
Car	1
Fuel	1
Health insurance	½
Rent	1
Expenses	1½
Wear and tear allowance	1
Maximum	10

6.1 **Sue**

(a) If the scheme has been approved then there are no tax consequences on the grant or exercise of the options.

When Sue comes to sell the shares she will have a chargeable gain and annual exempt amount as follows: (covered in the Capital Gains Tax section of the Text).

	£
Sale proceeds = 5,000 × £10.40	52,000
Cost = 5,000 × £4.00	(20,000)
Gain	32,000

TQT
Tax Qualification Training

(b)   As the scheme is unapproved, an employment income charge will arise on the exercise of the option as follows:

	£
Market value at date of exercise	10.00
Less exercise price	(3.00)
	7.00 per share

£7.00 × 5,000 shares =   £35,000

Sale of shares (covered later in the Text)

	£
Sale proceeds	52,000
Cost = MV at date of exercise (5,000 × £10)	(50,000)
Gain	2,000

> **Tutorial note**
>
> In general terms, there is little difference between an approved and an unapproved scheme if the shares are to be sold. The approved scheme gives rise to a capital gain. The unapproved scheme results in an employment income charge but a much smaller capital gain.
>
> However, most taxpayers would rather have profits taxed under the approved scheme rules (ie making their profit chargeable to CGT rather than income tax) as the CGT annual exempt amount of £10,100 is available and the rate of CGT is 28% compared to 40% for a taxpayer paying income tax at the higher rate, or 50% at the additional rate.
>
> You should revisit this question after you have covered the Capital Gains Tax section of this Study Text.

7.1   Mr Howe

Notes for meeting with Mr Howe:

(a)   *Employment income*

	Total income
	£
Salary	35,000
Company car benefit: £9,500 × 16% (W)	1,520
Fuel benefit: £18,000 × 16% (W)	2,880
Interest free loan – exempt as < £5,000	–
Laptop: £1,449 × 20%	290
Employment income	39,690

Working

Car benefit percentage:

$$*\frac{(135-130)}{5} = 1\% + 15\% = 16\%$$

(b)   *NIC*

Both Mr Howe and his employer must pay Class 1 NIC on his 'earnings', ie his salary of £35,000.
Only Mr Howe's employer has to pay Class 1A NIC on his taxable benefits:

Car benefit	£1,520
Fuel benefit	2,880
Laptop	290
Total liable to Class 1A NIC	£4,690

No Class 1A NICs are due on the interest free loan as it is an exempt benefit for income tax purposes.

8.1   Mr Matthews

(1)   REVIEW OF CALCULATION OF TAXABLE INCOME

	Total income £	Tax suffered £
Earned income		
Salary	48,750	9,430
Medical insurance	375	
Car parking space (Note 1)	–	
Less:		
Deduction for business mileage (Note 2)	(259)	
Subscriptions (Note 3)	(295)	
	48,571	
Unearned income		
Bank interest (Note 4)	400	80
Trust income (Note 5)	2,000	1,000
Net income	50,971	10,510

Notes

(1)   Provision of a car parking space at or near the place of work is an exempt benefit and therefore the reimbursement of the parking expenses does not form part of taxable income.

(2)   Payments received for business mileage are not taxable provided they do not exceed HMRC's Authorised Mileage Rates. Where an employee is reimbursed for business mileage at a rate less than the authorised rates then a claim can be made for the shortfall as a deduction from income.

	£
Amount due under authorised rates (925 × 40p)	370
Amount actually received (925 × 12p)	(111)
Amount to claim	259

(3)   Payments of a subscription to an approved HMRC body that relates to the individual's employment is allowable as a deduction from employment income under s.344 ITEPA 2003. Relief is given for the amount paid in the tax year.

(4)   The gross amount of the building society interest must be included in the computation of income. The tax deducted is £80, which means £320 is the net amount and gross income of £400 must be included. Tax of 20% of the gross income is deducted at source from building society interest.

(5)   The gross amount of the discretionary trust income must be included in the computation of income. The tax deducted is £1,000, which means £1,000 is the net amount and gross income of £2,000 must be included. Discretionary trust income comes with a tax credit of 50%.

(2)   Tax relief is available for donations made to charities if Gift Aid is claimed. The gift is deemed to be made net of basic rate tax, which the charity can claim from HMRC. If the donor is a higher or additional rate taxpayer, higher or additional rate tax relief is obtained by extending the basic or higher rate band respectively by the gross amount of the payment.

For example, Mr Matthews donates £120 per tax year to the Dogs Trust. Mr Matthews' basic rate band will be extended by £150 (£120 × 100/80) which means a further £150 of income will be taxed at the basic rate of tax rather than the higher rate. If he was an additional rate taxpayer, his higher rate band would also be extended by this same amount.

The above relief is available provided that the donor made a Gift Aid declaration. Such a declaration must contain the name and address of the donor, the name of the charity and a statement that the donor has paid sufficient income or capital gains tax to cover the basic tax relief due to the charity in respect of the gift.

In addition, the donor must not receive any significant benefit from the charity as a result of the gift – although an exception to this rules applies if the benefit is simply free entry to a charity's properties.

If Mr Matthews is in a repayment position for 2010/11 he can indicate on his tax return form that he would like the repayment to be donated to a charity of his choice. He can also indicate for Gift Aid to apply to this donation and therefore will be able to claim tax relief in respect of it for next year.

(3)   CALCULATION OF TAX PAYABLE/(REPAYABLE)

	£
Net income	50,971
Less: Personal allowance	(6,475)
Taxable income	44,496
£37,400 @ 20%	7,480
£375 (W) @ 20%	75
£6,721 @ 40%	2,688
Tax liability	10,243
Less tax deducted at source	(10,510)
Tax repayable	(267)

Working

	£
Donation to Dogs Trust (£10 × 12)	120
Donation to English Heritage (£15 × 12)	180
	300
Extension to basic rate band (£300 × 100/80)	£375

(4)   Contributions to a personal pension plan are made net of basic rate income tax.

If the taxpayer is a higher rate taxpayer higher rate tax relief is obtained by extending the basic rate band by the gross amount of the payment. The higher rate band is also extended by this same amount if the taxpayer is an additional rate taxpayer.

The maximum gross allowable contribution is based on the higher of:

(i)   £3,600 and
(ii)   100% × the taxpayer's relevant earnings.

Relevant earnings consist of his employment income (including benefits) less allowable expenses ie:

	£
Salary	48,750
Medical insurance	375
Car parking space	–
Less:	
Deduction for business mileage	(259)
Subscription	(295)
Relevant earnings	48,571

Mr Matthews can therefore contribute up to £48,571 and obtain tax relief. It is unlikely he would wish to contribute this entire amount to a pension and should therefore choose an amount that will leave him with sufficient income to maintain his current lifestyle.

For example if he chose to contribute, say, £6,500 (gross), this would result in a tax saving of £1,300, as a further £6,500 of income would be taxed at 20% rather than 40%. He would pay £5,200 (£6,500 × 80%) into the fund and HMRC would transfer £1,300 (£6,500 × 20%) into the pension fund.

Pension contributions must be paid in the current pension input period so it is not possible for Mr Matthews to claim relief against his 2010/11 income, as it is now mid February 2012.

Marking scheme

(1)	Insurance	½
	Car space	1
	Business mileage	2
	Subscriptions	1
	Interest	1
	Trust income	½
		6
(2)	Paid net of basic rate tax	1
	Basic and higher rate bands extended	1
	Illustration	1
	Declaration	1
	No benefits	1
	Repayment to charity	1
	Repayment under gift aid	1
	Maximum	**5**
(3)	Personal allowance	½
	Tax calculation	1
	Tax credit	½
	Donations	1
		3
(4)	Payment net of basic rate tax	½
	Extension of basic and higher rate bands	1
	Maximum contribution	2
	Relevant earnings	1
	Apply to Mr Matthews	2
	Relevant tax year	1
	Maximum	**6**
		20

8.2   Ed & Joan

(a)   Maximum contributions

Ed and Joan can contribute any amount to their pension regardless of the level of their earnings. However tax relief will only be given for contributions up to their earnings for the tax year.

Ed can contribute a maximum of £140,000 and Joan £35,000 and receive tax relief on their contributions.

They cannot obtain relief for 2009/10 as contributions must be made in the current pension input period.

(b)   Tax relief

Basic rate tax relief is given through the pension holder paying contributions net of 20% basic rate tax. This means that they pay only 80% of the gross payment into the pension. HMRC pays the extra 20% on their behalf to the pension provider.

Ed will pay £112,000 (£140,000 × 80%) and Joan will pay £28,000 (£35,000 × 80%).

In addition Ed will be entitled to higher rate relief. This is given by extending the basic rate band for the year by the amount of the gross contribution.

Joan's tax liability	£
Employment income	35,000
Personal allowance	(6,475)
Taxable income	28,525
Tax liability	
£28,525 @ 20%	5,705

Ed's tax liability

	£
Employment income	140,000
Personal allowance	(6,475)
Taxable income	133,525

Tax liability:
£133,525 at 20% (Note)   26,705

Note. Higher rate tax relief will be given by extending Ed's basic rate tax band for 2010/11 to £177,400 (£37,400 + £140,000).

(c) **No earnings**

There is no need for an individual to have earnings. A contribution of up to £3,600 gross per tax year may be made into a pension regardless of the level of earnings.

8.3 **Dwaine Pipe**

INCOME TAX COMPUTATION 2010/11

	Non savings income £	Savings income £
Earnings (W1)	35,105	
Interest on ISA		Exempt
BS interest £$(20,000 \times \dfrac{100}{80}) \times 50\%$		12,500
Premium bond winnings		Exempt
Net income	35,105	12,500
Less: Personal allowance	(6,475)	–
Taxable income	28,630	12,500

		£
Tax thereon:		
£28,630 @ 20%		5,726
£8,770 @ 20%		1,754
£2,750 @ 20% (W7)		550
£980 @ 40%		392
Tax liability		8,422
Less: tax deducted:		
PAYE		(6,000)
Interest (£12,500 @ 20%)		(2,500)
Tax repayable		(78)

Workings

1   *Earnings*   £

   Salary
   (£20,000 × $^9/_{12}$)   15,000
   (£22,000 × $^3/_{12}$)   5,500
                                                                  20,500

   Bonuses (Note 1)
       Awarded 30.9.10   3,850
       Awarded 31.3.11   4,250
                                                                  28,600

   Company cars:
       Vauxhall Cavalier (W2 + W3)   960
       Audi A6 (W4 + W5)   2,205
                                                                  31,765

   Mobile phone   Exempt
   Interest free loan (W6)   2,250
   Nursery fees (Note 2)   Exempt
   Pension contributions by employer   Exempt
   Central heating (cost to employer)   800
   Staff suggestion scheme   Exempt
   Round sum allowance   1,000
                                                                  35,815

   Less: allowable expenses
   Hotel bills   (710)
   Total   35,105

2   *Vauxhall Cavalier*   £

   £10,629 @ 20% × 7/12 (W3)   1,240
   Less employee contributions (7 × £40)   (280)
   Car benefit   960

   No fuel benefit as no private diesel provided.

3   $\left(\dfrac{140-130}{5}\right)$ = 2% + 18% (diesel) = 20%

4   *Audi A6*

   (£18,500 + £400) @ 28% × 5/12 = £2,205

   No reduction of benefit for time car in garage as unavailable for < 30 consecutive days.

   No fuel benefit as no private petrol provided.

5   $\left(\dfrac{195-130}{5}\right)$ = 13% + 15% = 28%

6   *Interest-free loan*

   Average

   $\dfrac{75,000+60,000}{2}$ × 10/12 × 4% = £2,250

                                                                       £
   Strict basis
   £75,000 × 7/12 × 4%   1,750

   £60,000 × 3/12 × 4%   600
                                                                   2,350

   HMRC may elect for strict basis; unlikely in practice.

7   *Personal pension contributions*

Dwaine pays £150 × 12   £1,800

$\times \dfrac{100}{80}$ £2,250

Basic rate threshold extended by £500 (£400 × 100/80 Gift Aid) + £2,250 = £2,750

Notes

(1)   Bonus becomes taxable in the year in which a director is *entitled* to the payment (even if this is before actual receipt).

(2)   First £55 per week of childcare costs paid by employer for approved childcare are tax-free.

9.1   **Ricardo Garcia**

Our address

Your address

Date

Dear Mr Garcia

UK taxation on moving to this country

Thank you for your recent letter informing me of your proposed move. I set out below the main points of UK taxation on income which would be relevant to you.

Domicile and residence

The tax treatment of individuals in the UK depends on three concepts – domicile, residence and ordinary residence.

'Domicile' is a person's 'permanent home country'. It is normally a 'domicile of origin', being the domicile normally of one's father, and so you are presumably domiciled in Spain at present. However, it can be changed to a 'domicile of choice'. This is not done merely by the act of emigrating: it requires very positive cutting off of ties in the previous domicile, to show that there is no intention to return.

If you were unwilling to cut such ties, you would retain your domicile in Spain. In fact, this may be to your advantage, as foreign domiciled individuals can be taxed more favourably in respect of their foreign income than UK domiciled individuals in certain circumstances.

'Residence' is broadly established by 183 days presence in the UK in a tax year, but if you come here to live permanently you will be treated as resident and also ordinarily resident in the UK from the date you arrive. This is the main factor which affects your UK tax position.

Remittance basis of taxation

As a foreign domiciled individual, you can make a claim to have your overseas sources of income taxed only if remitted to (ie brought into) the UK. This will initially at least have a cash flow advantage as you are only taxed when you bring the income into the UK. However there are certain disadvantages depending on the type of income remitted. These are explained where appropriate below.

This remittance basis applies automatically to foreign income in certain circumstances, for example if you have little or no unremitted foreign income. However, based on the information provided (ie your large sums of overseas income that you do not plan to bring into the UK) you do not appear to qualify for the automatic remittance basis.

Allowances

Normally, as an EEA resident, you are entitled to a personal allowance deducted from your income. However, if you claim to be taxed on the remittance basis, you will lose your entitlement to personal allowances. You would not lose your allowances if the remittance basis applied automatically.

Income

From the details given, you appear to have three main sources of income:

(1) **The pension**

On the basis that you retain your foreign domicile and claim for the remittance basis to apply, the pension income will be taxable only when remitted to (ie brought into) the UK. However, if you do not make a claim, or become UK domiciled, only 90% of the income from your Spanish pension will be taxable in the UK.

As it appears that you are planning to bring all of the pension income into the UK, you may decide not to make the claim for the remittance basis so that you are only taxed on 90% of the income. In this case, the income will be taxed at 20%, 40% and possibly 50% depending on your level of income.

(2) **Investment income**

Assuming the pension income takes you over the basic rate threshold, without a claim for the remittance basis your Spanish bank interest will be taxable at 40% and any dividend income from your portfolio will be taxable at 32.5% on an arising basis. The rates increase to 50% and 42.5% respectively if your taxable income exceeds £150,000.

If you make a claim for the remittance basis to apply you will only be taxable when you bring the funds into the UK. However, if and when it is remitted, it will be taxed as non savings income, so even the dividends will be taxed at 40% (or 50%).

This will need to be weighed against the position for your pension income before deciding whether or not to make the remittance basis claim.

(3) **The rent**

Your foreign rental income is taxable in the UK on an arising basis at 40% (assuming you are a higher rate taxpayer, 50% if you are an additional rate taxpayer) unless you make the remittance basis claim, in which case you will only be taxed on the amounts remitted to the UK. If rent does not cover expenses, there may be nothing to remit, so there will be no tax. Expenses of letting are deductible in arriving at the taxable amount.

Impact of long-term residence

Once you have been resident in the UK for seven tax years, from year eight you will need to pay an additional annual £30,000 tax charge onwards if you claim the remittance basis. Once you reach that stage, however, you can make a decision each tax year whether it is more beneficial to claim the remittance basis (and pay the £30,000 tax charge) or to be taxed on worldwide income and gains for that year on an arising basis.

Remittance planning

Assuming you retain your foreign domicile and would like to make a claim for the remittance basis to apply to your overseas income, I would advise you to have these amounts paid into a bank account in Spain separate from your savings. You can then spend that money when you visit Spain and not be charged to UK tax on it. If you bring across money from a different bank account (ie your previous savings) it cannot be taxed as it does not represent income arising while resident in the UK.

Note, however, that a 'constructive remittance' is taxable. For example, if you take out a loan in Spain, bring the money to the UK, and use the Spanish income and gains to pay off the loan, you are held to have remitted the income and gains to the UK.

Conclusion

I hope that the above comments are of use to you. If you wish to discuss these or any other matters further, please do not hesitate to contact me. I suggest that we have a meeting when you next come to the UK so that we can discuss your taxation affairs in more detail.

I look forward to meeting you.

Yours sincerely,

A Adviser

10.1 Peter Jones

(1) INCOME TAX REPAYMENT – 2010/11

	Non savings income £	Savings income £	Dividend income £
Building society interest × 100/80		4,000	
Dividends × 100/90			889
Rental income	5,289		
Net income	5,289	4,000	889
Less: personal allowance	(5,289)	(1,186)	
Taxable income	–	2,814	889

Tax:		
Savings income: £2,440 × 10%	244	
£374 × 20%	75	
Dividend income: £889 × 10%	89	
Tax liability	408	
Less: tax deducted at source:		
Credit on dividend		
(cannot give rise to refund)	(89)	
Building society interest		
£4,000 × 20%	(800)	
Repayment due	(481)	

Note. Remaining basic rate band is £33,697.

(2) CAPITAL GAINS TAX – 2010/11

	£
Chargeable gains (post 22.6.10 disposal)	40,000
Less: annual exempt amount	(10,100)
Taxable gain	29,900
Tax:	
£29,900 @ 18% (all within remaining basic rate band)	5,382

10.2 Simon James

Your address

Our address

10 March 2011

Dear Mr James

Relevance of residence, ordinary residence and domicile

Thank you for your letter of 3 March in which you refer to certain capital gains tax matters.

I assume you are aware of the meaning of these terms and are concerned with just the capital gains tax implications.

In order to be liable to UK capital gains tax on gains arising in a tax year the person to whom the gain accrues must be either resident or ordinarily resident in the UK at some time in the tax year.

If you cease to be UK resident and have been resident or ordinarily resident for four out of the last seven tax years, you remain within the scope of UK capital gains tax unless your absence covers at least five tax years. If you return within five years, any gains made during the period of non residence will be taxable in the year of return if the assets were acquired prior to leaving the UK.

An extra statutory concession applies for persons becoming resident part of the way through a tax year. Provided a new arrival has been non resident for the five years preceding his arrival in the UK, gains accruing in the part of the tax year before he became resident will not be chargeable. Similarly, a person becoming non resident part of the way through a tax year does not have to wait until the following tax year for his gains to be exempt, although this only applies to individuals who have not been resident or ordinarily resident for at least four out of seven tax years immediately before the year of departure.

Domicile status is of importance where gains are realised on overseas assets. A person domiciled in the UK is liable on gains arising on his assets wherever located. A person with a non UK domicile can make a claim to be only chargeable on overseas gains on a remittance basis, ie when the gains are remitted to the UK. The remittance basis can also apply automatically in certain circumstances, for example if you have little or no unremitted overseas income.

This does not, however, make gains realised prior to becoming resident, chargeable. If a foreign domiciled person wishes to bring funds into the UK it is advisable that he does not remit from sources which are chargeable to capital gains tax (or income tax) on a remittance basis. Thus proceeds giving rise to gains on a remittance basis should be paid into a separate overseas bank account and remittances to the UK should be made from past savings held in another account.

It should be noted however that if an individual has been UK resident for seven out of the preceding nine tax years, he will be subject to an additional annual £30,000 tax charge if that individual claims to be taxed on the remittance basis. It is therefore necessary to consider each tax year whether it is in fact advantageous to claim the remittance basis in respect of overseas income and gains.

If the non-UK domiciled individual makes a claim to use the remittance basis, he can only set losses on overseas assets against chargeable gains if he makes an irrevocable overseas capital losses election in the first year that he makes the remittance basis claim. This will allow the total of his overseas and UK losses to be set against remitted foreign gains of that tax year, then unremitted foreign gains and finally against any UK gains.

If you require any further clarification on this matter please do not hesitate to contact me.

Yours sincerely

A Adviser

11.1 Dorrit

	Pre-23.6.10 £	Post-22.6.10 £
Disposal 1 £(115,000 – 32,000)	83,000	
Disposal 3 £(47,000 – 16,000)		31,000
Less: Loss on disposal 2 £(45,000 – 62,000)		(17,000)
Chargeable gain	83,000	14,000
Less: Annual exempt amount		(10,100)
Taxable gain	83,000	3,900
CGT on pre-23.6.10 gain @ 18%	14,940	
CGT on post-22.6.10 gain at 28% (no basic rate band left)		1,092
	14,940	1,092
Total CGT	16,032	

11.2 Harbottle

(a) 2010/11 INCOME TAX LIABILITIES

(i) Fred

	Non savings income £	Savings income £	Dividend income £
Employment income	40,000		
NS&I interest (½ share)		1,000	
Dividends			7,000
Total income	40,000	1,000	7,000
Less: PA	(6,475)		
TAXABLE INCOME	33,525	1,000	7,000

TAX LIABILITY

	£
33,525 @ 20%	6,705
1,000 @ 20% (savings)	200
2,875 @ 10% (dividends)	287
37,400	
4,125 @ 32½% (dividends)	1,341
41,525	£8,533

(ii)   *Iris*

	Savings income £	Dividend income £
NS&I interest (½ share)	1,000	
Dividends		1,200
Total income	1,000	1,200
Less: PA	(1,000)	(1,200)
TAXABLE INCOME	Nil	Nil
INCOME TAX LIABILITY		Nil

2010/11 CAPITAL GAINS TAX LIABILITIES

(i)   *Fred*

	£
Gains – post-22 June 2010	10,700
Less: Annual exempt amount	(10,100)
	600
Capital gains tax at 28% (no basic rate band left)	168

(ii)   *Iris*

	£
Gains – post-22 June 2010	2,500
Less: Annual exempt amount	(10,100)
	NIL
Capital gains tax	£NIL

SUMMARY

	Fred £	Iris £	Total £
Income tax liability	8,533	NIL	8,533
Capital gains tax liability	168	NIL	168
	8,701	NIL	8,701

(b)   PLANNING ACTION

Currently, as the computations in (a) above show, Iris is not fully using her personal allowance of £6,475 nor her capital gains tax exempt amount of £10,100. The following action should be taken:

(i)   Ensure that Iris fully uses her 2010/11 personal allowance by the transfer of investments from Fred and/or the transfer of the NS&I account from joint names into her sole name. The effect of this would be to increase Iris's income and decrease Fred's income. To achieve the desired effect there must be an outright gift so that Iris is beneficially entitled; Fred must no longer participate in the income from the investments gifted.

(ii)   The value of assets transferred into Iris's name must be at least sufficient to yield £4,275 additional income (£6,475 – £2,200).

Ideally Fred's savings income should be reduced by £4,125 so that he is not a higher rate taxpayer in 2010/11.

(iii)   Fred and Iris should also make their maximum investment in an ISA – they could invest £10,200 each per annum in an ISA shares account. The dividends received on these shares will be exempt from tax.

(iv)   Assuming the couple continue to realise capital gains of £13,200 each tax year the gains should be shared such that each spouse may take advantage of their £10,100 annual exempt amount.

Investments may be transferred between spouses at no gain/no loss and this should be done before disposal of assets to third parties.

(c)   Fred and Iris are entitled to the following tax credits in 2010/11:

	£	£
CTC		
Family element	545	
Child element: 2 × £2,300	4,600	
		5,145
WTC		
Basic element	1,920	
Couple element	1,890	
30 hour element (Fred works full time)	790	
Child care (not available as Iris does not work)	—	
		4,600
		9,745
Maximum WTC & CTC before excess income restriction		
Restriction for excess income:		
Employment income	40,000	
Investment income (£8,000 + £2,200 - £300)	9,900	
	49,900	
WTC and CTC (excluding family element)	9,200	
Income reduction ((£49,900 - £6,420) × 39%) restricted	(9,200)	
		—
CTC family element (no reduction as income does not exceed £50,000)		545

Fred and Iris are entitled to the family element of the CTC of £545. This will be paid to Iris, by HMRC either weekly or four weekly.

Marking scheme

				Marks
(a)	Fred	–	income	½
		–	PA	½
		–	tax calculation	1½
	Iris	–	income	½
		–	PA	½
	Fred	–	AE	½
		–	CGT	½
	Iris	–	AE	½
				5
(b)	Use Iris's PA and AE			1
	Transfer of investments			1
	Outright gift			½
	Value of income transferred			1
	ISA			1
	Sharing of gains			1
	No gain/no loss transfer			1
	Maximum			5
(c)	CTC			1
	WTC			1
	Income			1
	Restriction			1
	Basic family element given			1
				5
				15

12.1 Julie Green

Share pool:

	No. of shares	Cost £
Purchase 1.6.93	50	1,000
Purchase 18.9.96	50	3,800
Purchase 21.5.97	100	9,300
	200	14,100
Bonus issue (1 for 2)	100	–
Purchase 15.1.02	100	8,200
	400	22,300
Sale 29.6.10	(75)	(4,181)
	325	18,119
Sale 16.8.10	(75)	(4,181)
c/f	250	13,938

Calculate gains:

	£
Disposal 29.6.10:	
Proceeds	10,150
Cost	(4,181)
Chargeable gain	5,969
Disposal 16.8.10	
Proceeds	8,500
Cost	(4,181)
Chargeable gain	4,319
Total chargeable gains	10,288

12.2 Mr Jones

Share pool:

	No. of shares	Cost £
Purchase Aug 1982	5,000	6,250
Purchase Sept 1982	2,000	3,000
Purchase Nov 1985	5,000	9,500
	12,000	18,750
Sale Oct 1987	(3,000)	(4,687)
	9,000	14,063
Purchase May 2001	1,000	3,000
	10,000	17,063
Sale July 2010	(7,000)	(11,944)
c/f	3,000	5,119

Calculate gain:

	£
Proceeds	31,500
Cost	(11,944)
Chargeable gain	19,556

12.3 Richard Price

Share pool:

	No. of shares	Cost £
Purchase 15.3.90	2,000	2,000
Purchase 17.12.96	4,000	10,000
	6,000	12,000
RI (1 for 5)	1,200	6,000
	7,200	18,000
Sale 4.10.10	(1,800)	(4,500)
c/f	5,400	13,500

Calculate gain:	£
Proceeds (1,800 × £7.50)	13,500
Cost	(4,500)
Chargeable gain	9,000

12.4 Eric James

Sale of shares in Toucan Play plc

	£
Proceeds	9,100
Less: Cost (working)	(2,049)
Chargeable gain	7,051

Working

	£
2,000 Ordinary shares (2,000 × £4.20)	8,400
4,000 Preference shares (4,000 × £2)	8,000
Total consideration received on takeover:	16,400

Allowable cost of shares sold:

$$\frac{8,400}{16,400} \times £4,000 \qquad 2,049$$

13.1 Doug

Summary

	£
Gains (W1 and W3)	8,533
Less: current year loss (W2)	(1,200)
	7,333
Less: AE	(10,100)
Taxable gain	–

Workings

		£
1	Ming vase:	
	Proceeds	8,000
	Allowable cost	(2,000)
		6,000

Gain cannot exceed 5/3 × £(8,000 − 6,000) = £3,333

	£
∴ Chargeable gain	3,333

		£
2	Leonardo cartoon:	
	Proceeds (deemed)	6,000
	Allowable cost	(7,200)
	Allowable loss	(1,200)

		£
3	Lathe:	
	Proceeds	9,500
	Allowable cost	(4,300)
		5,200

Restrict to $\frac{5}{3} \times £(9,500 - 6,000) = £5,833$ ∴ restriction does not apply.

13.2 Mr Cole

Summary (all post-22.6.10 gains)

	£
Car	–
Land	27,867
Chest	1,667
Painting	6,650
	36,184
Less: current year loss	(1,500)
Net chargeable gains	34,684
Less: Annual exempt amount	(10,100)
Taxable gain	24,584

CGT payable:

	£
£5,400 @ 18% £(37,400 – 32,000) (remaining basic rate band)	972
£19,184 @ 28% £(24,584 – 5,400)	5,371
Total CGT	£6,343

Workings

(1) Vintage Car

Disposal of a motor vehicle is exempt for CGT purposes.

(2)

Land

	£
Sale proceeds	38,000

$$\text{Less:} \quad \text{Cost} \times \frac{A}{A+B}$$

$$£32,000 \times \frac{38,000}{38,000+82,000} \qquad (10,133)$$

Chargeable gain	27,867

(3) Antique Chest

	£
Sale proceeds	7,000
Less: Cost	(4,000)
	3,000
Compared to	
5/3 × (7,000 – 6,000) =	
Lower gain taken	£1,667

(4) Painting

	£
Proceeds	11,500
Less: Costs of sale	(150)
	11,350
Less: Probate value	(4,700)
Chargeable gain	6,650
Compared to	
5/3 × (11,500 – 6,000) =	
Lower gain taken	£9,167

(5) Vase

	£
Deemed proceeds	6,000
Less: Cost	(7,500)
Loss	(1,500)

Marking scheme

13.3 CGT Leases

(1) Assignment of long lease

	£
Proceeds	79,000
Cost	(38,000)
	41,000

(2) Assignment of short lease

	£
Proceeds	79,000
Cost: £38,000 × $\dfrac{88.371}{100.000}$ % for 31 years / % for 57 years	(33,581)
Chargeable gain	45,419

(3) Grant of long lease – CGT part disposal

	£
Proceeds	30,000
Cost: £25,000 × $\dfrac{30,000}{30,000 + 7,500}$	(20,000)
Chargeable gain	10,000

(4) Grant of short lease out of freehold

	£
Proceeds: capital element of premium (W)	7,600
Cost: £25,000 × $\dfrac{7,600}{20,000 + 17,000}$	(5,135)
Chargeable gain	2,465

Working

Premium	20,000
Less: property income: £20,000 × [50 – (20 – 1)] ÷ 50	(12,400)
Capital element	7,600

TQT
Tax Qualification Training

14.1 Owning two homes (Pilot Paper)

A Tale of Two Properties!

(a) It is becoming increasingly common for a family to have not one but two homes that are occupied as residences. The purpose of this article is to set out the key capital gains tax implications of such a situation, using the case study of Mr and Mrs Hammond.

(i) On the sale of the current family home there will be no capital gains tax implications and the capital gains tax pages of the tax return do not need to be completed. This is due to the valuable relief known as principal private residence (PPR) relief which ensures that the sale of a property which has been the taxpayer's only or main residence is exempt from capital gains tax ie no gain chargeable (and no loss allowable).

(ii) However, where a taxpayer owns two properties, even if he actually resides in both, PPR relief can only apply to one property. It is worth noting at this point that a husband and wife living together such as Mr and Mrs Hammond can only have one PPR between them ie it is not possible for the flat to be Mr Hammonds' PPR and for the house to be Mrs Hammond's.

Instead, Mr and Mrs Hammond should elect which of the house and flat they wish to have treated as their main residence for the purposes of PPR relief. The election should be made within two years of residing in the two properties, in this case by May 2012. (If the election is not made then HMRC will make the decision for you!)

Mr and Mrs Hammond do have a right to vary the election by a further written notice which can take effect for any period starting not more than two years before the date of the second notice.

(iii) In this situation I would advise Mr and Mrs Hammond to elect for the flat to be treated as their main residence.

Although the country house is likely to be the property that has the largest gain on sale, we must also take into account their long term plans. Whilst the house is likely to be owned for the next 20 years, the flat is likely to be sold within five years and therefore a gain will arise on this property first.

If the election is made for the flat to be treated as the main residence, and it is sold after five years, any gains will be exempt from capital gains tax.

If the flat is let out after five years, it will cease to be the couple's main residence. However, as it has been their main residence at some point during their period of ownership, then on the subsequent sale of the property not only will the gain relating to the five years of residence be exempt, but also the gain relating to the last three years of ownership. The gain relating to the remaining two years of ownership is also likely to be completely exempt due to an additional relief known as letting relief.

This applies where a property which has been the taxpayer's main residence is then let out – the gain relating to this period is exempt up to the lower of:

   – The gain already exempt under the PPR relief rules
   – The gain relating to the let period
   – £40,000

(iv) Finally, on the sale of the country house, the gain relating to the period when the flat was the main residence will be chargeable to capital gains tax, but the balance of the gain will be covered by the PPR relief rules

(b) On a related point, I am often asked by couples – what is the difference between owning a property as joint tenants or tenants in common.

Under joint tenancy, the husband and wife own the property but each holds 100% of the property. If the husband and wife (as co-owners) wish to sell the property they must both agree to do so. It also means that on the death of one of the spouses, the ownership of the entire property is vested automatically in the surviving spouse.

However, as tenants in common each owner owns a share of the whole property eg Jane owns 60% and Paul owns 40% of the whole house, not a particular area which represents a percentage of the building. Each owner can dispose of their interest to whomever they want and do not need to seek the other owner's agreement.

On death the property passes according to the terms of the deceased's will (or under the rules of intestacy).

Scots Law

Under Scots Law where property is held jointly the owners have no separate estates but each holds 100% of the property. If co-owners wish to sell the property then must all agree to do so. It also means that on the death of one of the owners, the ownership of the entire property passes automatically to the surviving spouse.

In the case of common property each owner has a title to his own share which he may dispose of as he wishes and on death it will pass according to the terms of his will, legal rights or intestacy. However, this is the way that husbands and wives own property in Scotland as the owners can use a special destination to ensure that the property passes to the survivor.

Marking scheme

				Marks
(a)	(i)	No CGT on sale of home	½	
		PPR relief	½	
		Explanation	1	
				2
	(ii)	One property eligible for PPR	1	
		Husband and wife – one PPR	1	
		Election	1	
		Time limit	1	
		May 2012	½	
		Consequence of no election	½	
		Varying election	1	
		Maximum		5
	(iii)	Elect for flat	½	
		Bigger gain on country house	½	
		Flat sold earlier	1	
		Effect of election	1	
		Effect of letting	1	
		5 years' exemption	½	
		Last 3 years exempt	1	
		Letting relief	1	
		Amount of letting relief	1	
		Maximum		7
	(iv)	Part chargeable/part exempt	1	
				1
(b)		Joint tenancy:		
		Each has interest in 100% of property	1	
		Joint decision to sell	½	
		Treatment on death	1	
		Tenants in common:		
		Each has % share	1	
		No consent needed to sell	½	
		Position on death	1	
				5
				20

14.2 Peter Stamp

COMPUTATION OF CHARGEABLE GAIN ON SALE OF HOUSE

Period	Explanation	Occupation or deemed occupation (months)	Non occupation (months)
2.5.83 – 1.2.87	Actual occupation	45	
2.2.87 – 1.12.96	Letting		118
2.12.96 – 3.7.07	Absence		127
4.7.07 – 3.7.10	Last three years deemed occupation	36	
		81	245

Total ownership period = 326 months

	£
Proceeds (3.7.10)	270,000
Less: cost	(70,000)
Gain before PPR relief	200,000

Less: Exemption for main residence $\dfrac{81}{326} \times £200,000$

	(49,693)
	150,307

Less: letting exemption: lowest of
    £49,693 (gain exempted by private residence relief)
    £72,393 (chargeable gain attributable to letting) (W)
    £40,000 (maximum relief available for lettings)

	(40,000)
Chargeable gain	110,307

Working

Gain in let period: $\dfrac{118}{326} \times £200,000 = £72,393$

14.3 Mr Richman

Our address

Your address

9 May 2011

Dear Mr Richman

SALE OF 'RED BRICKS'

Thank you for your letter of 4 May regarding the sale of your property 'Red Bricks'. As requested I have set out below how the capital gains tax liability will be calculated, taking into account all possible reliefs.

Principal Private Residence Exemption

On the sale of a property which has at some time been used as your principal private residence (PPR) some of the gain arising will be exempt from Capital Gains Tax.

The amount of this exemption is calculated as:

$$\text{Total gains} \times \frac{\text{Period of occupation as PPR}}{\text{Period of ownership}}$$

In addition to any actual periods of occupation you are allowed to include certain deemed periods of occupation, whilst you were absent from the property.

Deemed Periods of Occupation

The following can be included as periods of occupation:

(1)   The last three years of ownership, since the property has at some time been used as your PPR; and

(2)   Four years of your period of absence whilst working abroad, since you used the property as your PPR both before and after the absence, and there was no other exempt residence during your period abroad (see below as regards the restriction due to use as offices); and

(3)   Up to three years for any reason whatsoever.

You will therefore see, from the appendix attached, that you are deemed to have occupied the house as your principal residence for 22 of the 28 years of ownership.

Business Use

During the period whilst part of the house was used exclusively as offices, the gain attributable to that part of the property will not be exempt as you are not occupying it as your PPR.

The last three years of ownership of both parts of the house will qualify as deemed occupation as you had occupied the whole of the property as a private residence at some point beforehand.

Capital Gains Tax Payable

Accordingly, I calculate that a gain of £55,714 (see appendix) will arise after all reliefs of which £10,100 is covered by your annual exempt amount. The rate at which the balance will be taxed depends on the level of your taxable income in the year. Gains falling within the basic rate band of £37,400 are chargeable at 18%, while gains in excess of this amount are chargeable at 28%.

Assuming your taxable income fully uses the basic rate band, tax of £12,772 will be payable on 31 January 2012. If you have part of your basic rate band left the tax liability will be lower as part of the gain will be taxed at 18%. Please let me have details of your income during the year so that I can calculate the exact amount due.

I trust the above answers your query, but if you require any further assistance please do not hesitate to contact me.

Yours sincerely

A. Jones

Appendix

1.   Calculation of chargeable gain

	£
Proceeds	370,000
Less: cost	(90,000)
Enhancement expenditure	(20,000)
Gain before PPR relief	260,000
Less: PPR relief (£260,000 × 22/28)	(204,286)
Chargeable gain	55,714

2.   PPR exemption

	Occupation	Non-occupation	Total
6.4.83 – 5.4.88 (actual)	5		5
6.4.88 – 5.4.95			
(deemed 4 years)	4	–	4
(3 years for any reason)	3	–	3
6.4.95 – 5.4.96 (occupation)	1	–	1
6.4.96 – 5.4.08			
(12 years joint use)	6	6	12
6.4.08 – 4.4.11			
(final 3 years deemed occupation)	3		3
	22	6	28

Tax Qualification Training

15.1 Fran and Anna

(1) *Fran's gain:*

	£
Proceeds (MV) June 2010	500,000
Allowable cost	(75,000)
	425,000
Excess of actual consideration over cost: £100,000 – £75,000	
Gain deferred	(25,000)
	400,000
Gain chargeable in June 2010	£25,000

(2) *Anna's gain:*

	£	£
Proceeds July 2012		520,000
Cost (MV)	500,000	
Less: gain deferred (from part 1)	(400,000)	
Base cost		(100,000)
Chargeable gain		420,000

15.2 Joe Bloggs

MR BLOGGS – CHARGEABLE GAINS 2010/11

	£
Chargeable gains (W1 + W2)	425,000
Less: annual exempt amount	(10,100)
Taxable gain	414,900

Workings

1   *Sale of flat*

	£
Sale proceeds	700,000
Less: cost	(200,000)
	500,000
Less: PPR relief (75% × 500,000)	(375,000)
	125,000

2   *Sale of shares:*

	£
Proceeds (market value)	450,000
Less: cost	(75,000)
	375,000

Part of the gain of £375,000 may be subject to a gift relief claim under s.165 TCGA 1992:

	£	£
Gain before relief		375,000
Less: excess actual proceeds:		
Actual proceeds	375,000	
Less: cost	(75,000)	
		(300,000)
Gain eligible for gift relief		75,000
Gain taxed now		£300,000

15.3   P J Laval

(i)   CAPITAL GAINS TAX PAYABLE 2010/11

	Pre-23.6.10 £	Post-22.6.10 £
House (W1)	60,000	
Vic plc shares (W2)		5,910
Lavaling Ltd (W3)		15,000
Total gains	60,000	20,910
Less: Annual exempt amount		(10,100)
	60,000	10,810
Tax		
£60,000 @ 18%	10,800	
£10,810 @ 28%	3,027	
Total CGT	13,827	

Workings

(W1)   House 'Chez Nous' – 14 May 2010

	£	£
Proceeds		99,000
Less:		
Cost	37,000	
Enhancement	2,000	
		(39,000)
		60,000
Chargeable gain		

(W2)   Vic plc shares – 18 July 2010

Share pool:

	No. of shares	Cost £
Purchase 10.2.83	1,400	3,500
Bonus issue (1 for 4)	350	–
	1,750	3,500
Sale 18.7.10	(1,400)	(2,800)
c/f	350	700

Calculate gain:

	£
Proceeds	8,710
Cost	(2,800)
Chargeable gain	5,910

(W3)   Lavaling Ltd shares – 31 March 2011

At the time of disposal, the market value of Lavaling Ltd's chargeable assets were:

	£
Chargeable business assets	
Freehold property	130,000
Other chargeable assets	
Quoted securities	30,000
	160,000

The proportion of the gain of £80,000 which is eligible for gift relief is found by applying the fraction:

$$\frac{\text{Market value of chargeable business assets}}{\text{Market value of chargeable assets}} = \frac{130,000}{160,000}$$

$$£80,000 \times \frac{130,000}{160,000} = £65,000$$

		£
Overall gain		80,000
Less: Gift relief		(65,000)
Chargeable gain		15,000

(ii) Freehold is an absolute interest in land. Subject to general law the freeholder can do as he wishes with the land.

A leasehold interest is qualified. The term is limited in time and the lease normally contains a range of covenants which are binding on the tenant.

Commonhold property must originally be freehold and must be owned by a commonhold association. Individual parts (commonhold units) are held as freehold by the unit holders. The commonhold is managed by the commonhold association which hold the common parts. Only the unit holders can be members of the commonhold association.

Marking scheme

		Marks
(i)	**CGT summary**:	
	Gains	
	AE set against correct gain	1
	Tax @ 18% on pre-23.6.10 gains	1
	Tax @ 28% on post-22.6.10 gains	1
	House 'Chez Nous'	1
	Enhancement expenditure	
	Gain calculation	1
	Vic plc shares	1
	Purchase	
	Bonus issue	1
	Disposal from pool	1
	Gain calculation	1
	Lavaling Ltd shares	1
	Identify CAs and CBAs	
	CBA/CA fraction	1
	Proportion of gain eligible for gift relief	1
	Chargeable gain	1
	Maximum	1
		13
(ii)	Freehold – absolute interest	
	Can do as wish with	1
	Leasehold – qualified interest	1
	Limited in time	1
	Limited by covenants	½
	Commonhold – originally freehold	½
	Ownership	1
	Management association	1
	Maximum	1
		5
		18

15.4 Simon

To: Simon Evans
From: Frances Ackland
Date: 5 December 2010
Subject: Deferral of gains

Thank you for your memorandum of 3 December.

First of all, I have calculated that the gain on the disposal of the Blue plc shares is £150,000 (see Appendix).

The relief you refer to is Enterprise Investment Scheme deferral relief. Briefly, you can obtain the relief if you subscribe for new fully paid up ordinary shares in an unlisted trading company provided it is not carrying on certain non qualifying trades such as farming or property development. The acquisition must be made within one year before your disposal (but I presume this is not the case here) and three years after the disposal (ie by 29 November 2013). At the time of the acquisition, you must be resident or ordinarily resident in the United Kingdom. You must make a claim by 5 April 2015. However, you may wish to make a claim sooner in order to avoid having to pay tax on the gain.

In order to defer the gain of £150,000 you would need to invest at least an amount equal to this gain. However, since you wish to invest about £100,000 of the proceeds in the French house, this leaves you only £100,000 to invest in the shares, so only £100,000 of the gain can be deferred. The remainder of the gain of £50,000 would remain chargeable to CGT. From this an annual exempt amount of £10,100 is deducted, leaving £39,900 chargeable to tax. As you are an additional rate taxpayer the tax rate is 28%, which would result in a liability of £11,172.

One other point to note is that if you become not resident and not ordinarily resident in the UK broadly within three years of the acquisition of the shares, the gain you have deferred will be treated as becoming chargeable immediately before this time. This is obviously a danger since you wish to move to France.

Please let me know if you require any further details.

Appendix	£	£
		200,000
Proceeds	65,000	
Less: cost	(15,000)	(50,000)
less: held over gain		150,000
Gain before EIS deferral relief		

15.5 Emily

Computation of taxable gains:	Pre-23.6.10 £	Post-23.6.10 £
		75,000
Factory (W1)	23,000	
Painting (W2)		
Less: current year loss relief (W3)		(21,000)
Net chargeable gains	23,000	54,000
Less: annual exempt amount		(10,100)
Taxable gains	23,000	43,900

CGT:	£
£23,000 @ 18%	4,140
£43,900 @ 28% (no basic rate band left)	12,292
Total CGT	16,432

Workings

1 Factory	£
	225,000
Proceeds	(150,000)
Less: cost	75,000
Chargeable gain	

TQT
Tax Qualification Training

2 *Painting*

Transfer to Emily on 1 July 2001 on no gain/no loss basis

Sale by Emily

	£
Proceeds	73,000
Less: cost (= cost to Arthur)	(50,000)
Chargeable gain	23,000

3 *Vase*

	£
Proceeds	19,000
Less: cost	(40,000)
Loss	(21,000)

15.6 Peter

Summary of gains:

	Pre-23.6.10 £	Post-22.6.10 £
Building (W1)	400,000	
Forum Follies plc (W2)		5,000
Dassau plc (W3)		7,100
	400,000	12,100
Less: losses b/f		(6,400)
Chargeable gains	400,000	5,700
Less: annual exempt amount	(4,400)	(5,700)
Taxable gain	395,600	NIL

	£
£395,600 @ 18%	
CGT due 31.1.2012	71,208

Workings

1 *Building*

	£
Proceeds	600,000
Less: cost	(200,000)
Chargeable gain	400,000

2 *Takeover of Forum Follies plc*

The elements in the takeover consideration have the following values:

	£
Ordinary shares (30,000 × £3.00)	90,000
Cash	10,000
Total consideration received	100,000

A gain only arises on the date of the takeover in respect of the cash element.

	£
Cash received (above)	10,000
Cost £50,000 × $\dfrac{10,000}{100,000}$	(5,000)
Chargeable gain	5,000

3   *Dassau plc shares*

   (i)   Share pool

	No. of shares	Cost £
Purchase: Dec 1984	1,000	2,000
Rights issue (1 for 2 @ £2)	500	1,000
	1,500	3,000
Disposal: Nov 2010	(1,200)	(2,400)
c/f	300	600

	£
Proceeds	9,500
Less cost	(2,400)
Chargeable gain	7,100

15.7   **Sarah Stone**

	Pre-23.6.10 £	Post-22.6.10 £
Summary		
Peterson Ltd (W1)	82,000	
Antique brooch (W2)	2,200	
House (W4)		37,000
Stamp collection (W3)		(1,000)
	84,200	36,000
Less: capital losses b/f		(15,000)
Net chargeable gain	84,200	21,000
Less: annual exempt amount		(10,100)
Taxable gain	84,200	10,900
£84,200 @ 18%	15,156	
£10,900 @ 28%	3,052	
Total CGT	18,208	

Workings

1   *Peterson Ltd shares*

   Share pool:

	No. of shares	Cost £
Acquisition 1.3.86	50,000	25,000
Purchase 1.8.99	5,000	10,000
	55,000	35,000
Rights issue (1 for 5 @ £3)	11,000	33,000
	66,000	68,000
Sale: 12 April 2010	(66,000)	(68,000)
	–	–

   Calculate gain:

	£
Proceeds	150,000
Less: cost:	(68,000)
Chargeable gain	82,000

2   *Antique brooch (15.6.10)*

	£
Net proceeds (£8,250 – £250)	8,000
Less: cost	(5,800)
Chargeable gain	2,200

Limited to: $^5/_3 \times (8,250 - 6,000) = £3,750$ (does not apply)

3   *Stamp collection (19.9.10)*

	£	
Proceeds (deemed)	6,000	(replace actual proceeds)
Less: cost	7,000	
Allowable loss	(1,000)	

4   *House (21.1.11)*

	£	£
Proceeds		75,000
Less: Cost	28,000	
Enhancement	10,000	
		(38,000)
Chargeable gain		37,000

Personal Taxation

Index

TQT
Tax Qualification Training

TQT
Tax Qualification Training

TQT
Tax Qualification Training

REVIEW FORM

Name: _____   Address: _____

_____

How have you used this Text?
(Tick one box only)

☐ Home study (book only)

☐ On a course_____

☐ Other _____

Why did you decide to purchase this Text?
(Tick one box only)

☐ Have used TQT Texts in the past

☐ Recommendation by friend/colleague

☐ Recommendation by a lecturer

☐ Saw advertising

☐ Other _____

During the past six months do you recall seeing/receiving either of the following?
(Tick as many boxes as are relevant)

☐ Our advertisement in *Tax Adviser*

☐ Our Publishing Catalogue

Which (if any) aspects of our advertising do you think are useful?
(Tick as many boxes as are relevant)

☐ Prices and publication dates of new editions

☐ Information on Text content

☐ Facility to order books off-the-page

☐ None of the above

Your ratings, comments and suggestions would be appreciated on the following areas of this Text.

	Very useful	Useful	Not useful
Introductory section	☐	☐	☐
Quality of explanations	☐	☐	☐
Examples	☐	☐	☐
Chapter roundups	☐	☐	☐
Exam focus points / Examiner's reports	☐	☐	☐
Legislative references	☐	☐	☐
Question bank	☐	☐	☐
Answer bank	☐	☐	☐
Index	☐	☐	☐

	Excellent	Good	Adequate	Poor
Overall opinion of this Text	☐	☐	☐	☐

☐ Yes   ☐ No

Do you intend to continue using TQT Products?

Please note any further comments and suggestions/errors on the reverse of this page. The TQT author of this edition can be e-mailed at: suedexter@bpp.com

Please return to: Sue Dexter, Tax Publishing Director, BPP Learning Media Ltd, FREEPOST, London, W12 8BR. BPP Learning Media Ltd is a member of the TQT joint venture.

REVIEW FORM (continued)

TELL US WHAT YOU THINK

Please note any further comments and suggestions/errors below.